Home–School Relations

Working Successfully with Parents and Families

Mary Lou Fuller
University of North Dakota

Glenn Olsen
University of North Dakota

Allyn and Bacon
Boston • London • Toronto • Sydney • Tokyo • Singapore

Senior Series Editor: Virginia Lanigan
Series Editorial Assistant: Kris Lamarre
Production Coordinator: Christopher H. Rawlings
Editorial-Production Service: Omegatype Typography, Inc.
Composition and Prepress Buyer: Linda Cox
Manufacturing Buyer: Suzanne Lareau
Cover Administrator: Jenny Hart

Library of Congress Cataloging-in-Publication Data

Home–school relations : working successfully with parents and families
/ [edited by] Mary Lou Fuller, Glenn Olsen.
    p.   cm.
    Includes bibliographical references and index.
    ISBN 0-205-18126-0 (alk. paper)
    1. Home and school—United States—Case studies.   2. Parent–teacher relationships—United States—Case studies.   3. Education, Elementary—Parent participation—United States—Case studies.
    4. Early childhood education—Parent participation—United States—Case studies.   5. Special education—Parent participation—United States—Case studies.   I. Fuller, Mary Lou.   II. Olsen, Glenn W. (Glenn William)
    LC225.3.H65   1998
    371.19'2'0973—dc21   97-20056
                                                                        CIP

Printed in the United States of America
10   9   8   7   6   5   4   3   2   1   02   01   00   99   98   97

Student artwork credits: Alex Guy, p. 1; Lindsey Johnson, p. 11; Jodi Langlois, p. 40; Sarah Olsen, p. 67; Amanda Carlsen, p. 87; Becca Olsen, p. 106; Megan Hulst, p. 127; Michelle Gourneau, pp. 151, 257; Amber Asman, p. 170; Brandon Waller, p. 208; Michelle Jalan, p. 235; Allison Bakken, p. 273; Tiffany Krause, p. 302; Lisa Moser, p. 332.

Dedication

*To my parents, husband, children, and grandchildren
for all of the lessons they have taught me, the love they have given,
and the joy they have provided. Thank you.*

*To Dr. Roger Kroth in appreciation for
his years of contributions to parent involvement.*
—Mary Lou Fuller

*To my wife, Barbara Hager-Olsen;
our three daughters, Sarah, Ann, and Becca;
and my parents. My family graciously allowed me the time to move
this book from an idea to a reality and helped me along the way.
My parents provided the early inspiration to continue learning
and to pursue teaching and writing.*
—Glenn Olsen

Contents

Foreword

Home–School Relations: Working Successfully with Parents is a thoughtful guide to more productive relationships between parents and teachers, homes and schools. It begins with the premise that parents are their children's first and most important teachers, and further, that the dispositions, language, values, and cultural understandings that help guide children and young people are learned most fully within families (and, importantly, this book makes the conception of families inclusive of the many child-nurturing arrangements that exist).

While those in schools often say that they value active parent participation, parents are not always treated as full partners. They typically don't learn enough about what their children will be learning in school, how their children's growth as learners will be assured, what special efforts will be made to support their children if they begin to struggle academically or socially or how they, as parents, can be most helpful to their children's academic learning beyond school. They need all of this information if they are to be the full partners they want to be.

Sometimes, the messages that come to parents about the foregoing are not in their languages. At other times, those in schools suggest times for meetings that are in conflict with other family related commitments. Moreover, when parent conferences occur, they are scheduled most often for a short time period, the teachers do most of the talking, the child is most often absent. It is an exchange teachers in most schools don't look forward to with great enthusiasm. And parents don't often come expecting to learn very much. Such conditions need to change. If the schools do not actively acknowledge and encourage a strong partnership role for parents, children's education will be limited, not as intense, as full, as it needs to be.

How does a productive partnership get constructed? What do teachers need to know to be a part of the construction? This book provides a useful map—an inspiring guide—that grows out of a set of solid commitments to parents as well as to the preparation of teachers able to extend themselves on behalf of parents. I suggest "able to" because I understand that the desire to involve parents is insufficient. Knowledge of how to proceed, the realities of family life across cultures, and skills are also needed. This book provides that kind of assistance.

The editors and contributors to *Home–School Relations* are people with experience as classroom and teachers, parents, and teacher educators. They use that experience well, providing numerous examples of productive home–school interchange. It is important to note that little attention has been placed on home–school relations in teacher education programs, in part because there hasn't been much credible literature. This book fills a large share of that void. It helps change the landscape, placing before us a vision of what is possible when teachers and parents work closely together. I am pleased the editors and contributors are sharing their work with the educational community and with parents.

Vito Perrone
Harvard Graduate School of Education

Preface

In order to be effective as educators, we must understand the families from which our students come and the opportunity and encouragement they receive to develop the skills necessary in creating positive working relationships. This book examines the nature of the contemporary family—what it looks like, how it functions, and its relationship to the schools. This includes the important related topics of diversity (cultural, racial, religious, sexual orientation) and the effects of income on families. To understand a family you must understand diversity. This book also includes topics which have been neglected by other work in the field, such as fathers' roles, poverty, and parents' perspectives of schools, in order to help educators better understand the complexities of home–school relations.

In addition to providing the reader with an understanding of what families look like and how they function, this book is highly practical. It provides descriptions of successful parent-involvement programs, has an excellent chapter dealing with communication skills and activities (newsletters, conferences, etc.), and provides the reader with much-needed information about family violence. Also, with the incorporation of students with special needs into the "regular" classroom, many teachers find they have not been prepared to work with the parents of these students. This text will be most useful to these teachers. Other chapters help educators understand the important and neglected areas of the legal and policy aspects of home–school relations.

Students

The organization of this book is based on the principles of good learning. First and foremost, the learners are actively involved in their own learning. Objectives are presented at the beginning of each chapter, allowing an overview of the material; there are also exercises throughout each chapter to help the reader reflect on the material they have read. Finally, there are lists of resources at the end of each chapter which allow students to pursue further any of the topics that were addressed in the chapter.

Instructor

College instructors have many demands on their time; this text has been designed to be as helpful to the instructor as possible. At the end of each chapter there are a variety of suggestions for activities designed to help make the class interactive, reflective, and stimulating.

This text employs the Internet as a teaching tool and provides World Wide Web (WWW) addresses to help students get started. There are also lists of articles, books, and videos that can be used as class resources for assignments or as resources for students' pursuit of their personal interests.

Important Features

Diversity

A chapter is devoted to diversity (cultural/racial, economic, religious, as well as family structure). Diversity is not only addressed in this single chapter, but is woven throughout the book. This is of particular importance since most pre-service teachers come from white, middle-class backgrounds. Most have had little meaningful interaction with families that differ from theirs.

Poverty

There is a chapter on the effects of poverty on the family. No other book that we reviewed looks at this important topic even thought the statistics are surprising—20 percent of all children live below the poverty line, and of those, 25 percent are children six and under. Economic status has a tremendous effect on the academic performance of children, yet this subject is often ignored.

Voice of the Parent

Generally the voices of parents are missing from books of this nature. This book not only includes parents' perspectives on parenting, but also their feelings about their relationships with the schools and educators.

Families of Children with Special Needs

Students with special needs were at one time the exclusive domain of special education programs. However, with the widespread movement of classroom inclusion, teachers must have an understanding of working with the parents of children with special needs.

Fathers' Roles

Fathers are generally only footnotes in educational literature. It is important to understand the father and his role if we are to understand the family in totality.

Home Schooling

Some families choose not to send their children to public schools. This is an examination of that experience.

We hope that you will find this book to be thorough, thought-provoking, current, and practical. We designed this book because of our frustrations with the limited available material, and are very happy with the results. We hope you will be too. Please feel free to call us if you have questions or comments about the book. We would love to hear about your successes so that we can pass them on to other teachers.

Mary Lou Fuller, Ph.D.
Distinguished Professor
Elementary Education
Teaching and Learning
University of North Dakota
Grand Forks, ND 58202
Phone: (701) 777-3140
Phone: (701) 777-3145
Email:mfuller@prairie.nodak.edu

Glenn Olsen Ph.D.
Associate Professor
Early Childhood Education
Teaching and Learning
University of North Dakota
Grand Forks, ND 58202
Phone: (701) 777-3145
Email: golsen@plains.nodak.edu

Acknowledgments

We would like to thank a number of people who helped us compile this book. During the planning stages, Dr. Sara Hanhan was one of the editors but due to demands on her time she was unable to continue. Some of the best ideas were hers and we hope that she will be pleased with the results. Thank you to Patricia Bohnet who was so much more than an excellent typist; she was a support system and a marvel at proofing and editing. Also, thank you to Sheri Torrance who not only provided "last minute" help but was always gracious, and Nancy Peotter for her organization and help. Thanks also to Owen Williams' talent as a librarian, who helped locate critical references and resources, and the young artists who provided us with pictures for this book. Finally, we'd like to thank the reviewers of this text, Colleen S. Bell, Hamline University; Milt Hoff, University of North Dakota; Roger Kroth, University of New Mexico; Margaret (Peggy) Shaeffer, University of North Dakota; and Roberta O. Shreve, Moorhead State University.

Chapter 1

An Introduction to Families

GLENN OLSEN
University of North Dakota

MARY LOU FULLER
University of North Dakota

This chapter provides the background information to help you realize the benefits of understanding families—how you, your students, and your students' families will benefit, and how you will become a more effective educator. More specifically, this chapter will help you consider:

- The purpose and behaviors of families
- The need for families to protect their children
- The need to socialize children into the familial culture
- The teacher's role
- Home–school relations of the past
- The changing family

The job of an educator is much more complicated today than it was in the past. Not only must educators understand the issues traditionally embodied in the subject matter of home–school relations, but also must view families in a sociological and educational framework in order to understand how they function. Only by doing so can teachers work with students' families in the most effective manner.

As always, teachers must conduct parent–teacher conferences and understand various parent involvement models—pre-school, elementary, middle school, as well as models for parents of students with special needs. Now, however, we also must know about changes in contemporary families and their effect on the ways that families function. We must understand how families are influenced by cultural backgrounds, financial resources (or lack thereof), and the changing roles of parents. Students may be from homes headed by single parents, foster parents, grandparents, or gay/lesbian parents; the family may practice a nontraditional religion or speak a language other than English in the home; the family may be "intact" or "blended." The variation in family types seems innumerable. The greater responsibilities that come with a more diverse group of families makes it imperative that teachers go beyond classroom walls to understand the relationship between families and schools.

Teachers must also be aware of ways in which education can be influential in supporting families. This involves understanding and using public policy, advocacy, and the laws that pertain to the issues involving families and schools. Without this knowledge, teachers can react only to the needs of individual students and their families, when it would be of more benefit to provide broad support for a greater number of families.

Defining "Family" and Determining Family Responsibilities

The U.S. Bureau of the Census (1993) defines a family as two or more persons related by birth, marriage, or adoption who reside in the same household. This is a legal definition, relying solely on relationships determined by blood or contract. In contrast, the sociological definition of families considers the way that families function. Though not a sociologist, a second-grader developed a sociological definition when he observed, "A family is people who live together who help and love each other."

The second-grader took the important step of focusing on what families do as opposed to how they look. Families, for example, do two important things for children: protect them from a range of harmful influences, and prepare them to function within their cultures, that is, society. Whether we look at pre-Colombian Mayan families in Central America, Chinese families of the Ming Dynasty, contemporary Buddhist families of Thailand, or middle-class families in Houston, the primary purpose of these families was and is the same—to protect and prepare their children. What makes these families different is the everyday conditions they face, and the manner in which they accomplish these similar goals.

Protecting Children from Danger

The nature of danger differs over time and with location. While prehistoric Aleutian parents feared saber-toothed tigers and parents of Dickens' industrialized England were concerned about their children working long hours in unhealthy environments, contemporary U.S. parents worry about their children's exposure to sex and violence in the media and on the Internet. Furthermore, parents in all times and places were, and remain, concerned about their children's health, nutrition, and safety. Again, what has changed is not the function of the family, but rather the nature of the dangers and the character of the society in which parents must prepare their children to live.

While families in the past worked hard to ensure their children's health and physical survival, contemporary parents can generally expect their children to survive and grow to maturity. Today, parents often include in their concerns their children's emotional health.

Preparing Children for Society

How did you learn the proper way to act in a place of worship, in a museum, at a party, or at a family reunion? While there usually is no formal instruction in these areas, most people know exactly what is expected of them, and behave accordingly. As children, we learned these skills through parental guidance and through observing members of our families and others as they interacted in various societal settings. Anthropologists refer to this learning as *enculturation*—the process by which a family and/or society prepares children to behave appropriately and appreciate their cultural values and traditions. Enculturation ensures that people in a given society understand and can interact appropriately with others within their society.

Families, Their Children, and Teachers

Stated simply, families strive to provide safe, nurturing environments in which children can learn to function in society. When most families lived in isolated rural areas, this socialization occurred predominantly under parental supervision. As the family was much more an isolated unit, these parents also played the roles of teachers, doctors, psychologists, and spiritual leaders for their children. Families continued to protect and nurture children as society became more industrialized and complex; however, this increasing complexity meant that parents found it more difficult to be totally responsible for all of their children's needs. Teachers, physicians, ministers, social workers, and institutions such as schools, public health services, churches, synagogues, community social services and others began to play greater roles in the upbringing of children. Although schools assumed more of the educational responsibilities, families continued to be the first and most important teachers of children, because it is through families that children learn how to live in their worlds.

Teachers now have some responsibilities that have historically been within the parents' domain. Teachers have taken on the responsibility of educating because it requires skill and knowledge beyond that which can be reasonably expected of lay people in contemporary society. Even if parents have the skill and knowledge needed to handle these responsibilities, they may not have the time to provide a formal education for their children. The result is that educators' skills and knowledge complement and overlap those of the family.

If teachers' professional efforts are to complement those of parents, they need to have a better understanding of families and how they function. Henderson's research (1987) provides the rationale for this need: First, since educators' efforts at school correspond with those of the parent(s) in the student's home, educators need to know about their students' families to be maximally effective. Second, by understanding those responsible for children at home, educators can work with parents to help children to be safe and move comfortably into society. And third, this understanding will help to produce better teachers.

Changing World—Changing Families

Schools are changing, families are changing, and society as a whole is changing. It hasn't been that long since you started communicating with others using email or your cellular phone. You probably use a computer rather than a typewriter, a microwave instead of a stove, watch movies on your VCR rather than in a theater, and withdraw money from an ATM instead of writing a check.

Schools have also changed. There are computers in the classroom. Children make use of the Internet and interactive television. Changes have also occurred in the cafeteria, which now includes salad bars and specialty foods. Yet, in spite of these changes, schools are still often viewed as being fixed and unchanging institutions. The cardboard replica of the red, one-room schoolhouse with a bell tower—which is often found on classroom bulletin boards in September—is as much like the schools of today as a No. 2 Pencil is like a word processor.

Schools also reflect the changes in the demographics of our society, changes including, but not limited to, the structure of the family, available economic resources and what those resources will (and will not) purchase. All these changes—technological, societal, demographic—are reflected in the demands placed on families. While families have always been under a certain amount of pressure, the nature of this stress seems to have changed and, in the process, increased significantly. Evidence of the changes can be seen with increased incidences of divorce, single-parenting, remarriage, blended families, adoption of children of other races, gay/lesbian families, mothers who never marry, the new sets of grandparents and other extended family members created by remarriage, and interracial marriages. The list could go on for pages.

REFLECTION ...

Consider your immediate and extended family. How many different types of families are present? Make a list and ask your parents, or someone from their generation, how many of those particular family styles were present a generation or two ago.

Home–School Relations in the Past

As educators, our relationship with parents has an interesting history that parallels the economic history of this country. While public schools were initially legislated in Massachusetts in the seventeenth century, it was many years before most parents saw public schools as a realistic opportunity for their children. At that time the economy was agrarian and the population rural; parents in these rural areas had a tremendous influence on the schools, the teachers, the teaching that took place, and even on how teachers could and could not behave outside of the classroom.

Initially, rural schools outnumbered urban schools and were governed by a school board made up of men from the community. As the United States became more industrialized in the mid-1880s, a mass migration from rural to urban areas occurred. As the size of communities increased, the influence of the individual parent on the school decreased. School board members, generally prominent business men, were not people most parents knew or could easily access. At the same time, school districts increased in size, and the boards came to rely more heavily on school administrators responsible for the day-to-day operation of the schools. Put simply, the power shifted from the parents, generally fathers, to male administrators and board members.

The role of parents shifted from that of being actively involved in running the school to that of guests of the school: they were invited to school for specific events and to confer about problems. Furthermore, whereas earlier it had been primarily fathers who dealt with schools and educational issues, the relationship between home and school gradually changed until the responsibility of dealing with schools rested with mothers. Dealings with the school became "women's work," and because the status of women was low at this time, mothers had little input and even less power in the education of their children.

During the 1950s–70s, the parental role remained that of little influence, and mothers continued to be the parent most likely to interact with the school. Parents' group meetings, parent–teacher conferences, and so forth, were generally held in the afternoon, thus making it difficult for working fathers to attend. For practical purposes, fathers were seen as not needing to be actively involved with the day-to-day care and education of children.

There were serious problems with this arrangement. Contrary to popular belief, a large number of mothers were part of the work force; these mothers were most often from ethnically/racially-diverse groups and/or low-income families. Because these women were not able to attend afternoon meetings, parent involvement in the schools became primarily an activity of white, middle-class women. This made a loud and clear statement about how minorities and poor people were valued by the schools during this period in time.

The U.S. economy has changed dramatically since the 1970s. Presently, it takes two salaries to provide an equivalent spendable income that a single wage-earner could make in 1970 (Sherman, 1994). Consequently, in order to maintain a middle-class standard of living today, most mothers of school children are a part of the work force. As a result, even middle-class mothers are generally not available during school hours. The unavailability during the school day of parents from all economic and ethnic/racial segments of society demands a rethinking of both how to involve parents in the schools and what the nature of that involvement might be.

At the same time, many parents want to be more actively involved in their children's education, as opposed to being merely recipients of test scores and grades. This desire is complicated by the amount of time (or lack of time) parents can devote to the schools. However, these issues and more will be discussed in detail in the following chapters.

Looking at Families

Because children bring their family experiences with them to school, educators must understand families in order to best understand the child. Most books on home–school relations focus on skills (parent–teacher conferences, parent-involvement programs, etc.), which are certainly important issues; indeed, they are covered in depth in this book. However, we feel strongly that knowledge and understanding of the family is a prerequisite to truly meaningful relationships between the school and the home.

To assist you in acquiring the skills to meet this goal, we will examine four factors influencing families and focus on their impact:

1. The spendable income available to a family
2. The ethnic, racial, and cultural background of the family
3. The structure of the family
4. Individual familial differences.

Changing Income Levels of Families

Income, more than any other single factor, determines the quality of life for most families. An alarming 25 percent of the children in this country live in poverty. The result of poverty, as Fuller and Tutwiler point out in Chapter 12, can be devastating to families, and make learning more difficult for the child.

The experiences that low-income families share with those from middle-class backgrounds are minimal. This is important to acknowledge because educators tend to come from middle-class homes (Webb & Sherman, 1989) and, therefore, have sensibilities and experiences that are very different from those of impoverished students. These middle-class sensibilities and experiences often restrict the understanding of poverty.

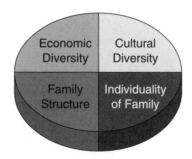

FIGURE 1-1   **Factors to Consider**
When Examining
Home-School Relations

While educators are generally caring, intelligent people who want the best for students, the disparity of life experiences between middle-class and poor families—a disparity that differs in both quality and quantity—is often not recognized. As a result, educators often hold stereotypes of low-income people that impede their abilities to work effectively with students from low-income families. While educators want to meet the needs of all children, their understanding of poverty is often inadequate to accomplish the task.

The Changing Demographics of Ethnicity/Culture/Race

The families of children in the public schools exhibit greater diversity than ever before, while teachers and pre-service teachers are still largely white, middle-class, and female (Fuller, 1994).

Approximately 31 percent of public school students are children of color. In fact, children of color make up the majority of school children in some states. Currently, 58 percent of school children in California are members of under-represented groups, and by 2020, these groups are expected to exceed the white mainstream population in schools (Wise & Gollnick, 1996). These children live in a range of ethnic, cultural, racial, familial, and economic milieus that are frequently different from those in which educators lived as children.

The ethnic/racial diversity of families has changed for a variety of reasons: Higher birthrates for people of color and changes in immigration patterns are two of the primary reasons for change. While early immigrants were generally from northern Europe or Canada (between 1951 and 1960, 67 percent of our immigrants came from Europe or Canada, 25 percent from Mexico or Latin America, and only 6 percent from Asia), between 1993 and 1994, 37 percent of immigrants came from Asia, 38 percent were from Mexico and Latin America, and only 22 percent from Europe and Canada. This results in a change in the traditionally northern European appearance of many of our students and their families. More importantly, it also means that in addition to cultural diversity, non-Judeo-Christian religions, such as Buddhism, Hinduism, and Islam are also adding to the richness and variety of our classrooms. Tutwiler, Chapter 3, discusses ethnicity, culture, and race in more depth.

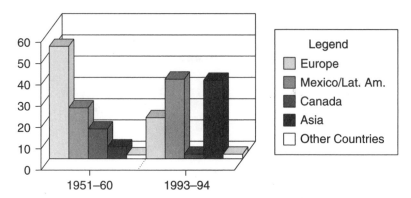

FIGURE 1-2   Immigration: A Changing Population

Changing Family Structure

Throughout history there has been a multiplicity of family styles: married, single parents (widow/widower), polygamous, polyandrogous, step families, and so on. In contemporary western society it is not new configurations of the family that society is experiencing but changes in the number of certain configurations. For example, single-parent households headed by women are not new; however, the number of such families has almost doubled since 1970 (Ahlburg & De Vita, 1992). In 1970, 45 percent of families had children, while in 1995, only 35 percent had children. These figures are of particular importance since they help teachers understand the changes that are occurring in the families of their students.

Another change in the family is the increasing age of first-time parents. In 1994, men were approximately 27 years and women 25 when they married for the first time. This is an increase of more than four years for both men and women over the 1950 data (U.S. Bureau of the Census, 1995). This means that, among the many other changes, schools will be dealing with an older parent population than in the past.

Among these many familial changes is the role of fathers—more and more men are actively involved in parenting than at any other time since the industrialization of society in the western world. Divorce has also created different roles for fathers. Non-custodial fathers may well want to continue to be involved in their children's education. In addition, there are a growing number of fathers who are now awarded custody. These are generally new relationships for most educators. Hennen, Palm, and Olsen discuss fathers in more detail in Chapter 13.

Individuality of Families

Every family is different. Each brings a unique history and attributes that affect their experience as a family, and all families have their successes and failures. Some families are more functional and some more dysfunctional than others. Fuller and Marxen will discuss families in more detail in Chapter 2. There are families with children who have special needs, which Reilly discusses in Chapter 8, and all educators—whether they are teaching children with special needs or not—need to understand the families of these children. Inclusion of children with special needs is all around us. In our classrooms today, we have students who not long ago would have been segregated into "special" classes, but who are now mainstreamed into the traditional classroom. School buildings and transportation have been modified to allow students with disabilities to become a more integral part of the schools. This means we must also rethink our relationship with the parents of special need students to ensure they are a more integral part of the educational system.

We must also be informed about the nightmare of violence experienced by numerous children and their families. Knowledge and skills for dealing with the aftermath of violence are imperative before we can be effective advocates for the abused. Knowlton and Muhlhauser will discuss the issues relating to violence in Chapter 11.

Parent Involvement

Hanhan, in Chapter 6, discusses the history of home–school relations to help give us a historical perspective. Currently, parent involvement is designed to return parents to the school. Parents must be team members in the education of their children. Educators are experts in their field—children and the education of children—and parents are the experts on their children. However, since past experiences have given either parents or teachers disproportionate power in the relationship, both now have to learn to work as a team. This starts with a basic understanding of families and their view of parenting responsibilities, as well as educators' views of these responsibilities. Zimmerman (Chapter 4), MacDonald (Chapter 5), and Sandell (Chapter 7) discuss parents, schools, and teachers and their interrelationship.

Understanding families is the initial step in working with the families of students. The next step must be to involve parents in their children's education. There are a variety of good parent-involvement models to consider: early childhood, elementary, middle-school, and special education (Chapter 9). In addition, it is helpful to understand the experiences of parents who have decided to remove their family and children from the traditional school experience and so Knowles (Chapter 14) discusses the history and rationale of the continued growth in numbers of home-schooled children.

Teachers have a responsibility to be knowledgeable about legal issues concerning home-schooling, and to inform parents of their legal rights and obligations. Thomas, in Chapter 10, analyzes the laws and responsibilities surrounding parents and their rights. We as educators are sometimes ill informed about advocacy and public policy, and this makes it difficult to make systemic changes in home–school relations. We must be knowledgeable if we are to be effective. Zimmerman (Chapter 15) discusses the most effective ways to advocate in the public policy arena.

This book has been written to meet the needs of early childhood, elementary, middle school, and special education teachers. It will allow them to better understand, and consequently work with, the contemporary family.

This book evolved out of a desire to better prepare teachers to work with families and so better serve students. We (Fuller and Olsen) teach in the area of home–school relations as well as write and conduct research in this important discipline. We have used a variety of different books with our classes and were impressed by the quality of most, but we had a different vision—a vision that teachers would develop an in-depth understanding of families. With this goal in mind, we spent considerable time deciding what should be included in this book. We then invited people with special expertise in these areas to contribute. We wrote this book for our students, you, your students, and their families.

References

Ahlburg, D. A., & De Vita, C. (1992). New realities of the American family. *Population Bulletin, 47*(2).

Fuller, M. L. (1994). The monocultural graduate in a multicultural environment: A challenge to teacher education. *Journal of Teacher Education, 43*(4) 269–278.

Henderson, A. (1987). *The evidence continues to grow.* Columbia, MD: National Committee for Citizens in Education.

O'Hare, W. P. (1996). A new look at poverty. *Population Bulletin, 51*(2).

Sherman, A. (1994). *Wasting America's future: The children's defense fund report on the cost of child poverty.* Boston, MA: Beacon Press.

U.S. Bureau of the Census. (1993). Poverty in the United States (*Current Population Series P60–185*). Washington, DC: US Government Printing Office.

U.S. Bureau of the Census. (1995, September). Household and family characteristics. *Current Population Reports,* P20–483.

Webb, R. B., & Sherman, R. R. (1989). *Schooling and society* (2nd ed.). New York: Macmillan Publishing Company.

Wise, A. E., & Gollnick, D. M. (1996). America in demographic denial. (National Council for Accreditation of Teacher Education). *Quality Education, 5*(2).

C h a p t e r 2

Families and Their Functions—Past and Present

MARY LOU FULLER
University of North Dakota

CAROL MARXEN
The University of Minnesota–Morris

Happy

Love
Lindsey Johnson

I'm happy when my family's together.

I love my brothers even when we fight.

By Lindsey Johnson

In order for educators to provide the best learning environment for students, they must understand the families from which the students come. The majority of families do not fit the stereotype of the "All-American Family." This chapter will introduce you to contemporary families. The purpose of this chapter is to help you:

- Trace the history of the family
- Identify the structures and needs of the contemporary family
- Compare historical and contemporary families
- Describe a functional and a dysfunctional family

This chapter provides the background information needed to help you understand families and consequently become a more effective teacher. More specifically, the chapter will help you: (1) take a historical perspective in viewing families of the past and the issues affecting them, (2) develop a perspective on how families look today, and (3) examine the characteristics of functional and dysfunctional families. In other words, reading and understanding the material in this chapter will provide you with a basic understanding of families and how and why they operate as they do. Because we are all fascinated by learning about ourselves and others, this chapter should be personally enlightening as well as informative.

The Evolution of the Family

Why Take a Historical Perspective?

While the structure of families is changing, our stereotype of families is not. Although observations tell us differently, our perception of the All-American family is still an intact family with children, father employed outside the home, and mother staying at home. The reality is that this family currently accounts for less than 4 percent of U.S. families, and this percentage is declining (Johnson, 1990). Is this decline (which some perceive as a breakdown in family values) the cause of societal ills such as poverty, crime, drug abuse, and school failure? Or are the societal ills the cause of family problems? In other words, does a stronger family unit create a more stable economic, social, and political environment? Or, does a growing, supportive, and prosperous economic, social, and political environment increase family stability? Looking at families from earlier times can help us consider these questions.

Skolnick (1991) encourages us to view families from other eras the way we would view families from different cultures. The comparison is appropriate because families at each point in history have their own sets of family values and family functions, which developed in response to the social, political, and economic environments of the time. They used those values and functions to do the same things contemporary families do: protect their children and prepare those children to take their places in society. Families have always struggled (as contemporary families do) with problems resulting from political, economic, and societal forces, so it is quite reasonable to look at earlier families in the same way as we look at present-day families. Indeed, doing so offers insights into how families develop their practices and values. Adopting a historical perspective may do more than document changes in families; it may offer insights concerning future trends. In particular, we will look at a range of historical families seeking to discover how they protected their children from threats to their well-being and how they prepared their children to be members of the societies in which they lived.

Early History

Prehistorical Families

Conditions faced by primitive societies dictated that families work together for survival; constant effort was needed to protect everyone—and especially children—from starvation, exposure to the elements, and disease. Practicality dictated that families sharing specific customs and beliefs band together for mutual security; these groups were called *clans*. *Tribes* were multiple clans living in the same vicinity and sharing the same culture. Tribes were better able than clans to protect their members against enemy tribes, and to ensure that everyone had sufficient food to eat and individuals who were disabled were cared for according to tribal custom. Children observed their parents, other adults, and members of their tribe and emulated what they saw. They learned from those responsible for them and, in so doing, became enculturated (socialized) into their culture. Because the continuation of the tribe was dependent upon children carrying traditions from one generation to the next, a measure of how much children were valued is found in the fact that they were taught traditions, rules, and customs (Berger, 1995).

As cultures learned to meet basic survival needs more effectively (e.g., as food supplies became more reliable through domestication of animals and the cultivation of crops), the threats to the family changed. In particular, new problems of social organization emerged both within and among populations. Internally, individuals became more dependent on others outside their families, and externally, groups of people needed to learn how to deal with other groups. In a word, society became more complex, and children needed to learn much more if they were to become productive adults.

Greek and Roman Period Families

We may speculate that this was the time when the task of educating children first became sufficiently complex that moving it out of the realm of parental responsibility might allow parents to better protect their children while ensuring that their children learned what they needed to take their places in society as they reached adulthood. More specifically, Plato (427–347 B.C.), Aristotle (384–323 B.C.), Cicero (106–43 B.C.), and Polybius (204–122 B.C.) were Greek and Roman philosophers who believed that educating parents and children was important for the benefit of the state. However, their interest was reserved only to boys born to wealthy families. Boys needed to learn about governing, military strategy, managing commerce, and so forth—all activities expected of those who would lead their cultures.

Such a view represented little departure from earlier times. Families were still responsible for protecting their children, and because formal education was reserved for boys from families of nobility, girls still learned domestic skills at home and boys from lesser families continued to learn within the family environment the skills and knowledge they needed to assume their roles in society. Although there were laws and customs allowing infanticide and the sale of children, Greek and Roman civilizations were generally supportive of families and children (Berger, 1995).

Family life and the role of children as members of family units changed considerably after the decline of the Roman Empire. Deterioration of the fabric of society meant that some threats which had been dealt with by large groups of people (e.g., defense of the community) again became the responsibility of families and family groups during the Middle Ages (400–1400). Simple survival re-emerged as the primary goal for many individuals, and so children came to be viewed as property. In addition, the harshness and brevity of life meant that children were expected to become adults at a very young age and there was no time for education. Indeed, family life for the children of peasants was a constant struggle to simply satisfy the basic needs of food, clothing, and shelter. Only those few children born to noble families were educated. In addition, they were also prepared to be responsible for the property and the traditions they would inherit.

European Medieval Families

While life for most children had always been difficult, a harshness became a predominant part of parenting behaviors during the Middle Ages. Although we now regard this view as misguided, families from both noble and peasant classes alike treated their children as miniature adults. Families had no appreciation of the developmental processes of childhood. The church of the time had an extraordinary influence on governmental matters, family life in general, and child-rearing practices.

The church taught that children were naturally evil, had to be told what to do, needed to be corrected constantly, and had to be punished harshly so that they could function well in society as adults. Children were thought to be evil and the term "beat the devil out of the child" came into existence because of this belief. It was very common for parents of all classes to emotionally neglect their young children or abandon them to a wet nurse, monastery, or nunnery. In other words, economic difficulties of the time and the church's view of children during Medieval times meant harsh treatment of children and little support for family life. Children generally were not well protected, and even though the boys of the wealthy were educated (as proposed by the Greeks and Romans), this experience was often a perversion of a healthy educational experience. We can be certain, however, that children learned how to behave as adults by watching and emulating the society surrounding them.

Renaissance and Reformation Families

The Renaissance (1300–1400) and Reformation (1500–1600) periods that followed saw increased concern about freedom for common people. This concern, accompanied by increased social organization that relieved some of the threats to families, and the important idea that a person is an individual rather than only a part of a group, made social classes less significant than during the Middle Ages. Individuality and freedom were extended to children and their schooling and better ensured that children were educated. The belief that children were pure and good was promoted in contradiction to the idea of original sin that the church had advocated during the Middle Ages.

Martin Luther (1482–1546), the father of the Reformation, proposed revolutionary child-rearing practices. He advocated that parents educate their children and teach them morals and the catechism. He maintained that families were the most important educators for children, that education was appropriate for both girls and boys, and that both genders would become better adults if they were educated.

Luther's ideas, followed by Johannes Gutenberg's invention of the printing press in 1439, meant that a few families would have access to books and could educate their children. In Europe, there were also more schools for the families who could afford them. However, school was still reserved for the sons of nobility, and education for the common person was not to come until much later.

The Age of Reason

The Age of Reason (1600–1700), also called the Period of Enlightenment, was an era of notable intellectual activity. Numerous religious leaders, philosophers, and educators introduced ideas about the way children learn and how families could best educate them. Comenius (1592–1670), a bishop, teacher, and writer, believed that all children were basically good; and Locke (1632–1704), an English philosopher, promoted the idea that children's minds are like "clean slates" on which parents and teachers could write what students were to learn.

While Comenius and Locke promoted education for maintaining a democracy, the philosopher Rousseau (1712–1778) took a social view of children. In his book *Emile,* he advocated a child's world that would be free from society's arrogant and unnatural ways. He introduced the concept of the whole child and promoted the idea that children needed a flexible, free atmosphere in which to mature according to their own natural timetables. Pestalozzi (1746–1827), a Swiss educator, was influenced by Rousseau, and he expanded upon Rousseau's belief of allowing a child's natural development by encouraging the child to learn basic skills. In addition, he believed that mothers from all socioeconomic classes should teach practical skills to their children at home, stressing the development of the whole child. Thus, the notion that families need to prepare their children for adulthood grew and included the important precepts that children are individuals and that they need to develop in a broad range of areas. Notice, though, that the family was still the central feature in the child's education.

Froebel (1782–1852) was a German educator who became known as the "father of kindergarten." He studied with Pestalozzi and eventually started a school for young children which promoted play for learning. Children's play, however, was guided by a trained teacher who planned activities that encouraged learning. Once again, a specially trained teacher relieved the family of some responsibilities for their children gaining the skills and knowledge they needed as adults.

Thinkers during the Age of Reason emphasized the worth and the dignity of humans and agreed with Francis Bacon's belief that "knowledge is power." In spite of the progress that was made toward valuing all individuals (including children), the Industrial Revolution changed how children were treated—in undesirable ways.

The Industrial Revolution

From the Age of Reason to the Age of Darkness—the Industrial Revolution was a period of child exploitation. The advent of the Industrial Revolution in the 1700s and 1800s brought social and political crises in France and England. During the Industrial Revolution, the economic condition was so desperate that families could no longer protect their children adequately; indeed, children became a liability to their families. Children from poor families, many as young as ten years of age, commonly worked ten- to fourteen-hour days in factories as cheap laborers.

This was not true for all children. Berger (1995) contends that "families tended to fit into three categories: the wealthy, who allowed others to rear their offspring and who exhibited indifference to children; the emerging middle classes, who wanted to guide, direct, and mold their children in specific patterns; and the poor and poverty stricken, who lacked the means to have much semblance of family life" (p. 44). Despite social class differences, children were still expected to act like adults from a very young age.

The political and economic structure of Europe during the Industrial Revolution changed how society viewed children and families. Concomitantly, colonies in the new world were developing their own political, economic, and social environment.

Colonial North American Family

While many city children were slaving in factories and living on the streets in the 1700s and 1800s, other children were helping on family-owned farms and businesses. Though economic life was a struggle, many colonial families were self-sufficient and so able to protect their children, and they were able to socialize them through secular and religious education—including opportunities for recreation (Seward, 1978).

It is important to realize that these families did not do this all on their own. Coontz (1995) reminds us that the government provided resources not available to families in Europe. "Prairie farmers and other pioneer families owed their existence to massive federal land grants, government-funded military mobilization that disposed [of] hundreds of Indian societies and confiscated large portions of Mexico, and state-sponsored economic investment in new lands, many of which were sold to settlers or spectators at prices far below the cost to the public treasury of acquiring them" (p. K6). During the 1700s, political and religious conflict, a growing economy, and free land allowed young families and individuals to move out on their own. The result was the emergence of the idea of a new independent family structure (Skolnick, 1991). But what about the children? Although children were viewed as important and necessary for the family economy in the new world, child rearing in Puritan families remained as it was in Europe, strict and humiliating. Children were perceived as corrupt and it was the parent's responsibility to break their wills to rid them of their basic evil natures. Physical punishment was common and legitimate in this patriarchal society for wives as well as children (Skolnick, 1991), and obedience to the father was strictly observed.

Despite the romantic image of the family of this period, many children died in early childhood, and a person's life expectancy was less than fifty years. A significant number of women died in childbirth and, because of women's high death rate, "only a third of the marriages lasted more than ten years" (Skolnick, 1991, p. 25). Widowers remarried quickly because of necessity, and, consequently, there were few single-parent homes and numerous blended families (step families) during Colonial times. Black families were brought from Africa as slaves and so did not have the advantages enjoyed by the new colonists. Because family members were frequently separated from one another, the structure of these families varied significantly from the rest of society. We continue to feel the effects of the devastation of the black family today (Berger, 1995).

American Industrialization and the Family

From the 1850s to the 1920s, there was a dramatic shift away from the Puritan ideas of colonial America. The country became more industrialized, urbanized, and prosperous. There was growth in manufacturing, with immigrants providing cheap labor for factories; gold was found in California; western lands were opened; and prosperous agricultural crops provided a surplus of food.

By 1920, the work week was shortened from six days to five, and the middle class had become larger. The working class profited, too; the strong economy and political climate allowed them many luxuries previously available only to wealthy. Because of the country's affluence, society altered its beliefs about the duties of the family, the role of its members, and the image of the child.

A change in the function of the family appeared in rural areas. Increased agricultural productivity meant farm families began to raise cash crops rather than providing solely for their immediate needs, and families began to rely on the money they received to buy goods produced by others. At the same time, larger and more prosperous farms were possible because of mechanization and the migration from rural to urban areas.

Skolnick (1991) reminds us that there is a "remarkable parallel between economic expansiveness and the expansion of 'personal life'—a concern with inner experience...and psychological development across the stages of life" (p. 42). Thus, economic growth was accompanied by an increase in the popularity of the writings of Locke, Rousseau, Pestalozzi, and Froebel, and childhood came to be viewed as a stage of development, with children being recognized as inherently good. Freud's psychoanalytic theory became popular and John Watson's behaviorist theory strongly influenced child rearing (Skolnick, 1991). In 1912, the government created the Children's Bureau to address concerns of undernourished, neglected, and abused children.

These changing attitudes toward children prompted further changes to the family unit. Relationships became more loving between husband and wife and between parent and child. Family members' roles were specific: fathers worked for financial security and mothers took care of the home and children. Middle- and upper-class mothers had servants to help take care of their children.

There was, however, a new middle-class working woman who challenged traditional gender roles and brought about the suffrage movement and, eventually, in 1920, earned women the right to vote. More women went to college as well.

The emergence of mandatory, free public schools was another major social change during the mid-1800s. While schools assisted families with the education of their children in the past (that is, families still maintained the major responsibility for children's education), the government now took over primary responsibility for formal education with the advent of public schools. The government believed that females were not able to properly teach their children to become effective citizens for a democratic society, especially women of immigrant families. Thus Horace Mann's Common School was created for the purpose of Americanizing all citizens (Keniston, 1977). While families were still responsible for protecting children and educating them for adulthood, much responsibility for the latter was now formally in the hands of the government.

World War I and the Great Depression brought many new ideas to a halt as mere survival became a daily struggle. As in the past, the functioning of the family and the roles of its members changed in response to economic and societal exigencies of the time.

The Great Depression and World War II

The political and economic impact of the Great Depression and World War II dramatically affected the functioning of the family. When men lost their jobs because of the Depression, they also lost their roles as family providers. They were further devastated as women joined the workforce and families moved in together to share resources and reduce expenses. The pattern of women working and families sharing housing continued through World War II as husbands and fathers became part of the military. In extreme cases, families were simply torn apart and children were often taken care of by their grandparents.

Educators saw the importance of education for young children, and child care centers were created because of a need for them. The government, through the Works Progress Administration (WPA), came to the aid of families by funding nursery schools using unemployed teachers. From 1941 to 1946, the Lantham Act War Nurseries were supported by the government to provide child care for children whose parents were part of the war effort. The most famous of these nurseries were the Kaiser Child Care Centers, which provided twenty-four-hour daycare for working mothers during the war. The centers were closed when the war ended and the mothers gave up their jobs and returned to their homes (Gordon & Browne, 1993). Indeed, women working outside the home were viewed as wartime sacrifices, with men assuming the breadwinner role when they returned home from military service. It appeared that traditional gender-specific roles had been reestablished.

REFLECTION...

Imagine yourself living during the time of the Depression. What would your life be like? How would the Depression affect your family? Compare a family of the Depression era with a contemporary family.

1950s to 1970s

Americans experienced the greatest economic boom in history from the 1950s through the 1970s. Many sociologists believe that, because of the strong economic and political climate during the 1950s, societies in general and families more specifically were secure and solid (Coontz, 1995; Skolnick, 1991). The nuclear family of the 1950s was thought to be the "main source of childhood socialization and center of all personal happiness" (Coontz, 1995, p. K7) and completely independent from all outside sources.

The idea of a completely self-reliant family is, however, a myth. Government assistance programs of the 1950s helped veterans (primarily middle-class white men) obtain college educations and buy homes. In other words, it gave them a head start. Unfortunately, these programs did not assist people of color; stigmatized ethnic groups; single, divorced, and working mothers; so that 30 percent of families lived in poverty during this supposedly "golden" period (Coontz, 1995). Moreover, women lost much of the independence they had gained before and during World War II.

At the same time, middle-class women were having more children and were tied to their suburban homes. Child-rearing practices of the 1950s were influenced by child development experts such as Erik Erickson, Arnold Gesell, and Benjamin Spock, whose messages were that children have individual differences that need to be nurtured and that each child proceeds through developmental stages at a rate that cannot be rushed. What each child needs, they argued, is not the stress that comes with being rushed through development, but love that comes with being recognized as unique and valued members of the family.

The 1960s and 1970s was a time of social and political revolt. The children of the 1950s were raised to be independent, critical, and creative rather than obedient (Skolnick, 1991), and when they entered colleges and universities (which they did in record numbers), they questioned and criticized "all institutions—family, education, religion, economics, and government" (Berger, 1995, p. 68). They witnessed a society which ignored poverty and sanctioned racial injustice, and they accepted neither (Skolnick, 1991). The Vietnam War also served to tear the country apart with protests against the United States' involvement—protests that frequently caused strife and strained family relationships. The lack of a unified effort in favor of the war meant family conflicts were magnified.

Economic and political upheaval again caused the family's structure and function to change. More women went back to work, either as single mothers or to supplement the family income, making child care an important issue. Jean Piaget, a Swiss psychologist, gained in popularity at this time. He proposed a theory of cognitive development in children and expressed concern for their intellectual development, in particular the intellectual development of young children. Upon reading Piaget and his followers, parents were eager to help their children develop cognitively rather than simply letting nature take its course.

At the same time, the government began its War on Poverty with hopes of providing children from low socioeconomic families educational, medical, and mental health services. Headstart, a preschool program that included parent involvement, provided disadvantaged children the opportunity to get a head start before entering school. Because of Headstart's success, other programs for young children expanded rapidly. An important feature of Headstart is that, in addition to having trained teachers work with children, parents are also involved and taught to work with their children.

In summary, families have had and will continue to have two responsibilities toward their children: they need to protect children from threats to their well-being, and they need to educate them so they can be productive members of the societies within which they live when they reach adulthood. What has changed has been the cultural matrix within which families function, a matrix to which families are bound by particular circumstances and events, and to which they react (Demos, 1996). Skolnick (1991) summarizes the relationship between families and society more generally by noting that "families are responsive to historical and cultural predicaments, and each such response invites new predicaments" (p. 48).

Changes have been both positive and negative. When they were positive, society grew in ways which made it easier for families to both protect and educate their children. This was the case, for example, in Greece and Rome, where social organization reduced the effort parents had to take to protect their children. It was also true of the Renaissance and Reformation periods when societal threats were reduced and the first recognition was made that children were individuals to be valued as such. And finally, after the Civil War and during the post-World War II period, the combination of economic prosperity and support from the government allowed families to expend more energy educating their children for adulthood.

Periods when families were most frustrated in addressing their responsibilities toward children were the Middle Ages and the Industrial Revolution, when economic deprivation threatened adults so severely that they were unable to look after their children. These were also times when society failed to recognize that being a child was different than being an adult, and that the proper maturation experiences for children did not include being treated like miniature adults.

Contemporary U.S. Families

We turn now to families in America at the close of the twentieth century and the ways in which they address the two tasks of protecting children and preparing them for adulthood. In doing so, we must consider the varieties of families commonly found in our contemporary society.

Most people think of children when they think of families. Yet only 37 percent of all families have minor children in their homes, and this number is expected to decrease to 34 percent in the next five years. Moreover, there is considerable diversity within that 37 percent (Ahlburg & DeVita, 1992). In addition to intact families (both biological parents and minor children), there are households headed by single-parents, cohabitating couples, and gay parents; blended families; and families headed by grandparents rearing minor children in addition to numerous other structures. To make matters even more complex, there is great diversity within each of these family structures.

It is true that the structure of families has changed since the end of World War II and continues to change. The advent of reliable, inexpensive birth control means that adults can put off childbirth until they have established themselves; consequently, families are smaller and women are older than their mothers were when they had children.

The number of single-parent families has also increased; indeed, it has doubled since 1970—due to divorce and the number of children born to unmarried mothers (up from 5 percent of all births in 1960 to 27 percent in 1989). In addition, the remarriage rate following divorce has grown, increasing significantly the number of blended families (Ahlburg & De Vita, 1992). Finally, because the Baby Boomers are largely moving out of the child-rearing years, there been a decrease in the number of married couples with children.

As an educator who shares responsibilities with families for educating children, you must be well informed about the range and nature of family structures in your classroom. Though there are many different familial structures and they are all equally important, we will focus primarily on three groups: single unmarried mothers, single divorced mothers, and blended families. These three were selected because they are more apt to be misunderstood than the intact (traditional) family.

Single-Parent Families

Currently, half of all children will spend at least part of their lives in single-parent homes, and the mother will most likely be the custodial parent (Coontz, 1995; Johnson, 1990). These children will be in your classroom, and you must be knowledgeable about them so you can effectively meet their needs. The two largest categories of children of single-parent families are families headed by an unmarried mother and single-parent homes created by divorce. Single-parent homes account for a large number of families and, unfortunately, single-parent households are perhaps the most stereotyped of all family structures.

Unmarried Mothers

Twenty-three percent of all children are born to unmarried mothers. Unfortunately, there is a lot of confusion as to just what that figure means. The public's perception of this population is that of an unmarried teen living on welfare. The reality is that there are two very different populations within this group—teenagers and women 20 and older. Contrary to the public's perception, "mothers 20 and older" is the larger of the two groups, accounting for two thirds of the births to unmarried mothers.

Twenty and Over

The twenty and over category can also be divided into two types: (a) those who chose to become pregnant and (b) those for whom the pregnancy was not planned (Ahlburg & De Vita, 1992). The first group is older, more affluent, better educated, and not in a position to marry. They are generally thirty or older and have decided that if they are going to have a baby they must, for biological reasons, have one soon. This is normally a well-thought-out decision with issues ranging from options for impregnation (invitro, artificial insemination, a male partner, etc.) to adoption. Also, financial security generally is considered well in advance for this population. Furthermore, these women generally report satisfaction with their decisions (Bing & Cowman, 1980; Fuller, 1989).

The second group tends to be in their early twenties and less well off financially and educationally. They do not plan the pregnancy and frequently have neither the maturity nor the resources available to properly rear a child. It is important to recognize that even though the pregnancy was not planned, this does not mean that the baby was not wanted or loved at the time of birth (Ahlburg & DeVita, 1992; Bing, 1980; Fuller, 1989).

> *REFLECTION...*
>
> Think about the structure of students' families when you were in elementary school. How do they differ from what you would see in a present-day classroom?

Teen Mothers

Unmarried teenagers give birth to approximately 13 percent of the children born in this country each year. While this is still a considerable percentage, it is a significant decrease in the number of births to unmarried teens in the 1970s. But what has increased is the number of young women between the ages of fifteen and seventeen who are having babies. These births are particularly problematic because they bring many serious complications to motherhood, including a lack of maturity and limited financial resources. These mothers are clearly more apt to live in poverty, be unemployed, have low-level employment skills, possess narrow educational backgrounds, and have limited parenting skills, to name a few (Ahlburg & DeVita, 1992).

Due to the increase in the numbers of very young unmarried teenage mothers, there has been an increase in another kind of family structure—households headed by maternal grandmothers who are rearing the children of these young mothers. Sociologists call this phenomenon *skip generation parenting.* As a teacher, you may well be working with your student's grandparents. To complicate matters even more, you may be working with both grandparents and the child's young mother.

There are those who point to the rate of unwed teenage mothers as evidence of a moral decline peculiar to the United States. However, this is an uninformed conclusion, since the rate of births to unwed teenagers in this country is about half of what it is in Sweden and about the same as other Western countries (Canada, France, and the United Kingdom) (Ahlburg & De Vita, 1992). Using this birthrate as an index of morality suggests that the United States is no better and no worse than many other countries and, indeed, better than some. Perhaps it would be more appropriate to consider the ability of unmarried teen mothers to protect and provide for their children than to attempt to assess the morality of the situation.

You will be teachers for children of unmarried mothers and, as with all families, you will find great diversity among these families. A student from a home headed by an unmarried mother may be the child of a mature, well-educated, financially secure woman who is interested and involved in her child's education. Or the student may be the child of a mother who was fifteen years old at his or her birth, and this could be problematic. The young mother may be unable to attend school functions because she cannot take time away from her job, either because her employer won't let her or because she cannot sacrifice the income. The variances in these families are innumerable, as they are within all family structures.

Patterns of Marriage, Divorce, and Remarriage

The demographics describing the transition of families can often be confusing. Consequently, Figure 2-1 is presented to help you visualize this statistical flow. Please note that this figure pertains to all marriages and the statistics used for the following families (single-parent families/divorced and blended families) pertain only to families with children unless otherwise noted.

The following two family configurations to be explored are single-parent families due to divorce and blended families. These two families share a common attribute: in both types parents are, or have been, married at least once.

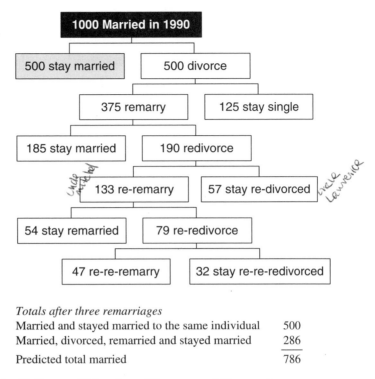

Totals after three remarriages

Married and stayed married to the same individual	500
Married, divorced, remarried and stayed married	286
Predicted total married	786

FIGURE 2-1   Patterns of Marriage, Divorce, and Remarriage

From: Family Science by W. R. Burr, R. D. Day and K. S. Bahr. Copyright © 1993 Brooks/Cole Publishing Company, Pacific Grove, CA, a division of International Thomson Publishing Inc. By permission of the publisher.

Single-Parent Families: Divorce

Though children of single-parent homes (divorce) also are part of a diverse group, they do share some commonalities. In particular, there are two factors which strongly influence the quality of the lives of children of divorced parents: (a) the length of time since the divorce, and (b) the family's economic resources.

Time Period

Children who have recently experienced a divorce are children in a crisis that generally lasts about eighteen months. During this period, children can be expected to display grieving-cycle behaviors: denial, anger, depression, and finally acceptance (or in the case of divorce—adjustment). All children don't necessarily go through each of these stages, and the intensity and duration will vary according to the individual child. However, the majority of children will. Grief is a response to loss (Kubler-Ross, 1969), and even if a child's home situation has been undesirable, they will still feel a loss. The loss in those cases is the loss of a dream—the dream that they will become a happy family (Fuller, 1989).

It is common for children to feel guilt and fear during this period—guilt that they are in some way responsible for the divorce and fear that they might also lose the other parent. During this crisis period, children need understanding, sensitivity, and emotional support so their lives can continue as normally as possible when they have worked through their crisis. Too often, people focus solely on the crisis period of divorce as it is a high-profile, dramatic time marked by increased stress, heightened needs, and new or intensified behaviors. It is easy to think that the crisis will continue forever, but children are resilient and the majority of them will work through their grief.

Finances

Income must be taken into consideration when trying to understand children from single-parent homes. A startling 57 percent of all female-headed households have annual incomes below the national poverty line (Ahlburg & De Vita, 1990), and because more than 90 percent of all custodial parents are women, lack of financial resources is often a very real problem for these families.

Living in poverty has implications for the family experience, from inadequate nutrition (which may appear in the classroom as lethargy) and medical concerns (inadequate immunization means the family is not protecting children well) to quality of both the physical and emotional environment (when the custodial parent is distracted by inadequate resources, it is difficult to pay attention to children and their needs). In other words, fiscal matters must be considered when trying to understand the quality of the lives of your students from single-parent families. Often, problems that children of divorce experience are blamed on the structure of the family as opposed to the stresses and restrictions of poverty. An important question to ask would be Are the problems your student brings to class due to the absence of a second parent or to the absence of adequate financial resources?

Stigmatization

We have all heard people explaining a child's behavior by saying, "She's from a broken home." If the divorce is recent, a better statement would be, "That child is going through a crisis," as that more correctly describes the situation. After your student has worked through his or her crisis, blaming the divorce for behavior is both inadequate as an explanation and inappropriate as a justification. Divorce (after the crisis period) no more produces juvenile misbehavior than marriage guarantees acceptable behavior. Moreover, the language that is used to describe these children and their families is often negative (for example, "broken home"). Broken means defective and surely no one would purposely purchase something that is defective. Yet the term is used frequently to describe divorced families. There was a break in the family at the time of divorce but then a new family evolved. Single-parent homes may be exemplary, undesirable, or, like most homes, somewhere in the middle—doing the best they can. Describing children of divorce as being from a broken home stigmatizes them and their families.

Unfortunately, such stereotyping of children of divorce is common. Much of the negative view of children of divorce in recent years has been promulgated by Judith Wallerstein (1989) through her book, *Second Chance: Men, Women, and Children a Decade after Divorce,* and subsequently, her numerous talk show appearances. Based upon her research,

Wallerstein asserts that over half the children of divorce experience long-term pain, worry, and insecurity that adversely affects their love and work relationships. The problem with these assertions is that they are based upon her research, which was faulty and does not support her findings. As Coontz (1995) points out, this supposedly definitive study was based on a self-selected sample of only sixty couples. It did not compare the children of divorced couples with those of non-divorced couples to determine whether their behaviors stemmed from other factors. Moreover, the sample was drawn from clients that were in therapy at a mental health clinic. Only one third of the sample was seen as mentally healthy *prior* to the onset of the study.

Unfortunately, Wallerstein influenced people who were either not acquainted with the specifics of her research or not knowledgeable about research on children of divorce. This included Barbara Whitehead (1993) whose article, "Dan Quayle was Right," in the *Atlantic Monthly* subsequently influenced President Clinton (Coontz, 1995). Not only did Whitehead base her conclusions on Wallerstein's faulty findings, she misused the research of other family researchers to support assertions about the inferiority of single-parent homes. Significantly, eleven of the family researchers quoted by Whitehead were misquoted. In fact, what they had actually said was that there were few differences between children from single-parent homes and those from two-parent homes, and that children of divorce do not generally experience long-term problems (Coontz, 1995).

Children from Single-Parent Homes

What are children from single-parent homes like? Amato and Keith (1991) did a meta-analysis of the major studies addressing this question, and they concluded that children from single-parent homes are similar to children from two-parent homes.

However, there are a few differences between the children of traditional (intact) homes and children from single-parent homes. After all, children of these two families live in different structures and environments. The following cite some of these differences.

The parents in single-parent homes talk more to their children than parents in two-parent homes (there are no other adults around to talk with), and children in single-parent homes are more mature and have greater feelings of efficacy than children from two-parent families (due, in part, from spending more time talking with adults). Also parents in single-parent homes are less likely to pressure their children into social conformity and more likely to praise good grades than parents of a two-parent household. On the other hand, single-parents on a whole spend less time supervising homework or interacting with the schools than do parents from two-parent homes (Demo & Acock, 1991). Also, two-parent homes can provide a more solid financial base and are less apt to be in poverty (Burr, Day, & Bahr, 1993).

It is important to note that there is often confusion about the statistics of single-parent homes. When you hear that half of all children will live in a single-parent home, it doesn't mean at a given time. Those figures mean at some time before they are eighteen years of age. Also, statistics concerning children from single-parent homes don't normally refer only to children of divorce. These figures generally include children of unmarried women and children who have lost a parent through death.

Blended Families

Blended families (step families) are growing in number. This is not surprising since there has been an increase in the number of single-parent families (unmarried and divorced).

The term *step,* as in stepparent, has an interesting history. It is derived from an early English term meaning deprived and describes the person who steps into a family after the death of an original parent. This was seen as a heroic act that often saved the family from economic ruin. Although the term step family is commonly used, the term "blended" better describes this family unit and is used in this chapter.

In the past, death was the most common cause of blended families; currently, however, the marriage of divorced and unmarried mothers is the most common reason. In the past, death of either parent was problematic, but the death of the father was the most disastrous. Women generally were not part of the workforce and, furthermore, for much of history they were not allowed to own property or have wealth. A remarriage could save a widow and her children from financial disaster.

Although children of single-parent homes are most apt to get the attention of the media, some researchers (Johnson, 1993) feel that blended families will eventually become the largest family structure. Presently, 35 percent of all children will live in a blended family at least once during their childhood (Glick, 1989).

The blended family is the most misunderstood of all family structures. Actually, the single-parent home is more like the intact home than the blended family. Educators are often uncomfortable with the single-parent family (Olsen & Haynes, 1993; Fuller, 1986) and tend to feel relieved when the single-parent family becomes a blended family. After all, it looks like the family we are most comfortable with—the traditional (intact) family.

However, the only thing that the intact family and the blended family have in common is their appearance. The blended family functions differently from other family structures. The members of a blended family bring with them to their new family a complex history as well as different traditions. Whereas there is diversity within any given family structure, none approach the complexity of the blended family. As an example of this complexity, the Institute for Clinical Social Work in Northbrook, Illinois, has defined thirty-two categories of blended families. As an educator, it is imperative that you have an understanding of this family if you are to serve them well.

Research on blended families is limited, and the findings are anything but conclusive. Some researchers view members of blended families as having more problems than those of the traditional family, while others view their problems as not greater but simply different. These latter researchers also see children from blended families as being as well adjusted as children from intact homes (Coontz, 1995, Fuller, 1989).

Facts about Blended Families
What is the truth about blended families? The following is a list of facts on which most researchers agree.

- Younger children tend to make the best adjustment to blended families.
- Adolescents, particularly those of the same sex as the stepparent, are apt to feel resentful of the stepparent.

- Generally, children adjust better to a stepparent after the death of a natural parent than after a divorce.
- Following divorce, the attitude of the adults involved (custodial, noncustodial, and stepparents) will contribute significantly to the child's adjustment to a blended family. Not surprisingly, positive attitudes are more apt to result in a healthier adjustment than negative attitudes.
- Most blended families report being happy.

REFLECTION...

Consider the stereotype of the fairy tale step-mother. How many negative portrayals can you remember? How many positive? How might you explain this disparity?

Myths about Blended Families

Unfortunately, too often the expectations for blended families are based on myths rather than facts. The following are four particularly dangerous myths (Fuller, 1992).

Myth 1.   Family roles in blended families are similar to those of intact families. Although another adult can replace a spouse, they cannot replace a parent. The role of the stepparent is ill defined and, as children often remind them, "You are not my parent!" While stepparents may nurture and support the children they seldom play the role assigned to the natural parent.

Myth 2.   The myth of instant love. It took the adults in the blended family time to build their relationship and yet there is an unrealistic expectation that the stepparent and stepchildren will automatically love one another. They need time to build a relationship, but even given time there are complicating factors. Mixed loyalties present problems for many blended families: "If I love my stepparent, am I being disloyal to my natural parent?" Also, jealousy of step siblings and stepparents is often a problem that must be addressed prior to the development of a functional family.

Myth 3.   Blended families function just like "traditional" families. While "traditional" families share common histories, traditions, and relatives, blended families do not. In contrast, blended families enjoy the richness that comes with diversity—although that diversity may require change. While family traditions (birthdays, Christmas, Hanukkah, family trips, etc.) provide opportunities for enjoyable and enriching new experiences, they also may result in conflict. In addition, relationships between step-siblings (custodial and noncustodial, etc.) must be negotiated.

Myth 4.   Life is just a family sitcom. Perhaps the most detrimental myth of all comes to us from television. Although the "step family" myths of the past (e.g., Cinderella, Hansel and Gretel, Snow White) have been examined and found wanting, we have replaced them with a new set of myths about the blended family (i.e., the *Brady Bunch* and more recent shows about blended families). The Brady Bunch technically may be a blended family, but the script writers have them acting just like an intact family. It is important that you as an educator be aware of the realities of blended families. The utopian adjustment made on television programs such as the *Brady Bunch,* and subsequently their never-ending reruns, is more dangerous than the myth of Cinderella. In Cinderella, the wicked stepmother is accepted as a storybook character while blended families may see the Brady Bunch as a real possibility and feel guilty when they don't live up to this contemporary fairy tale.

When examining any family which differs from the traditional family there is a temptation to dwell on the differences between the two. Often the behaviors that are unlike those of traditional families are seen as undesirable. Also, the strengths of the nontraditional family are apt to be ignored. Coleman and her associates help us examine the strengths of blended families (Coleman, Ganong, & Henry, 1984).

Flexibility

Stepchildren often learn to adjust to different value systems. Thus they may adapt more easily and become more flexible to new traditions and situations. These children generally know how to negotiate in new situations and compromise when necessary. Consequently, when situations require new behaviors (new schools, teachers, etc.), the child from a blended family may well have already developed some important coping skills that can be generalized to these other situations.

Multiple Role Models

There are generally more adults in the lives of children of blended families than those of other family structures, and these adults provide a variety of models from which a child can choose. Aunt Susan is a good business person, Cousin Jim is very creative, and Grandma Mae is a scholar, and they are all role models for the child from the blended family.

Experience with Conflict Resolution

It has been said that children from blended families should be excellent in politics or business management because they know how to negotiate. Their negotiation skills are generally well developed because they may have positive relationships with people who may otherwise be hostile to each other (i.e., their divorced parents).

An Extended Kin Network

The child of a blended family has more parents, grandparents, aunts, uncles, and cousins than children from other family structures. Not only are there more people to learn from, there are more people to love and support them.

Higher Standard of Living

Most children from blended homes previously lived in female-headed, single-parent homes with limited economic resources. With marriage, the total family income is generally increased. With the increase in resources, there is also a rise in the standard of living, as well as added opportunities available for the children. In addition, there is a decrease in the stress caused by worrying about financial instability.

Happy Parents

Remarriage may provide children with a more supportive emotional environment because their parents are happier. Children who have experienced hostility in a previous family may benefit greatly from a more caring, loving environment. Happier remarriages may also provide exposure to a good model of marital interaction.

Step-families are not traditional families warmed over. They are families with their own unique strengths and needs. By understanding the realities of the blended family and dispelling the myths, you can work with these children and their families more effectively. Knowledge allows us to look past the differences and appreciate the strengths of the blended family.

In summary, it is necessary that educators know about, and appreciate, the families of their students. It is also necessary to know how changing family structures play out in the lives of children. Families have become a fluid concept. Consider that the following scenario is about one of your future students, Angie. Angie was born into an intact family, her parents divorced, she then lived in a single-parent family, her mother then remarried, and she then lived in a blended family. Angie's father also remarried and she was part of his blended family, but he has since divorced and is planning to remarry. Angie will have been a member of a number of family configurations during her childhood, not only with her custodial parent but also with her noncustodial parent. Angie's experience is representative of a large number of children.

As families change, so do their needs. For example, as the number of single-parent families increases, so does the need for child care. There is continual change in all families, even within traditional (intact) families. There may be changes in the parents' employment, child care arrangements, or the economic status of the family. Furthermore, families are more mobile and move more frequently than they have in the past. Families are in a continual state of change.

REFLECTION...

Think of a family that you feel is a functional (good) family. What would be the adjectives that describe this family?

Functional and Dysfunctional Families

What are the characteristics of a functional "good" family? What do good families look like and what do they do? What are the effects of a dysfunctional family on the lives of your students?

It is important to be careful in making judgments about families. Contrary to popular belief you cannot determine the effectiveness of a family by its structure. The intact family with two children, in an upper income neighborhood, may or may not be more functional than the single-parent family with two children living in a working class neighborhood. It is not the way a family looks, but rather the way it acts. For many years the body of literature on families was on the dysfunctional family—they were more obvious and easier to study. Presently, there is a considerable body of literature on the functional family, and some identifiable characteristics have emerged. We have a sense of what healthy families are and what they are not.

Functional families are not perfect. All families have problems; only the nature, severity, and ability of the family to solve problems differ. Because a family seeks professional help does not mean they are dysfunctional. In fact, it may be a good example of their ability to address the problems (problem solving).

Characteristics of Functional Families

David Olson (1983) summarizes the research on the nature of "good" families. The following are characteristics generally present in functional families:

Family Pride
Good families show unity and loyalty to family members. Members of these families are cooperative, see the family in a positive light, and deal with problems in a positive way.

Family Support
A good family provides love and understanding to its members. It provides an environment that fosters growth and is sensitive to the needs of each individual member. An important aspect of family support is the commitment of time: good families spend time together.

Cohesion
A healthy balance between dependence and independence is found in good families. There is mutual respect and appreciation of the individuality of each family member.

Adaptability
In our rapidly changing world, healthy families are flexible and able to compromise. Role flexibility is an excellent example of the contemporary family's adaptability. For example, cooking is no longer "women's" work, nor do men have sole responsibility for the yard. Availability and skill, rather than gender, determine who performs a task in an adaptive family.

Communication
Not surprisingly, good communication skills are important to a well-functioning family. This implies time to develop and practice those skills. We are apt to think of communication as pertaining to talking, and yet those families that were superior in communicating with one another were particularly adept at *listening*. We all need to know that someone values what we have to say—we want to be heard.

Social Support
Just as members of good families feel a pride in and commitment to their families, they are also active in their communities, neighborhoods, schools, and so forth. In other words, they

demonstrate social responsibility. These families prepare their members to enjoy and feel a responsibility for the world in which they live.

Values

Good families have a core set of identifiable values and their goal is to adhere to them. Parents in these homes try to model the behaviors that demonstrate these values. For many families this may mean an active involvement in a religious organization while for some it does not.

Joy

I would like to add another characteristic to the above list. Good families have fun. In my experience working with families, I have observed in functional families a joyfulness, a spontaneity, and an enjoyment of life.

Note that none of these describe the appearance of a family. A good family may be a single man and his adopted child, a young couple with children, a couple over the age of thirty who have just had their first baby, or an infinite number of other family configurations. What is important is not the appearance but how well a family functions.

Dysfunctional Families

Where functional families allow children to grow to independence in a safe and supportive environment, dysfunctional homes do not. They may or may not provide for basic physical needs, but they do not provide for the development of an emotionally healthy individual.

Dysfunctional families are often unpredictable, with little or no structure, leaving the children anxious and unsure of themselves; conversely, they may be too structured, resulting in a lack of sense of self. Tolstoy said in *Anna Karenina,* "All happy families resemble one another, but each unhappy family is unhappy in its own way." In other words, it is difficult to identify an exhaustive list of characteristics for dysfunctional families. Consequently, it is more productive to examine some of the effects the dysfunctional family has on the developing child.

Distrust

Often children reared in dysfunctional homes have a difficult time learning to trust others. During those important developmental years when most children are learning to trust, they find that it is emotionally safer to distrust. Consequently, they rely on no one other than themselves. The price they pay is high—the cost of distrust is a lack of intimacy with others.

Low Self-Esteem

Frequently children from dysfunctional families are too self-critical, and often experience excessive feelings of guilt.

Inability to Have Fun

Children from dysfunctional families are often full of anger, disgust, depression, and sadness. They take themselves too seriously and find it difficult to laugh at themselves (Taylor, 1990).

Shame

It is common for children from dysfunctional families to feel that they deserve the treatment that they are getting. Their thinking is as follows: After all, adults are omnipotent so if they (children) are being treated poorly it must be because they deserve it. This is particularly true of children who are being physically or sexually abused, although shame is a common reaction of children from other dysfunctional settings as well. The result is that they grow up feeling that they are undeserving of better treatment.

What makes the effects of a dysfunctional family particularly disturbing is that these feelings do not cease, or in many cases even decrease, when children leave their dysfunctional home. Unless there is some sort of positive intervention, they will become adults that are handicapped by the messages they received from their dysfunctional families and are often doomed to repeat them. Their legacy is a lifetime of trying to prove that they are worthwhile people. In addition, they may become parents that perpetuate the pain of the dysfunctional family.

Summary

The family is a wonderful institution. It prepares children to fit into the larger world while teaching them that they have a responsibility to family, community, country, and others. It is a place where children are loved and nurtured and experiment with new behaviors in this secure social laboratory.

The idea of what constitutes a family has changed dramatically in the last fifty years. We know that it is the way a family functions, as opposed to its configuration, that tells us how successful a family is. No family is perfect. All families have problems and challenges, but in a functional family those become part of the learning experience.

We as educators handicap ourselves if we do not understand the nature of families. And, as part of this understanding, we are obliged to be generous with our appreciation of the efforts that parents make. We must also remember that the great majority of parents love their children and want the very best for them.

Recommended Activities

1. Write a description of your family of origin. Include a description of family roles, rituals, relationships, and so forth. You may wish to include pictures and mementos to support your description.
2. Select a period of history and describe family life and compare it to your family unit.
3. Interview a parent of a single-parent home, a blended family, and an intact family. You might want to ask about family rituals, roles, decision making, and so forth.
4. Examine popular magazines, cut out pictures of fifty families, and make observations.
5. Invite a family therapist to discuss with the class functional and dysfunctional families and the therapeutic intervention for the latter.

Additional Resources

Families

Books:

Ahlburg, D. A. & De Vita, C. J. (1992). *New realities of the American family.*

This report examines the social, economic, and demographic trends that have contributed to the rapidly changing structure of the American family and the implications of these trends.

> Population Reference Bureau
> 1875 Connecticut Avenue NW, Suite 520
> Washington, DC 20009-5728
> Phone: 800-877-9881

Coontz, S. (1992). *The way we never were.*

This an excellent book that helps the reader understand families of the present and the past. It examines some of the myths and misunderstandings about families. Coontz's investigation of families is both interesting and informative. ISBN: 0-465-00135-1.

> Basic Books
> 10 E. 53rd St.
> New York, NY 10022
> Phone: 800-242-7737

Hamner, T. J. & Turner, P. H. (1996). *Parenting in contemporary society* (3rd ed.).

This research-based book focuses on acquainting students with parenting in three major areas: 1. concepts, challenges, and changes; 2. diverse family types; and 3. risks and alternatives. Although mainly directed towards early childhood specialists, it would also be helpful to other educators. 400 pp. ISBN: 0-205-16105-7.

> Allyn & Bacon
> Paramount Publishers
> College Book Orders
> 200 Old Tappan Road
> Old Tappan, NJ 07675
> Phone: 201-767-5937

Articles:

Scherer, M. (1996). On our changing family values: A conversation with David Elkind, *Educational Leadership, 53*(7), 4–9.

Videos:

The Child in the Family

This compelling video shows the roles of parents and functions of the family through interviews and profiles. This focus on families provides information and insight significant to all who seek to understand the child and support the family. Produced in live action format.

> Magna System, Inc.
> 95 West County Line Road
> Barrington, IL 60010
> Phone: 800-523-5503

Families First

Bill Moyers examines a growing national movement that has achieved success in keeping troubled families together through the innovative strategy of working with them in their homes. It is modeled after a pioneer project called "Home builders." (90 minutes, color).

> Films for the Humanities & Sciences
> PO Box 2053
> Princeton, NJ 08543
> Phone: 800-257-5126

Families Matter

This program with Bill Moyers examines why America has become an unfriendly culture for families and children and explores ways to rebuild a web of support for families. (60 minutes, color).

> Films for the Humanities & Sciences
> PO Box 2053
> Princeton, NJ 08543
> Phone: 800-257-5126

Family Influences

This video illustrates how family background influences the way people view themselves and others. It defines four types of parents—authoritative, permissive, authoritarian, and uninvolved—and compares the characteristics of children raised by each. It also examines the importance of birth order and considers nontraditional families. 1991. (30 minutes, color). Purchase only.

> Insight Media
> 2162 Broadway
> New York, NY 10024
> Phone: 212-721-6316

On the Home Front the Influence of the Family

This program explores the effects of complex family interactions on child development. It defines bi-directional influences within the family and shows how different family structures (dual-income, single-parent, and blended family) affect children. 1991. (60 minutes, color).

Insight Media
2162 Broadway
New York, NY 10024
Phone: 212-721-6316

Our Families, Our Future

This video, hosted by Walter Cronkite, highlights successful programs across the country that are seeking to assess the multiple stresses of family life. Indeed, this documentary puts a human face on the problems facing the American family and examines programs that are part of the burgeoning "family support" movement, which offers comprehensive services for both parents and children. Winner of two awards. 1995. (58 minutes, color).

Filmaker Library
124 East 40th Street
New York, NY 10016
Phone: 212-808-4980

Organizations:

National Council on Family Relations
3989 Central Avenue NE, Suite 550
Minneapolis, MN 55421
Phone: 612-781-9331

National Congress of Parents and Teachers
330 Wabash, Suite 2100
Chicago, IL 60611
Phone: 312-670-6782

Single-Parent Families

Books:

Bienefeld, E. (1987). *Helping your child succeed after divorce.*

Bienefeld focuses on the problems children suffer as the result of divorce. She identifies problem areas and suggests ways to be supportive. ISBN: 0-89793-168-8.

Hunter House, Inc.
PO Box 2914
Alameda, CA 94501
Phone: 800-266-5592

Dinkmeyer, D., McKay, J. D. & McKay, J. L. (1987). *A new beginning: Skill for single parent & stepfamily parents.*

This book focuses on the needs of single- and stepparent families. It contains case examples and many illustrations. Covers areas such as self-esteem, relationships and behavior, communication skills, and discipline. Excellent to use with parents or to help students understand some of the issues confronted by single-parent and stepparent families. 222 pp., ISBN: 0-87822-286-3.

> Research Press
> Department 96
> PO Box 9177
> Champaign, IL 61826
> Phone: 800-519-2707

Gouke, M. N., Rollins, A. M., (1990). *One-parent children, the growing minority: A research guide.*

This is a very helpful book for those readers who want to examine the research on single-parent homes. This book contains over 1,100 abstracts of research, articles, and books. 494 pp., ISBN: 0-824-085-760.

> Garland Publishing, Inc.
> 1000A Sherman Avenue
> Hamden, CT 06514
> Phone: 800-627-6273

Chapters:

Hildebrand, V., Phenice, L. A., Gray, M. M., & Hines, R. P. (1996). Divorced single-parent families. In *Knowing and serving diverse families* (pp. 207–236). New York: Merrill Publishing Co.

Hildebrand, V., Phenice, L. A., Gray, M. M., & Hines, R. P. (1996). Single teenage parent families. Hispanic-American Families. In *Knowing and serving diverse families* (pp. 69–90). New York: Merrill Publishing Co.

Videos:

Do Children Also Divorce?
This film was produced to show teachers and parents the important role they must play in meeting children's needs during a divorce. It is normal for children to have negative reactions during the stress of divorce, with each age group exhibiting different behaviors. Special attention at this time will help them avoid serious psychological problems later on. 1988. (30 minutes, color).

The Bureau for At-Risk Youth
645 New York Avenue
Huntington, NY 11743
Phone: 800-999-6884

Single Parenting

Hosted by actor Dick Van Patten, this video focuses on ways to minimize the adverse effects that a divorce or death may have on children. It offers positive techniques of effective single parenting. This video is primarily meant for families but would be excellent for use with a class interested in home–school relations. (20 minutes, color). Purchase $99.

The Bureau for At-Risk Youth
645 New York Avenue
Huntington, NY 11743
Phone: 800-999-6884

Organizations:

Parents without Parents, Inc.
8807 Colesville Road
Silver Spring, MD 20910
Phone: 312-670-6782

Stepparents:

Books:

Dinkmeyer, D., McKay, G. D., & McKay, J. L. (1987). *New Beginnings: Skills for single parent & stepfamily parents.*

This book focuses on the needs of single- and stepparent families. It contains case examples and many illustrations. Covers areas such as self-esteem, relationships and behavior, communication skills, and discipline. Excellent to use with parents or to help students understand some of the issues confronted by single-parent and stepparent families. 222 pp., ISBN: 0-87822-286-3.

Research Press
Department 96
PO Box 9177
Champaign, IL 61826
Phone: 800-519-2707

Chapters:

Hildebrand, V., Phenice, L. A., Gray, M. M. & Hines, R. P. (1996). Step families. In *Knowing and serving diverse families* (pp. 237–259). New York: Merrill Publishing Co.

Videos:

An American Step Family

This video examines some of the problems faced by blended families. (26 minutes, color). Purchase and rental.

> Films for the Humanities & Sciences
> PO Box 2053
> Princeton, NJ 08543
> Phone: 800-257-5126

Organizations:

Stepfamily Association of America
215 Centennial Mall, Suite 212
Lincoln, NE 68508
Phone: 402-477-7837

Stepfamily Foundation
333 West End Avenue
New York, NY 10023
Phone: 212-877-3244

References

Ahlburg, D. A., & De Vita, C. (1992). New realities of the American Family. *Population Bulletin, 47,* 2.

Amato, P., Keith, B. (1991). Parental divorce and the well-being of children. *Psychological Bulletin, 110,* 30.

Berger, E. H. (1995). *Parents as partners in education: Families and schools working together* (4th ed.). Columbus, OH: Merrill.

Bing, E., & Cowman, L. (1980). *Having a baby after 30.* New York: Bantam Press.

Burr, W. A. R., Day, R. R., & Bahr, K. S. (1993). *Family science.* Pacific Grove, CA: Brooks/Cole Publishing Company.

Coleman, M., Ganong, L. H., & Henry, J. (1984). What teachers should know about stepfamilies. *Childhood Education,* 306–309.

Coontz, S. (1995). The American family and the nostalgia trap. *Phi Delta Kappan, 76*(7), K1–K20.

Demon, J., & Acock, S. (1994). *Family diversity and well being.* Thousand Oaks, CA: Sage Publishing.

Demos, J. (1996). Myths and realities in the history of American life. In H. Grunebaum & J. Christ (Eds.), *Contemporary marriage: Structure, dynamics, and therapy* (pp. 9–31). Boston: Little Brown.

Fuller, M. L. (1992). The many faces of American families: We don't look like the Cleavers anymore. *PTA Today, 18*(1), 8–9.

Fuller, M. L. (1989). Children of divorce: Things you should know. *PTA Today, 14*(5), pp. 11–12.

Fuller, M. L. (1986). Teachers' perceptions of children from intact and single parent homes. *School Counselor, 33,* 365–374.

Glick, P. (1989). Remarried families, step families and stepchildren. A brief demographic note. *Family Relations, 38,* 24–27.

Gordon, A., & Browne, K. (1993). *Beginning and beyond* (5th ed.). Albany, NY: Delmar.

Henderson, A. (1987). *The evidence continues to grow.* Columbia, MD: National Committee for Citizens in Education.

Johnson, H. J. (1990). *The new American family and the school.* Columbus, OH: National Middle School Association.

Keniston, K., & Carnegie Council on Children. (1977). *All our children: The American family under pressure.* New York: Harcourt Brace Jovanovich.

Kubler-Ross, E. (1969). *On death and dying.* New York: Macmillan.

Olson, H. (1983). *Families: What makes them work.* Thousand Oaks: Sage Publishing.

Olson, M. R., & Haynes, J. A. (1993). Success of single parents: Families in society. *The Journal of Contemporary Human Services, 7*(5), pp. 259–267.

Seward, R. (1978). *The American family: A demographic history.* Beverly Hills: Sage.

Skolnick, A. (1991). *Embattled paradise: The American family in an age of uncertainty.* New York: Basic Books.

Taylor, P. M. (1990). *Coping with a dysfunctional family.* New York: Rosen Publishing Group.

U.S. Census Bureau. (1993). *Poverty in the United States* (Current Population Research Series P60–185). Washington, DC: US Government Printing Office.

Wallersein, J., & Blakeless, S. (1989). *Second chances: Men, women, and children: A decade after divorce.* New York: Ticknor & Fields.

Whitehead, B. D. (1993). Dan Quayle was right. *The Atlantic Monthly, 271*(4), pp. 47–56.

C h a p t e r 3

Diversity among Families

SANDRA WINN TUTWILER
Hamline University

Diversity comes in many forms when discussing families. Even "mainstream" families (generally, white, middle class, etc.) are different from one another. However, there are some family characteristics that bind groups together into various groups, and this chapter examines some of those characteristics: ethnic/cultural, religious, and structural. The purpose of this chapter is to help you:

- Consider the degree of assimilation of ethnic/cultural families and recognize the importance of this information
- Understand what cultural pluralism means in relationship to ethnic/cultural families
- Consider some of the familial characteristics of Latino, American Indian, Asian, and African American families
- Consider how religious diversity affects families
- Become better informed about non-traditional families: gay and lesbian families and grandparent-headed families

The Changing Family

Families in the United States historically have varied in structure, social and economic status, ethnic/cultural background, and religious tradition. These characteristics contribute to differences among families that suggest the diversity among the peoples of this nation. They underpin differences in language, customs, attitudes, behaviors, values, and everyday living circumstances existing among family units.

This chapter focuses on three attributes that contribute to family diversity: family structure, ethnic/cultural background, and religious traditions. While each of these family characteristics is discussed separately, it is the particular combination of attributes that comprises a family's distinctiveness. But just as importantly, these family characteristics influence the manner in which the family conducts its day-to-day functioning. Understanding differences among families allows school personnel to structure a variety of strategies for working with families. School and home connections are likely to be enhanced when teachers and other school personnel are respectful of a family's living circumstances, as well as the unique ways a family might support the education of their children.

As noted in the previous chapter, conventional notions of a traditional or typical family are influenced by a family structure that gained prominence in the late eighteenth and early nineteenth centuries, and again in the 1950s. However, the family as a social institution has experienced many transformations that profoundly influence not only the ways in which we understand what constitutes "family" but also the function of the family unit as well. A discussion of diversity among families promotes more awareness and acceptance of differences among family units as they exist in contemporary life.

The relationship between parents and schools may be affected by faulty perceptions schools hold of given groups. Typically, school expectations of families reflect behaviors, value orientations, and capabilities of middle-class nuclear families. In this way, uniform standards for measuring familial competency exist that often ignore or negate the diversity among families as well as the contributions families bring to the educational setting. Stephanie Coontz, author of *The Way We Never Were,* points out that "myths (based on middle-class experience) that create unrealistic expectations about what families can, or should, do tend to erode solidarities and diminish confidence in problem-solving abilities of those whose families fall short" (p. 6).

While traditional bonds between white middle-class families and schools must be maintained, a need exists for recognition of the variety of ways in which families not fitting this form conceive of their roles in the educational lives of their children.

Family Structure

There are perhaps as many family types as there are individual families, but broad configurations of these families allow us to consider and understand families more easily. The previous chapter carefully examined single-parent families and blended families. This chapter will briefly examine the functioning of two-parent families, grandparents as parents, and the gay and lesbian family, but it is primarily dedicated to the ethnic/cultural diversity of families.

We all know the stereotype of the family—a mother, a father, and two children. In actuality, only 31 percent of families fits this picture of the stereotypical American family, with twice as many families fitting into some other family model (Outtz, 1993).

Married-Couple Families

One form of married-couple families includes a husband, wife, and their biological and/or adopted children. Sociologists often call this family form an *intact family.* It is important to note that this is not a value judgement but merely a descriptive term. Another configuration of the married couple with children is the blended family, and although these two families function very differently, they have a similar appearance.

Slightly more than one third of all family households consist of married couples with children. This family structure is represented at all economic levels, as well as among all ethnic/cultural groups in the United States. A growing number of married couples, however, are childless. In fact, Outtz (1993) points out that, in 1990, married couples without children outnumbered those with children!

Families are not static. Throughout the history of humankind they have and continue to change. A change that has greatly influenced married-couple families over the last fifty years is the increased number of women working outside the home. The number of married women with children under the age of eighteen in the work force has grown to a point that, currently, only three out of ten women in married-couple families are "stay-at-home-moms." While some women entered the work force out of economic necessity, others have entered to further a career.

Even though there have been dramatic changes in the structure and functioning of families, some things have not changed. Women still are the primary caretakers of children and have primary responsibility for the home. According to Demo and Acock (1993), household labor responsibilities for women that emerged with the nuclear family form are well established and resistant to change. Although men's contributions to household labor has increased over the last thirty years, mothers working outside the home add nearly forty hours a week in domestic labor to their outside-the-home employment responsibilities.

Women's entry into the work force dramatically changed the day-to-day needs and functioning of the married-couple family. The quandary over how to best attend to the needs of "latchkey" children has reached national discussion, and provides an excellent example of the impact of women's labor force participation on the nuclear family. Affordable and quality child care, flexible working schedules, and more flexible maternal and paternal leave policies from employers are major concerns, not only for married couple families but also for other families who have children home alone while adults are working. Just as employers are considering ways to accommodate the needs of working couples, many schools have also made changes to facilitate involvement of these parents in their children's education. A modification such as scheduling parent–teacher conferences for evening hours acknowledges the need for change in some school practices to adapt to the living circumstances of working couples.

Some working married couples meet the challenges caused when both parents are working by reaching out to an extended family. Ethnic minority couples who have maintained culturally valued extended family ties may not experience the same child-care dilemmas as those families who adopted a more nuclear family form. In this way, current issues facing working married couples are more closely related to the decline of the white middle-class nuclear family as the predominant family form.

Alternative Family Structures

The American family is diverse in a variety of ways (culture/ethnicity, economic status, etc.). We tend to see this as a recent phenomenon when in fact there always has been diversity within and between family groups, but the numbers—if not the nature of them—are certainly changing: father-headed homes, foster homes, children living with a variety of relatives, and so forth. This section examines two of the non-traditional families: grandparent-headed homes and gay/lesbian families.

Grandparents as Parents

The number of homes where grandparents are rearing the children of their children is increasing. This has long been a cultural practice with some American Indian groups but generally has not been a practice within mainstream society (Hildebrand, 1996). With the age of unwed mothers decreasing and substance abuse increasing, many mothers are unable or unwilling to care for their children. The increase in the number of grandparents rearing young children has reached such proportions that support groups for these grandparents have been formed across the country.

Although the number of grandparents as primary care givers has increased due to a variety of societal problems, there are other—more positive reasons—for this family configuration. It is common for grandmothers in some cultures (many American Indian groups, for example) to assume parental responsibilities.

Gay- and Lesbian-Headed Families

The gay and lesbian family is more conspicuous and more numerous than in the past. Whereas this family structure may be controversial in some sections of society, an increasing number of children are being raised in gay and lesbian households. While there are societal hesitations to label these households "families," their numbers are estimated to range from four to fourteen million (Hare & Richards, 1993; Outtz, 1993). The reluctance of many gay and lesbian parents to let their sexual orientation be known accounts for much of the difficulty in gathering exact numbers for this family type. Gay and lesbian parents often fear discrimination and the possibility of custody battles, as they are automatically assumed to be unfit parents in some states.

For many gay and lesbian parents, children were the result of a previous heterosexual bond. However, alternative insemination and adoption are increasingly used as means for becoming parents. Gay and lesbian families may take a number of forms and span the social and economic ladder. Many families are headed by two women or two men in a partner relationship; some are blended families in which both parents bring a child or children to the family unit; some are single-parent families; and in some instances, a gay man may father a child with a lesbian and parenting is shared.

REFLECTION...

Explore your thoughts and feelings about gay/lesbian parents. How will your attitude affect the child of gay/lesbian parents?

Lesbian and gay parents differ in the extent to which they prepare their children for possible negative experiences in reaction to the parent's lifestyle. Some children are accepting of their parent's lifestyle, while others may feel they have a secret that must be kept. School personnel must reflect on their views of families headed by homosexuals. Behaviors that inhibit or support school/home relations will not go unnoticed by these parents. Attitudes that allow parents to interact on school/family-related issues based on their chosen level of openness about their sexual orientation are more likely to enhance school/home relations.

Ethnic and Cultural Diversity

A position of dominance for European-American culture occurred in the seventeenth century. The English language, customs, laws, and religion were transported to the colonies by English immigrants, who made up the majority of early settlers. While cultural shifts have evolved over the centuries, Euro–American cultural dominance has been maintained, and is now known as mainstream America—white and middle class. Native Americans and blacks who inhabited the colonies in the seventeenth century were viewed as unsuitable for assimilation into the Anglo-American way of life. Immigrants from Germany, Ireland, and Scandinavia were more readily accepted than were Italians, Jews, Croatians, Poles, and other southern and eastern Europeans who immigrated to United States.

Assimilation versus Cultural Pluralism

Immigrant groups were expected to conform to the established way of life in the United States. Families and schools were pivotal institutions in the process of conformity, with the latter positioned to play a major role in the process of assimilation. *Assimilation* is a gradual process in which one set of cultural traits is relinquished over time and a new set is acquired through participation in the mainstream culture. In the United States, assimilated individuals conform to the standards of life as set by European Americans, while abdicating cultural characteristics of their ethnic group. However, assimilation into a mainstream culture represents but one possible outcome of interaction between a dominant culture and various ethnic groups.

An earlier notion of the United States as a great "melting pot" of ethnicities never came to fruition. The melting pot ideology suggests a coming together of all ethnic/cultural groups would result in a new culture, one that melded the characteristics of both. However, rather than "melting" into a common culture, each new wave of immigrants was expected to give up distinctive cultural practices and to assimilate into an "American" culture which had been heavily influenced by populations from northern Europe. Many immigrant groups were pressured to take on the characteristics of the mainstream population while denying the richness of their own culture. The myth has been that the dominant culture would also change, influenced by other ethnic groups; the reality is very different.

A third possibility is enculturation. Bernal and Knight (1993) describe *enculturation* or *ethnic socialization* as a process by which developing individuals acquire cultural teaching from family, peers, and the ethnic community that allows for development of qualities necessary to function as a member of the ethnic group. The individual develops an ethnic identity. Ethnic group members, to varying degrees, may engage in enculturation.

These distinctions are especially important in attempting to understand how families identify themselves with respect to their ethnic backgrounds. Differences among various ethnic/cultural groups in language, customs, child-rearing practices, and values existing in the home could be explained in part by a family's beliefs in the value of assimilation and enculturation.

A number of issues emerge as families, particularly ethnic minority families, try to find a balance between their culture of origin (enculturation) and mainstream culture (assimilation). However, according to Ramirez and Cox (1980), society pressures minority parents to rear their children to be as much like mainstream children as possible. Unfortunately, this ignores the concern these parents have with regard to the cultural identity of their children. Will they lose their connections with the parents' culture(s) of origin?

While it is important for school personnel to understand characteristics attributed to a given ethnic/cultural group, it is important not to stereotype.

Traditional to Assimilated

Members of a culture whose behaviors, beliefs, and cognition are determined by a single culture are called *traditional* (e.g., a Navajo Medicine Man on the Navajo reservation), while those who forego their own cultural practices to take on all of the characteristics of the mainstream culture are said to be *assimilated.* Those people who are equally knowledgeable and comfortable in two cultures are *bicultural.*

Hence, it is important to view ethnic/cultural distinctions routinely associated with a particular group, not so much as prescriptions for the functioning of particular families, but rather as descriptions of possible characteristics, behaviors, or attitudes a family may incorporate into their day-to-day existence.

REFLECTION ...

Consider the cultural behaviors of your family. Do your family traditions include special foods, activities, celebrations, etc.? How do these tie into your cultural background?

Mainstream Families

As mentioned early in this chapter, a "typical" American family does not exist. Still, values, customs, and behaviors exist within certain families that are more reflective of values and attitudes accepted as mainstream cultural norms. For example, when compared with the norms of some minority ethnic group families, mainstream culture families tend to be more democratically oriented, with children having the opportunity to express their views and wishes. It would not be disrespectful for the child to question or challenge authority figures, including parents themselves.

Children are encouraged to be individuals and to make decisions for themselves early on, with parents in the role of providing support and guidance. Parents have high expectations that children will develop a sense of responsibility for their actions, learn to rely on themselves, and, over time, develop a level of independence believed necessary to function as an adult.

This focus on individualism envelops the family unit as well, because the nuclear or immediate family is valued over an extended one in the day-to-day functioning of the family. In fact, mainstream culture families generally confer less respect to the elderly when compared with some minority ethnic group cultures.

Another characteristic generally attributed to mainstream culture families is the focus on the importance of punctuality and attention to schedules. An adherence to both is seen as a sign of politeness and responsible behavior. The maxim "getting the job done" is an expression of an orientation toward completing tasks in a timely manner.

A competitive spirit underlines a drive for personal accomplishment in education, work, and play. A mainstream culture belief that the individual has some control over his or her destiny supports the notion that adversity can be overcome through hard work.

While formal education is highly valued, children are given the opportunity, and expected, to achieve in other learning and performing situations as well. Activities such as athletics and vocal or instrumental music, whether an extension of school activities or privately arranged, are examples of areas in which hard work leads to personal accomplishment and contributes to the development of a well-rounded individual.

It is important to note that these family characteristics may be observable in any number of family situations. However, they are more likely observable in European-American middle-class families, as well as in more assimilated middle-class ethnic minority families.

African American Families

The history of African Americans in the United States, including two hundred years of enslavement, followed by years of segregation, discrimination, and both overt and institutionalized racism, plays a large role in characteristics exhibited in varying degrees among these families. Today, African Americans make up about 12 percent of the population nationally, with substantial numbers living in urban areas where crime, poor housing, high unemployment, and the lack of adequate services persist. Despite an increase in the number of African Americans having middle-class status, substantial numbers continue to live in poverty. Inequities continue in health, employment, and quality of life between African Americans and European Americans.

Even with differences in social and economic class, survival and protection of one's family remains a predominant theme among African Americans. Concern over racism and biased treatment from both individuals and institutions influences many behaviors and attitudes among African American families. Valuing of an extended family, for example, represents a belief that a larger, interdependent group stands a better chance of moving through barriers to survival. As part of the value of an extended family, the elderly are held in a position of respect, and African American children learn early to value and obey the elderly, even those to whom they are not related. Indeed, a sense of kinship often extends beyond blood relations to other members of the community.

Kinship ties also play a role in assuring that children are cared for. When parents and children were sold away from each other during slavery, children were taken care of by other adults on the plantation. Today informal adoptions by an aunt, uncle, grandmother, or even a cousin are common. Additionally, single parents (mother or father) faced with raising children without a spouse may turn to their kinship network for help and support.

Generally, the nurturance and protection of children is highly valued among African Americans. A strong belief that children need to be disciplined is complemented by the belief that children need time to be children. Hence, in many African American families, there is less focus on pushing the child toward independence and/or detachment from the family. When compared to peers in other ethnic groups, it is common to find African American young adults remaining with the family of origin for longer periods before establishing a home as an independent adult.

African American families tend to have flexible family roles, a characteristic borne out of the social and economic circumstances faced by many African American families. Traditional gender roles for males and females may be reversed, based on the needs of the family. Children may also assume some roles normally taken by parents. Generally, family members adapt to whatever role is needed in order for the family to function (Burnett & Lewis, 1993).

Education is viewed as the way to a better life and thus has traditionally been held in high esteem by African Americans. This characteristic was supported by a recent study conducted by Ritter, Mont-Reynaud, and Dornbusch (1993), which focused on minority parent attitudes toward the education of their children. The study included students and parents from various ethnic minority groups, at various social and economic levels. Based on survey responses, African American parents emphasized hard work in academic areas (e.g., math, English, social studies) and more frequently reacted both positively and negatively to grades of their high school students. While these parents also appeared to have more working knowledge of "school ways," including awareness of homework, school schedules, and the importance of course selection, they also tended to have higher levels of mistrust toward schools than some of the other ethnic minority parents included in the study.

Many African American families believe that it is necessary for children to understand racism, as well as the history and the status of African Americans in the United States, as a means for the child's self-protection and survival. African Americans are particularly sensitive to acts perceived as racist. They want children to be able to discern negative actions directed toward them that are based on the color of their skin and have little to do with their character. This distinction is seen as important in helping the child develop a positive self-esteem. The current movement by some African American parents and educators toward Afrocentric schools, particularly for African American males, highlights, in part, the importance of the development of this self-protective capacity.

> ### REFLECTION...
>
> Do you have African American or other ethnic minority friends? If not, why not? Describe ways we can develop friendships with people of different ethnic backgrounds and how we can model this for the children we teach.

Like many other ethnic minority families, African American families are challenged by the assimilation/enculturation dilemma. Historically, African Americans have come together as an interdependent group in order to address issues that might improve life circumstances (e.g., education, employment, housing) of the group. In fact, it is common to hear African Americans speak of "the community" as an entity which embraces all African Americans. There is an underlying expectation that the community should receive benefits from the successes of the individual. However, being successful in academic and work settings is often tantamount to leaving the community, an action believed to be an integral part of upward social mobility. This circumstance presents a dilemma for some African American families. Broadway (1987), for example, found that African American middle-class families were specifically concerned that their children learn to function in Euro-American middle-class contexts, while at the same time, maintain close cultural ties with the African American community.

Implied is a recognition among some African American families of the bicultural nature of African Americans. For example, many African Americans, particularly middle-class African Americans, are well versed in both standard and black English and can switch into using either, depending on the situation. African Americans have a prized oral tradition in which the use of language is highly valued. Indeed, some African Americans describe themselves as bilingual as well as bi-cultural, believing that some expressions lose the richness of meaning when translated into standard English.

As is the case with other ethnic minority groups, African Americans are a very diverse group. The extent to which they embrace the characteristics cited above will vary. School personnel are thus challenged to get to know individual families in order to understand more clearly how they identify themselves with respect to ethnic group characteristics.

Asian American Families

Asian Americans are the fastest growing minority group in the United States. With groups originating from countries including China, Japan, Korea, Cambodia, Laos, Vietnam, and India, Asian Americans are clearly a very diverse people. The experiences of Asian American families will depend to some extent on the circumstances surrounding their immigration to the United States. Some Asian Americans arrived in the United States as highly educated professionals, having marketable skills, and/or as bilingual and familiar with the mainstream culture in the United States. Still others arrived with low levels of education, languages other than English, and experiencing high levels of culture shock due to a lack of familiarity with this country. For example, Korean Americans have one of the highest levels of education among all ethnic groups, as well as high rates of self-employment. Like the first wave of Vietnamese, they were well educated in their homeland. More recent refugees from Vietnam, Cambodia and Laos tend to have lower levels of education and experience higher levels of unemployment in the United States (Chan, 1992).

The assimilation/enculturation balance also influences the experience of Asian Americans. Throughout their history in the United States, Asian Americans have experienced varying levels of acceptance and rejection. For example, Chinese Americans, a culturally diverse group among themselves, were the first Asians to immigrate to the United States. Forty-two years later, they were banned from immigration as a result of the Chinese Exclusion Act of 1882. Anti-Chinese sentiment, fueled by racism and economic tension led to this federal law, which was not repealed until 1943. We might also remember the imprisonment of people of Japanese ancestry, the vast majority of whom were U.S. citizens, in relocation centers during World War II. Today, however, Asian Americans are stereotypically looked upon as a "model minority."

Like other racial/ethnic minority groups, Asian American families are subjected to additional stereotypes that function to minimize the diverse cultural and historical backgrounds existing in this group. As Yao (1993) points out, it is impossible to describe a typical Asian American family. Although there is great diversity in the backgrounds, languages, religions, and customs among Asian Americans, there are some generalizations that can be stated about Asian American families.

The family is the primary social unit among Asians, hence its preservation is important to the maintenance of the social, political, religious, and economic order. The strongest familial bonds are between parent and child, rather than between parents themselves. The male is perceived as the head of the family. Unlike the democratic model existing in many mainstream culture families, parents are clearly the authority figures in Asian American families. Unquestioning obedience to parental control is expected from the child. In fact, the close supervision children receive from their parents is perceived as a sign of parental love. It is considered disrespectful for a child to question parental love and authority.

Asian Americans have high expectations for their children academically, and also value upward mobility. Achievement is considered part of the child's obligation to the family, rather than a personal accomplishment. The child's success, or lack thereof, is a source of pride or embarrassment to parents. Asian American parents believe that children should not be rewarded for what they are expected to do. In fact acknowledgment of accomplishments comes in the form of encouragement to do better, while failure to meet parental expectations results in punishment. The child may be chastised verbally and excluded from family social life.

At the same time, parents make many personal sacrifices for their children in order to facilitate their success. Family goals of achievement and upward mobility result in a high number of families where both parents work outside the home. For recent immigrants who may have education and job skill limitations, it is not uncommon for parents to work long hours and/or have more than one job.

Asian American families tend to have distinct boundaries between educational responsibilities of the home and school. Teachers are highly respected and parents are not likely to contradict what is said by the teacher in his or her presence. Concurrently, matters more directly connected to the process of schooling (e.g., curriculum, discipline) is believed to be the province of the school. Within the home, parents closely watch the progress of the child, while encouraging the child to increase his or her performance.

Despite striking differences between behaviors, attitudes, and values of Asian American and mainstream culture families, it is often suggested that other ethnic minorities adopt Asian American child-rearing practices. Indeed, the label of "model minority" is viewed as a burden by some Asian Americans. The concomitant label of "superior students" assigned to Asian American children adds to the pressure these students already feel from high expectations emanating from the home. Additionally, the academic difficulty experienced by some Asian American students is often overlooked because of a perception that Asian American children are "smart students" (Shen & Mo, 1990). Academic pressures and other difficulties felt by Asian American students may go unnoticed, owing to some extent to the lessons taught in the home regarding social and emotional restraint. Discussing problems may be difficult for students, as well as for their parents.

Tradition passed through the ages continues to have a valued position within some Asian-American families. The differences between Eastern and Western beliefs, customs, and values are often the basis of conflict between Asian American children and their parents. In fact, some families attempt to protect their children from outside influences by controlling those with whom the child comes in contact (e.g., peers, playmates). Nonetheless, influences of Western customs and values inadvertently cause tension in many Asian American families, especially families of more recent immigrants who may be less familiar with customs in this country. Schools and other social service institutions working to assist and support the transition of these families into their new home in the United States, must take care not to undermine parental authority in the process.

Latino Families

Latinos in the United States include Mexican Americans, Cuban Americans, Puerto Ricans, and other Central and South Americans. Each of these groups has a different historical background that continues to influence their experience in contemporary U.S. society. Many Mexican Americans, or Chicanos as many prefer, trace their ancestry to those who lived on the land that is today California, Texas, New Mexico, and Colorado. This land was ceded to the United States at the conclusion of the Mexican War of 1848. Others trace their ancestry to immigrants who fled Mexico in search of work during the Mexican Revolution of 1910.

Like Mexican Americans, Puerto Ricans are United States citizens as a result of land ceded to the United States following a war. The United States obtained Puerto Rico at the end of the Spanish American War, and later made the inhabitants of the island citizens of the United States. Today, Puerto Ricans live on both the island and mainland United States.

Cuban Americans immigrated to the United States as refugees beginning in 1959, with the reign of Castro. Early Cuban immigrants were wealthy professionals. However, the last wave of Cuban immigrants, those who were a part of the Mariel exodus of 1980, consisted of what Cuba referred to as its "social undesirables" (Suarez, 1993). The experience of the earlier Cuban Americans differs from that of the general population of Puerto Ricans and Mexican Americans, who tend to experience more discrimination, poverty, and higher school dropout rates. Approximately 26 percent of Latinos live in poverty (Ramirez, 1993), and, as noted earlier, this number increases when the family is headed by a single parent. Additionally, Fillmore (1990) estimates that approximately 40 percent of Latino children will drop out before completing high school.

Even with these differences, there are commonalities shared by Latino families that provide insight into the dynamics operating within these families. Regardless of class, religion, and length of time in the United States, Latinos traditionally value the family as an important resource for coping with life's stresses. Family is defined as a closely bonded group that may extend beyond blood lines. It is common for family members to prefer living close to each other, in order to more easily accommodate the financial and emotional support extended to family members.

Children hold an exalted position in the family. In fact, the birth of a child validates a marriage (Zuniga, 1992). Zuniga also points out that Latino families are generally less concerned about children reaching developmental benchmarks and tend to be more permissive and indulgent with young children when compared to mainstream culture families. Still, children have family-related responsibilities, such as helping with household chores or caring for siblings. Children are taught to respect elders and are expected to interact with others in a respectful and polite manner. Child-rearing practices among Latinos are traditionally geared to prepare children for their role in sustaining the function of the family in Latino culture.

There is concern, however, among some Latinos over what appears to be an erosion of traditional supports expected of the family. More-assimilated, younger Latinos who are focused on upward mobility are leaving the more traditional customs behind, including the traditional values of sharing and support among family members. The concern over the rift between old ways and new, more assimilated ways also extends to the implications these divisions have for the Spanish language as essential to maintaining a Latino culture. Younger Latinos may not speak Spanish, while the elderly may not speak English. This lack of communication contributes to the erosion of traditional ways.

Parents of children in public schools may have limited English as well. When combined with poverty, this lack of English proficiency often results in barriers between schools and Latino families, as well as for other language minority parents (e.g., Asian American parents). Language proficiency is to not be confused with parental competency. Hence, a number of schools seek ways to minimize language barriers (e.g., through translators), in order to maintain communication between the school and the home.

Native American Families

At the time of the arrival of Columbus in 1492, an estimated five million Native Americans (commonly labled "Indians" based on European explorers' mistaken belief that they had traveled to the far east) lived in North America. Nearly four hundred years later, the Native American population had decreased to approximately 600,000. Warfare and death due to new contagious diseases introduced by Europeans decimated tribes who inhabited the land before the Europeans' arrival. The remaining Native Americans were left without benefit of their warriors and their elders. While the continuous loss of warriors left tribes unable to defend themselves in battle, among some tribes the loss of elders equaled loss of historical and cultural knowledge that sustained the social order and way of life for tribal members.

The Native American way of life was further assaulted by continuous attempts at assimilation by European Americans. The English initially viewed Native Americans as unworthy of the land they lived on because they were not Christian, and later as unworthy of being included in an evolving European-American way of life. By the late 1800s, however, concerted efforts were initiated to assimilate the now conquered indigenous peoples of North America. History is replete with descriptions of methods aimed at purging Native Americans of their culture. The young have been the major target of these efforts. Perhaps the most widely known effort of assimilation is the removal of Native American children from their families on the reservation. These children were sent to boarding schools where they were discouraged from using traditional ways and inculcated with European-American culture and values. Today, there is an effort among Native Americans to reestablish traditional values.

As we have observed with other ethnic minorities in this chapter, Native Americans are also culturally diverse. Similarly, as noted with other families, the discussion of family characteristics of Native Americans is generally applicable to the group as a whole. The issue of assimilation and enculturation exists for Native Americans as for other groups, with families fitting at various points along a continuum of traditional and more European ways of life.

Not surprisingly, children are prized in Native American families. The family has traditionally played an intimate role in the education of children. In Native American families, the term *family* is broadened to include the immediate and the extended family, and all adults in the family are responsible for teaching children. In fact, biological parents may not have primary responsibility for the child's care. There is traditionally a strong bond between grandparent and grandchild in Native American cultures. The elderly are highly revered for their wisdom and experience in all areas, and are thus consulted on issues of child rearing as well. Aunts and uncles are also involved with child rearing; in fact, the same kinship terms are used for mother-aunt and uncle-father (Sipes, 1993).

Children are accorded respect in Native American families and are not scolded or admonished. Rather, they are taught through explanation and example and provided with the reason a behavior is expected. The lessons of an expected behavior may be embedded in stories, which are also commonly used to provide children with knowledge of Indian traditions, rituals, and beliefs.

The structure and functioning of Indian families is consistent with a value in collectivism over individualism. Actions that support the needs of the community are more positively regarded than accomplishments and achievements motivated solely by self-aggrandizement. One's personal well-being is enhanced by giving to and sharing with others. As a result of this focus on the group rather than the individual, some Native American children may exhibit behavior that could be labeled as shyness. They would rather not draw too much attention to themselves as individuals.

Native American families currently have the lowest income and employment rates in the United States, and their children have the highest drop-out rates of any group of students. In keeping with their cultural tradition, Native American parents are calling for a larger role in making decisions about their children's education. They are especially interested in a culturally relevant curriculum and an increase in the number of Native American teachers (Noley, 1992). Assimilationist educational practices historically disparage Native American culture. Thus, parents are also interested in cross-cultural training for teachers in order to reduce the discontinuity between home and school (Szasz, 1991).

REFLECTION...

Too often we focus on the negative stereotypes and characteristics of ethnic groups. What are some common strengths of African American, Latino, Asian American, and Native American families?

Religious Diversity

A majority of European immigrants during the colonial period were members of Protestant denominations. Not surprisingly, public education was founded on Protestant beliefs and values. Protestant denominations, including Lutherans, Methodists, Presbyterians, and Baptists, collectively make up the majority of religious affiliations in the United States today.

Students live in homes ranging from those in which religion is of little consequence, to those in which religion is integral to the everyday functioning of the family. In some cases, religious tradition is intimately tied to ethnic/cultural traditions. For example, among some Native American tribes spirituality is manifested through a belief that every living thing on earth is interconnected. Respect for all living things leads to harmony, an important attribute of Native American culture. Among Asian Americans, life values, social norms, and beliefs are supported by the religious-philosophical teachings inherent in Confucianism, Taoism, and Buddhism (Chan, 1992). And while Judaism provides a link among many Jewish Americans, some Jews view themselves as a cultural minority as well.

The previously mentioned assimilation/enculturation dilemma becomes an issue for ethnic/cultural groups for whom particular religious teaching is part of an ethnic/cultural group identity, because mainstream assimilation may lead to changes in religious beliefs and practices as well. In a similar manner, members of ethnic groups may follow non-mainstream religious practices and beliefs, albeit those that are not traditionally associated with their ethnic/cultural group. African Americans, for example, traditionally belong to Protestant denominations, although they may also follow the teachings of Catholicism, Judaism, and growing numbers are becoming Muslims. Latinos in the United States are traditionally associated with the Roman Catholic church; however, this number has decreased approximately 20 percent over the last twenty-five years, as immigrant Latinos as well as those living in poverty are shifting to denominations believed to better serve their needs ("Latinos Shift Loyalties," 1994).

Even though schools have improved in their efforts to be more sensitive to the impact of school activities and practices on diverse religious traditions, instances continue to occur in which families perceive their religious values and beliefs to be in conflict with school practices. Moreover, the possibility of misunderstanding increases as religious beliefs and practices veer further away from traditional Protestantism. For example, the doctrine of Jehovah Witnesses forbids the celebration of holidays and birthdays. The children of these families will be in conflict if you expect them to join in the celebration. In addition, the rights of the family would be violated. Lunch menus with ham as the only entree overlook the Muslim and Jewish practice of not eating pork.

The freedom to worship at the church, synagogue, or mosque of one's choice contributes to the religious diversity of the United States. As educators, we must guard against making assumptions about the religion of our students. School personnel need only be prepared to listen to the family to accommodate the family's wishes, while taking care not to infringe on the rights of other families.

REFLECTION ...

Consider your attitudes towards various religions. Do you have biases concerning other religions? Are there stereotypes that have affected your thinking? How could you investigate the accuracy of your perceptions?

Summary

Diversity among Families: Impact on Home–School Collaboration

Any general discussion of diversity among U.S. families is necessarily hindered by the richness and extent of that diversity. Additional family customs and values could be discussed within each of the broader ethnic/cultural groups mentioned. Characteristics of mainstream culture families discussed above, for example, do not include the diversity of customs inherent in Euro-American families. Additional families of African descent (e.g., Haitian, Ethiopian); Asian/Pacific Island families (e.g., Hawaiian, Samoan, Filipinos); and Native American Eskimo families could be discussed within the context of their respective ethnic groups. At the same time, the needs and challenges facing the growing number of transracial families could be addressed as well. Extension of a discussion on family structure might include the growing numbers of grandparents now raising their children's children, as well as families with adopted children.

Addressing family diversity is central to building constructive home/school relations. The combination of family characteristics (e.g., middle class, African American, single parent, United Methodist) provides important information for understanding how to work with a particular family. It is even more important, however, to learn from families how they define themselves within the context of observable characteristics in order to understand more clearly the attitudes and values operating within the family.

Teachers must be prepared to work with families who challenge their personal notions and experiences of what constitutes family. For this reason, it is important to read and become familiar with cultures that are different from one's own. We may well be facing the eradication of the conforming role historically assigned to schools. An understanding of diversity among families is not meant to provide information for development of strategies to change families so that they fit the needs of the school. Rather, it provides information that allows schools to change, so that they are inviting to the variety of families represented in contemporary school settings.

Recommended Activities

1. Interview (or video tape) families of two different ethnic/cultural groups and identify unique familial behaviors and those that are generally universal to all families.
2. Invite gay and/or lesbian parents to visit your class and share with you their family experience.
3. Volunteer to work in a day care center with children and families that are different from yours.
4. Visit churches different than your own and speculate how the doctrine of these churches would affect family life.

5. If families of particular ethnic/cultural backgrounds are not available in your community, identify such families in other communities and have a telephone conference call. It would be helpful to the family for you to send pictures of the class members so that they can visualize the people to whom they are speaking. Also, ask them to send you some family pictures.
6. Identify the cultural characteristics of your family and how those characteristics have affected your family life. Describe a family with a different cultural background you have known and compare and contrast the two families.

Additional Resources

Cultural Diversity

Books:

Dickenson, G. E., & Leming, M. R. (1990). *Understanding families: Diversity, continuity, and change.*

As a primary text for sociology of the family courses, *Understanding Families* delivers up-to-date research and a life-cycle approach spanning parenting, middle years and retirement. Updated discussions of family crises include death and violence as well as traditional divorce.

> Allyn & Bacon
> Paramount Publishers
> College Book Orders
> 200 Old Tappan Road
> Old Tappan, NJ 07675
> Phone: 201-767-5937

Hildebrand, V., Phenice, L. A., Gray, M. M., & Hines, R. P. (1996). *Knowing and serving diverse families.* Englewood Cliffs, NJ: Merrill.

This book, divided into four parts, offers suggestions on how to serve individual families, and explores ethnic diversity and lifestyle variations among contemporary American families. It contains chapters that foucs on African-American, Hispanic-American, Asian-American, Arab-American, Native American and Amish-American families.

Kendall, F. E. (1996). *Diversity in the classroom: New approaches to the education of young children* (2nd ed.).

This is a book of contributions by some of the leading proponents of multicultural education. This book has a number of selections that will be helpful to a classroom teacher (talking with parents, preparing for a multicultural classroom, affirming diversity, etc.), 192 pp.

Teacher College Press
PO Box 20
Williston, VT 05495-0020
Phone: 800-864-7626

Chapters:

Dauber, S. L., & Epstein, J. L. (1993). Minority parents and the elementary school: Attitudes and practice. In N. F. Chavkin (Ed.), *Families and schools in a pluralistic society* (pp. 73–84). Albany, NY: State University Press.

Ritter, R. L., Mount-Reynaud, R., & Dornbusch, S. M. (1993). Minority parents and their youth: Concerns, encouragement, and support for school achievement. In N. F. Chavkin (Ed.), *Families and schools in a pluralistic society* (pp. 107–120). Albany, NY: State University Press.

Organizations:

Institute for Responsive Education
605 Commonwealth Avenue
Boston, MA 02215
Phone: 617-353-3309

Intercultural Development Research Association
5835 Callaghan, Suite 350
San Antonio, TX 78228
Phone: 512-684-8180

African American Families

Books:

Hutchinson, E. O. (1992). *Black fatherhood: A guide to male parenting.*

Black men of different generations tell what it means to be a father in America. The book features interviews with fathers of different occupations, incomes, and family circumstances. 144 pp., ISBN: 1-881032-08-6.

Highsmith Company, Inc.
W5527 Highway
PO Box 899
Fort Atkinson, WI 53538-0800
Phone: 800-558-2110

Johnson, A. E., & Cooper, A. M. (1996). *A student's guide to African American genealogy: Oryx American family tree series.*

This book is an excellent way to help African American students learn about their family history as well as informing non-Native American teachers about native families. This book provides cultural background, an annotated bibliography, and interesting historical facts. In addition, it comes with color and black-and-white photographs and features a glossary and index. ISBN: 0-89774-975-8.

Oryx Press
Customer Service Department
4041 N. Central Avenue, Suite 700
Phoenix, AZ 85012-9759
Phone: 800-279-6799

Staples, R., & Johnson, L. B. (1992). *Black families at the crossroad.*

This book addresses the black family in America. It offers a comprehensive examination of the black family unit as it has evolved in contemporary society by considering how economics, racism, culture, and politics affect the dynamics of family relations. 315 pp., ISBN: 1-55542-486-4.

Empak Publishing Company
212 East Ohio Street
Chicago, IL 60611
Phone: 323-642-8364

Williams, R. (1990). *They stole it but you must return it* (4th ed.).

Williams examines the historical roots of the African American family. He examines what slavery did to the black family. The book is intended as a guide for black families. 130 pp., ISBN: 0-938805-01-0.

Highsmith Company, Inc.
W5527 Highway
PO Box 899
Fort Atkinson, WI 53538-0800
Phone: 800-558-2110

Chapters:

Hildebrand, V., Phenice, L. A., Gray, M. M., & Hines, R. P. (1996). African American families. In *Knowing and serving diverse families* (pp. 69–90). Englewood Cliff, NJ: Merrill.

Staples, R. (1988). The black American family. In C. Mindel, R. Haberstein, and R. Wrights (Eds.), *Ethnic families in America* (pp. 303–324). New York: Elsevier.

Articles:

Jones, E. (1993). An interview on the topic, "Changing church confronts the changing Black family." *Ebony, 18*(10), 94–100.

Massaquoi, H. (1993). The Black family nobody knows. *Ebony, 18*(10), 28–31.

Videos:

Black History: Lost, Stolen, or Strayed

Although this film is old, starring a very young Bill Cosby, it is not dated. It is still the best video available that provides an in-depth examination of some of the influences which affect the African American. 1965. (60 minutes, color).

> Insights Media
> 2162 Broadway
> New York, NY 10024
> Phone: 212-721-6316

I'll Fly Away

This is a PBS video series which helps the viewer understand a white and a black family in the 1960s. This series is not only very well done and entertaining but also allows the viewer to better understand the functioning and stresses of black families of that period, consequently better understanding today's families. (60 minutes).

> PBS Television Series
> Washington Educational Television Association
> Box 2636
> Washington, DC 20009
> Phone: 703-998-2600

Organizations:

> National Black Child Development Institute
> 1023 15th Avenue NW, Suite 600
> Washington, DC 20002
> Phone: 202-387-1281

Latino Families

Books:

Ryskamp, G., & Ryskamp, P. (1996). *A student's guide to Mexican American genealogy.*

This book is an excellent way to help Mexican American students learn about their family history as well as informing non-Native American teachers about native families. This book provides cultural background, an annotated bibliography, and interesting historical facts. In addition, it comes with color and black-and-white photographs and features a glossary and index. ISBN: 0-89774-975-8.

Oryx Press
Customer Service Department
4041 N. Central Avenue, Suite 700
Phoenix, AZ 85012-9759
Phone: 800-279-6799

SotoMayor, M. (Ed.). (1991). *Empowering Hispanic families: A critical issue for the 90's.*

This book is a collection of essays on various issues pertaining to Hispanic families. It deals with educational, sociological, and mental health issues. 214 pp., ISBN: 0-87304-243-3.

Family Service America
11700 West Lake Park Drive
Milwaukee, WI 53224
Phone: 414-359-1040

Vades, G. (1996). *Con Respeto: Bridging in the distance between culturally diverse families and the schools—An ethnographic portrait.*

A study of ten Mexican immigrant families, describing how such families go about the business of surviving and learning to succeed in a new world. Valdez examines what *appears* to be a disinterest in education by Mexican parents. This book examines a number of important issues and helps the teacher have a better understanding of these families. This is a well-written and informative book. 256 pp.

Teacher College Press
PO Box 20
Williston, VT 05495-0020
Phone: 800-864-7626

Valdivieso, R., & Davis, C. (1988). *U.S. Hispanics: Challenging issues for the 1990s.*

This booklet provides demographic information that will help the reader better understand the Hispanic population and consequently better understand the Hispanic family. ISBN: 0736-7716.

Population Reference Bureau
1875 Connecticut Avenue NW, Suite 520
Washington, DC 20009-5728
Phone: 800-877-9881

Chapters:

Carrasuillo, A. L. (1991). The family of Hispanic children and youth. In *Hispanic children & youth in the United States: A resource guide* (pp. 69–87). New York: Garland Publishing, Inc.

Hildebrand, V., Phenice, L. A., Gray, M. M., & Hines, R. P. (1996). Hispanic-American Families. In *Knowing and serving diverse families* (pp. 69–90). Englewood Cliff, NJ: Merrill.

Videos:

The Latino Family

This video shows both the changes in and the endurance of traditional Latino families. In following three generations of one Mexican American family, it traces the pattern of migration and cultural change. It shows how the traditional roles of the Latino elderly are being altered by their families' needs and also how the traditional pleasures can still be celebrated.

Films for the Humanities & Sciences
PO Box 2053
Princeton, NJ 08543
Phone: 800-257-5126

The Status of the Latina Women

This video compares the Latina of the United States with those of Latin America. It also examines how Latino men perceive Latina women—the myth and reality, as well as the Latina woman's role in the family and in the community. 1993. (26 minutes, color).

Films for the Humanities & Science
PO Box 2053
Princeton, NJ 08543
Phone: 800-257-5126

Organizations:

Mexican American Legal Defense and Education Fund
634 South Spring Street, 11th Floor
Los Angeles, CA 90014
Phone: 213-629-2512

Gay & Lesbian Families

Books:

Sherman, S. (Ed.). (1993). *Lesbian and gay marriages: Private commitments, public ceremonies.* ISBN: 0-8772-297-5-9.

Bulk of book consists of interviews with "long-term couples," some who had public ceremonies, some who did not. Appendices include directory of organizations.

Temple University Press
USB Room 305
Broad and Oxford Street
Philadelphia, PA 19122
Phone: 800-447-1656

Articles:

Hare, J., & Richards, L. (1993). Children raised by lesbian couples: Does context of birth affect father and partner involvement? *Family Relations, 42*(3), 249–253.

Videos:

We Are Family: Parenting and Foster Parenting in Gay Families

We Are Family won four major film awards. This video deals with what life is really like in three homosexual families. First, two gay fathers tell of their efforts to create a secure environment for their 16-year-old foster son. In another family, two lesbian mothers have helped their adopted 11-year-old boy overcome early neglect. In the third family we hear how two adolescent daughters have accepted their father's homosexuality. 1988. (57 minutes).

Filmakers Library
124 East 40th Street
New York, NY 10016
Phone: 212-808-4980

Organizations:

American Civil Liberties Union (ACLU)
Lesbian & Gay Rights Project
132 West 43rd Street
New York, NY 10036
Phone: 212-944-9800, ext. 545

Miscellaneous

Books:

The following three booklets pertain to families and military life. They are part of The Family Forum Library.

The Military Life Style and Children

Military families experience a number of influences, both positive and negative, that are generally not part of other families' experiences. How children adapt to this special lifestyle is discussed in this booklet.

School and the Military Family

This booklet will help military parents better understand and deal with their children's schooling. Although the intended audience is the military family, this booklet provides educators with some excellent insights.

Stress and the Military Family

This booklet examines some of the causes of stress which impact military families, in particular, military youngsters. It will assist educators in understanding some of the problems their students from military families are experiencing.

Videos:

Teenage Pregnancy

This video follows several teenagers through the births of their children and subsequent changes in their lives. It is a sobering look at the problems these girls face. (26 minutes, color).

> Films for the Humanities & Sciences
> PO Box 2053
> Princeton, NJ 08543
> Phone: 800-257-5126

Websites:

African American

> African American Resources
> http://www.rain/org/~kmw/aa.html

> NAACP
> http://www.shoga.wwa.com/~desktop/naacp.htm

> National Urban League
> http://www.nul.org/

Asian American

> The Asian American Cybernaats
> http://vc.apnet.org/%7ebihara/wataru_aaecyber.html

> Asian American Resources
> http://www.mit.edu:8001/afs/athena.mit.edu/user/i/r/irie/www/aar.html

> Hmong Home Page
> http://www.stolaf.edu/people/cdr/hmong/

Hispanic/Latino

    Azteca Web Page
    http://www.azteca.net/azteca/

    Chicano/Latino Net
    http://www.latino.sscnet.ucla.edu/

    Informatica PR-NET
    http://www.geocities.com/capitolhill/1033/

    Latino Interest Site
    http://www.latino.sscnet.ucla.edu/latinos.links.html

Native American

    American Indian Movement
    http://www.netgate.net/~jsd/AIMintro.html

    Indian Defense League of America
    http://www.tuscaroras.com/IDLA

    Native American Education
    http://www.pitt.edu/%7E/mitten/ indians.html#education

    Native American Home Page
    http://www.pitt.edu/~mitten/indians.html

    Resources for Native American Families
    http://www.familyvillage.wisc.edu/frc_natv.htm

Other Diversity Sites

    CLNet Diversity Page

    Diversity Resources
    http://www.siue.edu/~jandris/htmldocuments/andric/diversity.html

    National Center for Research on Cultural Diversity and Second
       Language Learning
    http://zzyx.ucsc.edu/cntr/cntr.html

    Pathways to Diversity on the World Wide Web
    http://www.usc.edu/library/QF/diversity/

References

Ascher, C. (1988). Improving the school–home connection for poor and minority urban students. *The Urban Review, 20*(2), 109–123.

Baca Zinn, M. (1987). Structural transformation and minority families. In L. Beneria & C. Stimpson (Eds.), *Women, households, and the economy* (pp. 155–171). New Brunswick: Rutgers University Press.

Banks, C. M. (1993). Restructuring schools for equity: What have we learned in two decades? *Phi Delta Kappan, 75,* 42–44, 46–48.

Bernal, M., & Knight, G. (Eds.). (1993). *Ethnic identity: Formation and transmission among Hispanics and other minorities.* Albany: State University of New York Press.

Broadway, D. (1987). *A study of middle class black children and their families: Aspirations for children, perceptions of success, and the role of culture.* Ph.D. Dissertation, Ohio State University.

Burgess, E., & Locke, H. (1945). *The family: From institution to companionship.* New York: The American Book Company.

Burnett, M. C., & Lewis, E. A. (1993). Use of African-American family structures to address the challenges of European-American post-divorce families. *Family Relations, 42,* 243–248.

Carter, M. (1994). Supporting the identity and self esteem of children in gay and lesbian families. Anaheim, CA: Annual Conference of the National Association for the Education of Young Children. (ERIC Document Reproduction Service No. ED 377 985)

Chan, S. (1992). Families with Asian roots. In E. W. Lynch & M. J. Hanson (Eds.), *Developing cross-cultural competence* (pp. 181–257). Baltimore: Paul H. Brookes Publishing Co.

Chavkin, N. F. (Ed.). (1993). *Families and schools in a pluralistic society.* Albany: State University of New York Press.

Coontz, S. (1992). *The way we never were: American families and the nostalgia trap.* New York: Basic Books.

Demo, D., & Acock, A. (1993). Family diversity and the division of domestic labor: How much have things really changed? *Family Relations, 42,* 323–331.

Fillmore, L. (1990). Latino families and the schools. *California Perspectives, 1,* 30–37.

Fraga, L., Meier, K., & England, R. (1986). Hispanic Americans and educational policy: Limits to equal access. *The Journal of Politics, 48,* 851–876.

Hare, J., & Richards, L. (1993). Children raised by lesbian couples: Does context of birth affect father and partner involvement? *Family relations, 42,* 249–255.

Hildebrand, V., Phenice, L., Gray, M., & Hines, R. (1996). *Knowing and serving diverse families.* Columbus, OH: Merrill.

Hill, R. B. (1993). Dispelling myths and building on strengths: Supporting African American families. *Family Resource Coalition Report, 12*(1), 3–5.

Hiner, N. R. (1989). Look into families: The new history of children and the family and its implications for educational research. In W. Weston (Ed.), *Education and the American family: A research synthesis* (pp. 4–31). New York: New York University Press.

Lasch, C. (1977). *Haven in a heartless world.* New York: Basic Books.

Latinos shift loyalties. (1994, April). *The Christian Century* (p. 344).

McAdoo, H. P. (Ed.). (1993). *Family ethnicity: Strength in diversity* (pp. 164–176). Newbury Park: Sage Publications.

McLemore, S. D. (1983). *Racial and ethnic relations in America.* Boston: Allyn and Bacon.

Mintz, S., & Kellogg, S. (1988). *Domestic revolutions: A social history of American family life.* New York: The Free Press.

Noley, G. (1992). Educational reform and American Indian cultures. (ERIC Document Reproduction Service No. ED 362 341).

Outtz, J. H. (1993). *The demographics of American families.* Santa Monica, CA: Milken Institute for Job and Capital Formation. (ERIC Document Reproduction Service No. ED 367 726).

Pasley, K., Dollahite, D., & Tallman, M. I. (1993). Clinical applications of research findings on the spouse and stepparent roles in remarriage. *Family Relations, 42,* 315–322.

Ramirez, E. W. (1993). The state of Hispanic education: Facing the facts. Washington, DC: ASPIRA Association, Inc., Institute for Policy Research. (ERIC Reproduction Service No ED 357 132)

Ramirez, M., & Cox, B. (1980). Parenting for multiculturalism: A Mexican American model. In M. Fantini & Russon, J. (Eds.), *Parenting in a multicultural society.* New York: Longman Inc.

Ritter, P., Mont-Reynaud, R., & Dornbusch, S. (1993). Minority parents and their youth: Concern, encouragement, and support for school achievement. In N. Chavkin (Ed.), *Families and schools in a pluralistic society* (pp. 107–119). Albany: State University of New York Press.

Shen, W., & Mo, W. (1990). Reaching out to their cultures: Building communication with Asian-American families. (ERIC Document Reproduction Service No. ED 351 435)

Sipes, D. S. B. (1993). Cultural values and American-Indian families. In N. Chavkin (Ed.), *Families and schools in a pluralistic society* (pp. 157–173). Albany: State University of New York Press.

Suarez, A. (1993). Cuban Americans: From golden exiles to social undesirables. In H McAdoo (Ed.),

Family ethnicity: Strength in diversity. Newbury Park: Sage Publications.

Szasz, M. C. (1991). Current conditions in American Indian and Alaska Native communities. Indian Nations At Risk Task Force. (ERIC Document Reproduction Service No. ED 343 7556)

U.S. Bureau of the Census. *Poverty in the United States: 1988 and 1989.* Current population report, Series P-60, No. 171, Washington, DC: Author.

U.S. Bureau of the Census. Statistical abstract of the United States: 1990 (110th Edition). Washington, DC: Author.

Wetson, W. (Ed.). (1989). *Education and the American family: A research synthesis.* New York: New York University Press.

Yao, E. L. (1993). Strategies for working with Asian immigrant parents. In N. Chavkin (Ed.), *Families and schools in a pluralistic society* (pp. 149–156). Albany: State University of New York Press.

Zuniga, M. (1992). Families with Latino roots. In E. W. Lynch & M. J. Hanson (Eds.), *Developing cross-cultural competence* (pp. 151–179). Baltimore: Paul H. Brookes Publishing Co.

C h a p t e r *4*

Parents' Perspectives on Parenting

KAREN W. ZIMMERMAN
The University of Wisconsin–Stout

Too often the study of the relationship between home and school fails to address the component of parenting. Schools will be able to form better working relationships with the home if they understand parenting practices and problems. This chapter uses the parent's voice to investigate parenting. Sections 1 and 2 examine families from the perspective of demographics and structure. This chapter takes a different perspective—that of the parenting present in these families. The purpose of this chapter is to introduce the reader to:

- How parenting affects the lives of parents
- The nature and complexities of dual-employed parents
- The views of single-parent families
- The parenting concerns of non-custodial fathers
- The complexities of parenting in a step family
- How parenting adults and children differ

Kenneth and Grace, a dual-employed couple, have two children. Joyce is raising her child as a single parent. Robbie and Kathy, along with their children from a previous marriage, form a stepparent family. In this chapter, we will be looking at each of these family situations and the perspectives these mothers and fathers have on parenting.

This chapter focuses on parents and how they see themselves. It begins by examining how becoming a parent changes one's life and affects the marital relationship. Parenting styles and the parents' perspectives are explored. In addition, this chapter explores several familial structures from a parenting perspective. Dual-employed parents identify the coping patterns they use in dealing with role overload and role conflict between work and family. Viewpoints of single parents, divorced parents, and stepparents are shared. Finally, this chapter concludes with a discussion of what parents perceive as the rewards and satisfactions of parenting.

Becoming a Parent

New Parents

New parents are generally very concerned with how to raise their children. They want to incorporate their personal beliefs about child rearing and develop healthy parent–child relationships. These parents seek to understand and explore their feelings as they assume the parental role for the first time.

The changes in becoming a parent for the first time are abrupt (LeMasters, 1957; LeMasters & DeFrain, 1989). Newlyweds usually interact with each other as personally as possible, trying to mesh as a couple. But when the first child arrives, the couple will likely begin to respond to each other as mommy and daddy instead of as marriage partners. The responsibilities of parenthood take priority over personal gratification. LeMasters (1957) reports that new mothers feel tired, lose sleep, worry that their personal appearance and the appearance of the home are not up to par. In addition, they feel frustrated about having less time for friends and not having a social life.

New fathers also have many of the same complaints, but men and women differ in how they adjust to the new circumstances. Women tend to think of themselves in a *new* role, while men are more inclined to see themselves in an *additional* role. This can be especially frustrating for the husband, as the wife becomes more of a mother and less of a wife. Women are quicker to identify the change in the couple's relationship. One young mother describes this change as follows:

> We aren't able to pay much attention to each other, because Amy needs so much. She's great, don't get me wrong. But Daniel comes home from work cranky, I'm cranky because I haven't talked to anyone who says anything back to me, Amy's cranky because she wants to eat right now, and we don't have time to find out how each other's day went. So I'm making dinner for three cranky people. And as a consequence, we have not been as close as before she came. (Cowan & Cowan, 1992, p. 77)

Marital satisfaction declines somewhat in the early stages of the family life cycle when children are added to the family (Belsky & Rovine, 1990; Belsky, Spanier, & Rovine, 1983; Rollins & Feldman, 1970). Infants and young children demand much time, energy, and attention, and parents have less time for each other. Both mothers and fathers miss the attention of their partner. Having children reorganizes the marriage along traditional sex-role lines (Cowan et al., 1985; LaRossa & LaRossa, 1981). Women assume more of the parenting and household tasks than men, even if they are employed outside the home.

One new mother of a six-month-old, who is doing more housework than ever before, describes this vividly:

> He wasn't being a chauvinist or anything, expecting me to do everything and him to do nothing. He just didn't volunteer to do things that obviously needed doing, so I had to put down some ground rules. Like if I'm in a bad mood, I may just yell: I work eight hours, just like you. Half of this is your house and half of this child is yours too. You've got to do your share. We planned this child together, and we went through Lamaze together, and Jackson stayed home for the first two weeks. But then—wham—the partnership was over. (Cowan & Cowan, 1992, p. 98)

Most educators agree that children thrive best in a home where some consistency between the parents is present. Significant differences between parents on developmental expectations, discipline, and nurturing styles could signal potential problems for the family. In a recent study, mothers and fathers of young children (ages one to four years) were asked to assess their own parenting and that of their spouse. Three parenting categories were examined: developmental expectations, discipline, and nurturing (Platz, Pupp, & Fox, 1994). Mothers and fathers had similar developmental expectations for their young children.

However, fathers tended to see themselves as having a more disciplinarian approach than mothers. Furthermore, fathers gave mothers higher discipline ratings than mothers gave themselves. Mothers rated themselves as more nurturing than fathers. Mothers gave fathers higher ratings in developmental expectations than fathers gave themselves.

After the First Year

How does the role of parenting change during the second year of life? This is the question asked in a study of fathers and mothers (Fagot & Kavanagh, 1993). Parents with twelve-month-old children (infants) reported greater marital adjustment and more pleasure in parenting than parents of eighteen-month-olds (toddlers).

Meeting the daily hassles of parenting adds to parental strain as children make the transition from infancy to early childhood. Perceptions about the minor daily hassles and inconveniences associated with parenting were studied in families with young children (Crnic & Booth, 1991). Three groups of parents were studied: those with children aged nine to twelve months, eighteen to twenty-four months, and thirty to thirty-six months. Such things as "continually cleaning up the same messes," "difficulty getting privacy," "being nagged or whined to," "kids resisting or struggling over bedtime," and so on, were rated.

Parental reports of the daily hassles of parenting increased across the age groups—that is, as children grew older, the hassles increased. It seems that as children are developing and gaining more abilities, they may be presenting a greater range of behaviors and situations that parents find stressful. Furthermore, as the daily hassles of parenting increase, life satisfaction and parenting satisfaction decrease (Crnic & Booth, 1991).

Parenting Styles

Parenting styles are shaped by values, attitudes, and beliefs of the parents. Baumrind (1967) identified three parenting styles that emerge when children are at the preschool stage of family development. These three parenting styles are *authoritarian, authoritative,* and *permissive.*

Authoritarian Parents

The authoritarian parenting style emphasizes total parental control and the obedience of the child. The parent is definitely the person in power; conforming to the parent's standards is required. If necessary, the parent may use physical punishment to force the child to comply. The parent dominates the child by use of rewards and punishment. The child is not allowed to question nor given opportunities to discuss directives.

Authoritative Parents

Authoritative parents make use of reasonable limits and controls for the child's behavior, considering the child's stage of development and individuality. Authoritative parenting falls between authoritarian and permissive parenting. In this parenting style, the authoritative parent wants to develop responsible children by allowing input into discussion on rules and responsibilities. Children have some freedom, but not at the expense of rights and responsibilities of others.

Permissive Parents

Permissive parents strive to promote the child's regulation of his or her own behavior rather than regulating the child's behavior by intervening. In this approach, the child has more power than the parent. The permissive parent allows a child to regulate his own activities as much as possible, avoids the exercise of control, and does not encourage him to obey externally defined standards (Baumrind, 1966).

Most American parents see themselves as raising their children in an authoritative parenting style. When parents were asked to respond to problems dealing with children's misbehavior, most of the people selected responses that would fit with the authoritative parenting style (Carter & Welch, 1981).

In addition, the popularity of the three parenting styles varies by social class. The authoritarian style is found to be more popular with blue-collar families. They are more likely to insist on obedience and to value teaching children to control their impulses. Middle-class parents are more likely to value explaining rules to the child, using verbal discipline, and prizing the child's individuality; this is consistent with the authoritative parenting style. Perhaps more important than style of parenting is that the parents provide guidance, consistency, and an atmosphere of caring.

> ### *REFLECTION...*
>
> Which parenting style did your parents use? What would be examples of your parents discipline behaviors that would support your selection? If you are a parent, what parenting style do you use and why? If you plan to be a parent, what discipline style will you use?

Parents Seeking Help

Good parenting includes the willingness to seek, and accept, help when it is needed. McDade (1993) asked parents to respond to statements which indicated their attitudes toward seeking help with parenting. These parents agreed with the following attitude statements:

- Occasionally even good parents need help or advice with their kids.
- Parents should not be embarrassed to ask for help.
- It's important for parents to have someone to talk to when they need help or advice.
- Because it's more difficult today to be a parent, it's okay to ask for help.
- Some of the tips other people offer on raising kids can be very helpful.
- Most parents need help or advice about parenting.

Most of these parents (87 percent) noted they were likely to seek advice or help with parenting from another source. Preferred sources mentioned were print and video material

(94 percent), family members (88 percent), and parenting classes (84 percent). In other words, good parenting doesn't mean not having problems, but rather finding appropriate help when needed.

> ### REFLECTION...
>
> Think of the stresses present in your life. How would these affect your parenting if you were a parent? If you are a parent, how are your life stresses evidenced in your parenting? How could you reduce these stresses?

Parenting Behaviors in Diverse Family Structure

Dual-Employed Parents

Kenneth (36) and Grace (38) are a middle-class, African American family with two children, Alicia (12) and Francine (10). They live in a four-bedroom house in a small city in California. Kenneth is an accountant for a large clothing firm and Grace teaches math in a local high school.

Kenneth, Grace, Alicia, and Francine experience a lot of family stress, as do most families in which both parents work. While Kenneth and Grace value enrichment experiences for their children, these activities do add to the complexities of their family life. The children are busy with Scouts, music lessons, ballet, after-school sports, and family activities. There is never enough time.

Kenneth and Grace, as dual-employed parents, are facing the many challenges of multiple roles: worker, parent, and a marital partner. People who have multiple roles gain benefits from each of their roles (e.g., a sense of accomplishment, financial gains, and enhanced self-esteem). These benefits can help to balance the role strain they also encounter. Role strain refers to the problems, challenges, conflicts, and difficulties one has as a result of being in a particular role and fulfilling the tasks and responsibilities that role requires.

Role Conflict and Conflicting Demands

Two types of role strain are role overload and role conflict. Role overload is the feeling that there is not enough time to accomplish everything one has to do. Grace teaches school all day and shuttles Alicia and Francine to music lessons, ballet, and Scouts before rushing home to fix supper. After supper, Grace has housework, a stack of math papers to grade, and "catch up" with Kenneth on how his day went. The heavy work schedules of dual-employed families often leave limited time for parenting, the marital partner, household work, and leisure. Role conflict occurs when the demand of one of these roles interferes with doing what needs to be done in another role.

Kenneth's job requires that he be at the office until 6:00 P.M. each weekday. He is thankful that Grace can do the driving so Alicia and Francine can take part in after school activities. He hates missing Alicia's soccer games and Francine's ballet and piano recitals.

Managing the demands of competing life roles, which Kenneth and Grace do daily, has become a common experience for many American men and women. Grappling with multiple life-role commitments is a key source of stress in dual-employed families, especially those with children in the home. Today dual-employed couples frequently have ambitions and commitments in both the work and family areas simultaneously. Men report career interests intruding on fathering roles. Women say that parenting is interfering with career roles. One first-time mother in her thirties described this conflict as follows:

> *For the first time in my life I was having to make tradeoffs—work, to have a child, to be a wife, to take care of a home, and to try to do all of these things well meant that something had to get cheated a little bit in each area. Not enough so that anybody else would notice, maybe, but I did. I noticed it. (Daniels & Weingarten, 1984, p. 224)*

Prioritizing Life Roles

Dual-employed couples' personal expectations concerning occupation, marital, parental, and home-care roles were examined in a study of parents with children (Zimmerman, Skinner, & Muza, 1989). Surprisingly, both husbands and wives independently rated their commitment to four life roles in the same priority order: parental as first, marital as second, home care as third, and occupational as fourth.

REFLECTION...

Which of your life roles (school, family, work, etc.) do you consider to be most important? How is this reflected in the life choices you make?

Although dual-employed couples agreed on the relative importance of these four life roles, they weighed these commitments differently. That is, wives were significantly more committed to the parental role than husbands, although both groups agreed that this was their highest priority. In contrast, husbands were significantly more committed to the occupational role than wives. Thus, both men and women placed a higher value on commitment to familial roles, particularly parental roles, than other life roles. For example, Kenneth and Grace are committed parents but, as discussed earlier, Kenneth's job prevents him from taking the girls to their after-school activities.

These dual-employed couples were divided into two employment orientation groups, worker and career, based on their education and the type of employment. Worker couples were significantly more committed to marital roles and to home-care roles than career couples. It is interesting to note that worker men, career men, and worker women all valued home-care commitment (e.g., working to have a neat, well-kept, and attractive home) to a greater extent than career women. Perhaps this dual-career mother's attitude toward housework illustrates this:

You must begin with what one does not do. I have a cleaning woman…and what she doesn't do, doesn't get done. My kitchen shelves are cruddy, but it doesn't bother me. Dust sits around. It doesn't bother me that everything isn't shipshape. … The way a house is kept is not the most important thing in the universe. (Holmstrom, 1973, p. 71)

Moreover, the scores of career women on occupational commitment were similar to those of both worker and career men. Both groups of men and career women were committed to their occupation significantly more than worker women.

Coping Patterns in Dual-Employed Couples

What coping patterns do dual-employed couples use to deal with stress from their work-family roles? Several studies have addressed this question. In one study of dual-employed parents with children, coping patterns parents identified using most frequently were examined (Zimmerman, Skinner, & Muza, 1989). Coping patterns are a broad range of behaviors used together to manage various dimensions of the dual-employed lifestyle simultaneously (Skinner & McCubbin, 1991). Maintaining a positive perspective on the lifestyle and reducing tensions and strains were the most frequently used coping patterns. This pattern includes behaviors that attend to personal needs focusing on reducing individual stress and maintaining an optimistic perspective on the situation. Examples include "maintaining health," "encouraging children to be more self-sufficient where appropriate," and "believing that there are more advantages than disadvantages to our lifestyle." Husbands and wives felt more positive during their children's adolescence than when children were very young. One mother, in describing her lifestyle advantages, stated the following:

Also I feel that children are better off the more different people they associate with. I think that a child who grows up only with a mother has an awfully narrow outlook on life. And when a mother does go away, it's traumatic. (Holmstrom, 1973, p. 79)

The second most frequently used coping pattern was modifying roles and standards to maintain a work/family balance. These couples modified their roles and standards by buying convenience foods, leaving things undone, and limiting involvement on the job.

Maintaining and strengthening the existing work/family interface was the third most frequently used coping pattern. The focus of this approach was using organizational skills in meeting family, work, and homemaking demands efficiently. An example would be planning schedules ahead of time.

Schnittger and Bird (1990) have identified the coping strategies that dual-career couples have found successful in dealing with the stresses in family life. Among these coping strategies are encouraging their children to help out whenever possible, eliminating some community activities, cutting down on outside and leisure activities, and lowering household standards. Also, parents find spending time alone with their spouses and making friends with other two-career couples helpful.

Coping with work and family demands by subordinating their careers, compartmentalizing work and family roles, and avoiding some responsibilities are strategies used both by career husbands and career wives. These couples contend with stress by limiting their involvement on the job, saying "no," and reducing the amount of time spent at work. They practice making efficient use of their time at work, plan ahead, and postpone certain tasks.

Single-Parent Families

Joyce Anderson, twenty-eight, is a single parent. Joyce, her daughter, Beth, a six-year-old, and Joyce's mother Helen are a family. They live in an apartment in a low-income neighborhood in Minneapolis, and Joyce has worked at the same minimum wage job for a little more than two years. Beth is in first grade in a neighborhood school. One of their chronic problems is lack of health insurance. Although most single-parent families are functional families, their situation has lately become even more precarious than usual. Helen has suffered from a severe respiratory problem for a few years, and her doctor wants her to move to Arizona and live with her other daughter. If Helen leaves, not only will Joyce's resources be greatly reduced, she will have to pay for child care. The stresses Joyce and her family experience are good examples of those experienced by single-parent families.

Financial Concern

Problems occur in every family type, single-parent families included. Most studies have identified financial problems as a major problem of this type of family. One thirty-five-year-old single mother who is on welfare describes her current situation:

> *I can't pay rent, I can't buy Keith clothes that will fit him, I don't have enough money for food, furniture, or clothes for Erin and myself. Everything and anything is a burden, right down to buying a roll of toilet paper. Not to mention Christmas …things are so bad that the thing the kids want most for Christmas is a kitchen table. (Richards, 1989, p. 398)*

Worrying about finances can have a negative impact on parent–child relationships. One mother adds the following, "The lack of money is a real problem for all of us. My anxiety over not being able to find a job makes it hard to be attentive and concerned with the everyday demands of my children" (Richards, 1989, p. 398).

Other Areas of Concern

Whereas the lack of money is the single biggest problem reported by single parents, there are a number of other problematic areas. In a more recent study of single parents, lack of money was the number one problem reported by mothers (77 percent), followed by role/task overload (55 percent), and the lack of social life (30 percent) (Richards & Schmiege, 1993). For fathers, role/task overloads and problems with the ex-spouse were tied for first (35 percent), followed by lack of social life and lack of money (18 percent). In addition, problems with role overload were reported by over half the mothers and a third of the fathers. A mother of three adolescents describes role overload in her own words, "In this day and age of child rearing, it sure would be nice to be sharing the responsibility with someone else. I get tired of being a full-time policeman and everything else" (Richards & Schmiege, 1993, p. 280). A single-parent father also mentioned a task and role overload. He especially hates cooking and believes a role overload has affected his parenting. He noted, "I would have to say that I tended to be more lenient than I should have been simply because I just didn't have the energy after I worked all day" (Richards & Schmeige, 1993, p. 280).

Children were also reported as a major source of stress. Most of these stressful encounters (50 percent) involved negative challenging behavior on the part of the child. These included noncompliance ("my youngest refused to take his nap," "fought with the kids to clean up their room"), irritating behaviors ("my daughter began whining during her nap," "the kids ran in and out all day and made a lot of noise"), defiance ("sassing and rebelling"), temper tantrums, and rule violations. These were followed by sibling conflict, demanding attention, being slow in getting ready for outings, illness, school failure and misbehavior, as well as stressful interactions with child care providers (Olson & Banyard, 1993).

Single parents, like all parents, have strengths as well as problems. Single mothers and fathers see themselves as supportive of their children, being patient, helping children to cope, and fostering independence in their children. They also describe themselves as well-organized, dependable, and able to coordinate schedules in managing their family. In an interview, one mother said of her parenting strengths:

> *I think just communicating with my kids and listening to them and letting them make decisions and giving them choices.... They're very independent and responsible and they have very high self-esteem. I think I've helped them reach their potential and be good caring kids. (Richards & Schmiege, 1993, p. 281)*

When these parents were asked whether single parenting becomes easier or more difficult over time, the majority agreed that single-parenting becomes easier over time. One father said, "Things go more into a routine, so it got a little bit easier that way.... You would learn how to do things, and again, I had a lot of support from my parents" (Richards & Schmeige, 1993, p. 282).

Divorced Noncustodial Fathers

The divorce rate in the United States is high. Half of all marriages in the United States end in divorce and approximately 60 percent of these divorces involve minor children. Mothers are still much more likely to become the custodial parent than fathers. Relationships between divorced fathers and their children are often strained and interaction may be infrequent.

Umberson and Williams (1993) held in-depth interviews with forty-five divorced fathers in Texas to identify the stress involved in noncustodial parenting. They found that visitation and custody issues presented major problems along with relationships with the ex-wife, as well as personal and social identity issues. Child support was also an area that these fathers found to be problematic. The unfairness of the system was pointed to by one divorced father:

One thing that really irritates me about the court system here is that…you can be married for 10 years, and you can be a loving, wonderful father for 10 years. And…in my instance, she met this other guy and decided to run off with him, and the minute that she left, I was no longer a worthy father. I got visitation! (Umberson & Williams, 1993, p. 389)

Some fathers in this study described the pain they felt after dropping off their children following a visitation. One father of a six-year-old son noted:

I don't perceive any stress from being a single parent. When he's with me, it's not stressful at all. It's just hard bringing him back home.… All the way going back home he'll tell me how he wishes he could stay with me, he's going to miss me. (Umberson & Williams, 1993, p. 389)

Other divorced fathers reported that their former wives were good mothers. Knowing that their children are receiving good care is important to many divorced fathers. In the words of one of these fathers: "I think she does a real good job considering all the circumstances and everything" (Umberson & Williams, 1993, p. 392). In a second study, Thompson and Lawson (1994) examined divorced African American fathers in Kentucky and Missouri. These fathers had working- and middle-class jobs. From these in-depth interviews, two themes emerged: fathers seeing their children as the most important reason for marriage, and fathers seeing their children as the most significant reason for not divorcing. Most of these fathers were willing to stay married for the sake of their children. After divorce these fathers did not disassociate or think about disassociating from their children. The findings of this study conflict with the results of the study by Umberson and Williams (1993). Clearly, more studies need to be done to better understand the views of noncustodial divorced fathers.

While the noncustodial father is a common occurrence and evident in most classrooms, the number of noncustodial mothers is significantly less. We can only speculate that the modest number of noncustodial mothers accounts for the sparse literature on the subject. However, this is a growing phenomenon, and we can expect to see an increase in this parent population. With this growth, we as educators must inform ourselves as to the needs and special circumstances of noncustodial mothers.

Stepparent Families

Challenges of Stepparenting

Kathy (35) is of Euro-American extraction and the mother of Amy (9) and Jack (14). Both children are from a previous marriage. Robbie (35) is a Native American who also has children from a previous marriage—Amanda (14), Jim (12), and Fred (7). Kathy and Robbie have been married four years and are both custodial parents. They live in a three-bedroom house in a medium-sized community in Colorado.

Robbie and Kathy started their new marriage with five children in the household—a blended family. In addition to working hard to form a strong, marital bond, Robbie and Kathy each had the challenge of performing in new roles as stepparents. Neither the role of stepfather nor stepmother is easy to carry out. Lacking clear role definition and being uncertain about how family roles should be carried out is called *role ambiguity.* Stepparents, such as Robbie and Kathy, frequently become confused and frustrated as they work out the role ambiguity of being a stepparent by the trial-and-error method.

Who Is in Charge?

Although Robbie was experienced in disciplining his own three children, he felt uncomfortable and wondered what he should be doing regarding disciplining Jack and Amy. The disciplining of stepchildren is a major issue confronting stepfathers. Even stepfathers who had children prior to stepparenting find it difficult; that is, in one study, 30 percent of stepfathers believe that it is more difficult to discipline stepchildren than their own children (Marsiglio, 1992). Moreover, it is more challenging when the stepchild is an adolescent. One stepfather complained about his adolescent stepson as showing a "complete lack of any acknowledgment of my right to correct him or have him obey when asked (told) to do something—like clean up his room or be home at a certain time" (Giles-Sims & Crosbie-Burnett, 1989, p. 1071).

Stepfathers were asked what they would advise a friend about being a stepfather. Here is what they said:

> *Live with them first, don't expect to ever replace the natural father in their eyes; win their respect; treat them as your own; love them and discipline them as your own; let nothing come between you and your woman—especially the kids. (Giles-Sims & Crosbie-Burnett, 1989, p. 1071)*

A national study of stepfathers who were also natural parents found that the majority disagreed with the notion that it is harder to love stepchildren than their own children (Marsiglio, 1992). However, a third of these stepfathers also reported that they were apt to be more a friend than a parent to their stepchildren although the majority still felt that they had assumed the full responsibilities of parenthood. Kathy was concerned about Jack and Amy's reaction when Robbie tried to discipline them, especially during the first year of marriage. Mothers question how much to rely on the stepfather and how much authority he should have in disciplining the children. Typically, mothers remain in the disciplining role and stepfathers gradually begin assuming more of this role when they feel more comfortable with stepparenting. This is how Kathy and Robbie handled the situation. However, some mothers remain in the disciplining role. One mother relates:

> *I have never counted on their stepdad to provide discipline, not even to put them to bed. That is not his responsibility. Those children are my responsibility and it is one that I choose to have. He married me, he only has to live with them, not discipline them. (Giles-Sims & Crosbie-Burnett, 1989, p. 1071)*

Stepmothers report greater dissatisfaction with their family roles and higher levels of stress in carrying out family responsibilities than stepfathers (Ahrons & Wallish, 1987). Women are usually more responsible for the daily contact with and management of children. Therefore, they have the daily hassles of making decisions that may be unpopular with the children.

Successful Stepparenting

Six characteristics of adults who have successfully adapted to step-family life have been identified by Emily and John Visher, founders of the Step Family Association of America (Visher & Visher, 1990). These characteristics are:

1. These adults have mourned their losses and are ready for a new pattern of life.
2. They have a realistic expectation that their family will be different from a first marriage family.
3. There is a strong, unified couple.
4. Constructive family rituals are established and serve as a basis for positive shared memories.
5. Satisfactory step-relationships have formed (which takes time).
6. The separate households cooperate in raising the children.

Healthy step families may differ from healthy intact families according to Pill (1990). They are more flexible and adaptable because of the comings and goings of family members, and they allow for differences among family members. For example, they allow their children to decide whether to go on a family vacation or when to spend time with their other birth parent.

Adult Parenting

Dividing parenting into two stages, Feldman and Feldman (1975) saw parenting as active parenting and adult parenting. Active parenting reflects the dynamic and busy roles parents play from birth to the end of adolescence when children are dependent. Although the parent role continues throughout life, both adults and their adult children must make a transition to the adult parenting stage. In adult parenting, relationships between the parents and the adult children are more equal. Whereas the transition to active parenthood (when the child is born) is abrupt and well-defined, the transition to adult parenting is less abrupt and may be reversible. Many mothers of adult children report delight when their children reach adulthood and leave home (Boss, 1988). Research suggests that couples experience a renewed interest in each other and that martial satisfaction increases at this time (Rollins & Feldman, 1970).

Adult parenting may, however, lead to increased dissatisfaction in another area of a parent's life. Generally, parents in the adult parenting stage reduce involvement with schools and other organizations such as Scouts, 4-H, and youth sports in which their children were involved. As a result, these parents may lose social support and connections with other parents with whom they have shared children's activities and friendships over a number of years (Atkinson & James, 1990).

Rewards and Satisfactions of Parenthood

Nurturing children and being needed are sufficient rewards for parenthood. But would parents do it again? In a recent study, 93 percent of parents said yes—they would have children again. These parents felt that the greatest advantages of having children were the love and affection children bring; having the pleasure of watching them grow; the sense of family they create; the fulfillment and satisfaction they bring; and the joy, happiness, and fun they bring (Gallup & Newport, 1990).

Research studies on parental satisfaction have shown consistently that an overwhelming majority of parents report being satisfied with their parenting role (Cheng, Taylor, & Ladewig, 1991; Chilman, 1980; Ishii-Kuntz & Ihinger-Tallman, 1991). For some people, living childless, even with a partner one loves, is unacceptable. They want children as a creative expression of themselves. These parents find their own lives enriched by having children: to love and to be loved by them (Chilman, 1980).

In a study of the satisfying aspects of parenting, Langenbrunner and Blanton (1993) conducted in-depth interviews with mothers and fathers. Their statements regarding satisfaction clustered into six major areas: (a) the child's growth and accomplishments, (b) verbal and physical interactions between parent and child, (c) the child showing affection toward the parent, (d) parent–infant attachment processes, (e) positive evaluations of their performance of the parental role, and (f) experiencing a sense of cohesion in their family. Overall, these parents received the greatest amount of satisfaction from seeing their children's developmental accomplishments. One parent described this:

> *I also derive a great deal of satisfaction from watching both of them, I have two children now, learning things. It's very interesting for me to see James learn to talk. I have also taken a great deal of satisfaction in seeing James take an interest in books. (Langenbrunner & Blanton, 1993, p. 184)*

All the parents in this study expressed the good feelings they felt from physically interacting with and talking with their children. As one father said, "It is surprisingly relaxing to spend time with a small child and for me it is good therapy" (Langenbrunner & Blanton, 1993, p. 184).

The primary source of satisfaction for fathers in this study came from their experiencing a sense of family cohesion or family unity. For these fathers, a feeling of connectedness to the family was very important. As one father concluded:

> *Well, I was thinking about it a lot. And the most satisfying times are just "feelings" that I have. There's not really anything happening specifically. But I have a sense of being a family unit or we're sharing our feelings. (Langenbrunner & Blanton, 1993, p. 185)*

> **REFLECTION...**
>
> How do you think your parent(s) would respond to the question, "What has been the greatest satisfaction in your parenting? After considering this question, call or write your parents and ask them.

Summary

Marital Satisfaction

Becoming a parent involves a major transition for the couple and taking on a new life role. This changes the relationship between the husband and wife. Typically marital satisfaction decreases somewhat in the early stages of the family life cycle when children are in the home. The daily hassles of parenting add to parental strain especially when children are preschool age and younger.

Parenting Style

Baumrind (1966) identified three parenting styles: authoritarian, authoritative, and permissive. These styles can be seen in the preschool years. Working-class parents usually prefer the authoritarian style, while middle-class parents prefer the authoritative style. Consistency, guidance, and caring are very important in parent–child interactions.

Dual-Employed Parenting

Dual-employed parents encounter role strain as they try to meet the expectations of their various roles. Role strain includes: role overload (having too much to accomplish in a limited time) and role conflict (demands of one life role interfere with meeting the demands of another life role). Dual-employed parents rate their life role commitments in the following order: parent, spouse, home care, and occupation.

Coping patterns used by dual-employed parents to deal with work/family demands include (a) maintaining a positive perspective on the lifestyle to reduce tensions, (b) modifying roles and standards to maintain a work/family balance, (c) maintaining and strengthening the existing work/family interface, and (d) finding support to maintain the family unit.

Single Parenting

Single parents are faced with financial problems, role overload, and daily hassles of interactions with children. They see their parental strengths as parenting skills, managing a family, communicating, growing personally, and providing financial support. They believe that single parenting becomes easier over time.

Divorced, Noncustodial Fathers

Divorced, noncustodial fathers report parental role strain due to visitation and custody issues, relationships with ex-wives, and personal and identity issues. They believe that the children are the most important reason for staying married.

Stepparenting

Stepparent families find that the roles of stepfather and stepmother are not easy to carry out and lack clear role definition. They experience role ambiguity. Disciplining children is a major issue confronting stepfathers. Stepmothers report greater dissatisfaction with their family role and higher levels of stress. Healthy step families differ from healthy intact families. They are more flexible, adaptable, and allow for more differences.

Adult Parenting

Parenting can be divided into two stages: active parenting and adult parenting. Active parenting occurs while children (ages 0 to 18) are still in the home. Adult parenting is a more gradual transition and relationships between parents and their adult children are more equal. Marital satisfaction tends to increase.

Would parents have children again? The overwhelming answer is yes. The greatest rewards of having children are the love and affection they bring, watching them grow, and the sense of family they help create.

Recommended Activities

1. Watch the video "Parenthood" (with Steve Martin) and analyze the parenting styles of the five families depicted in the film.
2. Invite an attorney and two noncustodial fathers to speak to the class about the legal and parenting concerns of this group.
3. Put together pamphlets of resources that will help parents in your community with their parenting (e.g., organizations, mental health services, videos on parenting, books, etc.) and distribute them.
4. Monitor an evening of prime-time television and document the parenting behaviors you observe.
5. Invite parents from dual-income families to class to discuss the mechanics of running a dual-income family. What are the rewards and the stresses?
6. Have various students in the class interview custodial parents, noncustodial parents, a family therapist, and children from these homes, and share the various positions in class.
7. Examine the role of mediation in working out problems between the custodial and noncustodial parent. A panel comprised of a psychologist, family mediator, and an attorney could be helpful in reviewing this topic.

Additional Resources

Parenting

Books:

Binger, J. J. (1989). *Parent–child relations: An introduction to parenting* (3rd ed.). New York: Macmillian Publishing Company. ISBN: 0-02-309831-7.

This is an excellent text that covers parenting from a developmental perspective. It has a short, but good, section on the cultural meaning of parenthood and also includes contemporary parenting concerns (e.g., latch-key children, etc.).

Brooks, J. B. (1991). *The process of parenting* (3rd ed.). Toronto: Mayfield Publishing Company. ISBN: 1-55934-013-4.

This is a superb resource book about parenting. It is thorough and well written. It explores parenting and the life cycle as well as the process of parenting. Brooks then looks at each stage of parenting and examines some special topics (e.g., children with special needs, etc.), 545 pp.

Curran, S. (1987). *Stress and the healthy family.* New York: Harper & Row.

This book examines the stresses experienced by families. Curran groups the stresses into ten categories and discusses how they affect families.

Galinsky, E. (1987). *The six stages of parenthood.* New York: Addison-Wesley.

Galinsky points out that parenting has stages just as childhood does. He examines these stages and discusses their implications as they relate to the individual parent.

Articles:

Anderson, C. (1995, Winter). Parenting issues in rural areas. *Views on Parent Involvement,* 18–19.

Foster, R. (1995, Winter). The national parenting association: Building a voice for parents. *Views on Parent Involvement,* 12–13.

Videos:

Basic Parenting Skills

This entertaining program examines the "three Rs" of parenting—routine, respect, and resources. Viewers learn specific skills and techniques for dealing with difficult behaviors constructively. The video also presents strategies for coping with the frustrations of being a new parent. 1990. (60 minutes, color).

> Insights Media
> 2162 Broadway
> New York, NY
> Phone: 212-721-6316

My Family, Your Family

Emily has a mother, a father, and a brother. Sam has no siblings. Cindy has a mother, father, stepfather, stepbrother, and a half sister. Pointing out that there are all kinds of families, this program helps students understand that what makes a family a family doesn't depend on who is in it, but on the caring feeling members have for one another. Recommend by *School Library Journal.* Grade level K–2. (16 minutes, color).

Sunburst Communication
39 Washington Avenue
PO Box 40
Pleasantville, NY 10570
Phone: 800-231-1934

On Being an Effective Parent

This video is well done and is popular with parent groups. It helps parents develop positive skills in communicating with their children. It is often used with *Basic Parenting Skills.*

Single Parenting

This program teaches single parents how to respond effectively to the difficulties of raising children. It details a four-step plan for raising children after divorce, and illustrates ways to minimize the adverse effects of the loss of a parent on a child. It also suggests ways to handle discipline, financial problems, and family crises. 1988. (20 minutes, color).

Insights Media
2162 Broadway
New York, NY
Phone: 212-721-6316

Organizations:

Family Resource Coalition
200 South Michigan Avenue, Room 1520
Chicago, IL 60604
Phone: 314-341-0900

National Congress of Parent and Teacher Associations
700 North Rush Street
Chicago, IL 60611
Phone: 312-670-6782
http://www.pta.org/

National Council on Family Relations
33989 Central Ve. NE, Suite 550
Minneapolis, MN 55421
Phone: 612-781-9331

Websites:

Children, Youth, and Families
http://www.cyfc.umn.edu/

Early Childhood Education and Family Web Corner
http://www.nauticom.net/www/cokids/index.html

Family Com
http://www.family.com/

National Child Care Information Center
http://www.ericps.crc.uiuc.edu/nccic/nccichome.html

National Coalition for Campus Children's Center
http://www.ericps.crc.uiuc.edu/n4c/n4chome.html

National Parent Information Network
http://www.ericps.crc.uiuc.edu/npin/npinhome.html

Parent's Place
http://www.parentsplace.com/

Parent's Soup
htp://www.parentsoup.com/

References

Abbot, D. A., & Meredith, W. M. (1988). Characteristics of strong families: Perceptions of ethnic parents. *Home Economics Research Journal, 17*(2), 141–147.

Ahrons, C. R., & Wallisch, L. (1987). Parenting in the binuclear family: Relationships between biological and stepparents. In K. Pasley & M. Ihinger-Tallman (Eds.), *Remarriage and stepparenting* (pp. 225–256). New York: Guilford.

Atkinson, A. M., & James, D. (1990). The transition between active and adult parenting: An end and a beginning. *Family Perspective, 25*(1), 57–67.

Baumrind, D. (1966). Effects of authoritative parental control on child behavior. *Child Development, 37*, 887–907.

Baumrind, D. (1967). Child care practices anteceding three patterns of preschool behavior. *Genetic Psychology Monographs, 75*, 43–88.

Belsky, J., & Rovine, M. (1990). Patterns of marital change across the transition to parenthood: Pregnancy to three years postpartum. *Journal of Marriage and the Family, 52*, 5–19.

Belsky, J., Spanier, G., & Rovine, M. (1983). Stability and change in marriage across the transition to parenthood. *Journal of Marriage and the Family, 45*, 567–579.

Boss, P. (1987). Family stress. In M. B. Sussman and S. K. Steinmetz (Eds.), *Handbook of marriage and the family* (pp. 695–723). New York: Plenum.

Boss, P. (1988). *Family stress management.* Newbury Park, Calif.: Sage Publications.

Carter, D., & Welch, D. (1981). Parenting styles and children's behavior. *Family Relations, 30,* 191–195.

Cheng, T. C., Taylor, M. R., & Ladewig, B. H. (1991). Personal well-being: A study of parents of young children. *Family Perspective, 25,* 97–106.

Chilman, C. (1980). Parent satisfactions, concerns, and goals for their children. *Family Relations, 29,* 339–345.

Cowan, C. P., & Cowan, P. A. (1992). *When partners become parents: The big life change for couples.* New York: Basic Books.

Cowan, C. P., Cowan, P. A., Heming, G., Garrett, E., Coysh, W. S., Curtis-Boles, H., & Boles III, A. J. (1985). Transition to parenthood: His, hers, and theirs. *Journal of Family Issues, 6,* 451–481.

Crnic, K. A., & Booth, C. L. (1991). Mothers' and fathers' perceptions of daily hassles of parenting across early childhood. *Journal of Marriage and the Family, 53,* 1042–1050.

Daniels, P., & Weingarten, K. (1984). Mothers' hours: The timing of parenthood and women's work. In

Voydanoff, P. (Ed.), *Work and family: Changing roles of men and women* (pp. 204–231). Palo Alto, CA.: Mayfield.

Fagot, B. I., & Kavanagh, K. (1993). Parenting during the second year: Effects of children's age, sex and attachment classification. *Child Development, 64,* 258–271.

Feldman, H., & Feldman, M. (1975). The family life cycle: Some suggestions for recycling. *Journal of Marriage and the Family, 37,* 277–284.

Gallop, G. H., & Newport, F. (1990). Virtually all adults want children, but many of the reasons are intangible. *The Gallop Poll Monthly, 297,* 8–22.

Giles-Sims, J., & Crosbie-Burnett, M. (1989). Adolescent power in stepfather families: A test of normative-resource theory. *Journal of Marriage and the Family, 51,* 1065–1078.

Holmstrom, L. L. (1973). *The two-career family.* Cambridge, MA: Schenkman Publishing Co.

Ishii-Kuntz, M., & Ihinger-Tallman, M. (1991). The subjective well-being of parents. *Journal of Family Issues, 12,* 58–68.

Langenbrunner, M. R., & Blanton, P. W. (1993). Mothers' and fathers' perceptions of satisfactions and dissatisfactions with parenting. *Family Perspective, 27*(2), 179–193.

LaRossa, R., & LaRossa, M. (1981). *Transition to parenthood: How infants change families.* Beverly Hills, CA: Sage.

LeMasters, E. E. (1957). Parenthood as crisis. *Marriage and Family Living, 19,* 352–355.

LeMasters, E. E., & DeFrain, J. (1989). *Parents in contemporary America: A sympathetic view* (5th ed.). Belmont, CA: Wadsworth.

Marsiglio, W. (1992). Stepfathers with minor children living at home. *Journal of Family Issues, 13*(2), 195–214.

McCubbin, H., and McCubbin, M. (1988). Typologies of resilient families. *Family Relations, 37,* 247–254.

McDade, K. (1993). Multi-cultural perspectives on parenting. *Family Perspective, 27*(4), 323–346.

Muza, R. A. (1988). *Family stress as related to coping strategies and life role salience of dual earner couples.* Unpublished M.S. thesis. Menomonie, Wisconsin, University of Wisconsin-Stout.

Olson, S. L., & Banyard, V. (1993). Stop the world so I can get off for a while: Sources of daily stress in the lives of low-income single mothers of young children. *Family Relations, 42,* 50–56.

Pill, C. (1990). Stepfamilies: Redefining the family. *Family Relations, 39*(2), 186–193.

Platz, D. L., Pupp, R. P., & Fox, R. A. (1994). Raising young children: Parental perceptions. *Psychological Reports, 74,* 643–646.

Richards, L. N. (1989). The precarious survival and hard-won satisfactions of white single-parent families. *Family Relations, 38,* 396–403.

Richards, L. N., & Schmiege, C. J. (1993). Problems and strengths of single-parent families: Implications for practice and policy. *Family Relations, 42,* 277–285.

Rollins, B., & Feldman, H. (1970). Marital satisfaction over the family life cycle. *Journal of Marriage and the Family, 32,* 20–28.

Schnittger, M. H., & Bird, G. W. (1990). Coping among dual-career men and women across the family life cycle. *Family Relations, 39,* 199–205.

Skinner, D. A., & McCubbin, H. I. (1991). Coping in dual-employed families: Gender differences. *Family Perspective, 25*(2), 119–134.

Thompson, A., & Lawson, E. J. (1994). Fatherhood: Insights from divorced black men. *Family Perspective, 28*(3), 169–181.

Umberson, D., & Williams, C. L. (1993). Divorced fathers: Parental role strain and psychological distress. *Journal of Family Issues, 14*(3), 378–400.

U.S. Census Bureau. (1989). Studies in marriage and the family: Singleness in America, single parents and their children, married-couple families with children. *Current Population Reports,* Series P-23 (162). Washington, DC: U.S. Government Printing Office.

Visher, E., & Visher, J. (1990). Dynamics of successful stepfamilies. *Journal of Divorce and Remarriage, 14,* 3–12.

Zimmerman, K., Skinner, D., & Muza, R. (1989). *The relationship of lifecycle stage and employment orientation to work/family stress, coping and life role salience in dual-earner families.* Paper presented at the meeting of the National Council of Family Relations, New Orleans, Louisiana.

$$C \quad h \quad a \quad p \quad t \quad e \quad r \quad \mathit{5}$$

Teachers and Parenting

Multiple Views

JUDITH B. MACDONALD
Montclair State University

This chapter begins by identifying why it is important for teachers and parents to be aware of each other's viewpoints and attitudes. A range of perceptions teachers have about parents—from an understanding of their vulnerability to a puzzlement about their indifference to school matters—is presented. In the last section, the attitudes various groups of parents have about teachers and parents are described. We believe students will ultimately benefit when parents and teachers better understand each other's frames of reference.

The purpose of the chapter is to help the reader to:

- Describe the similarities and differences of teaching and parenting

- Explain the changing roles of the teacher and the parent in the schools

- Compare the teachers' perspectives on parents to the parents' perspectives on teachers

- Identify ways for teachers to deal with parents' vulnerability and sensitivity about their children

- Compare and contrast time and work constraints for both parents and teachers

- Identify ways that the parent is a partner with the teacher in the education of their children

It is understandable that teachers and parents have been called "natural allies." They share the common goal of wanting children to develop their potential as fully as possible. But despite their similar aims, teachers and parents don't always work comfortably together to achieve them. The complexity of life in the 1990s makes it hard for teachers and parents to connect with each other at a time when understanding one another may be even more critical than in the past. How teachers perceive parents and how parents view teachers and schools are subtle, but important, elements in providing optimal educational service to students.

When we talk about groups we tend to make generalizations. While it may be easier or more efficient to talk "globally" about a group, we also know that talking in a general way can mask differences within a group that should be identified to understand its range and complexity. Just as we know that adolescents have certain characteristics and are driven by feelings that are particular to that age and stage of development, we also know how much they can differ from each other. When we talk about teachers and parents in this chapter, we will describe the varied perceptions that people from each group have about the other. We will explore teachers' views about parents and parents' perspectives on teachers and schools. We will consider how to help beginning teachers prepare for relating to the parents of the students they will teach.

Teaching and Parenting

Similarities

Although teaching and parenting are different experiences, as we have noted, they do share some common elements. We teach and nurture in both roles. The settings we work in as teachers and parents have similarities. The privacy (some teachers have called it loneliness) of the classroom has been compared to what Madeleine Grumet (1988) has termed "the exile of domesticity." Being a teacher or parent requires an energetic giving of oneself. Just listening to students and children demands a special attentiveness. Last, but certainly not least, is patience, an attribute essential in both teaching and parenting.

Differences

When teaching has been compared to other kinds of work, it is called unique because teachers, unlike other workers or professionals, confront "a unique set of difficulties…working with inherently changeful materials" (Lortie, 1975, p. 136). But parents also contend with the changeful nature of children and for longer periods of time than teachers. In fact, teachers who are also parents would be the first to say that hard as teaching can be, its challenges can't compete with those a parent faces. The vast number of books on raising children suggests that parents seem to need guidance and support.

In comparing teaching to parenting, the most obvious difference is the feeling of attachment one has to one's child versus one's student. Although the bond between teacher and student can be strong and meaningful, it lacks the elemental and enduring connections that usually develop between a parent and child. Lillian Katz (1980) identified important differences between mothering and nursery-level teaching, and the distinctions she identified also apply to parenting and teaching at higher levels.

Knowledge of Parents versus Pedagogical Knowledge

At this point in your preparation to become teachers, you may not yet have thought much about relationships with the parents of your prospective students. You are probably more concerned with issues of classroom management or of academic and pedagogical knowledge. Understanding parents, their views about their children, and those of the school may seem like a "back burner" issue. Without passing judgment on where it belongs in your hierarchy of topics in education, we suggest that knowing a parent's perspective will enrich your understanding of students. Because teaching is so fluid and unprescribed, and because there are concurrent classroom demands for attention, we contend with gaps in understanding students. Learning more about parents and their perspectives is one way of learning more about students.

Teacher Morale

Just as it is useful for you to know about parents, the parents should know about the challenges inherent in teaching. We know that parent attitudes affect teacher morale. Feeling valued and respected is crucial for teachers (and for most people), and its absence is the chief cause of teacher burnout or depression. A major cause of teachers leaving the profession is their perception of a lack of respect from parents.

Rob is an example of a teacher who became disenchanted with teaching due to a sense of growing disrespect from parents (and students). He teaches social studies in an ethnically, racially, and religiously diverse middle school. Rob is forty-two years old, married, and has two adolescent children. He has taught for twenty years and enjoyed teaching until the last five years. Rob told me that in recent years the parents in his school treated him as if he were their employee rather than a respected member of a profession.

> *I had a student say to me, "Hey, take it easy, I'll have my mother get you fired"....*
> *So that lack of respect, the lack of returning the caring attitude that I have for them*
> *is very demoralizing. (MacDonald, 1994, p. 60)*

We know that teachers are less valued in contemporary society than in the past. Reasons for this change in attitude deserve more analysis than we can provide here. But we do know that if teachers are to function effectively, efforts must be made to correct the misunderstandings that exist between parents and teachers who feel disrespected.

Changing Role of Parents in Schools

It is helpful in understanding how teachers perceive parents to note how the parent's role in schools has changed. In the first quarter of this century when "children were to be seen and not heard," parents, too, were not very visible or vocal in schools. Parents viewed teachers as experts and accorded them the respect appropriate to their position. Until the 1960s parent participation in schools was mainly confined to attending PTA meetings and was limited to those parents who were interested in school issues. Today, PTA events are still mainly supported by groups of interested parents, but most schools would welcome more parent involvement. A recent Gallup poll showed lack of parental interest and support is one of four factors contributing to teacher dissatisfaction.

> **REFLECTION...**
>
> Consider the responsibilities of working parents. Many parents' home and work responsibilities are such that they don't have enough time for everything they must do. Make a list of these responsibilities and consider the time required for each.

At the same time that teachers want parent support, they are also "wary of activist parents who have become more numerous since the 1960s and who act as if the schools belong to them" (Newman, 1994, p. 252). According to Lortie's study (1975) of teachers, "the good parent" is one who doesn't intervene and also supports teacher's efforts or acts as a "distant assistant." It is obvious there is a range of attitudes that teachers have toward parent involvement. It is a bit of a paradox that as parents have more opportunities to make educational choices—through the development of magnet schools and, in some systems of school vouchers—they have less time to make use of the expertise of teachers. Parents' stressful, busy lives and work schedules often prevent them from consulting with teachers on issues with which they could provide assistance.

Teachers' Perspectives on Parents

Teachers develop ideas about parents based on their interactions with them. As we consider teachers' perspectives, you will note the variety of opinions teachers seem to have about parents.

The Perspectives of Teachers Who Are Also Parents

It may surprise you to learn that more than 70 percent of teachers in the United States are also parents. Teaching parents are a useful source of knowledge about parents. Their perspective is especially instructive if they taught before becoming parents—which is the case for most teachers—and can compare their attitudes toward parents before and after being a parent.

Teaching parents find that a main effect of the dual role is an increased empathy for parents. They understand the complexities of the role of parent when they become parents themselves, and this positively affects their relationships with parents of students (MacDonald, 1994).

We think that sharing some of the attitudes teaching parents have about parents will be useful to you. Perspectives of teachers who are not parents are also presented in this section.

Attachment to Children

When teachers become parents they understand the profound attachment parents can have to their children. Although you may lack actual experience as a parent, awareness of a parent's attachment to a child may help you understand how it can affect the parent's perspective.

Consider Max, a forty-eight-year-old elementary school principal who began his career as a kindergarten teacher. He has a ten-year-old son and has been teaching and working in elementary education for more than twenty years. Max is the principal of a suburban school outside of New York City. Parents in this community are high achievers academically and economically, and, as Max said, "They are quite ambitious for their children.... You understand a parent's investment in their own child and how attached parents can be to their children.... As a parent you can understand why somebody would want everything for their child." So having his own child and feeling what he calls "that inexplicable love" helped Max, as a principal, understand and better cope with "irrational" attitudes of parents.

Understanding Limitations in Parents' Power

It goes without saying that parents are responsible for their children. Parents' values and priorities determine how they raise their children. Clearly they have the responsibility of setting rules and limits. Yet, there are situations in which a parent lacks control. For example, you might want your child to study for a test before doing something more enjoyable. Alice, a science teacher with two young children of her own, found that she could not actually force her child to study for a test. Alice teaches science in a white, middle-class school. She says she loves teaching science although, as a single mother and conscientious teacher, she is exhausted at the end of a school day. She said, "Prior to having my own children, I wouldn't understand how a parent couldn't make a child do his homework. Now I understand you can't force Johnny to study for a test, you can't force your kid to get A's."

Stanley is the father of three adolescents. He teaches English in a middle school which is ethnically, racially, and religiously diverse. He said, "you become sensitive to some of the problems that parents have. Before being a parent I thought 'well, you're the parent, you're in charge, why don't you do something about it.'" But Stanley also talked about parental responsibility:

> *On the other hand being a parent also gives you the sense of what it is that parents aren't doing that they should be doing. You see children who come to school whose parents aren't involved in their lives, and that makes you wonder and get angry. So I think I'm more sensitive to that as well because I know what goes into parenting.*

Awareness of Vulnerability, Sensitivity, Defensiveness

Teachers who realize how vulnerable and sensitive parents can be about their children will have an easier time communicating with parents. It is hard for parents to hear negative news about their child even when they ask you to tell them the truth.

Selma is an experienced fifty-year-old fifth-grade teacher in a suburban elementary school. She was very puzzled by her student Collin's lack of interest in school and lack of connection with the other students. Collin's mother is a well-educated woman in her forties who seemed worried about her son's lack of well-being and inability to fit in to the school. During a conference with Collin's mother, Selma focused on Collin's positive aspects. (He was a kind, sweet-natured boy who loved music.) The atmosphere Selma created encouraged Collin's mother to ask direct questions about Collin's adjustment to school. Selma was able to share more of the truth about Collin than if she had started the discussion with her very real concerns about him. Because the conversation was an honest sharing of knowledge about Collin, both the teacher and mother felt good about it and made plans to meet again.

We think it is useful to realize that if a student is not happily engaged in school, the parent may know it but may not know what to do about it. When a teacher is aware of the pain that a child's unhappiness causes the parent, the teacher is seen as an ally and not a judge. Together they can take steps to address the problem.

Maureen teaches elementary school and has four children. A parent of one of her students who had a learning disability was "resisting referral," as Maureen put it. After Maureen told the parent about her own learning-disabled child and how hard it was for her to face what she felt was the shame of this condition, the parent agreed to have her child evaluated.

When parents are hurting, it is hard for them to use their usual common sense. Parents feel vulnerable when school life isn't going well for their child. Parents of children with difficulties in school, such as learning disabilities, can be defensive about their child's condition, often denying it and thereby depriving the child of better educational alternatives.

Just as teaching isn't formulaic, there is no formula for helping parents see their child impartially. We suggest that you be aware of how sensitive parents of children with problems can be. It may be helpful to remember situations in which you felt vulnerable so as to become attuned to the parents' feelings. You may need to give them time to reveal their concerns, and often it is useful to talk first about less sensitive issues.

REFLECTION...

Why does there appear to be an uneasy tension between teachers and parents? Why can't teachers and parents trust each other to have children's best interests at heart?

Awareness of Insufficient Time, Being Overworked

Parents today, and especially mothers, have layers of responsibility. Many women work and have to juggle children and their activities, and take some if not all responsibility for household duties. Women who don't work outside the home may have other obligations such as caring for their parents.

Walter is a math teacher in an urban high school. He is in his early forties and has two children in elementary school. When his wife went back to work, he gained a new perspective on working women:

> *When my wife went back to work, I really appreciated how hard it is for women who work.... You work all day just to come home and make the dinner, correct papers, and prepare for the next day's classes, and make lunches for the next day, and pretty soon it gets to be 10:00 at night.*

We know that people today have less leisure time than their parents despite the labor-saving devices that many families have. Mothers with young children have the least free time and seem to have profited least from advances in labor-saving technology (Hall, 1991).

An awareness of parents' lack of free time will help you understand the constraints and stresses they contend with. Parents may not have the time to help with homework or other school-related tasks. Knowing the time limitations of parents may affect your decisions about what schoolwork should be done at home.

The Educated and/or Affluent Parent

In this section we describe the negative attitudes teachers have reported that some educated and/or affluent parents exhibit. These behaviors clearly don't apply to all educated or affluent parents. New teachers, in particular, feel uneasy teaching students of highly educated parents who may lack the sensitivity to understand the vulnerability of a new teacher. You might expect that the parent who is as educated or more educated than you would be your natural ally in school. Unfortunately, this isn't necessarily so. Teachers have varying perspectives about educated parents. They are clearly valued when they share an understanding of the teacher's educational objectives, but teachers also report that educated parents can be demanding and aggressive.

Experienced teachers claim that parental respect has declined in the last ten to fifteen years. Two groups in particular, educated and affluent parents, seem to be the culprits. Affluent parents can undervalue the teacher if they assess accomplishment in strictly monetary terms.

Cathleen, a high school teacher for twenty-five years, claims that affluent parents in her school (a suburb in the Northeast) are subject to a "stock market syndrome." She said, "When the economy is weak and people are in danger of losing their jobs, they show more disdain for teachers. Since they pay the teachers' salaries, they resent their security at a time when their own may be threatened."

We know it is difficult to work in a community where you expect educated parents to support your efforts but instead perceive themselves as experts and question your professional expertise. It is important for teachers, and especially beginning teachers, to realize that their professional knowledge is distinct and not interchangeable with the knowledge that educated parents may have. It may be a misnomer to call parents "educated" when they are disrespectful of teachers. We alert you to the existence of these parents but also reassure you that the truly educated parent will value and respect you as a teacher.

The Indifferent Parent

Teachers have found it frustrating to work with a parent who seems indifferent to their efforts. It is hard to understand why a parent wouldn't be responsive to a teacher's overtures for contact. We are usually not privy to the origins of a parent's indifference, although knowing why a parent seems apathetic might help you better connect with her or him. Consider Melinda, a thirty-year-old kindergarten teacher who teaches in Newark, New Jersey, a large city with typical urban problems. She has felt frustrated over the parents' lack of involvement and interest in their children's development and schoolwork. She feels it diminishes her job as a teacher when she cannot follow through on her commitment to children by connecting with parents.

We know that "Back to School" nights usually draw the parents who don't need to come. That, too, is frustrating for teachers because it deprives them of the chance to interact with parents whose children they want to know more about. You should realize that the appearance of indifference may be masking other conditions. We know that life can be complicated for parents. They may be unable to come to school due to work or other familial obligations. They may feel uneasy in a conference situation. They may have unpleasant associations with school based on their own educational experience.

What can you do? Generally speaking, parents sense a teacher's earnestness. If you send home a note or make a telephone call that reveals your commitment to reaching the parent, that is an important step in connecting. We realize that you may ultimately have to accept the fact that, despite your efforts to reach out to parents, some will not be there for you.

The Bewildered Parent

Being a parent has never been easy. Parenting is one of the few jobs for which there is no preparation. Parents today may be more isolated and vulnerable than in previous generations. The extended family which provided psychological support has largely disappeared. In most two-parent households both parents work. In single-parent families, the parent bears even more responsibility. Today's parents may be more enlightened about child-rearing than their parents were. They clearly have access to more literature on the subject. But they have less first-hand knowledge of children. When both parents work, they not only have less time with their children, they also have less familiarity with their children's friends, and so have limited knowledge of the range of normal behavior. Teachers today are often called upon to provide support for bewildered parents.

Teachers expressed a range of opinions about bewildered parents. Rachel teaches English to special education students in a large, racially mixed suburban high school. She loves teaching and enjoys her students. However, she is appalled by the lack of maturity on the part of parents: "They simply don't know how to be parents. They don't know how to set limits; they don't know the importance of consistency." Her reaction to what parents didn't know was one of annoyance with what she felt was a lack of parental responsibility. She felt her students were being short-changed because of the parents' ignorance about their responsibilities.

Linda, a third-grade teacher in a suburban school, strongly believes that parents today need parenting skills. She was astonished at the lack of know-how a professional couple demonstrated regarding their child. They seemed to not know when a third grader should go to bed, let alone the kinds of limits and responsibilities they should set. Linda is troubled by the parents' fundamental lack of common sense. .

Other teachers were more empathic toward parents who were unsure about how to cope with their children. Alex teaches social studies in a middle-class middle school. He empathized with parents who had adolescent children and found it "hard to know if you're doing the right thing." He understood how peer pressure can make life very difficult for parents as well as for children.

> **REFLECTION...**
>
> What is so difficult about parenting? Isn't it better we learn from our parents? If not, where do we learn how to parent and why do some parents seem to have such a hard time with parenting?

Max, the elementary school principal whom we described earlier, empathized with parents of pre-adolescent children, because he was going through the throes of that experience himself. He said:

I feel for parents who are confused. My son is a pre-adolescent…he wants to be a baby one minute and the next minute he wants to be the independent teenager going off on his own and not wanting any questions asked of him. I know this is typical adolescence, but it's my first and only child, so the first time it hits you, it's a growth experience for the parent.

Being a parent means that you contend with uncertainty and change. Max enjoyed the challenge of growing as a parent and understood that parents must adapt to the stages their children go through. Alex understood the dilemmas of adolescents and their parents. Rachel and Linda are disturbed by what they perceive is a lack of parental responsibility where they believe it is sorely needed.

The Parent as Partner

Teachers found particular satisfaction when they encountered parents who seemed to profit from a relationship with them. These parents defy categorization in terms of age or socio-economic status. What they seem to have in common is open-mindedness, respect for the teacher's knowledge, an eagerness to learn from the teacher, and a feeling of being at ease in a school setting.

> *Dorothy, a second-grade teacher enjoyed having Jessica assist as a mother: She was so involved with all the kids, not just her own. Of course, we tell parents who come on trips with us or come to school to help out that those are the rules of the game—that you are there for all the children. But Jessica really was interested in all of them and in my behavior with them. She watched me very closely and was very interested in picking up on my routines. She asked me a lot of questions. I could tell that she was storing away what she saw for use at home. I love having parents like that around because I do think after thirty years I know a lot and I wish I could share what I know more specifically with the parents. Jessica is like a sponge and I get such pleasure from sort of teaching her, too.*

Dorothy isn't the only teacher to experience the satisfactions of developing a relationship with a parent. One of the pleasures of teaching is sharing what you know or have learned, and a likely recipient of this knowledge is a parent. But the parent has to be ready to receive and use this knowledge.

Understandably, teachers develop a perspective about parents based on the nature of their experiences. They feel frustrated with parents they cannot reach and they also know the satisfaction of connecting meaningfully with parents who need their help. We believe that in general parents want to do the best they can for their children. We think it is useful to have some familiarity with the perspectives teachers have about parents. These perspectives are presented to show the variety of ways parents present themselves to teachers, although parents may not be conscious of the effect they have.

As you know, teaching is more than teaching subjects. Who the students are and what they contend with at home affects the attitudes they bring to school. It may be helpful for you to think of your students as someone's child who goes home to a family after being in school and blends the school experience with the realities of home life.

Teachers are required to take on many roles today. We don't suggest that your teaching world extend to the home life of children. But we do believe that the parent is your partner in education, and you can learn from and teach each other—for the benefit of your students.

Parents' Perspectives on Teachers and Schools

For some people, one of the perks in growing up is not having to go to school anymore. But that advantage ends when you become a parent and your child goes to school. The discomfort you felt as a student can return when you are in an environment you never liked in the first place. Why talk about negative feelings as we begin to consider parents' perspectives on teachers and schools? Because many of us have them. Just walking into a school can suddenly make you anxious, remembering the tests on Friday and the Sunday night feeling that Monday was coming.

Are we exaggerating? Yes and no. For many people school was a haven—a place to learn, be with friends, and be nurtured intellectually and emotionally. For others, it was a place where people felt genuinely uncomfortable. The reasons vary. They may have been the victims of poor teaching; they may have had difficulty learning; they may have had problems with social adjustment. As we consider parents' perceptions about teachers and schools, we should remember that parents vary greatly, and the more we know about the range of their attitudes, the better we can address their needs.

Why Should Parental Perspectives Be Considered?

There are two principal reasons to pay attention to parents' feelings about school. First, their attitudes toward school influence their children's attitudes and affect their behavior in class (Seligman, 1979). Second, when parents demonstrate a supportive attitude about school, it has a beneficial effect on teachers. It makes them feel valued and contributes to keeping them in the profession (Newman, 1994).

Shift in Parents' Attitudes

We have already noted that before the 1960s most parents were not active in school affairs. School was the domain of teachers and children. Children went to school either knowing implicitly or being told explicitly that they should cause their parents no shame. Nowadays, however, according to one fifty-year-old teacher, "The parent is likely to blame the teacher for what the child hasn't taken the trouble to learn." While this shift in parent attitude is not universal, it is sufficiently widespread to concern teachers.

Defining Parental Perspectives on Teachers and School

It can be difficult to assess parents' attitudes about school, and that isn't your primary task as a teacher. Still, if you have some sense of the feelings parents bring to school, you will better understand them and the environments from which your students come. We present viewpoints parents have about teachers and schools to make you aware of the array of feelings and beliefs parents can have on these issues. The circumstances of parent's lives—whether they are single parents, working parents, or stepparents, for example—will also affect their relationships with teachers and schools.

When we describe parents of a particular group, we don't mean to imply that all parents will have the attributes we have used in our example. We are identifying tendencies that people in a specific group may have.

Negative Feelings

Parents with a "Good Old Days" Mentality

This view represents the belief that teachers are not as dedicated as they were in the past. These parents believe that teachers don't work as hard as they used to and that teaching isn't the "calling" that it once was. Parents assert that the caliber of people entering the profession has declined. They contend that teachers are in the profession for the security it provides and that they don't care sufficiently about students.

Parents who have these beliefs can undermine their child's education by their lack of support for the teacher. It is confusing to a child to hear his or her parent denigrate teachers. A student's success in school can be hampered by a parental attitude of alienation from school. We identify this attitude because you may encounter it. We think the mind-set of these parents can be altered as their children have positive school experiences.

Feelings of Discomfort Due to Disliking School

As we have said, not everyone liked school as a student, and these feelings can re-emerge as a parent. Consider Joyce who never enjoyed school. She saw it as a chore she had to get through. When her daughter, Beth, began going to school, Joyce felt the old apprehensions about school return. Fortunately, Beth seems to enjoy school and this pleases Joyce because of the potential for the better life education can give Beth. Joyce's jobs have been confined to minimum wage work from which she derives little satisfaction.

One of Joyce's lingering worries is that because she wasn't a good student, she will be unable to help Beth when she gets into higher grades. Being a single parent, she sees herself as having sole responsibility for helping Beth at home. In a conference setting, a teacher can usually sense a parent's uneasiness. Joyce would feel reassured learning how well Beth was doing in school. Beth's positive adjustment is likely to contribute to Joyce's level of comfort in school. With reduced anxiety about school, Joyce could get the help she might need to assist Beth if or when she will need it.

Effects of Feeling Discomfort in School

It may be hard to understand how a parent's discomfort about school could be more important than attending to her child's problems. But there are such parents. Linda is an educated woman but she is also depressed by the emotional aspects of her life. She is not a joiner and has avoided school and parent association events. She has a son with learning difficulties and, despite being an educated person, she feels a sense of shame about her son's condition. Her uneasy feelings about school, coupled with an unwillingness to face her child's problems, interfere with finding an appropriate course of action for her son's problems.

A teacher cannot know a parent's frame of mind. We include Linda in our example of parents because, as we have said earlier, parent vulnerability is a subtle but frequent condition. With parents such as Linda, listening to them in a nonjudgmental, supportive way is a first step toward making them less anxious in school.

Positive Feelings

Single Parent—Child's Advocate

As you might expect, not all parents of children with disabilities are vulnerable and take a "head in the sand" approach to solving problems. Louisa is a forty-year-old single mother of two elementary school-age daughters. The family lives in an integrated suburb. Louisa has sole responsibility for her children and is also working toward a college degree. One of her daughters has learning difficulties in math and reading. Louisa sees herself as the child's advocate and maintains frequent contact with the teacher. Although she describes herself as having emotional problems, she has the focus and the energy to get what is best for her child.

Maria is a single mother of three children, one of whom is severely learning disabled. Like Louisa, she does not shy away from finding solutions for her son. She has an optimistic outlook about what school can do for her son. She sees teachers as being on her side and feels nurtured by the efforts they have made for him.

Effects of Feeling Comfortable in School

Parents who feel comfortable in a school setting tend to take leadership roles in parent–teacher associations. They are in a good position to use the school beneficially for their children.

Jean has three children. Her two daughters were very school oriented but her youngest child Tim was not interested in school. Jean did not work outside the home and so was fortunate in having the time to talk to Tim's teachers about him. She felt that informing teachers about one's child makes an important difference in their understanding of a puzzling student. Beside having the time to talk to Tim's teachers, Jean also had the inclination to work with them. She felt at ease in school and with teachers and so was able to help them address Tim's needs. She felt it was her obligation to share what she knew about Tim with his teachers.

Blended Family Perspectives

Blended families have many adjustments to make at home. Sometimes the school can be a haven of retreat from family conflicts. In other cases, family problems demand more solutions than the school can successfully provide. Gail was a thirty-eight-year-old teacher with a five-year-old son and three-year-old daughter when her husband died of a heart attack. After a period of three years she married a widower, Martin, who was ten years her senior. He had three children—daughters aged eighteen and eight, and a son aged fifteen. When they married, Gail moved into Martin's house. There were marked differences in Gail and Martin's style of parenting. Gail set very clear limits and was consistent while Martin was unable to deny his children anything. Martin's children were unaccustomed to rules, which made home life very hard for everyone.

Gail's children adjusted well to school because the orderliness their mother provided at home resembled the structure of school. Martin's children, however, were poorly adjusted at school (and at home). They no longer had the freedom at home that they were used to, and they were not involved at school.

With the help of psychological school services and family therapy, Martin's children began to function in school. They were moved to smaller schools where they could get more professional attention. Gail's children functioned well in their regular school but continued to have conflicts with their siblings at home.

As you can see, the different and conflicting parenting perspectives of Gail and Martin had an impact on their children at school as well as at home.

Teaching–Parenting Perspectives

It goes without saying that parents who also teach are comfortable in schools although they may not necessarily be in total agreement with a teacher's method of teaching. In general, though, parents who also teach feel a rapport with teachers and view them as colleagues and allies. Paula and Larry are both teachers and have three adolescent children. Paula said both she and Larry are very sympathetic to teachers. She described the atmosphere of her children's schools as "comfortable, inviting and homey." She acknowledged that she and her husband are on the same economic and social level as the teachers, which she feels adds to the ease of communicating with them. She and Larry hold teachers in high regard and believe that most teachers work hard and seek to improve their teaching by taking courses to keep up with educational innovations. Ruth is an example of a teaching-parent who is less contented with her children's teachers than Larry and Paula are. She has two pre-adolescent children and said:

> *On several occasions my children have had teachers who were, in my judgment, doing a very poor job. Teachers who are parents must be very careful in the way they approach their own child's school and teachers. Over the years, I have felt uncomfortable at times having to walk that very thin line. To remember my place, and then when necessary to "go to bat" for my child.*

Being a teacher and parent gives a parent the opportunity to interact as a colleague with her child's teacher. The success of the relationship depends on having similar educational goals. As we know, not all teachers share a common perspective. So while being an insider as a teacher is beneficial for a parent, it doesn't guarantee the parent the understanding he or she might expect.

Effects of Culturally Diverse Backgrounds

We know that different cultural groups have their own priorities, and as a teacher it is useful to be familiar with the values of your students' families. We include two perspectives which differ somewhat from the majority culture. As mentioned in previous chapters, it is important not to over-generalize about any population. Where we can make some general observations about groups, there is too much variation within any population to apply them to all people of that group. Factors such as culture, socioeconomic status, age, gender, and so forth all influence the experiences and behaviors of individual members of a group.

The Hispanic Parent's Perspective

In the Hispanic community, a woman's priority is first to care for her husband and children, and then if time permits she will attend a school meeting (Finders & Lewis, 1994). For Hispanic parents, the child's education is his or her responsibility and not one which the parent oversees. This behavior is intended to foster independence in the child. So for example, if, as a teacher, you expect parent involvement in homework, it is useful to know the parent's perspective about her role in the child's education. Actually this minimalist approach resembles the behavior of "mainstream" parents fifty or more years ago when parents were much less involved in their children's school life.

Hispanic parents have their own perspective about the status of children. If you have a conference with a parent whose understanding of English may require an interpreter, don't ask the child to translate. Doing so would go against a cultural norm and be perceived as putting the child on an equal status with an adult.

The Asian Parent's Perspective

Valuing educational achievement knows no cultural boundaries but it may be more ostensibly prevalent in Asian communities. "Cram schools" or "juku" in Japanese, "buxiban" in Chinese, and "hagwon" in Korean, are a flourishing industry in places such as New York, New Jersey, California, and other regions where Japanese, Chinese, and Koreans have settled. These schools hold classes on Saturdays and are intended to supplement students' public education. They developed because Asian parents perceived American education to be lax and insufficiently challenging compared to schools in Asia. Participation in Saturday schools is not confined to the well-to-do. Students from a variety of economic backgrounds attend these schools.

Since this is a private school phenomenon, what relevance does it have for you as future public school teachers? It is, in fact, an example of Asian parents' perspective of education. Asian parents send their children to public schools but don't trust them to do a satisfactory job of educating their children (Dunn, 1995). Instead of participating in public school affairs to achieve their objectives, parents choose alternatives that are familiar to them as Asians. "We try to make sure that our children have as much opportunity as possible.... They will have a better life," said Sung Kim, the father of one student attending a Saturday school.

One of the challenges we face as teachers is in reaching out to parents who don't feel comfortable in their child's school. Asian parents, like Hispanic parents, don't see themselves as partners of teachers in the process of educating their children. If Asian parents believed the public school could effectively serve their children's needs, would they seek their own alternatives? We think through dialogue with school people, some Asian parents might alter their attitudes.

REFLECTION...

How can teachers enable parents to better understand the joys of teaching? How can parents help the non-parent teacher understand the total responsibility of parenting?

The Parent as Learner and Partner

We have referred to the parent, Jessica, in the section on teachers' perspectives, as someone who the teacher, Dorothy, perceived as benefiting from being in her classroom. Jessica valued what she learned from the teacher, such as routines and consistency, which she had not learned elsewhere. She sees the classroom as a unique setting in which to learn about children and then to use this knowledge as a parent. It is both instructive and nurturing for her. From Jessica's perspective, the school and teachers are sources of learning and collaboration.

Summary

We have presented a range of attitudes parents have toward teachers and schools. Despite the differences in their feelings about school, parents have a common desire for their children to succeed there.

We see the school as a place for teachers and parents to exchange knowledge and perspectives. The expertise of teachers should not be confined to the classroom. Most teachers have a natural desire to communicate what they know and this knowledge can be used by parents. Teachers have honed their skills in the laboratory setting of schools and parents can adapt these skills for use at home. Classroom techniques, such as questioning to stimulate thinking and giving students (children) time to think and respond, could be used by parents if they aren't engaging in these practices. Sigel (1991) has clearly described how parents' verbal interactions with children can affect their intellectual development.

We believe parents should know more about what it is like to be a teacher in today's society. Parents may not be sufficiently aware of the varied roles teachers are required to assume (i.e., social worker, surrogate parent) and the impact of these responsibilities on their teaching lives. We think that if parents better understood the complexity of teachers' professional lives, it would positively affect their relations with them.

Schools where the development of teacher–parent collaboration and trust is given priority produce students who take learning seriously and enjoy school. [Note: Two examples are James Comer's work in schools in New Haven, Connecticut, and Deborah Meier's in the Central Park East schools in New York City.] We hope this trend will grow, and as teachers you will contribute to it.

Recommended Activities

1. Invite a panel of parents into class to discuss, from their perspective, the relationship between the parent and teacher. Make sure to include parents of children in preschool, elementary, middle, and high school classes.
2. Invite a panel of teachers into the class to discuss, from their perspective, the relationship between the teacher and parent. Make sure to include teachers from preschool, elementary school, middle school, and high school.
3. Interview teachers and/or administrators that have been teaching for over twenty years. Ask them to compare teaching today with teaching twenty years ago. Ask them specific questions about changes they see in the roles of teachers, parents, and children. What do they see as changes that are positive as well as negative?
4. Have a parent educator come into class and discuss the types of questions he/she hears from parents about parenting issues. How do these questions relate to teachers?
5. Identify various parenting discussion groups on the World Wide Web. Describe the different groups and the emphasis of their discussions. Ask parents you know if that is the type of format they would like to have available to answer their questions or if they prefer the face-to-face contact.

6. Interview parents and teachers and ask them what they perceive the role of the parent is in the school. If they identify roles, ask them to describe the differences they see with parent involvement in schools today compared to when they were growing up.

7. Survey different ages of children to determine what kind of role they would like to have their parents play in schools. Make sure to survey different age groups from four-year-olds to seventeen-year-olds.

Additional Resources

Parental Participation

Books:

Comer, J. B. (1989). Home, school, and academic learning. In J. Goodlad & P. Keating (Eds.), *Access to knowledge* (pp. 23–42). New York: College Board.

Delgado-Gaitan, C., & Trueba, H. (1991). *Crossing cultural borders: Education for immigrant families in America.* Washington: Taylor & Francis.

Meier, D. (1995). *The power of their ideas: Lessons for America from a small school in Harlem.* Boston: Beacon.

Reitz, R. (Ed.). (1990). *Parent involvement in the schools.* Bloomington, IN: Phi Delta Kappa.

Winters, W. G. (1993). *African American mothers and urban schools: The power of participation.* New York: Lexington Books.

Articles:

Comer, J. B. (1986). Parent participation in the schools. *Phi Delta Kappan, 67*(6), 442–446.

Hulsebosch, P. (1992). Significant others: Teachers' perceptions on relationships with parents. In W. A. Schubert & W. C. Ayers (Eds.), *Teacher Lore* (pp. 107–132). New York: Longman.

Organizations:

Alliance for Parental Involvement in Education
PO Box 59
East Chatham, NY 12060
Phone: 518-456-1876

Center for Study of Parent Involvement
John F. Kennedy University
12 Altarinda Road
Orinda, CA 94563
Phone: 510-254-8820

National Committee for Citizens in Education (NCCE)
900 2nd Street, NW
Washington, DC 20002
Phone: 800-NETWORK

Parents as Teachers National Center
9374 Olive Blvd.
St. Louis, MO 63132
Phone: 314-432-4330

Parents' Rights Organization
12571 Northwinds Drive
St. Louis, MO 63146
Phone: 314-434-4171

Videos:

For Children's Sake: The Comer School Development Program Discussion Leader's Guide Videotape C—The Parents Program

Describes the Comer process, which puts children at the center of the educational process by calling on all significant adults in the community to work together to support and nurture every child's total development. 1992. New Haven, CT: Yale Child Study Center.

Involving Parents in Education

Examines how two schools, one rural and one urban, involve parents in their operations. Offers suggestions on how to build parent–teacher partnerships. 1992. Alexandria, VA: ASCD. (30-minute video and 54-page leader's guide).

Partnerships with Parents

Discusses how parents and teachers can work together for the benefit of preschool children, foster communications, and resolve difficulties with schedules of both parents and schools. 1989. (28 minutes).

Teacher TV: Parents as Partners, Episode #5.

Explores ways that teachers can get parents involved as their partner in education. (22 minutes). 1993. Washington, DC: National Education Association.

Working with Parents: Home School Collaborations

Examines how to improve communication between teachers and parents when they meet at parent–teacher conferences to better serve the student. 1984. (30 minutes).

Websites:

COMPASS Resource: Parents and Teachers
http://www.compassinc.com/resources.html

National Association for the Education of Young Children (NAEYC)
http://www.america_tomorrow.com/naeyc/

Teacher/Parent/Trainer Site List
http://www.edpro.com/link.html

References

Dunn, A. (1995, January 28). Cram schools: Immigrants' tool for success. *New York Times,* pp. 1, 5.

Finders, M., & Lewis, C. (1994). Why some parents don't come to school. *Educational Leadership, 51*(8), 50–54.

Grumet, M. (1988). *Bitter milk: Women and teaching.* Amherst, MA: University of Massachusetts Press.

Hall, T. (1991, July 3). Time on your hands? It may be increasing. *New York Times,* pp. 1, 7.

Katz, L. G. (1980). Mothering and teaching: Some significant distinctions. In L. G. Katz (Ed.), *Current topics in early childhood education* (Vol. 3) (pp. 47–64). Norwood, NJ: Ablex.

Lortie, D. C. (1975). *Schoolteacher.* Chicago: University of Chicago Press.

MacDonald, J. B. (1994). *Teaching and parenting: Effects of the dual role.* Lanham, MD: University Press of America.

Newman, J. W. (1994). *America's teachers.* New York: Longman.

Seligman, M. (1979). *Strategies for helping parents of exceptional children.* New York: Free Press.

Sigel, I. E. (1991). Parents' influence on their children's thinking. In A. L. Costa (Ed.), *Developing minds* (Vol. 1) (pp. 43–46). Alexandria, VA: Association for Supervision and Curriculum Development.

Chapter *6*

Parent–Teacher Communication: Who's Talking?

SARA FRITZELL HANHAN
University of North Dakota

My family is sad because my grandpa died.

my dad   Ann   my mom   me   Sarah

Becca Olsen

> After reading this chapter, the student will be able to:
>
> - Identify principles for establishing two-way communication with parents
> - Distinguish between effective and ineffective non-verbal communication
> - Describe ways to establish a positive atmosphere for parent–teacher conferences

Although many of you may believe strongly that parents and schools should form true partnerships in order to maximize the benefit of parent involvement (Swap, 1993), this is not always an easy thing to achieve. It requires mutual commitment, action, trust and understanding on the part of both parents and school personnel. One of the first steps teachers can take towards successful parent involvement and the possibility for true home–school partnerships is to learn the ins and outs of communicating with parents. This is not so different from skillful communication with anyone else, of course, but there are some purposes and nuances that can be particular to parent–teacher relationships.

In many teacher education programs, students are required to take a course in communication, usually a course in fundamentals of public speaking. When a rationale for the requirement is offered, it is usually that teachers need to learn to feel comfortable speaking in front of a group and to make an organized and articulate presentation. Although there are few occasions for teachers to give formal speeches to groups of parents, the direction of much parent–teacher communication nonetheless tends to be one-way, flowing from teacher to parent, with an expectation or perhaps even a hope that parents will receive teacher wisdom passively. As examples, some of the most common methods teachers use to communicate with parents are newsletters, parent handbooks, orientation meetings, and report cards, which typically involve the teacher *telling* parents about activities, school policies and procedures, student progress, curriculum, and so on. Even parent–teacher conferences are sometimes viewed as opportunities to *tell* parents how their children are doing in school. The idea is to have parents informed. Although just as important as the teacher education emphasis on speech, courses on *listening* are not only not required for teacher certification, they are seldom even available at any college or university in the country. Teachers, in other words, despite rhetoric about the importance of good home–school communication, are taught to talk rather than to listen to students and parents. To reap the benefits of parent involvement, however, parents too must speak and be heard. Communication must flow in at least two directions, and for this to happen both parent and teacher need to consider each other their equal.

In most cases teachers need to take the initiative in order for this to happen. Problematic for a parent–teacher relationship based on equality is the inherent inequality of the relative positions of teacher and parent within the school. For many parents, their own children's initial school enrollment is their first contact with teachers and schools since they themselves were students, and school memories for many adults are not very pleasant (Seligman, 1979). Whether memories of school are pleasant or not, however, parents' childhood relationships with teachers were inherently unequal, and for many the nature of that relationship lives on, even though they are now adults.

> **REFLECTION...**
>
> Think about your teachers from elementary or secondary school. Which teacher would you look forward to having a frank conversation with—and which would you not? What makes your memories different?

In addition to a perceived inequality between the teacher and the parent, parents are also keenly aware that they have placed the welfare of their children in the hands of teachers and that each teacher potentially has the power to make children's school lives either comfortable or difficult. For this reason, many parents tread lightly within the parent–teacher relationship, unwilling, from their perspective, to upset the child-teacher relationship for fear that the teacher might take it out on the child (Swap, 1993).

Finally, an important idiosyncratic quality of the teacher–parent relationship is that the stakes are so high. To be sure, this is true of some other relationships that rely on good communication as well, but in this case the quality of the relationship may affect what happens to a child's life—something that for many of us is of ultimate importance.

Building a Coequal Relationship

Although it may be difficult for teachers to affect the relationships children have with their parents, teachers can affect the nature of their own relationships with their students' parents. Most parents and many teachers consider schools to be teacher territory, not parent territory. The majority of parents probably feel uneasy, like fish out of water or guests in a strange place. They view teachers as authority figures, the experts in teaching and learning, and they are often even uncertain about their own expertise in parenting. When the relationship is unequal to begin with, the flow of communication generally goes from the person in the superior position (the one perceived to have more expertise) to the person who is viewed as inferior (parenting is seen as something everyone can do).

It is very difficult, under these circumstances, for the water (or conversation) to flow from lower vessel to higher vessel. If we truly want parents to be partners in our educational efforts, we must change the perceived positions of the pitchers (or players). Communication must begin to flow two ways. And considering the relatively powerful position of teachers, it becomes their responsibility to make the first move. Unfortunately, this is not always easy either, as there are many barriers that need to be avoided or overcome.

Barriers to Two-Way Communication

Language

In addition to the barrier of perceived inequality, language itself poses a number of stumbling blocks for those teachers and parents who wish to establish open and two-way communication. Language is often ambiguous. Mutual understanding requires both clear

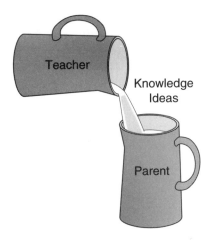

FIGURE 6-1

articulation on the part of the speaker/writer and accurate interpretation on the part of the listener/reader. The very acts of speaking, listening, writing, and reading, however, leave much room for misinterpretation. Teachers may, for instance, in the hopes of lessening parental disappointment, couch what they have to say about children in gentle terms, which in turn may be interpreted by one parent as teacher satisfaction or by another as a cover-up of serious problems. Another example which illustrates the importance of specificity and clarity comes from a first grade parent–teacher conference. The teacher told the parent in this conference that her child was "what we call immature." When the parent inquired further about his immaturity, the teacher offered that "he was reluctant to try new things." The parent in turn asked what he was reluctant to do. The teacher said that he was unwilling to climb some bleacher-like stairs. At this point, the teacher's comments made sense to the mother because she knew of her son's fear of heights; only now could she be of some help to the teacher in offering both an explanation and the beginnings of a solution.

Although there is ambiguity in cases such as the above example, parents at least have the background to make some interpretation. When educational jargon is used, however, parents can be left feeling inept, ashamed or even stupid or embarrassed to ask for an explanation. What does it mean to have an "auditory processing problem" or good "visual-spatial abilities" or "learning disabilities?" It seems best for teachers to forego jargon of all kinds in favor of using everyday language that is as descriptively specific and as free of value judgments as possible.

Body Language

The influence of nonverbal messages can also complicate the communication process. Body positions (e.g., arms and legs folded tightly), gestures (e.g., a shrug of the shoulders), facial expressions (e.g., a quivering lip or flaring nostrils), voice intonation or rate of speech (e.g., a firm and monotone voice), or an involuntary behavior (e.g., a quick inhale of breath) can all carry signals to the listener. If our nonverbal behaviors do not correspond with the message we wish to convey, or if we are unfamiliar with the meanings of nonverbal behaviors in other cultures, these behaviors can become obstacles to clear and sensitive communication.

Body language can provide information about a person's emotional state (see Table 6-1). The person who folds his or her arms and quickly turns away is most likely upset; this can be useful information. On the other hand, you do not want to over interpret every movement. Some people are more comfortable sitting with their legs or arms crossed and it is their desire for comfort, rather than a nonverbal message, that may be the reason.

TABLE 6-1   Nonverbal Communication

Attitude	Nonverbal Cue	Attitude	Nonverbal Cue
Openness	Open hands Unbuttoned coat	**Nervousness**	Clearing throat "Whew" sound Whistling
Defensiveness	Arms crossed on chest Crossing legs Fist-like gestures Pointing index finger		Cigaretter smoking Picking or pinching flesh Fidgeting in chair Hand covering mouth while speaking Not looking at the other person Tugging at pants while seated
Evaluation	Hand to face gestures Head tilted Stroking chin Peering over glasses Taking glasses off, cleaning Earpiece of glasses in mouth Pipe smoker gestures Putting hand to bridge of nose		Jingling money in pockets Tugging at ear Perspiration, wringing of hands
		Frustration	Short breaths "Tsk" sounds Tightly clenched hands Wringing hands Fist-like gestures
Suspicion	Arms crossed Sideways glance Touching, rubbing nose Rubbing eyes Buttoning coat—drawing away		Pointing index finger Rubbing hand through hair Rubbing back of neck
		Cooperation	Upper body in sprinter's position Open hands
Insecurity	Pinching flesh Chewing pen, pencil Thumb over thumb, rubbing Biting fingernails Hands in pockets		Sitting on edge of chair Hand to face gestures Unbuttoning coat Tilted head
		Confidence	Steepled hands Hands behing back Back stiffened Hands in pockets with thumbs out Hands on lapels of coat

You need to be aware of clusters of behaviors that seem unusual for that person. You can then use this information to help you rethink how you can best deal with the situation. It is also a good idea to monitor your own body language when dealing with parents—especially if it is a tense moment. What is it saying about you? Are you demonstrating defensiveness?

In addition, teachers sometimes deal with parents who are exhibiting contradictory nonverbal messages. Most seasoned teachers have had the experience of talking with a parent and—although the parent's voice is calm, and there may be a smile on his or her face—there are tears running down the mother or father's face. In situations such as these you can say something such as, "I noticed that while we were talking about Beth's reading scores you were upset." It is then important to give them a few moments to think about what they are going to say about this emotional topic. This is also just as necessary with the parent whose body language suggests anger and hostility.

Still other barriers to effective two-way communication include such things as fatigue, lack of time, ego involvement (often manifested in defensiveness), differences in personality or communicative pace (most of us can think of people who speak annoyingly slowly or quickly), preoccupation with personal circumstances or other distractions, differing communicative purposes, or simply differences in status, age, sex, race, or culture. Obviously no matter how hard an individual teacher tries to establish a communicative flow that is two-way, there may be other contributing factors that make it impossible. But there are strategies that can be used successfully to lessen the impact of such factors.

Aids to Two-Way Communication

Active Listening

Speakers who are able to use everyday, but descriptive, language to clearly articulate ideas in nonjudgmental ways are obviously important in conducting effective two-way communication; but if he or she does not listen, even the most gifted speaker will not support a reciprocal conversation. A key to establishing a relationship in which two (or more) people communicate effectively is *active listening.* If you think of someone you consider a good listener, you can probably identify some of the visible outward characteristics that communicate close listening. Active listeners tend to maintain eye contact with the speaker; their posture communicates attentiveness, often with a forward lean; they may encourage the speaker by nodding, raising eyebrows or smiling appropriately in response to what the speaker is saying; they ask pertinent questions, sometimes to check their perceptions; they get rid of or ignore potential distractions; they acknowledge the feelings of the speaker; and mostly, they stop talking.

These are behaviors that are practicable and learnable, but active listening is more than just outward behavior: it is an attitude. The active listener *wants* to hear what is being said, and he or she listens with the goal of hearing—and empathetically understanding—what the speaker is saying; he or she is nonjudgmental. Active listening on the part of a teacher can communicate a wish to engage in real two-way communication, and this in turn begins to equalize the position of those in the relationship. Communication begins to flow two ways, with each party truly hearing the other and therefore responding appropriately.

When the teacher begins to listen and respond with empathy and understanding, mutual trust and respect begin to develop, and the parent(s) are able to speak out (and to listen actively and intelligently themselves).

Honesty

In addition to a context of mutual respect and trust, active listening and the use of descriptive and nonjudgmental language, communication must be based on a commitment to openness and honesty. If parents (and teachers) feel they are being manipulated or lied to, communications will break down. All of these qualities simultaneously interact to provide the atmosphere in which true partnerships can be developed and maintained. The foundation for the success of the following kinds of teacher–parent communication is the early establishment of relationships which embrace and enact the above qualities.

Initial Communication

There are many ways of initiating the parent–teacher relationship, and each of them should be planned with an eye to establishing a context in which teacher and parent are co-equal, leading, in turn, to the establishment of communication that is two-way, respectful, honest, and productive.

Some schools or centers have *intake interviews* for parents when they enroll their children. These interviews should be viewed as occasions on which parents can ask for and receive information about the school and as occasions for the school to gather important information about the child from the parents. Parents can, for instance, provide medical information which could be relevant for teachers, especially in emergency situations. The name and phone number of the child's doctor, food allergies or other diet restrictions, medical conditions which might require special responses or which might affect the child's school performance are a few examples. The initial intake interview may also ask parents about such things as the child's interests or preferred ways of spending free time, or the family's linguistic, religious and/or cultural background, which in turn can help teachers build a relationship with the child as well as build a curriculum responsive to children's interests and needs. Schools, in turn, can use the intake interview to orient the family to the physical space, rules, and expectations of the school.

Information from and to parents may be made in writing (e.g., an enrollment form to be filled out by the parents or a policy manual for parents to take home), or the information may be offered and received verbally. Many educators advise using both an oral and a written method of communicating initial information—oral because it is more personal and written because there is no guarantee verbally stated information will be remembered. And in the case of the school receiving personal information about children, the sheer number of children precludes the possibility of a person remembering details for each child with any accuracy. Although such intake interviews are often conducted by principals or directors, teachers should attend, if at all possible, as a way of establishing initial communicative and two-way relationships as early as possible and as a way of coming to know and value the parents' perceptions of their children.

In the event that teachers cannot attend such interviews (often the case, as teachers have class preparation to attend to, and initial intake interviews most logically complement the administrative processes of registering), there are many other kinds of activities that can help establish early relationships both with families and among families, and with students. Some that I've heard about or used myself are: a beginning-of-the-year family picnic, a personal phone call to welcome each family to the school, a welcoming postcard sent prior to the beginning of school, a home visit by the teacher, a family/teacher start-of-the-year social, or an invitation to families and students to visit the classroom together. Such activities can take many forms, but the objective should be to exchange information and to make initial contacts; these efforts are crucial in building relationships that facilitate two-way communications on a regular and co-equal basis. This requires initiative and a personal and attentive manner from the teacher.

> ### REFLECTION...
>
> Describe how you would establish effective communication between yourself as a teacher and a family. Do you think your feelings about home–school communication would change if you had children in school and were teaching?

Regular Communication

Once initial communication has been established, methods of building and maintaining a communicative relationship need attention. Such methods, too, may be informal or formal, written or oral.

Informal Communication

The most common method of informal regular communication, especially with families of young children, is the casual conversation parents have with teachers while dropping off or picking up their children from school. For parents who do this, this may, in fact, be the most important place for tone setting. A casual conversation, if done with respect and with genuine interest in the parent's child, can go a long way simply because it does not occur in a more formal setting, such as a parent–teacher conference where parents may feel as if formal feedback is what goes on record. In the daily conversations parents have with teachers, feedback (two-way) is generally considered more helpful than threatening, more flexible than permanent.

For parents of children who are old enough to get themselves to school or for parents who are too busy or unable to make daily trips to the school or whose children ride buses, other means of regular informal communications can substitute. Perhaps one of the most common is the phone call. Although teachers may view this as an imposition on their personal time, a call to a parent of each child, well-spaced over the course of the first month of school, can be a key to parents realizing the teacher is approachable and genuinely concerned about children and parental opinions. You should be warned, however, that despite many classrooms now having their own phones, most teachers do not do this, and as a result a phone call out of the blue from a teacher may initially be frightening to parents. If no one has ever called the parent from school or there have only been calls when something is wrong (the child is sick or misbehaving), it may take more than one call to convince the parent that you are calling just to check in or to describe an interesting event. It is for this reason that I recommend that the first call of the year be a positive one. If this is the case, later calls that might not be so pleasant will be received much more willingly.

Written Communication

Written communication has a permanence about it that demands a particular kind of attention. Although it can take many forms and can be informal or formal, it is expected to be written in proper English with correct spelling. When this is not the case, negative judgment of the teacher may occur, interfering with expectations of co-equality.

Newsletters

One of the most common methods of written communication with parents, besides the narrative report, which is discussed below, is the *newsletter.* These are written and regular publications which most often inform parents of the events in the classroom either prior to or following the events themselves. While many parents like these because they are interested in school curriculum and school happenings, others may find them relatively boring. One method that teachers employ to entice parents into reading the newsletter is to be sure to write something about each child in the class, highlighting their names. Another is to include announcements and news about things that would interest parents in general, interspersed with specific classroom news.

Computers have made the production of newsletters easier than ever, particularly if you use the same format each time. Most newsletters are sent biweekly or monthly, but how often it is published is up to the individual. Newsletters should not be more than two pages long. Parents are very busy and may feel put off by a multi-page document.

The newsletter provides you with an opportunity to share with parents the exciting things that are occurring in the classroom. It is important to use students' work, articles written by the students, and illustrations drawn by the students. Make certain that every student is mentioned several times over a period of time. The following is a list of possible newsletter items:

- Samples of the students' work
- Relevant quotations from the students
- Announcements
- Requests for needed materials (We need 2-gallon milk cartons, etc.)
- Special community announcements

- Reprints of short articles that might be of particular interest to parents
- Suggestions of things that parents and children can do together
- Thank you notes to parents who have in some way helped the class
- Suggestions for age-appropriate books for your students and books dealing with education, parenting, etc. for the parents
- Welcomes to new class members and their families
- A brief synopsis of what is being studied in class
- Articles or notes from parents for other parents

Unfortunately, most newsletters are a method of teacher-to-parent communication, which by itself is no problem, but which when put together with other one-way communication has the potential for perpetuating the distance between parents and teachers. As teachers, you might want to consider how to involve parents in writing and planning part of the newsletter. This not only opens up possibilities for parental involvement in the program, it opens up possible parent-to-parent communications, may identify items more parents would like to see, and has the potential for lightening your own work load!

School–Home Journal

A form of two-way written communication, used most often for children with special needs, is the *school–home journal.* This is especially helpful when parents do not or cannot visit the school on a daily basis. It consists of a notebook in which teachers make comments about the child's school day on a regular basis. It is then sent home with the child, and the parent(s) respond to what the teacher has said and comment on the child's day at home. Of course, its success depends on the diligence of both the parent and the teacher, but you should not get discouraged easily. A parent may not be able to write in the journal every day, but may find the time to do so twice a week. Encouraging the child to write or draw his or her own occasional entry may also perk up the parent(s)' or the child's interest (and children can then help remind parents and teacher about their commitment to the journal).

Narrative Report

Another means of describing to parents the child's life in school is through *narrative reporting.* Although many parents cling to the traditional report card as a way of comparing their children with others, teachers who write narrative reports for parents are often rewarded for their time and effort with increased parental appreciation and support. It is important, however—especially because such reports are time-consuming for teachers—that the reports speak to the child's unique presence in the classroom. Comments such as "great student" or "needs some work" tend to be so generic that they are not helpful to parents. Nor do such remarks give specific enough information to enable the parent's helpful response. A good narrative report is one that describes only one child and is therefore not interchangeable with or substitutable for narrative commentary about other children. It is descriptive and sufficiently detailed to make the child's classroom work come alive for the reader.

Parent–Teacher Conferences

Although there was a time when parent–teacher conferences were not used except when there was trouble afoot, they are now probably the single most frequently used (and most institutionalized) method of parent–teacher communication in schools and other educational settings. The parent–teacher conference may vary in its frequency, length, and even purpose, but most often it occurs twice a year, lasting about fifteen or twenty minutes, largely for the purpose of parents becoming informed of their child's progress in school (Swap, 1993). Perhaps one reason that it has become such a stable method of home–school communication is that it has been relatively successful. For the most part, parents appreciate a time to talk to the teacher about their child's school life, and when done at regular intervals, with administrative time and support, it affords teachers an organized means of ensuring that each family has an opportunity to be personally informed. It is also interesting to note, however, that many teachers come to view these conferences as a chore rather than an opportunity and that both teachers and parents report some nervousness about them (Swap, 1993). The conferences can be emotionally draining for teachers and parents. Parents and teachers further complain that there is usually not enough time for meaningful conversation, and teachers often note, with regret, that the parents whom they most need to see do not come.

Even though it is improbable that parent–teacher conferences on their own can create two-way communication patterns between teachers and parents, there are a number of strategies which can be brought to bear at conferences that will maximize their potential for supporting other efforts at good parent-teacher communication. They can be scheduled, for instance, to accommodate parents' work schedules. Many schools now have parent–teacher conferences scheduled during one evening as well as during the day. It can also be helpful to parents to schedule conferences for siblings back-to-back, so that one trip to school will suffice to see the teachers of all the children in the same family.

The conference environment can be made less threatening as well. Seating parents next to the teacher at a table, rather than on the other side of a desk, can reduce the perception of unequal positions. Making parents comfortable with adult-sized chairs can help put them at ease. When possible, not keeping parents waiting and getting up to greet them at the door can communicate care and interest and help make parents feel welcome and valued. Engaging in a minute of small talk before addressing the conference agenda can also help put parents at ease and make the atmosphere more friendly.

Although fifteen or twenty minutes is a very short time to accomplish much in the way of communication, there are other things which can be kept in mind that can help maximize the success of the conversation itself. Experts recommend, for instance, that discussion about the child start out and end with something positive. If there is a concern to be communicated, it is best done in the middle of the conference (Rockwell, Andre, & Hawley, 1996). It is also important to limit the number of areas of concern expressed at any one time, especially if the advice and help of the parent is desired, as it is difficult for anyone to effectively deal with a litany of concerns at once. It is also important and very effective to be able to describe something about the child that shows the parent that you know the child in ways that go beyond grades on tests and academic performances. What engages her in class? Who are his friends? What role does he play in a group project? How does she express herself?

Two controversial activities related to parent–teacher conferences are note-taking and parents bringing others to the conference. Although there are some advantages to either a parent or a teacher taking notes at conferences, there are also disadvantages. Note-taking both helps the note-taker remember what has been said and conveys to the other person that he or she takes what is said seriously. On the other hand, note-taking can convey an impression that the note-taker is creating a written record which could be used against the speaker. This becomes a particularly touchy issue in a litigious time and culture such as ours. Whatever your inclination, however, permission to take notes should be asked before doing so.

Although some teachers react strongly to the presence of anyone but the parents in a conference, parents do have a right to bring others with them, and there are sometimes sound reasons for doing so (Schulz, 1987). Especially when issues such as special education diagnosis or placement are being discussed, it helps to have a second pair of ears. When we take in difficult or disappointing information, we tend to focus on only the most shocking elements of the conversation. We can miss such things as suggestions for action or possible alternative interpretations. For this reason, we should welcome friends or relatives who come to help parents hear. We should also welcome child caregivers when parents have invited them to be part of the conference, as they often have as much information to contribute to the conversation as the parents do. For non-English speaking parents, a friend who can serve as a translator, if the school or center does not provide one, is often a welcome relief for both teacher and parent. If, however, parents have been accompanied by someone and they seem to be uneasy about the person's presence, or if a neighbor has just come along for the ride (and may be a possible gossip), it is appropriate to request that such individuals wait outside while you confer with the parent(s). Decisions about children attending their own or their siblings' conferences depend on the preference of the teacher and the parent, the age of the children, and the purpose for their attendance, and need to determined on an individual (or class) basis.

> ### *REFLECTION...*
>
> How would you make sure fathers are included in conferences? What if both parents were female (a lesbian relationship)?

These suggestions can help make the parent–teacher conference pleasant and productive, but they don't go very far toward increasing the reciprocal nature of information flow. It's important to save time for parents' questions and discussion of any agenda they might bring to the conference. And if time runs out during the regularly scheduled conference, arrangements should be made for a second conference. In fact, parents need to feel that they can request a conference with the teacher at any time during the year, without suspicion. Since you know the child and his or her family background, what happens if the parents are divorced or separated? Frequently the teachers, when presented with those situations, will hold separate conferences with the parents.

Effective parent–teacher conferences require planning, thoughtful action, and timely follow up on the part of the teacher and the parent. Figure 6-2 offers a helpful checklist for teachers as they engage in their parent–teacher conferences. Of course the most important element in supporting parental participation in a conference is to stop talking and start listening!

Pre-Conference

_____ 1. Notify—Purpose, place, time, length of time allotted

_____ 2. Prepare
      –Review child's folder
      –Gather examples of work
      –Prepare materials

_____ 3. Plan agenda

_____ 4. Arrange environment
      –Comfortable seating
      –Eliminate distractions

Conference

_____ 1. Welcome
      –Establish rapport

_____ 2. State
      –Purpose
      –Time limitations
      –Note taking
      –Options for follow-up

_____ 3. Encourage
      –Information sharing
      –Comments
      –Questions

_____ 4. Listen
      –Pause once in awhile!
      –Look for verbal and nonverbal cues
      –Questions

_____ 5. Summarize

_____ 6. End on a positive note

Post-Conference

_____ 1. Review conference with child, if appropriate

_____ 2. Share information with other school personnel, if needed

---

FIGURE 6-2   Conference Checklist

This has been modified from material developed by Roger Kroth and the Parent Involvement Center, University of New Mexico.

Communication with Parents of Middle School Students

Student–Parent–Teacher Conferences

A fast-growing model for conferences includes the student in the conference. This model can be used from first grade through high school but is particularly successful with middle school students. Because middle school takes a team approach, this "team" conference is particularly appropriate.

It is important to note that the student must be an active member of the team who has input into the conference. There are several methods of conducting this type of conference and numerous variations. The following is one possible scenario.

Beginning of the School Year

Meet during the first weeks of school to set goals for the school year and discuss how these goals will be met. At this time the responsibility of each participant should be determined and written down for future reference. At this point, the time and date for the next conference might be determined.

Mid-Year

This conference should begin with an evaluation of the success of the previously set goals. At this time, adjustments to the goals and responsibilities should be made as needed. These adjustments may involve knowledge not available to the participants earlier in the semester. Make an appointment for the next conference.

Final Conference

Again, it is important to review the original goals and the modifications made during the second conference. This is a time to evaluate the year's progress. It is important that all areas be evaluated—areas of strength as well as areas of weakness. It is also a time for the parents, teachers, and students to enjoy the successes of the year.

Teachers and parents both have reported this as a productive format. By including students in conferences, not only are parents and teachers responsible but students are also. The number of conferences may vary according to individual need and school policy.

Homework Hot Line

Parents often feel intimidated by their middle school child's homework. They may have found a subject difficult when they were in school, not have been exposed to the material, or have forgotten it—after all, it has been a number of years since these parents were the age their children are presently. Whatever the reason, parents and students may need additional help. Schools that have implemented *homework hot lines* have found this a positive way to help both parents and students.

Homework hot lines can be used in a variety of ways. For example, they could be used to assist callers with their assignments or to verify homework assignments. The following is a list of guidelines for running a successful homework hot line. It is important to remember that there are many variations of this program and that a school must tailor it to meet its own needs.

- Determine what the greatest homework need is for your school; in most schools, it is math—particularly pre-algebra and algebra. The second pertains to writing skills and is very broad in nature—everything from punctuation and grammar to how one structures a term paper. After determining your needs, decide how you are going to meet them.
- How often is this service going to be available? Mondays through Thursdays are generally busy homework nights for middle school students. Remember that it is usually better to start small and increase the service as needed.
- Who is going to staff the homework lines? Some schools use volunteers as "homework helpers" and some used paid personnel. Those programs that pay "helpers" tend to be the most successful. If volunteers are the most practical option for your school, then consider hiring a part-time coordinator who will set up schedules, find replacements for those helpers who cancel, and so on. If this program becomes an added burden for busy teachers and/or administrators, it will fail.
- After the program is planned, determine how to best inform parents and students about the Homework Hot Line.
- Have regular meetings of the hot line staff to identify problems and improve the service.
- Give the program time before trying to determine its success. It generally takes a while to build a clientele for any program of this nature.

Reaching Out to Parents through Computer Classes

Many parents are not computer literate and feel uncomfortable that their children are so much more knowledgeable about computers and their use than they. Many schools have provided evening classes to teach parents some basic computer skills and the response is normally excellent.

These classes should be as informal as possible. Classes offered for credit with homework assignments are generally not as well received. You must remember that the parent may already feel inadequate due to lack of computer skills. Those classes that are friendly, less structured, and reinforce success are the most successful. Parents that have been in the class for awhile, or who have computer skills, can be used to help new class members. This has been a particularly successful strategy.

Although many parents don't have computers in their homes, it doesn't mean that they are not interested in computers. And, as libraries and other public facilities make computers available to the public, those parents without computers can now more easily find access to computers. Still, a lack of a computer is a handicap. Schools generally have computer labs that are not utilized in the evenings, making these labs an ideal parent resource. If parents can drop by the lab to use the word processor, learn programming skills, or "surf the Net," they can develop better feelings about themselves and feel more a part of the school. The benefits to the school are numerous: The parents feel more a part of the school community, see the school as being concerned about the family as a whole, can better understand the child's curriculum, and develop a relationship with other parents in the school community. Everyone wins!

Other Ways of Communicating on a Regular Basis

Parent Bulletin Boards

Still another vehicle for communicating with parents is a *parent bulletin board.* Strategically placed so that parents come upon it when they are at the school or center, a bulletin board containing attractive and interesting information for parents can be an effective way to communicate with parents. Unfortunately, depending on the program, all parents may not come to the school or center, and the communication on bulletin boards moves from displayer to onlooker, generally not in the other direction. This kind of communication tends to be one-way. Nonetheless, there are strategies that can be employed to encourage both parent attention and parent participation. One key to interesting bulletin boards is the relevance and attractive display of information. Interesting information for parents might include pictures and documentation of children's work at school (both product and process) (Edwards, Gandini, & Forman, 1993), information about parenting, notices of community events that might be interesting for parents, children, or families, interesting (and positive) news clippings about the parents, announcements about school events, and so forth.

To ensure continued attention over time, the bulletin board needs to be changed on a regular basis. Although using a bulletin board for parents to communicate to teachers is probably inappropriate, given other more direct modes of communication, using the bulletin board as a place for parents to communicate with one another is certainly possible. The bulletin board then becomes interactive, not passive. If a section of the bulletin board were set aside for parents' use, they could bring in items that they know would be of interest to other parents, which in turn could lead to more parental interest and ownership as well as the establishment of a vehicle for parents to find and communicate with others who share similar interests and concerns related to their children in school.

Home Visits

Teachers in some schools and other educational programs such as Head Start visit parents in their homes for a variety of reasons. Although a frequently cited reason for such home visits is that they allow teachers opportunities to see the home contexts of children as a way of understanding them better and gaining some empathy for their families, other reasons may be just as compelling. Home visits at the beginning of the school year can establish an early context for two-way communication. Parents generally appreciate the teacher's efforts to come to their territory—a place where they are in charge and where the teacher is a guest in a strange place. Making a home visit can signal to a parent that the teacher is interested in the family and a partnership, and when this occurs, parents often start the year ready to work together rather than spending valuable time trying to find their role with the teacher (Burian, Haveman, Jacobson, & Rood, 1993). In addition, children are often quite taken by the presence of their teacher in their home, and they too start the school year more enthusiastically. The relationships in these cases are already initiated before school even gets started.

There is need for some caution related to home visits as well. It is important to allow parents to refuse a home visit. They may be self-conscious about the conditions of their home, or they simply may not be individuals who are pleased to welcome others into their home. Also, some teachers recommend doing home visits in pairs, both to help collect multiple perspectives and to guard against the possibility of a threatening visit. It should be noted, however, that each additional person from the school upsets the balance of equality. Unfortunately, lack of funding often means that teachers cannot be paid to conduct home visits, but many teachers, after experiencing the good will that comes from them, are willing to do them on their own time.

Communication on Special Occasions

Initial communication and regular communication are important contexts for parent–teacher communication, as they first set the stage and later work towards maintaining relationships that are open and productive for all concerned, and especially for the students. There are, however, times that require other strategies for other kinds of communication.

Communication with Groups

There are occasions when those required classes in public speaking can come in handy. Parent nights, parent education classes, school programs, and even school orientation programs all are events at which teachers may be asked to speak to groups of parents en masse. When such opportunities arise, however, there must also be room for parent voices to be heard. Whenever such meetings occur, for instance, there needs to be ample time for parents to ask questions and to give their opinions. Parent speakers might share the podium with teachers and other school personnel. Structuring the schedule for parent or parent/teacher discussion groups can help parents feel ownership in the events and know that their opinions also have weight.

Times of Crisis and Truly Difficult Parents

Even given the most successful and productive efforts at open and effective parent–teacher communication, there are both times and individuals which can test the commitment of the most well-meaning teacher. Despite parents who are generally cooperative (if sometimes or initially reluctant) about working with the teacher in partnership, a few, no matter what the teacher does, cannot easily be reached. Some examples are the very irate parent or the chronic complainer. Parents who are irate are obviously unhappy people, but frequently they are people who have had trouble getting themselves heard. If a parent is irate, one strategy is to swallow your pride and your defensiveness and concentrate on listening alone, without responding. Try, in such instances, to hide your own emotions, take out pencil and paper and concentrate on writing down every complaint the parent has. Do not interrupt them with explanations or even apologies. Simply write. When they begin to slow down, ask if they have anything else to add. Continue this until they exhaust their list. Doing this will generally have an effect on their demeanor. Anger will usually dissipate, and in the meantime, you have a clear record of what the complaints are. When you have everything recorded, calmly read the parent(s) what you have listed and assure them that you will look into the issue(s) and then get back to them. Give yourself some time, and then return to the list when you have more emotional distance from it (usually overnight will do it). Confer with others who can help you think about the course of action you can take, changes you can make, and principles on which you wish to take a stand. Be prepared and calm when you get back to the complainer. Chances are, he or she will be much more willing to hear your thoughts on the matter now.

Chronic complainers can also benefit from knowing they are being heard, but sometimes such individuals continue looking for problems no matter how many you've solved for them. One strategy for working with such parents is to invite them into the classroom to observe and participate, as appropriate, in classroom activities. (They can, for instance, be invited to read to children.) When they become part of the inside, rather than staying on the outside, and when they discover the difficult and complicated nature of teaching and learning, they often become the teacher's best allies, spreading the word to other parents about the teacher's good work.

We as educators work toward a cooperative environment where individuals are respected. We work with students to resolve their problems in non-confrontational ways. In fact, many schools employ conflict resolution as a way of dealing with conflict. Consequently, we often feel uncomfortable with discord. Table 6-2 provides some guidelines for working with aggressive people. It also helps you to be less defensive and more centered on solving the problem at hand.

Some parents prove difficult for teachers because they come to rely on their listening skills *too* much. For some parents, you will be the only other adult who cares about them enough to listen to their problems. You, after all, have a mutual concern for their child, and

TABLE 6-2   Tips for Dealing with Aggression

DO	DON'T
1. Listen—without interruptions.	1. Argue.
2. Write down main points of what has been said.	2. Defend or become defensive.
3. When they slow down, ask if anything else is bothering them.	3. Promise things you can't produce.
4. Exhaust the list of complaints	4. Own problems that belong to others.
5. Ask for specific clarifications when complaints are too general.	5. Raise your voice.
6. Show them the list of complaints.	6. Belittle or minimize the problem.
7. Ask for suggestions in solving the specific problems, and write down the suggestions.	
8. As they speak louder, you speak softer.	

These practices take practice. Our first reaction is almost always anger or hostility and these only serve to make matters more volatile. Also, remember that all of us have, upon occasion, acted in an angry, inappropriate way, and usually wish we had behaved with more temperance. Give the parent the same understanding that you would like to receive.

This has been modified from material developed by Roger Kroth and the Parent Involvement Center, University of New Mexico.

you may have chosen this profession to be of help to others. Although such parental trust can be helpful for two-way communication, if it gets out of hand and becomes excessive, the teacher may feel (uncomfortably) as if he or she is expected to be a counselor to the parent. Under such circumstances it is important to remember that you have been trained as a *teacher,* not as a counselor. Having knowledge of community resources is helpful in such situations, as the most appropriate help you can give such individuals is probably to refer them to professional services that meet their counseling needs.

Summary

Working with parents can be very rewarding—for you, for parents, for your school or center, and especially for the children who are under your care and tutelage. In order for this work to be most fruitful for all concerned, a concentrated effort at open and two-way communication is required. Without communication, mutual goals are less likely to be met. Here is a list of some principles to keep in mind when planning for such an effort:

Principles for Effective Communication with Parents

- Choose or create an environment that puts parents on an equal footing with you.
- Care about the parent(s)' child. Ask about him or her.
- Care about the parent(s). Ask about them.
- Listen to understand.
- Use descriptive, rather than judgmental, language when relating a child's school life. Avoid educational jargon.
- Don't talk about other parents or their children. Respect the confidentiality of all families.
- Take the initiative to establish a co-equal relationship. Don't be discouraged by limited initial success.
- Establish communications early in the school year, before problems occur.
- Find time to spend with parents.

Recommended Activities

1. Think of a time when you know you were not being listened to. How did you know? What was the behavior of the person to whom you were speaking? How did you feel? What was your response?
2. Ask three friends to think about a person they consider a good listener. Interview them about the qualities they think makes the person so. Make a list of these qualities and compare them with what you know about yourself as a listener.
3. Interview three teachers. Ask them about the principles and the techniques they use for communicating with parents. Where appropriate and possible, obtain examples of

written communications, such as newsletters. Analyze what was described and given to you for communicative flow. Note especially where parent voices were heard.

4. Interview three parents of school age children. Ask them about parent–teacher conferences. How do they prepare for them mentally and emotionally? Ask them to describe the worst and best conferences they have had with teachers.
5. Interview three teachers. Ask them about parent–teacher conferences. How do they prepare for them mentally and emotionally? Ask them to describe the worst and best conferences they have had with parents.
6. Ask teachers about the role technology—other than the telephone—plays in their communication with parents.
7. Interview parents of children in early childhood, elementary, middle, and secondary schools. Ask them to describe the most effective style or pattern the school/center or teacher(s) use with them. How could it be more effective? Compare the results among the four groups.
8. Interview teachers to discuss how report cards or narrative reporting is being done. Does it change from elementary to middle to secondary? If so, how does it change?

Additional Resources

Communicating with Parents

Books:

Henderson, A. T., Marburger, C. L., & Ooms, T. (1986). *Beyond the bake sale.* Columbia, MD: National Committee for Citizens in Education.

This book is a guide for educators to help them work with parents to improve schooling. It is particularly geared to dealing with some of the problems that have become greater in recent years owing to changes in family life such as high divorce rates, teenage parents, and working mothers.

Kroth, R. L. (1985). *Communicating with parents of exceptional children.* Denver, CO: Love Publishing.

This book serves as a practical handbook for educators and parents of children with disabilities. It combines innovative strategies with daily activities designed to improve communication between the school and the family.

Articles:

Gomby, S S., Larson, S. L., Lewit, E. M., & Berhman, R. E. (1993). Home visiting: Analysis and recommendations. *The Future of Children, 3*(3).

Weiss, H. B. (1993). Home visits: Necessary but not sufficient. *The Future of Children, 3*(3).

Videos:

Conducting Effective Conferences with Parents

This program offers suggestions about how to prepare and conduct conferences with parents. It considers what kind of questions to ask, what information should and should not be exchanged. 1998. (22 minutes). #TP93.

> Insight Media
> 2162 Broadway
> New York, NY 10024
> Phone: 212-721-6316

Working with Parents: Home-School Collaboration

This video will help teachers understand the concerns and fears of parents, Parents explain what they want from parent–teacher conferences and ways to improve the exchange of information. The video provides specific suggestions for how teachers and parents can work together to create a positive learning environment, and discusses when counselors should be called upon to resolve an impasse. 1984. (30 minutes). #TP93.

> Insight Media
> 2162 Broadway
> New York, NY 10024
> Phone: 212-721-6316

References

Burian, B., Haveman, S., Jacobson, M., & Rood, B. (1993). Implementing a multi-age level classroom: A reflection on our first year. *Insights into Open Education, 26*(2), 23–32.

Edwards, C., Gandini, L., & Forman, G. (Eds.). (1993). *The hundred languages of children: The Reggio Emilia approach to early childhood education.* Norwood, NJ: Ablex.

Kroth, R. (1985). Communicating with parents of exceptional children. Denver, CO: Love Publishing.

Rockwell, R. E., Andre, L. C., & Hawley, M. K. (1996). *Parents and teachers as partners.* Fort Worth, TX: Harcourt Brace.

Schulz, J. B. (1987). *Parents and professionals in special education.* Newton, MA: Allyn & Bacon.

Seligman, M. (1979). *Strategies for helping parents of exceptional children.* New York: Free Press.

Swap, S. M. (1993). *Developing home–school partnerships: From concepts to practice.* New York: Teachers College Press.

Chapter 7

Parents in the Schools

ELIZABETH J. SANDELL
Meld Director, Minneapolis, Minnesota

Everyone seems to agree that parent involvement is a wonderful idea. In fact, researchers tell us that the single fastest way to improve a student's academic performance is to involve the parents. Given this widespread agreement, it is perplexing that we don't have more actual parent involvement in our schools. The purpose of this chapter is to introduce you to:

- The rationale for parent involvement
- A parent-involvement model
- Ways in which you can involve parents
- Ways of evaluating a parent-involvement program
- Issues and concerns in parent involvement

The National Education Goals panel has defined one of the eight goals to be achieved by the year 2000 as: "Every school will promote partnerships that will increase parental involvement and participation in promoting the social, emotional, and academic growth of children" (U.S. Department of Education, 1994). This goal is very important for achieving the other seven goals, which relate to student achievement in school. According to a review of sixty-six studies of how students succeed in school (Henderson & Berla, 1994), when parents become involved in children's education at school and in the community, the results include one or more of the following:

- Higher grades and test scores
- Better attendance and regularly completed homework
- Fewer placements in special education or remedial classes
- More positive attitudes and behavior in school
- Higher graduation rates
- Greater enrollment in post-secondary education

The challenges which face America's children cannot be solved by schools alone, and they cannot be solved by families alone. Children in the United States face critical social, emotional, and environmental problems.

Parental involvement in helping children succeed in school was among the necessary factors identified for positive development. This particular asset, however, was the least frequent found among more than 46,000 youth surveyed across the United States. Only 26 percent of these young people reported that they received strong support from, and involvement by, parents in school-related activities.

School districts need to establish and implement parent-involvement policies, with input from parents. As district policies are developed, schools need to encourage and support parent involvement in the schools. In addition, school policies and support are needed to show teachers how to involve parents in their classrooms.

208	children under 10 years old are killed by firearms.
560	children 10–14 years old are killed by firearms.
2,234	children and youths under 20 years old commit suicide.
4,173	children 15–19 years old are killed by firearms.
73,886	children under 18 years old are arrested for drug abuse.
112,230	children under 18 years old are arrested for violent crimes.
124,238	children under 18 years old are arrested for drinking or drunken driving.
232,093	babies are born to women who received late or no prenatal care.
531,591	babies are born to teen mothers.
613,514	Students are corporally punished in public schools.
928,205	babies are born to mothers without high school degrees.
1,047,000	babies are born into poverty.
1,200,000	latchkey children come home to houses where there is a gun.
1,213,769	babies are born to unmarried mothers.
1,939,456	children under 18 years old are arrested for all offenses.
2,695,010	children are reported abused or neglected.

FIGURE 7-1   One Year in the Life of American Children

From: Reprinted with permission from *The State of America's Children Yearbook 1994.* Washington, DC: Children's Defense Fund, 1994.

From extensive work with parents, administrators, and teachers, Epstein (1988) has identified five major types of parent involvement in education:

1. The basic obligation of parents
2. The basic obligations of schools
3. Parent involvement in the schools
4. Parent involvement in learning activities at home
5. Parent involvement in governance and advocacy

Please note that two are related to parent involvement in the schools directly: parent involvement at school (type 3) and parent involvement in school governance and advocacy (type 5). This chapter will provide definitions and examples of these two types of parent involvement, as well as summaries of outcomes which school personnel might expect as a result of implementing these forms of parent involvement in schools.

> *REFLECTION...*
>
> Think about your elementary school experience. How were your parents and your friends' parents involved in school? How and why has the philosophy of parental involvement changed since then?

In order to facilitate these two types of parent involvement, it is important to recognize diverse family structures, circumstances, and responsibilities that might impede parent

**Board of Education
Parent Involvement Policy Statement**

The Board of Education recognizes the necessity and value of parent involvement in education to support student success and academic achievement. In order to assure collaborative partnerships between parents and schools, the Board, working through the administration, is committed to:

a. Use schools to connect students and families with community resources that provide educational enrichment and support.

b. Establish effective two-way communication with all parents, respecting the diversity and differing strengths and needs of families.

c. Develop strategies and program structures at schools to enable parents to participate actively in their children's education.

d. Provide support and coordination for school staff and parents to implement and sustain appropriate parent involvement in education from early childhood education through grade twelve.

e. Involve parents as partners in school governance, including shared decision-making.

FIGURE 7-2

participation. Programs and activities should be flexibly scheduled in order to facilitate the participation by diverse parent groups. The person responsible for the child may not be the child's biological parent. Policies and programs should include participation by all persons interested in the child's educational progress. The community's historic, ethnic, linguistic, or cultural backgrounds will greatly influence types and levels of participation by individual parents.

Parent Involvement in the School

Parent involvement at school (type 3) refers to parents who come to school as visitors to support school events or to attend workshops or other programs for their own education. It also refers to parents who volunteer to assist teachers, administrators, and children in classrooms or in other school activities (Epstein, 1988).

Comer (1993) reported that about 10 to 25 percent of the parents served as volunteers at School Development Program schools. This type of involvement demonstrated strong parent participation in the schools in the study. Other research has demonstrated that even small numbers of volunteers are important. Becker and Epstein (1982) found that in schools with an active core group of volunteer parents teachers were more likely to try to involve all parents at home in their children's learning activities.

Parents as Visitors

School personnel and volunteers can help all parents feel welcome at school. In addition, various other groups (such as grandparents, community groups, recreation center participants, and businesses) may enjoy coming to school as audiences for student performances, athletic events, or demonstrations of student learning. Parent workshops are another way to involve parents in their children's education.

When school personnel encourage parents to visit the classrooms and schools of their children, several important outcomes have been documented:

- Parents better understand the teacher's job and the school programs
- Parents become better acquainted with their child's teacher
- Parents feel more comfortable interacting with school personnel
- Teachers become better acquainted with the parents of children in their classrooms (Epstein, 1988).

When school personnel provide parent workshops, numerous goals are achieved:

- Workshops provide a bond between home experiences and the education program
- Parents strengthen their ability to provide a positive family home environment
- Parents acquire skills and ideas that can enhance home learning
- Parents and school staff build partnerships in informal settings
- Workshops help dispel parents' fears about involvement in their child's education (Gelfer, 1991).

There are many possible activities that are related to the inclusion of parents as visitors in the schools. A few methods of fostering such inclusion are:

- Encourage classroom visitations and observations; make the front door obvious; place a "Welcome" sign on the front door; create a welcome/information desk near the school's entrance; use signs to direct visitors to the office
- Create Parent Resource Centers, places for parents to relax with informal seating and refreshments, to have meetings, to borrow parent education resources, to get acquainted, to get information about community resources
- Create Parent Activity Leader positions (paid or volunteer, bilingual as needed and sensitive to the needs of the non-English speaking community) to organize activities and act as a liaison between parents and school personnel
- Create Translation Service Centers to facilitate parent and staff communication; provide interpreters who speak the languages of families of children enrolled in the school; establish a game, computer, and book lending library to encourage parent and student interaction
- Conduct parent workshops on: school programs and goals; communication and behavior guidance; how to supervise homework, monitor student progress, collect information on college and career opportunities, or emphasize family math or reading activities
- Host frequent curriculum or back-to-school nights or weekend enrichment courses for parents with "make-it-take-it" activities, parent work parties to make classroom materials, mathematics nights and science fairs, hands-on experiences with computers, family writing conferences to record family stories
- Hold meals with "elders" in which parents and community leaders learn together
- Be sure parents are informed and involved in special events, family nights and field trips, talent shows, athletic competitions, and so forth.

Figure 7-3 provides a checklist for evaluating the degree to which a school provides a welcoming environment for parents.

How Welcome Are Parents in Our School?

We want you to feel comfortable and welcome at school. Please think about your experiences and circle your response. Your name will not be identified with your answers. Thank you for your time. Your answers will be used to help improve our school.

Am I always greeted in a friendly, courteous way when I contact the school on the phone or in person?	Yes	No	Do not know
Does the school have a reception area for visitors, equipped with information so that I can find my way around the building?	Yes	No	Do not know
Did the school conduct some kind of orientation program for my family when I first enrolled my child?	Yes	No	Do not know
Do school staff and parents have informal occasions when we can get to know each other during the school year?	Yes	No	Do not know
Does the administrator have regular office hours when parents and students can stop in?	Yes	No	Do not know
Are programs and activities for parent involvement provided at times which are convenient for me?	Yes	No	Do not know
Does the administrator ask for parents' ideas when making decisions that will affect the school, and are our ideas implemented when possible?	Yes	No	Do not know
Does the school encourage me to visit my child's classroom outside of planned occasions (after checking first with the teacher involved)?	Yes	No	Do not know
Am I and other parents welcome to use the building after school hours for community purposes?	Yes	No	Do not know
Are limited-English-speaking parents given opportunities to understand and fully participate in the school's activities?	Yes	No	Do not know
Does the school give written material to parents in their first language about rules, parent-teacher conferences, and other important items?	Yes	No	Do not know

FIGURE 7-3

From: Planning Your PTA Year! planning kit, copyright © 1994, by the National PTA. Permission to reprint is granted by the National PTA.

Parents as Volunteers

School personnel recruit and train volunteers who assist in classrooms, in other areas of the schools, on trips, or with other activities. An organized volunteer program will provide a method to match the volunteer's skills, talents, and available time with the needed assistance. Creative scheduling will be necessary to allow volunteers to work after school hours in evenings, on weekends, and during holidays. Community groups, businesses, and senior citizens organizations may be able to organize volunteers for the schools.

When school personnel encourage parents to volunteer on behalf of their children's classrooms and schools, several important outcomes have been documented:

- Parents become more comfortable in interactions with staff at the school
- Students increase their learning skills and receive more individual attention
- Students develop an ease of communication with adults
- Teachers and school staff acquire an awareness of parent interest in school and children and parent willingness to help
- Teachers and school staff are more ready to try programs that involve parents in many ways (Epstein, 1988).

There are many possible activities that are related to the inclusion of parents as volunteers in the schools. A few methods of fostering such inclusion are:

- Develop a parent/community volunteer program: develop job descriptions, recruit and train volunteers, provide translation if necessary, recognize and award volunteers
- Conduct a family strengths and assets survey to assess parent resources for working with the schools and to create a talent bank
- Develop a process whereby parents earn "coupons" or "credits" for their work at school or off-campus on behalf of the school; as coupons are accumulated, they are redeemable for premiums, prizes, or services
- Encourage parents to share skills and expertise at school as a way of extending the class curriculum (computers, crafts, storytelling, etc.)
- Organize after-school, parent-led school enrichment programs for students
- Involve parents as volunteers for listening to students read, staff a computer laboratory, translate children's books, share hobbies and collections, or lead classroom cooking activities
- Create opportunities for family volunteers to assist as tutors, cafeteria helpers, teachers' assistants, door greeters, chaperons, typists, organizers, career mentors, parent mentors
- Use support activities (such as fund raisers, social events, carnivals, etc.) to reinforce the school's academic focus (for example, a school carnival might have a literary character costume focus; a marathon might have reading or math activities and raise funds)

REFLECTION...

As an educator which of the volunteer activities seem to be the most helpful to you? Why? Which do you think the volunteers would find most satisfying? Why?

Facilitating Parent Involvement in the Schools

Established policies and procedures about recruitment, supervision, and recognition will facilitate parent involvement in the schools.

Recruitment

Parents, grandparents, relatives, and community members can be supportive volunteers in the school. Contacts with local colleges, high schools, retirement homes, churches, synagogues, and civic groups might encourage others to respond. Think about the goals and interests of the individuals in order to match them to the needs of the school program. Volunteers are motivated to get involved because of many factors, such as:

* Helping others and improving the community
* Gaining work experience or testing a new career
* Learning new skills or using untapped skills
* Meeting new people
* Building self-confidence and learning responsibility
* Using natural gifts and talents
* Empowering others
* Being a role model
* Giving back what was received
* Demonstrating care for others

Create clear, brief job descriptions for the volunteer opportunities. They should be well thought out and clearly defined. Each job description should include information about its title, purpose, function, role in the school, necessary skills and abilities, time commitment needed, and training provided. The job description will be a useful recruiting tool, because parents are becoming more selective about the commitments they make. They will compare their own interests, background skills, time available, and personal goals with the information in the job description. If they match, parents may volunteer and participate. If they do not match, parents can automatically screen themselves out.

School staff and parent organizers will want to use a variety of recruitment strategies to communicate the opportunity for involvement to parents and others. Here are some methods that other parent-involvement programs have found effective:

1. Appeal to current volunteers and staff members to recruit their friends by attending an introductory coffee time.
2. Recruit people for less time-consuming jobs by breaking down large projects into smaller components.
3. Be honest and up-front; do not lie or minimize the time needed; do not use guilt.
4. When recruiting businesses, use their advertising slogan in your presentation.
5. When recruiting a group or organization, use its mission statement in your presentation.
6. Find leaders from communities of color and ask them to recruit their peers.

7. Ask company personnel directors to direct retirees and current employees to yc school.

8. Participate in a volunteer fair to present opportunities at a shopping mall or company.

9. Ask organizations to give you time on their agenda, distribute written information, or post notices on bulletin boards.

10. Ask the cable television station to present programs on your school and its volunteer opportunities.

Supervision

Each school or classroom will need to decide how to coordinate their volunteers and parent events. A volunteer coordinator can develop the parent handbook, the recruitment strategy, the job descriptions, the publicity, the orientation, and the recognition program.

The parent or volunteer handbook should include general information needed by participants. Such information might include:

- Program definition and philosophy
- Description of parent program
- Benefits of participating
- Insurance coverage
- Tax information for volunteers
- Statement of behavior standards and ethics
- Behavior guidance strategies when working with children at school
- Volunteer time sheets
- Requirements about child abuse and neglect reporting
- Emergency procedures
- Signed statements about confidentiality and staff-volunteer relationships

Recognition

The highest form of recognition is making sure the parents know they are needed and valued in the school by staff and administrators. Ideas for recognition and appreciation might include:

- Smiling; calling the parent by name
- Sending birthday cards and greetings for special family events
- Awarding a volunteer certificate
- Enlisting the parent to help train or orient other parents
- Devoting a page in the school newsletter to volunteer recognition
- Writing thank you notes
- Awarding recognition pins for hours of training or service
- Providing gift certificates or small volunteer gifts
- Bringing treats for the parent room
- Recognizing parents at a dinner or evening celebration

Considering Diversity

Those who organize opportunities for parent involvement as visitors and as volunteers will want to carefully consider the diverse needs of families from different backgrounds. For example, despite diversity among Hispanic families in terms of background, custom, and tradition, it is income and education level that show the greatest effects on how Hispanic parents relate to schools and learning (Nicolau & Ramos, 1990). Many low-income parents share common beliefs that present barriers to parent involvement in schools. Parents may see teachers as experts who are not to be questioned, and they do not feel that they even belong in school unless their youngster has caused trouble or had some difficulty. However, most parents want their children to succeed. School staff can explain to parents in a non-threatening way about how the school system in their locale works.

Successful outreach efforts for Hispanic parents will be built on personal outreach; warm, nonjudgmental communication; and the ability to communicate respect for the parents' feelings and needs. The personal outreach should be by home visit or a personal chat with the parent outside the school building. Letters, especially on school letterhead, may not be effective because they are perceived as communicating bad news. Use of the parent's primary language must also be considered.

Contemplate holding events for parents outside the school building where families will be more comfortable, such as a neighborhood center, apartment community room, or a home. Carefully consider the timing of the meeting and the needs for transportation and child care. Nicolau and Ramos (1990) reported that effective parent events at school included: make-it-take-it workshops, community projects (such as murals or gardens), parent activity corners in classrooms, informal small workshops, and parent resource rooms. As Hispanic families become involved in the schools, they will contribute many strengths: respect for education and educators; value for cooperation, courtesy, and loyalty; emphasis on discipline and correct behavior; and dignity that requires relationships to be built on mutual respect.

REFLECTION ...

What are the diverse populations in your community and how involved are the under-represented groups? Are they involved in the school?

Parent Involvement in Governance and Advocacy

Parent involvement in governance and advocacy (type 5) refers to participation in parent groups, advisory councils, or other committees or groups at the local, district, or state level. It also refers to parents who take advocacy roles to monitor the schools and work for school improvements (Epstein, 1988).

This type of parent involvement may pose more problems than the other types, in which parents are more clearly the recipients of information from the schools. In practice, Comer (1993) found only about 1 to 5 percent of the schools' parents were engaged as active decision-makers. Even experienced parent groups and leaders may have a difficult time successfully representing other parents and communicating clearly with them.

Parents in Governance

Parents can play key leadership roles in parent councils, parent–teacher groups, planning teams, budget review committees, individualized educational plans, family impact statements, evaluation teams, program advisory councils, interview committees, school boards, and other committees and school groups. Schools should provide training in decision making and leadership so parent leaders can communicate effectively with all families they represent. School-based management models which involve parents in meaningful decision-making roles may improve the skills of parents of students at risk for school failure (Comer, 1993).

When parents are involved in governance of the schools of their children, several important outcomes have been documented:

- Parents provide input to policies that affect their child's education
- Parents feel in control of their child's learning environment
- Parents' and children's rights are protected
- Specific benefits for children and parents are linked to specific policies
- Teachers and school staff become aware of parent perspectives for school policy development (Epstein, 1988).

There are many possible activities that are related to the inclusion of parents in governance for the schools. A few methods of fostering such inclusion are

- Involve parents in student goal setting at regular parent–teacher conferences
- Involve parents and the community in developing the school's mission and goals
- Keep parents informed of leadership opportunities on school committees and in the community
- Form a parent council (such as a parents' club or parent–teacher organization), with advisory committees to support each academic area
- Provide training for parent leaders in collaboration and problem-solving skills
- Involve the parent council in reviewing monitoring procedures, reporting of student progress, and conducting curriculum reviews
- Involve the parent council in planning ways to extend learning opportunities
- Involve parent council representatives on any site-based management teams and on all school committees

Parents as Advocates

School personnel can provide parents and community members with the information they need to support school improvement. Groups and individuals may be connected to national organizations, such as the National Parent Teacher Association and the National Parenting Association. Parents may become linked to political groups and elected representatives who design and approve educational programs, funding appropriations, and budgets.

When parents are involved in advocacy for the schools of their children, several important outcomes have been documented:

- parents provide input to policies that affect education
- parents feel in control of their child's learning environment
- parents' and children's rights are protected
- benefits for children and parents are linked to educational policies
- educators give equal status to interaction with parents to improve educational programs
- educators become aware of parent perspectives for school policy development (Epstein, 1988).

There are many possible activities that are related to the role of parents as advocates for the schools. A few methods for promoting parent advocacy include:

- forming an alliance with other agencies and community resources to extend advocacy opportunities
- training parent leaders to organize community action through telephone calls, petitions, and letters
- encouraging parent council representatives to attend all school board meetings and community meetings that affect the school

Figure 7-4 provides some useful suggestions for training parents for leadership and advocacy roles.

Facilitating Parent Involvement in Decision Making

In order to get parents involved in governance and advocacy, it is necessary to provide opportunities for involvement and training for advocacy.

Providing Opportunities

Parent involvement in governance or decision making may be nurtured and strengthened in important ways, such as decentralized decision making, adequate resource support, training for school staff, local school incentives for coordination, and community representation.

To encourage parent involvement, school districts should consider decentralizing governance to the building level. When building administrators have decision-making authority, school parent councils should have greater decision-making authority. These partnerships can make decisions about school budget, personnel, and programming.

Building councils should have adequate resources to take action on specific issues. This support can include staffing support, budget, access to school information, a family resource center, defined procedures for handling parent concerns, skill development workshops, leadership training, and timely feedback on actions and recommendations.

A comprehensive staff development effort would include workshops and follow-up sessions to individualize the staff response to parent councils. Staff need adequate time to work in partnership with parent councils.

School councils should integrate their activities with other groups and efforts. Unique coordination patterns may be created at the school and district levels.

Session 1: Issues which affect children. Milestone and transitions in child development and family life.

Session 2: Thriving with diversity. What are the strengths of our diverse backgrounds? What are the strengths of collaborating?

Session 3: A look at how change happens for children and families from within our own experience. Tools we can use to change our environment and to shape our response to change.

Session 4: Parents as change agents. How family life experiences influence ideas about parent leadership. How parents can become a greater force for change.

Session 5: Problem solving. How to define a problem and work toward solutions. Examination of community strengths and needs from a parent perspective.

Session 6: The power of language. Kinds of communication. Constructive ways to make a point. Public speaking with success.

Session 7: How a community works. Maximizing community resources and assets. Discussion of how community meetings work.

Session 8: Identification of decision-makers in the schools, in the city, and at the state level. How are policies developed?

Session 9: Joining together in coalitions. Expanding influence. Determining who should become part of the joint efforts.

Session 10: How to use the media (television, radio, and print). Public speaking. Presenting public statements with success.

FIGURE 7-4 Suggested Outline for Parent Training in Leadership and Advocacy

From: The National Parenting Association of Minnesota, 1030 University Avenue, Saint Paul, MN 55104.

School councils should be representative of the building's parents, teachers, administrators, students, and community. Special outreach and training efforts may be necessary to include low-income and diverse populations in meaningful ways.

> ***REFLECTION...***
>
> What are the advantages of using volunteers in decision making? There has been some resistance on the part of educators in involving non-educators in decision making. Reflect as to why.

Training for Advocacy

Parents clearly have the most at stake concerning decisions which affect their children. School staff and others can provide them with training which develops skill in communicating with policy-makers in writing, by telephone, in person, or through the media.

When communicating with policy-makers in writing, encourage parents to avoid professional jargon, emotional ranting, and form letters. Parents should focus on one issue per letter, keep it short, and use their own real-life examples to illustrate their message. Show strength: mention the number of parents represented by the writer or through the program. Parental input is critical at three stages: urging the policy-maker to introduce the issue for consideration, encouraging committees to pass the proposal, and urging the representative to vote for the proposal. Parents should include their name and address on their letter and request a response. Write a letter of appreciation if the representative acts in accordance with the recommendations.

Communication by telephone is usually handled by the staff members of policy-makers. Parents can leave a brief message to express their opinion, urge action, and give their name and address. Telephone calls by many people on the same issue may have an impact. It may be advantageous to create a telephone tree. Use the telephone tree to give parents information about issues that concern them and to let them know the results of their advocacy. To organize a telephone tree:

1. Gather names of interested parents and their telephone numbers.
2. Appoint a group to organize the names and telephone numbers. One or two persons might start the tree. To be effective, each person should not have more than three people to call.
3. Strategically organize the tree so the people most likely to follow through with calls receive notice first, followed by people who may be least available to continue calling others.
4. Provide a copy so each person on the telephone tree has one handy at home.

Parents may want to get involved by visiting policy-makers to express their concerns. Be sure to call in advance to make an appointment and ask for directions. Decide ahead of time about the points to make. Bring materials about the program along with information they can use to contact parents at a later date. Encourage parents to follow-up with a letter of thanks.

Newspapers, community newsletters, radio, and television are important tools that can shape public opinion on education and family issues. Parents can write letters to the editor or submit guest columns and editorials. Make two or three important points succinctly and identify yourself by name and address. Relate the main points to important facts and personal interest stories. On television, comments have the best chance of being used if they are between twenty and thirty seconds long. Suggest related stories or other persons to interview.

Considering Diversity

Those who organize opportunities for parent involvement in decision making and as advocates will want to consider cultural and economic differences among families. Successful programs learn about other cultures and respect their beliefs and strengths. Stepparents, grandparents, and other family members can get involved on behalf of children. Ask parents what they are interested in accomplishing and work with the families' agendas first. Parent involvement in decision making requires site-specific program development and leadership.

Partnership with diverse families can be facilitated through collaboration with culturally specific community agencies. Community groups can work independently, yet cooperatively, with the schools to assist parents to understand their children's school program and practices. Bilingual advocacy groups can monitor school decisions on behalf of parents and community members.

A parent coordinator or leader who understands the languages, cultures, and backgrounds of parents is needed to communicate with parents. A leader with time to do the job is the single most essential element (Nicolau & Ramos, 1990). Child care, transportation, interpretation, and meals will make a big difference for including parents.

Additional Considerations in Facilitating Parent Involvement

Obstacles to Parent Involvement

As educators have become more professional and organized, parents have gradually been removed from the decision-making process. Although research and experience reported elsewhere in this textbook has documented the importance of parent involvement in the schools, parents often are perceived as peripheral and tangential rather than essential to education. Why does this continue? Teachers and administrators face realistic time constraints. They are busy maintaining the educational operation as it currently exists. Any changes mean that something will receive less attention, and it may be parent involvement.

The acknowledgement of the importance of parental involvement in education, however, does not mean that school staff and administrators are well-prepared to facilitate such involvement. Radcliffe, Malone, and Nathan (1994) found that the majority of states do not require most teachers or administrators to study parent involvement or to develop skills in promoting parent involvement. Only seven states (14%) required principals or central office administrators to study parent involvement or to become proficient in promoting parent involvement. Only fifteen states (30%) required most or all teachers to study or develop abilities in parent involvement. And only twenty states (40%) required early childhood educators to study or develop skills in parent involvement. Teachers and school personnel report that they have received little training on ways to help parents get more involved in their child's education.

It may be difficult to establish relationships with numerous families within the nine months of a traditional school year. Contemporary classrooms are filled with diversity. Teachers and administrators must be sensitive and knowledgeable about the unique cultures and background of their students. This takes time, effort, and dedication.

In today's mobile society, there is always some natural transition; families move away during the school year and others take their places. There is a constant turnover of parent leadership as their children grow up and leave specific classrooms or specific school buildings. The "next generation" of parents is always arriving, ready to get involved, but needing to build relationships and receive training.

Role of School Administrators

It is the administrator of a school who sets the climate for parental interaction. The goal of the schools is the education of students. School personnel are concerned with the teaching–learning process. Parents are essential to this process. It is the administrators who must motivate teachers to include parents. Administrators encourage activities to bring parents into the schools. Administrators can help school staff be successful at parent involvement by

Session 1:   Meeting parents as people—part 1: Greeting parents, creating an inviting and non-threatening climate; using positively phrased language; learning why schools intimidate some parents.

Session 2:   Meeting parents as people—part 2: Learning and understanding cultural, racial, ethnic, and economic groups different from ourselves.

Session 3:   Involving parents as parents: Planning activities that involve parents in their child's learning; facilitating parent-teacher conferences; providing informative student progress reports.

Session 4:   Involving parents as volunteers: Identifying parent skills and strengths and matching them with classroom and building needs.

Session 5:   Involving parents with decision-makers: Identifying parent leadership strengths; sharing power.

FIGURE 7-5   Suggested Outline for School Staff Training in Parent Involvement

coordinating, managing, supporting, funding and recognizing parent achievement. They can further facilitate parent involvement by:

- Sharing relevant research findings with school staff
- Leading staff meetings and workshops on the influence of parents on student grade achievement
- Coordinating information on programs in the school and documenting the efforts at parent involvement
- Encouraging teachers to work together to share practices
- Providing small grants for creating materials or compensating teachers for after-school time spent with parents
- Coordinating school recognition programs for parents and teachers who participate in parent-involvement programs
- Building a positive attitude for improving parent involvement at school (Epstein, 1987).

Handling Disagreements

Partnerships in a democratic system can help parents get involved before problems arise over curriculum changes or school environment developments. However, as parents get more involved in the schools, there will still be frequent contradictions and frustrations. Here are seven guidelines for school staff responses to parental concerns and complaints:

1. Staff should understand school policies on materials selection, academic freedom, instructional hearings, handling complaints and grievances, and school board protocol. Share clear policies and guidelines with parents.
2. Continue to be courteous and make parents feel welcome. Acknowledge the community's and parents' rights to express themselves and be involved in decision making.
3. Listen carefully to get a deep understanding of the parents' concerns, the issues they see, and their guiding assumptions.

Protecting Family Integrity

1. Support the development of healthy, stable relationships among family members
2. Encourage acceptance, valuing and protection of a family's personal and cultural values and beliefs
3. Minimize intrusion upon the family by those who hold external resources needed by the family
4. Promote acquisition of behavior incompatible with maltreatment
5. Mobilize resources necessary for family reunification

Strengthening Family Functioning

1. Create opportunities for family members to acquire knowledge, skills, capacities necessary to become more capable and competent
2. Primarily identify and build on family strengths rather than correct weaknesses
3. Permit families to establish interdependencies with personal social network members
4. Maximize the family's control over the amount, timing, and methods of support, resources, or services
5. Provide information about options and their consequences and encourage informed decision-making by the family

Proactive Human Service Practices

1. Encourage adoption of resource-based rather than service-based intervention models and practices
2. Encourage adoption of a holistic family and community orientation
3. Encourage a consumer-driven rather than a professional-driven approach to resource mobilization
4. Encourage promotion and enhancement models rather than prevention or treatment models

FIGURE 7-6   Checklist of Family Support Principles

Adapted with permission from C. J. Dunst, (1990). *Family Support Principles: Checklists for Program Builders and Practitioners.* Morganton, NC: Family, Infant and Preschool Program, Western Carolina Center.

4. Avoid arguing about who is right and who is wrong. Most issues have many viewpoints.
5. If possible, explain the background and rationale for the action or materials in question. Avoid resorting to educational jargon.
6. Arrange for the parents to meet with other school staff and administrators.
7. Remember that students and parents learn about democratic liberties by observing how school administrators and policy-makers deal with disagreement.

Evaluation

As efforts are made to increase parent involvement programs, it is important to evaluate them on a regular basis. The evaluation might include consideration of the *amount,* the *quality,* and the *outcomes* of parent involvement.

Reports about the amount of parent involvement will include information about the parents who are involved as visitors, volunteers, decision-makers, or advocates. Possible topics for assessment include:

- Number of opportunities offered
- Changes in involvement opportunities offered
- Numbers of participants
- Number of hours of participation
- Change in type of participation
- Description of resources provided to encourage parent involvement
- Parent self-report about understanding of and comfort with school programs and policies
- Description of the changes in the school environment to encourage parent participation

Parent involvement in the schools as visitors, volunteers, decision-makers, and advocates may be considered a form of family support because it is aimed at strengthening student and family functioning. Dunst (1990) has developed a checklist of family support principles which might be used as indicators of the quality of such programs. School staff and parents could use the checklist to stimulate discussion about the ways in which the particular school's parent-involvement program influences family strengths.

Research in the resources cited earlier in this chapter mentions many outcomes that may result from parent involvement in the schools. Evaluation of a classroom's or school building's biases may show how such outcomes affect the particular parent-involvement strategies implemented. Table 7-1 lists some of these outcomes and their correspnding indicators.

Conclusion and Recommendations

Direct interaction happens when parents go to the school that their children attend and communicate with teachers and administrators. Admittedly, there are complexities to changing the traditional one-way relationship (in which parents are clients and recipients of educational services) to the two-way relationship (in which parents are citizens and colleagues in delivering educational services). Parents need schools and their education and support services. However, schools also need parents as co-educators and political allies, now more than ever.

Several areas still need to be reviewed in relation to parent involvement in the schools and in decision making. First, resources are needed to genuinely involve parents in education. This means adequate budgets and priorities are needed for school building, local

TABLE 7-1   Outcomes and Indicators of Parental Involvement

Outcome	Indicators
Student achievement in school	• higher grades • higher test scores • reduced placements in special educatin or remedial classes • remedial classes • higher graduation rates • higher enrollment in post-secondary education
Student attitudes and behavior	• more positive attitude about school • more positive behavior at school

school districts, and state policies. Second, more information is needed about the effect of specific forms of parent involvement on students and parents at various grade levels. Finally, teachers and administrators need pre-service and in-service education on culturally sensitive and appropriate parent-involvement practices.

Recommended Activities

1. Survey schools in your area as to the nature of their parent-involvement programs.
2. Inquire to see if your local school district(s) have a written parent-involvement policy. Request a copy and discuss in class.
3. Using the information provided in this chapter, design your own parent-involvement program.
4. Invite a parent, teacher, and administrator to share their experiences and perspectives concerning parent involvement.
5. Visit a Head Start program and investigate their parent-involvement program.
6. Review the parent-involvement part of James Comer's model and after watching the movie "Dangerous Minds," speculate as to how his program could be implemented into the school.

Additional Resources

Encouraging Parental Involvement

Books:

Epstein Getwici, C. (1991). *Home, school and community relations: A guide to working with parents* (2nd ed.).

This parent–home book emphasizes communication and working with parents of preschool children.

> Delmar Publishers
> PO Box 15015
> Albany, NY 12212-5015
> Phone: 800–824-5179

Kroth, R. (1996). *Communicating with parents of exceptional children* (3rd ed.).

Kroth's work in the area of parent involvement acts as a foundation for many other researchers and writers. You will see his influence in most major works in this area. Although this book was specifically written for those working with parents of students with special needs, it is also valuable in working with parents in general. He provides the reader with a philosophical basis for planning as well as practical suggestions. This is a book that all educators interested in parent involvement need for their library.

Love Publishing Co.
PO Box 22353
Denver, CO 80222
Phone: 303-757-2579

Articles:

Comer, James. (1986). Parent participation in schools. *Phi Delta Kappan, 67*(2), 442–446.

Dodd, A. W. (1996). Involving parents: Avoiding gridlock. *Educational Leadership, 53*(7), 44–49.

Epstein, J. L. (1987). Parent involvement. *Education and Urban Society, 19*(2), 119–136.

Hoover-Dempsey, K. V., Bassler, O. C., & Brissie, J. S. (1987). Parent involvement: Contributions of teacher efficacy, school SES, and other school characteristics. *American Educational Research Journal, 24*(3), 417–435.

Videos:

Latino Parents as Partners in Education

Latino children have the highest school dropout rates in the United States. This video looks at how parental involvement helps increase the opportunities for and potential of Latino children.

Films for the Humanities & Science
PO Box 2053
Princeton, NJ 08543
Phone: 800-257-5126

Parent Involvement

This video examines techniques for encouraging parents to become more involved in their children's educations. It makes some very specific suggestions. With the busy schedule of today's parents this video is most timely. 1994. (22 minutes, color).

Films for the Humanities & Science
PO Box 2053
Princeton, NJ 08543
Phone: 800-257-5126

Partnership with Parents

Young children benefit most from programs in which teachers and parents work together as partners. The program dramatizes the importance of the parent–teacher relationship for children and demonstrates how to establish and maintain positive communication. It also shows how to handle common problems teachers face when working with parents. 1989. (28 minutes, color).

Insight Media
2162 Broadway
New York, NY 10024
Phone: 212-721-6316

Shared Decision Making

This video examines two school communities that involve parents, teachers, school-board members, and students working together to make decisions that result in better schools. 1994. (22 minutes, color).

Insight Media
2162 Broadway
New York, NY 10024
Phone: 212-721-6316

Working with Parents: Home–School Collaboration

This video will help teachers understand the concerns and fears of parents. Parents explain what they expect from parent–teacher conferences and discuss ways to exchange information. The video provides specific suggestions for how teachers and parents can work together to create a positive learning environment. 1984. (30 minutes, color).

Organizations:

Alliance for Parental Involvement
   in Education
PO Box 59
East Chatham, New York, NY 12060-0059
Phone: 518-392-6900

Center on Families, Communities, Schools and Children's Learning
The John Hopkins University
3505 North Charles Street
Baltimore, MD 21218
Phone: 401-516-0370

Center for Social Organization of Schools
Johns Hopkins University
3505 North Charles Street
Baltimore, MD 21218
Phone: 301-338-7570

Family Resource Coalition
200 South Michigan Avenue, Suite 1520
Chicago, IL 60604
Phone: 312-341-0900

Hispanic Policy Development Project
Suite 5000A, 250 Park Avenue South
New York, NY 10003
Phone: 212-523-9323

The Home and School Institute
1201 16th Street NW
Washington, DC 20036
Phone: 202-466-3633

Institute for Responsive Education
704 Commonwealth Avenue
Boston, MA 02215
Phone: 617-353-3309

National Coalition for Parent Involvement in Education
Box 39
1201 16th Street, NW
Washington, DC 20002
Phone: 703-684-3345

National Committee for Citizens
   in Education
10840 Little Patuxent Parkway, #301
Columbia, MD 21044-3199
Phone: 800-NETWORK

National Congress of Parent
   Teacher Associations
700 North Rush Street
Chicago, IL 60611-2571
Phone: 312-670-6782
http://www.pta.org/

National Parent Teacher Association
700 Rush Street
Chicago, IL 60711
Ogibe 312-787-0977

National Parenting Association
Suite 1D, 65 Central Park West
New York, NY 10023
Phone: 212-362-7575

Parents in Touch
Indianapolis Public Schools
901 North Carrollton
Indianapolis, IN 46202
Phone: 317-266-4134

Parent–Community Involvement

Books:

The child development center. (1994). *A guide to schoolwide activities that build community: At home in our schools.*

This book shares ideas from the Child Development Project for parents, teachers and administrators. *At Home in Our Schools* gives wonderful suggestions for schoolwide activities and offers a process for rethinking our existing activities. ISBN: 1-885603-00-2.

> Child Development Project
> 2000 Embarcasero, Suite 305
> Oakland, CA 94606
> Phone: 800-666-7270

Cibulka, J. G., & Knitek, W. J. (Eds.). (1996). *Coordination among schools, families, and communities.*

Improving the connection among school, families and communities has emerged as a recent focus of the education reform movement, posing many challenges for educators and parents. This book provides information on the diverse goals of the coordinated services movement and the problems of reconciling competing goals within the movement. Different models of coordination are presented. 456 pp. ISBN: 0-7914-2858-3.

> State University of New York Press
> c/o CUP Services
> PO Box 6525
> Ithaca, NY 14851
> Phone: 607-277-2211

Gestwicki, C. (1991). *Home, school, and community relations: A guide to working with parents* (2nd ed.).

This book makes a number of excellent suggestions that can be used in working with many parents, but it is meant primarily for working with pre-school children.

> Delmar Publishers
> PO Box 15015
> Albany, NY 12212-5015
> Phone: 800-824-5179

Chapter:

Moles, O. C. (1993). A new paradigm for parent involvement. In N. F. Chavkin (Ed.), *Families and schools in a pluralistic society* (pp. 229–234). Albany, NY: State University Press.

References

Becker, H. J., & Epstein, J. L. (1982). Parent involvement: A study of teacher practices. *Elementary School Journal, 83,* 85–102.

Benson, P. L. (1993). *The troubled journey: A portrait of 6th–12th grade youth.* Minneapolis, MN: Search Institute.

Children's Defense Fund. (1994). *The state of America's children yearbook.* Washington, DC: Children's Defense Fund.

Comer, J. P. (1993). *School power: Implications of an intervention project.* New York, NY: Free Press.

Dunst, C. J. (1990). *Family support principles: Checklists for program builders and practitioners.* Morganton, NC: Family, Infant and Preschool Program, Western Carolina Center.

Epstein, J. L. (1987). Parent involvement: What the research says to administrators. *Education and Urban Society, 19*(2), 119–136.

Epstein, J. L. (1988). How do we improve programs in parent involvement? *Educational Horizons, 66*(2), 58–59 (special issue on parents and schools).

Gelfer, J. (1991). Teacher–parent partnerships. *Childhood Education, 67*(3), 164–167.

Henderson, A. T., & Berla, N. (1994). *A new generation of evidence: The family is critical to student achievement.* Columbia, MD: National Committee for Citizens in Education.

Nathan, J., & Radcliffe, B. (1994). *It's apparent: We can and should have more parent/educator partnerships.* Minneapolis, MN: Center for School Change, Humphrey Institute of Public Affairs, University of Minnesota.

Nicolau, S., & Ramos, C. L. (1990). *Together is better: Building strong partnerships between schools and Hispanic parents.* Washington, DC: Hispanic Policy Development Project.

Radcliffe, B., Malone, M., & Nathan, J. (1994). *The training for parent partnership: Much more should be done.* Minneapolis, MN: Center for School Change, Humphrey Institute of Public Affairs, University of Minnesota.

U.S. Department of Education. (1994). *Goals 2000: Educate America.* Washington, DC: U.S. Department of Education.

C h a p t e r 8

Families and Their Children with Disabilities

AMYSUE REILLY

The lives of families with special needs children are the same as other families and, at the same time, very different. Family love, affection, and pride are similar, but families of children with disabilities often experience stresses not normally a part of other families' lives. This chapter examines the dynamics of these special families. The purpose of this chapter is to help the reader explore the:

- History of special education and parental involvement
- Legislation that has affected students with special needs and their families
- Reaction of family members upon learning of their child's disability
- Accommodations and adjustment made by the family
- Adjustment of fathers, siblings, and mothers
- Community response

Two Sculptors

I dreamed I stood in a studio
And watched two sculptors there,
The clay they used was a young child's mind
And they fashioned it with care.

One was a teacher; the tools she used
Were books, music and art.
One, a parent who worked with a guiding hand
And a gentle, loving heart.

Day after day the teacher toiled
With touch that was deft and sure,
While the parent labored by her side
And polished and smoothed it o'er

And when at last their task was done,
They were proud of what they had wrought;
For the things they had molded into the child
Could neither be sold nor bought

And each agreed he would have failed
If he worked alone,
The parent and the school,
The teacher and the home.

Author Unknown (in Salisbury, 1992).

Author Unknown. *From: Collaborative Teams for Students with Severe Disabilities: Integrating Therapy and Educational Services.* Reprinted with permission from Brookes Publishing Co.

Families of children with disabilities are no different from others in wanting their offspring to have an opportunity to develop, learn, socialize, and enjoy life. In order to enhance these possibilities, however, families and professionals must work together to ensure that these children are provided with the needed experiences to grow through exploration of the world around them.

This chapter will familiarize the reader with the dynamics surrounding families who have a child with a disability. By way of introduction, a useful synopsis of the progression of integrating individuals with disabilities into homes, schools, and community settings will be provided. This will be followed by a statistical overview of the numbers of students with special needs being served in recent years. Finally, a summary of relevant legislation will be offered.

Historical Perspective

For centuries, a societal laissez-faire attitude has been responsible for the generally insensitive treatment of people with disabilities. Consider, for example, that some cultures abandoned or destroyed babies and toddlers if they developed or exhibited disabilities, while others used youngsters with disabilities as social curios and sideshow entertainment. Twentieth-century history reveals that most institutions for the disabled were more reminiscent of penal, rather than medical, facilities.

Antiquity and the Middle Ages

Interestingly, however, two significant visionaries of ancient times spoke of a more humane social treatment of these individuals. Hippocrates (physician, c. 460–377 B.C.) believed emotional problems were a result of natural forces rather than supernatural powers. Likewise, Plato (philosopher, c. 427–347 B.C.) hypothesized that people who were mentally unstable were not accountable for their behaviors.

During the Middle Ages, a limited number of religious orders provided basic care and shelter for individuals with disabilities who were removed from their families. These children were often cared for in monasteries. They participated within their range of ability in the day-to-day activities of the monasteries, performing housekeeping chores, grounds-keeping duties, and tending crops. Unfortunately, these persons were often thought to be possessed by demons and subjected to cruel treatments intending to exorcise these demons.

Nineteenth-Century Developments

Jean Marc Gaspard Itard found an abandoned, naked boy living in a dense forest near Aveyron, France. Given the name Victor, this "Wild Boy of Aveyron" was reared in a nondomestic and isolated environment. Jean-Marc Gaspard Itard, who was a physician and researcher for the deaf, believed that learning was best acquired through hands-on experiences that provided challenging opportunities. Based on Itard's success with Victor, he came to believe that anyone could learn if properly stimulated. Edouard Sequin, a student of Itard's, brought this educational philosophy to the United States in the mid-nineteenth century, and actively promoted it in residential programs for people with mental retardation.

In the nineteenth century, residential schools for individuals who were deaf and/or blind were established in the United States. These schools were based on European residential schooling which had demonstrated the benefits of appropriate education. In 1817, Thomas Gallaudet established this country's first residential school for the deaf at Hartford, Connecticut.

In 1829, Samuel Howe founded the Perkins School for the Blind in Watertown, Massachusetts. Anne Sullivan was trained at the Perkins School and, subsequently, recruited by the Keller family to provide an on-going intense education for their daughter Helen. Through Ms. Sullivan's teachings and the family's perseverance and unwavering commitment, Helen became a nationally recognized inspirational speaker and a respected author. What was once thought to be impossible now became possible. In essence, individuals with severe sensory disabilities could become functional community members.

Twentieth-Century Developments

Pearl Buck's *The Child Who Never Grew,* a heartfelt story about raising a child with mental retardation, provided parents of similarly affected youngsters a level of support and encouragement sorely missing in their lives. By sharing her frank and moving account of raising her child, many parents of children with disabilities also began to share their experiences with each other, thus fostering a grass-roots prototype for parental support groups.

Other twentieth century efforts were prompted by the increase in society's concern with the incidence of infant mortality, childhood diseases, and abusive child labor. Coupled with these concerns was John Dewey's educational reform, which emphasized a more child-centered philosophy of teaching and parenting. The results of these outcries and teachings, which were influenced by involved families, educators, and physicians, led to significant reform of societal attitudes toward those with disabilities, especially the treatment and services provided individuals with mental retardation and mental illness.

The mid-twentieth century was distinguished by an international leader with a disability. President Franklin D. Roosevelt demonstrated through his own perseverance that he could perform efficiently despite his ineffectual polio-afflicted legs. He was a productive chief executive despite performing the majority of his duties from a wheelchair.

President John F. Kennedy grew up with a sister who was mentally retarded, and, while in office, he established the Task Force on National Action to Combat Mental Retardation, the President's Commission on Mental Retardation, and the Bureau of Education for the Handicapped (now the Office of Special Education Programs). President Kennedy's strong convictions regarding the right to full opportunities for individuals with mental retardation (and all other disabilities) strongly influenced the development of special education.

Several years later, Vice President Hubert Humphrey, whose granddaughter had Down Syndrome, showed a strong interest in early education for young children with disabilities. He also supported the notion that early stimulation would provide a youngster the additional learning opportunity necessary to progressively acquire skills later in life.

Another contemporary public official who supported the development and passing of landmark legislation was Connecticut Senator Lowell Weikert, whose son had a disability.

The Education for All Handicapped Children Act, known as Public Law 94-142, was implemented in 1975 and laid the ground work for this country's educational reform and commitment to infants, toddlers, children, youth, and young adults with disabilities.

Number of Children Receiving Special Educational Services

A national count of children receiving special education services began in 1976 with the passing of Public Law 94-142 (Education for All Handicapped Children Act), which required special educational services be provided for all children with disabilities. Since 1976–77, there has been a steady annual increase (overall, approximately 25 percent) in the numbers of children receiving special education services.

Over 4.5 million children with disabilities, ranging from six to twenty-one years of age, or approximately 10 percent of the population, received special education services during the 1991–92 school year (*Fifteenth Annual Report to Congress,* 1993). This was a 3.9 percent increase from 1990–91, the largest increase since 1976–77 (U.S. Department of Education, 1993).

The increase of younger children served in special education was due directly to early intervention programs implemented in 1986. Public Law 99-457 mandated state-determined services for infants and toddlers (birth to age 2) and required appropriate educational opportunities for preschoolers (3 to 5 years of age). Since then, the population growth of youngsters receiving early intervention services has increased significantly. An estimated 35,000 infants and toddlers (birth through age 2) and 422,226,000 preschoolers (ages 3–5) were among those receiving special education services during 1991–92 (U.S. Department of Education, 1993).

The empirical data presented above indicate that an even larger number of young children with disabilities and their families will be seeking various early intervention and transition services into community educational programs. The legislation concerning special education is critical to these children and their families.

Legislation

Parental involvement in the legislative process dates back to the early 1950s, with the establishment of the National Association of Parents and Friends of Mentally Retarded Children (now, the American Association for Retarded Citizens). ARC has a long history of representing the interests of people with mental disabilities and their families. Other parent groups have been organized through the strong efforts of family involvement (e.g., United Cerebral Palsey Association and the National Society for Autistic Children). In the late 1960s a group of parents of children with mental retardation collaborated with the Pennsylvania Association for Retarded Citizens to sue the state. They won their lawsuit and the court held that all children with mental retardation must be provided with a free public program of education and training (*Pennsylvania Association for Retarded Citizens* v. *Commonweath of Pennsylvania,* 1972). As a result, the time was right to establish federal legislation (Turnbull, Turnbull, & Wheat, 1982).

Public Law 94-142

The various parental organizations (ARC and other parental organizations representing all areas of exceptionalities) joined to develop a strong political advocacy. These groups were striving for federal legislation mandating that all students with disabilities be provided with a free, appropriate public education. Through the concerted efforts of parents and professionals, congress passed the Education for All Handicapped Children Act in 1975. In addition, this law recognized the critical role that families play in the decision-making process in their children's lives.

One of the earliest programs for youngsters considered disadvantaged by society's standards was established by President Lyndon B. Johnson in 1965. To remedy the lack of learning opportunities, Johnson initiated the development of a federally funded educational project called "Head Start." Prior to the late 1960s and early 1970s, few programs existed for any preschoolers, much less for those with disabilities. Even fewer programs were available for infants and toddlers.

In 1975, President Gerald R. Ford signed landmark legislation that dramatically altered the educational rights of individuals with disabilities and their families. Among other things, the spirit of this legislation, the Education for All Handicapped Children Act (Public Law 94-142), advocated families to be actively involved with their child's educational programs.

Congress has amended Public Law 94-142 three times (1983, 1986, and 1990). In the most recent amendments, the title of the law also was changed to the Individuals with Disabilities Education Act (IDEA). This change reflects the philosophy that the main focus should be on an individual's *abilities* rather than his or her *disabilities*.

The overall basic features and requirements of the original 1975 act have remained essentially unchanged despite its three amendments, including the rights of parents of children with disabilities. These entitlements have strengthened parental participation and input by guaranteeing to parents their legal rights and opportunities for involvement (Hanson, 1985).

Five fundamental rights are guaranteed to parents of children with disabilities, as is their subsequent involvement in the special education process. Specifically, parents and the served child are to:

1. Be provided free appropriate public education
2. Be provided safeguards by the school system to protect these rights (e.g., parental consent must be given for any assessments or placement regarding the served children)
3. Be educated with their nondisabled peers to the maximum extent possible. This is also referred to as the concept of *least restrictive environment*
4. Participate as full members of the individual education plan (IEP) team developing and implementing the child's IEP
5. Play an active role in the educational decision-making process concerning their child. If the parents are not satisfied with any educational decision regarding their child, they have recourse

Public Law 99-457

The second amendment, made in 1986 (Public Law 99-457), required states to develop and implement, within five years, comprehensive interdisciplinary services for infants and toddlers (birth through age 2) with disabilities, and to expand services for preschool children (aged 3 through 5). As a result, individual states now provide free, appropriate education for all 3- to 5-year-olds with disabilities who are eligible for federal preschool funding.

An extension of the comprehensive interdisciplinary service for infants, toddlers, and preschool programs was the *Individualized Family Service Plan* (IFSP), which required educational services to develop a family plan that would enhance both the child and the child's family. Too frequently, professionals need to be reminded of the various dimensions of a child's life and behavior. The educators' and parents' perceptions of the child often differ depending on the context and depth of discussions (Dunst, Trivette, & Deal, 1988). Some professionals may present a picture of the child that is not an accurate representation of the child as a whole.

> *To sit and listen—as one after another of the other participants (teachers and therapists) describe Bill's deficiencies and the almost minuscule progress that he has made from year to year—has almost left me feeling sad and hopeless. For that one day each year, I see Bill as I know other people see him and not the unique person I live with and know and love. (Statum, 1995, p. 65)*

How a child performs in one setting rarely constitutes a complete picture of how that given child performs in all settings. It is for this and other reasons that professionals should readily provide the family ample opportunity to share their perspectives regarding their child (Salisbury, 1992). Parental input has definite value in that it may furnish the professional(s) with critical information not easily obtained during the course of clinical observation or the teaching regimen. Also, such input reminds the professional that the child is a unique individual with various needs which are met in different settings by many providers.

In summary, these significant pieces of legislation have provided a tremendous increase in new educational programs and opportunities for all infants, toddlers, preschoolers, school-aged children, youth, and young adults with disabilities. The importance of family involvement in the collaborative educational pursuit of their children's opportunities is central to much of this legislation. It is for this reason that professionals must continue to learn how to work more effectively within the family system.

Family Systems

This section is based on the premise that families of children with disabilities, like families of all other children, want their offspring to have meaningful, enjoyable, and successful lives. Furthermore, it recognizes that in order for this to be possible professionals must respect and appreciate each family's unique position as they strive toward this end. The overall family dynamics that are impacted by the presence of a child with a disability are first presented. Second, the reader is introduced to fathers and siblings and their perspectives, which are often neglected in a literature that has traditionally emphasized the mother's role within the family system. Finally, the parental viewpoints and opinions regarding community inclusion for their children with disabilities is discussed.

Adjustments: Dealing with the Disability

Reactions

When a family is first told their long awaited "bundle of joy" has a disability, it is not easy to predict how each family member will react (Powers, 1993). Most families first receive this information from medical professionals while they are dealing with the hospitalization of their infant or toddler (Long, Artis, & Dobbins, 1993; Pearl, 1993). Receiving information pertaining to the birth (or diagnosis) of such a child is indeed overwhelming (Buck, 1950; Long, Artis, & Dobbins, 1993; Meyer, 1986b).

Each family member's reactions stem from intense feelings and draining emotions, often leaving them in a state of confusion, questioning, and bewilderment. Of course, a major key to working effectively with such families is to respect their right to express this intense and constantly varying range of emotions (Fewell, 1986; Gibbs, 1993).

> *Over the years I have often heard that parents must learn to accept the fact that their child has disabilities. I know no parent who hasn't accepted their child's disabilities. When you get up in the morning and force your child's legs into braces, put them in a wheelchair, feed them breakfast, give their antiseizure medication, you have accepted and are dealing with your child's disability. (Statum, 1995, p. 68)*

Professionals naturally may make generalizations regarding how parents might react and respond to their child with a disability. This action is usually in hope of working more effectively with the families. Often, however, the parental feelings, emotions, and behaviors are unpredictable. After all, few families are prepared to face the complex issues confronting them (Singer & Powers, 1993).

Emotional Impact

Parental expectations regarding their child's disability can be strongly influenced by the different types and severity of the disability (Fewell, 1986). Parents have long anticipated the birth of their child and their anticipation is full of hopes and dreams. Parental grief and reactions to the birth of their child with a disability is a result of the loss of their "normal" child (Murray & Cornell, 1981).

Thus the birth of a child with a disability is frequently a stressful event for families due to the variety of feelings, reactions, and responses felt by the various family members (Featherstone, 1980; Murray & Cornell, 1981; Turnbull, Brotherson, & Summers, 1985). Farber (1975) indicated several adaptations that families develop when having a child with a disability. Murray (1980) indicated that families frequently go through a series of reactions and responses. Kirk & Gallagher (1989) and Kubler-Ross (1969) found that some parents and other family members, including siblings, grandparents, and other extended family members, are faced with a variety of feelings, reactions, and responses when having a child with a disability. These feelings, reactions, and responses may change as life goes on, especially as the internal and external resources increase.

Professionals have become more aware of how family members are affected by the presence of a child with a disability. Professionals also need to take into consideration the roles and needs of each family member (Goldenberg & Goldenberg, 1980; Turnbull, Brotherson, & Summers, 1985). Turnbull's and Turnbull's (1990) framework for understanding the emotions, dynamics, and elements of family systems has allowed professionals to work more effectively with these families. The four elements of this framework are (a) family resources, (b) daily interactions among family members, (c) different individual family needs, and (d) changes that occur over time which affect family members (Turnbull & Turnbull, 1990).

Accommodations: Getting On with life

Adaptiveness

Families are remarkable adapters to the needs of their child (Seed, 1988; Lobato, 1990; Pearl, 1993). Moreover, the role of each family member assumes varying dimensions depending on the respective attitudes and behavior displayed regarding the child's disability (Meyer, 1986b; Nixon, 1993; Seed, 1988).

A broad range of emotion is experienced while attempting to reconcile those feelings regarding the family's child with a disability (Hawkins, Singer, & Nixon, 1993; Meyer, 1993; Seed, 1988). The anguish and stress is often tremendous, yet somehow each family member learns to cope with a mechanism that is frequently quite efficient to carry other family members through the substantial turmoil. In other words, the family often draws closer as they depend on one another.

Balanced Lifestyle

A family's daily routine typically focuses around the child with the disability. Thus, their attempt to find a balance in a family routine is an arduous task at best, given they often are having to juggle appointments dealing with various medical specialists, therapists (physical, occupational, speech and language), and early interventionist home visits. Clearly, it is time-consuming to visit a multitude of professional offices while trying to find answers to questions regarding the diagnosis or treatment of a child with a disability. Also, it is an exhausting pursuit for families to find the best services and newest information regarding their child's condition. Again, the family's attempt to find a requisite balance and perceived normalcy is an issue with which they frequently wrestle.

Child-Peer Relations

Parents are constantly seeking opportunities for children with disabilities to actively engage in typical early childhood experiences with their peers (Boswell & Schuffner, 1990; McLean & Hanline, 1990; Ruder, 1993; Statum, 1994). Also, critical to these children's development is the growth they continually experience from interactions as members of their own families (Frey, Fewell, Vadasy, & Greenberg, 1989; Pearl, 1993; Statum, 1995). Thus, an additional difficulty is the family's effort to continually locate positive peer-interactions so their exceptional child has an opportunity to enhance his or her learning experiences (Bailey & Bricker, 1984; Guralnick, 1990; McLean & Hanline, 1990; Ruder, 1993).

Day Care

Finding an appropriate day care program for any family often is a trying event and even more stressful to families attempting to locate such a program that will accept a child with a disability (Fewell, 1986). Quite frankly, day care providers are not customarily informed on how to work with young children with disabilities and thus are reluctant to accept responsibility for such children.

Seeking Services

Families seek the best services to provide for their child. Consequently, their homes are often like New York's Grand Central Station in trying to schedule various needed services. Furthermore, opening one's home to the numerous specialists arriving to provide services to their child and family is an intrusion on family privacy with which other families do not have to contend (Hanson, Lynch, & Wayman, 1990; Pearl, 1993). Nevertheless, these families are frequently required to carry out the programs prescribed for their child if they want to ensure their child's progress.

Early childhood special education interventionists attempt to work with families and their children with disabilities in a caring, sensitive, and supportive manner (Fewell, 1986; Pearl, 1993). Obviously, the services provided must be flexible and responsive to the diversity of family needs and resources (DeGangi et al., 1994; Hanson et al., 1990).

In addition to handling everyday life stressors, families learn how best to provide for the various needs of their child. Therefore, early intervention services must strive to be family-friendly, family-focused, and family-centered. Moreover, services need to be provided to families in the various settings that each family requires, such as home, day care, or community.

Values

Cultural and religious values heavily influence a family's structure as well as their views of disabilities (DeGangi et al., 1994; Hanson et al., 1990). Families will differ by cultural, economic, and religious influences, as well as by membership and structure of the family itself (Hanson et al., 1990). Such values can impact the effectiveness of the family's acceptance and willingness to implement intervention strategies. Therefore, professionals must be respectful of families' value systems and their services flexible enough to be in accordance with differing family value systems and cultures (DeGangi et al., 1994; Hanson et al., 1990).

Extended Family

Another important factor is the extended family, which is often a wonderful resource for providing that additional assistance needed in dealing with their child. An extended family can include grandparents, aunts, uncles, cousins, neighbors, and close friends who have joined the family circle. These members frequently provide the continual encouragement, respite relief, moral support, comfort, and unconditional understanding needed by the parents and other family members (Fewell, 1987; Gallagher, Cross, & Scharfman, 1981; Long et al., 1993; Pearl, 1993).

Support Groups

Parents of children with disabilities often need additional support other than that provided by professionals (Long et al., 1993; Meyer, 1993). Consequently, there is a growing network of parent support groups across the nation. Networking is a process linking parents interested in talking to other parents who have coped with similar situations—felt anguish, needed relief, and paved the road for tomorrow (Frey et al., 1989; Gibbs, 1993; Grossman, 1972). These networks of extended support allow family members to grow through personal shared experiences.

Perspectives of Family Members

Fathers

Traditionally, professionals have focused on mothers' perspectives regarding parental concerns of families and their children with disabilities. Interestingly, however, these mothers have long recognized the need to facilitate the father's involvement with their child's intervention program (Gallagher et al., 1981). In response, professionals have begun to address the significant needs of fathers and their active involvement in their child's intervention program (Lamb & Meyer, 1991; Young & Roopnarnine, 1994).

"A man's pride in his child's abilities influences his perspective of his parenting abilities, which increases his pride in his abilities as a parent" (Meyer, 1993, p. 83). A father's attitude toward his child's disability frequently influences the attitude of the family as a whole (Frey et al., 1989; Lamb & Meyer, 1991).

Typically, when a man becomes a father he evaluates his future in respect to his ability to provide and influence the development of his child. He assesses his accomplishments, career satisfaction, family, and marriage. The diagnosis of a disability can directly influence how a man assesses his family life (Meyer, 1986b), which in turn can directly influence the overall family unit's perception.

As a result of their recognized importance, there are now support programs specifically designed to meet the individual needs of fathers (Meyer, 1986; Young & Roopnarnine, 1994). One example provides an opportunity for fathers to participate in discussions regarding how their views of accomplishment and family have changed in the wake of the child's diagnosis (Meyer, 1993). Fathers bring their children to the program and are given the opportunity to be primary care givers, thus increasing their feelings of "expertise" regarding their child's disability. Father-focused support groups assist the family in handling everyday life stressors while attending to the various needs of their child.

> When people speak of acceptance, they imply that parents must learn that their child's disability prevents them from having all the things normal people have, that these children can't be a real part of our society. They must be separate even though it is bad and painful. But it isn't the job of a parent of a child with disabilities to accept things the way they are. It is our job to do anything we possibly can do to change things. (Statum, 1995, p. 68)

Siblings

Professionals, while providing services to the child with a disability, have also unintentionally overlooked siblings. Fortunately, professionals now have begun to address the significant need of siblings, and their sincere interest to be involved in the intervention program.

Siblings are curious about their brother's or sister's disability and genuinely want to increase their knowledge and understanding of their sibling's condition. Also, according to

Meyer (1993), "Nondisabled siblings frequently complain about people who view their sibling *as* the disability" (p. 85). Thus, siblings need more information as well as the skill to share with others what they have learned.

Several sibling programs have been established to provide brothers and sisters opportunities to meet others who share the experience of having a sibling with a disability (Meyer, Vadasay & Fewell, 1985; Powell & Ogle, 1985). Through these programs, "participants share strategies to address common sibling concerns, such as what to do when classmates make insensitive comments about people with disabilities or when siblings embarrass them in public" (Meyer, 1993, p. 84).

In spite of the challenges due to their brother's or sister's disability, there are unanticipated benefits that contribute to their lives (Gibbs, 1993; Meyer, 1993). Some of the reported sibling benefits of these shared experiences include increased understanding of other people, more tolerance and compassion, and greater appreciation of their own good health and intelligence (Grossman, 1972). After acquiring these (and other) benefits, "brothers and sisters frequently express pride in their siblings' accomplishments and view their siblings in terms of what they can do" (Meyer, 1993, p. 85).

Mothers

Mothers, like fathers and siblings, are individuals and respond accordingly. But there are also some experiences that are common to many mothers. It is not uncommon for some mothers to feel a personal responsibility for the their child's condition. They blame themselves for not having been more careful during pregnancy. They wonder if it is something they did, or perhaps something they didn't do. Thoughts such as these often result in feelings of self-recrimination and condemnation (Buscaglia, 1975).

Mothers often find their lives dramatically changed after the birth of a child with a disability. The woman who had been actively involved in the community, with personal interests, employment, and so forth, may find that her world becomes very small. Because of the demands of time, energy, and emotion, the mother may find that her whole life is changed, leaving little time for her own interests and needs. Burnout is often a consequence of this change in life circumstances (Berger, 1995).

As with the other family members, the mother will need to grieve her loss—the loss of the dream of the "perfect child." This may be complicated by the fact that mothers often feel they are responsible for helping other family members deal with their grief, and neglect their own need to grieve, thus prolonging it.

Community

> *Full inclusion affords children with disabilities an opportunity given to other people: to live a meaningful life. I know that every day Anna spends in an integrated environment is a meaningful day. Every transaction she has with another child counts for something. Every day she is teaching lessons that no one else can teach. She is bringing out the best in others who bring out the best in her. She deserves that opportunity, and so do they. (Statum, 1995, p. 68)*

As expected, parents and families are concerned with providing supportive and nurturing environments for their children with disabilities (Rainforth, York, & Macdonald, 1992).

The new IDEA legislation (PL 102-119) specifically ensures that professionals will address the issue of transition from early intervention programs for infants and toddlers to preschool programs. The smooth and successful transition of these children (and their families) from early intervention programs to community-based programs should be a primary concern of all individuals involved (Seed, 1988; Singer et al., 1993).

Parents and families are often concerned that children with disabilities will experience isolation from their nondisabled peers. The fact is that all children (disabled or not) can and do learn through shared experiences with their peers. In return, nondisabled peers also benefit and begin to recognize that these new friends are a part of their neighborhood. Several studies have shown that in integrated settings, nondisabled children develop at the expected rate, and children with disabilities make progress (McLean & Hanline, 1990; Odom & Strain, 1984). An important lesson is that children are cruel only because such experiences are lacking (Seed, 1988).

> *I withdrew her from the special center she had attended for several years and enrolled her in a Head Start program. Anna was the only child in her class in a wheelchair, the only one who couldn't speak. The teacher had never taught a child with severe disabilities before. That first morning when we came rolling into that room full of noisy, active 4-year-olds, the teacher said to me, "Go home and don't worry; everything will be fine." And it was. Whatever problems we had, we worked out together. By year's end, Anna was beginning to speak. And I learned that it doesn't take a special person to teach children with disabilities. It simply takes a special person to be a good teacher. (Statum, 1995, p. 66)*

Summary

The general perspectives held by professionals, communities, and families of children with disabilities have matured. No longer is the birth of a child with a disability viewed as a "burden." As families and parents are empowered through their experiences (e.g., coping, adapting, seeking support), they have become active leading members in their child's learning opportunities. Families have also learned to effectively implement strategies and techniques that best fit their families' goals and objectives.

All families, including families of children with disabilities, have hopes, dreams, and desires for their children. For families with children with disabilities these expectations are more difficult to attain. In order to pursue their goals, families and professionals must learn to work in a collaborative partnership. Together, professionals and parents must in turn learn how to be more respectful and genuinely sensitive in their collaborative partnership efforts. There is always an undying hope and belief that, as a result of their efforts, the community will accept their children with dignity and respect (Santelli, Turnbull, Lerner, & Marquis, 1993; Seed, 1988).

> *There is a hitherto unacknowledged place in the world for our children and we need to claim it. The current movement toward full inclusion gives us a hope that no other generation of parents of children with disabilities has had; the hope that when our children are grown they will be accepted as full members of the human community. We are luckier than we thought. (Statum, 1995, p. 68)*

Additional Resources

Families of Children with Disabilities

Books:

Alper, S. K., & Schloss, P. J. (1994). *Families of students with disabilities: Consultation and advocacy.*

This book is designed to help teachers assist the families of children with disabilities become full members in the educational process. It is a comprehensive look at this subject. 368 pp. ISBN: 0-205-14038-6.

> Longwood Division
> Allyn & Bacon Order Processing
> PO Box 10695
> Des Moines, IA 50381-0695

Buzzell, J. (1996). *School and family partnership: Case studies for special educators.*

This book is a collection of case studies to help prepare students for the real world of teaching. Each case is a short story that describes a problematic situation that a teacher has actually faced. It includes a number of cases that help special education students better understand these special families and develop skills they will need to be supportive. 160 pp. ISBN: 0-8273-7164-0. Instructors Guide ISBN: 0-8273-7164-0.

> Delmar Publishers
> PO Box 15015
> Albany, NY 12212-5015
> Phone: 800-824-5179

Curran, D. (1989). *Working with parents.* Circle Pines, MN: American Guidance Service.

Topics covered in this book for professionals working in the parent education field include: conducting groups that empower parents, reexamining traditional assumptions about parents, and listening to identify parents' needs.

Cutler, B. C. (1993). *You, your child, and "special education:" A guide to making the system work.* Baltimore, MD: Paul Brookes.

A handbook for parents describing and explaining the special education system. Topics covered: rights to education, school system's power structure, and effective strategies for dealing with school personnel.

Featherstone, H. (1980). *A difference in the family: Living with a disabled child.* New York: Penguin Books.

A woman shares her own personal story regarding the impact a disability has on the family as a whole as well as on each individual family member. She shares the family dynamics and frank discussion of their decisions regarding the child with a disability.

Harry, B. *Cultural diversity, families, and the special education system: Communication & empowerment.*

This timely and thought-provoking book explores the quadruple disadvantage faced by the parents of poor, minority, handicapped children whose first language is not that of the school that they attend. 296 pp. ISBN: 0-807-73119-6.

Teacher College Press
PO Box 20
Williston, VT 05495-0020
Phone: 800-575-6566

Kroth, R. (1996). *Communicating with parents of exceptional children* (3rd ed.).

Kroth's work in the area of parent involvement acted as a foundation for many other researchers and writers. You will see his influence in most major works in this area. Although this book was meant for those working with parents of special needs students in particular, it is also valuable in working with parents in general. He provides the reader with a philosophical basis for planning, as well as practical suggestions. This is a book that all educators interested in parent involvement need for their library. 250 pp. ISBN: 0-89108-248-4.

Love Publishing Co.
PO Box 22353
Denver, CO 80222
Phone: 303-757-2579

Lobato, D. J. (1990). *Brothers, sisters, and special needs: Information and activities for helping young siblings of children with chronic illness and developmental disabilities.* Baltimore: Paul Brookes.

This is a curriculum and activity guide for children 3 to 8 years of age with siblings who are disabled. Provides workshop activities to assist children in understanding their "disabilities."

Meyer, D. J., & Vadasy, P. F. (1994). *Sibshops: Workshops for siblings of children with special needs.* Baltimore, MD: Paul Brookes.

The easy-to-use Sibshop is a practical resource that brings together 8- to 13-year-olds to express their feelings about brothers and sisters with disabilities.

Powell, T. H., & Gallagher, P. A. (1993). *Brothers & sisters: A special part of exceptional families* (2nd ed.). Baltimore, MD: Paul Brookes.

This contains personal stories shared by brothers and sisters of exceptional siblings. Topics include sibling adjustment, effective listening, and innovative teaching programs.

Rainforth, B., York, J., & Macdonald, C. (1992). *Collaborative teams for students with severe disabilities: Integrating therapy and educational services.* Baltimore, MD: Paul Brookes.

A text on how to establish effective transdisciplinary teaming with professionals and parents. Various models of effective collaboration in educational settings are discussed.

Rosenkoetter, S., Hains, A., & Fowler, S. (1994). *Bridging early services for children with special needs and their families.* Baltimore, MD: Paul Brookes.

A practical guide for service providers via a step-by-step process of planning coordinated, uninterrupted services for children and their families. A series of case studies illustrate a variety of early childhood transitions.

Stainback, W. & Stainback, S. (1990). *Support networks for inclusive schooling: Interdependent integrated education.* Baltimore, MD: Paul Brookes.

Written for administrators, educators, parents, students, and interested citizens as a primary tool for developing schools into inclusive communities. A guide for designing classrooms where students are valued for their talents and not characterized only by their limitations.

Articles:

Davern, L. (1996). Listening to parents of children with disabilities. *Educational Leadership, 53*(7), 61–63.

Videos:

Parents' Views of Living with a Child with Disabilities

This video features candid interviews with parents of children with disabilities and shows the daily life conflicts and frustrations they encounter. (30 minutes, color). Purchase.

The Bureau for At-Risk Youth
645 New York Avenue
Huntington, NY 11743
Phone: 800-999-6884

Parenting Special Children

A two video set which discusses issues parents face when their newborn has health problems. It contains three interviews with parents of exceptional children. The video addresses the psychological stages that parents experience and discusses early intervention, communication with caregivers, applicable federal laws, and ways of dealing with health care professionals.

Organizations:

Council for Exceptional Children
1920 Association Drive
Reston, VA 22091
Phone: 703-620-3660

National Clearinghouse on Family Support and Children's Mental Health
Portland State University
PO Box 751
Portland, OR 97207-0751
Phone: 800-628-1696

National Information Center for Children and Youth with Disabilities
PO Box 1492
Washington, DC 20013
Phone: 800-999-5599

Websites:

The Arc (a national organization on mental retardation)
http://www.metronet.com/-thearc/welcome.html

The Council for Exceptional Children
http://www.cec.sped.org/

Disabilities Interest Group
http://www.wce.wwu.edu/info.html

Disability Resources
http://www.icdi.wvu.edu/Others.htm

EDLAW Home Page
http://www1.access.digex.net/~ed/awinc/

Family Village (new site with broad range of disability-related information for
   parents and professionals with lots of links to other sites)
http://familyvillage.wisc.edu/

Friends of Inclusion Resource Page
http://www.inclusion.com/resource.html

Internet Resources in Disability and Knowledgework
http://www.cais.net/danw//piduk/dlinks.html

Special Education Distance Learning Course
http://141.218.70.183/speddistedwww/independentsped.html

References

Americans with Disabilities Act of 1990, Pub. L. No. 101-336.

Bailey, E., & Bricker, D. (1984). The efficacy of early intervention for severely handicapped infants and young children. *Topics in Early Childhood Special Education, 4*(3), 30–51.

Berger, E. (1995). *Parents as partners in education: Families and schools working together* (4th ed.). New York: Merrill Publishing Co.

Boswell, B., & Schuffner, C. (1990). Families support inclusive schooling. In W. Stainback & S. Stainback (1990), *Support networks for inclusive schooling: Interdependent integrated education* (pp. 219–230). Baltimore, MD: Paul Brookes.

Buck, P. (1950). *The child who never grew.* New York: John Day.

Buscalglia, L. (1975). *The disabled and their parents.* Thorofare, NJ: Charles B. Slack, Inc.

DeGangi, G., Wietlisbach, S., Possison, S., Stein, E., & Royeen, C. (1994). The impact of culture and socioeconomic status on family–professional collaboration: Challenges and solutions. *Topics in Early Childhood Special Education, 14*(4), 503–520.

Dunst, C. J., Trivette, C. M., & Deal, A. G. (1988). *Enabling and empowering families: Principles and guidelines for practice.* Cambridge, MA: Brookline Books.

Education for All Handicapped Children Act (1976) (EHA), 20 U.S.C.A. 1400 *et seq.*

Farber, B. (1975). Family adaptations to severely mentally retarded children. In M. J. Begab & S. A. Richardson (Eds.), *The mentally retarded and society: A social science perspective* (pp. 247–266). Baltimore, MD: University Park Press.

Featherstone, H. (1980). *A difference in the family: Living with a disabled child.* New York: Penguin Books.

Fewell, R. (1986). A handicapped child in the family. In R. Fewell & P. Vadasy (Eds.), *Families of handicapped children: Needs and supports across the life span* (pp. 87–104). Austin, TX: PRO-ED.

Frey, K. S., Fewell, R. R., Vadasy, P. F., & Greenberg, M. T. (1989). Parental adjustment and changes in child outcome among families of young handicapped children. *Topics in Early Childhood Special Education, 8*(2), 38–57.

Gallagher, J., Cross, A., & Scharfman, W. (1981). Parental adaptation to a young handicapped child: The father's role. *Journal of the Division of Early Childhood, 3,* 3–4.

Gibbs, B. (1993). Providing support to sisters and brothers of children with disabilities. In G. Singer & L. Powers (1993), *Families, disability, and empowerment: Active coping skills and strategies for family interventions* (pp. 27–66). Baltimore, MD: Paul Brookes.

Goldenberg, I., & Goldenberg, H. (1980). *Family therapy: An overview.* Monterey, CA: Brooks/Cole Publishing Company.

Grossman, F. K. (1972). *Brothers and sisters of the retarded children: An exploratory study.* Syracuse, NY: Syracuse University Press.

Guralnick, M. (1990). Major accomplishments and future directions in early childhood mainstreaming. *Topics in Early Childhood Special Education, 10*(2), 1–17.

Hanson, M. J. (1985). Administration of private versus public early childhood special education programs. *Topics in Early Childhood Special Education, 5*(1), 25–38.

Hanson, M. J., Lynch, E. W., & Wayman, K. I. (1990). Honoring the cultural diversity of families when gathering data. *Topics in Early Childhood Special Education, 10*(1), 112–131.

Hawkins, N., Singer, G., & Nixon, C. (1993). Short-term behavioral counseling for families of persons with disabilities. In G. Singer & L. Powers (1993). *Families, disability, and empowerment: Active coping skills and strategies for family interventions* (pp. 317–341). Baltimore, MD: Paul Brookes.

Kirk, S. A., & Gallagher, J. J. (1989). *Educating exceptional children* (6th ed.). Boston: Houghton Mifflin.

Kubler-Ross, E. (1969). *Death and dying.* New York: Macmillan.

Lamb, M. E., & Meyer, D. J. (1991). Fathers of children with special needs. In M. Seligman (Ed.), *The family with a handicapped child* (pp. 151–179). Boston: Allyn & Bacon.

Lobato, D. J. (1990). *Brothers, sisters, and special needs: Information and activities for helping young siblings of children with chronic illness and developmental disabilities.* Baltimore: Paul Brookes.

Long, C., Artis, N., & Dobbins, N. (1993). The hospital: An important site for family-centered early inter-

vention. *Topics in Early Childhood Special Education, 13*(1), 106–199.

McLean, M., & Hanline, M. (1990). Providing early intervention services in integrated environments: Challenges and opportunities for the future. *Topics in Early Childhood Special Education, 10*(2), 62–77.

Meyer, D. J. (1986a). Fathers of children with special needs. In M. E. Lamb (Ed.), *The father's role: Applied perspectives* (pp. 227–254). New York: John Wiley & Sons.

Meyer, D. J. (1986b). Fathers of handicapped children. In R. Fewell & P. Vadsey (Eds.), *Families of handicapped children* (pp. 35–73). Austin, TX: PRO-ED.

Meyer, D. J. (1993). Lessons learned: Cognitive coping strategies of overlooked family members. In A. Turnbull et al. (Eds.), *Cognitive coping, families & disability* (pp. 81–92). Baltimore: Paul Brookes.

Meyer, D. J., Vadasy, P. F., & Fewell, R. R. (1985). *Sibshops: A handbook for implementing workshops for siblings of children with special needs.* Seattle: University of Washington Press.

Murray, J. N. (1980). *Developing assessment programs for the multi-handicapped child.* Springfield, IL: Charles C. Thomas.

Murray, J. N., & Cornell, C. J. (1981). Parentalplegia. *Psychology in the Schools, 18,* 201–207.

Nixon, C. (1993). Reducing self-blame and guilt in parents of children with severe disability. In G. Singer & L. Powers (1993), *Families, disability, and empowerment: Active coping skills and strategies for family interventions* (pp. 175–201). Baltimore, MD: Paul Brookes.

Odom, S., & Strain, P. (1984). Classroom-based social skills instruction for severely handicapped preschool children. *Topics in Early Childhood Special Education, 4*(3), 97–116.

Pearl, L. (1993). Providing family-centered early intervention. In W. Brown, S. Thurman & L. Pearl (1993), *Family-centered early intervention with infants & toddlers: Innovative cross-disciplinary approaches* (pp. 81–101). Baltimore, MD: Paul Brookes.

Pennsylvania Association for Retarded Children v. Commonwealth of Pennsylvania, 343 F. Supp. 279 (E.D.Pa., 1972).

Powell, T. H., & Ogle, P. A. (1985). *Brothers & sisters— A special part of exceptional families.* Baltimore: Paul Brookes.

Powers, L. (1993). Disability and grief: From tragedy to challenge. In G. Singer & L. Powers (1993), *Families, disability, and empowerment: Active coping skills and strategies for family interventions* (pp. 119–149). Baltimore, MD: Paul Brookes.

Rainforth, B., York, J., & Macdonald, C. (1992). *Collaborative teams for students with severe disabilities: Integrating therapy and educational services.* Baltimore, MD: Paul Brookes.

Ruder, M. (1993). The provision of early intervention and early childhood special education within community early childhood programs: Characteristics of effective service delivery. *Topics in Early Childhood Special Education, 13*(1), 19–37.

Salisbury, C. (1992). Parents as team members: Inclusive teams, collaborative outcomes. In B. Rainforth, J. York, & C. Macdonald (1992), *Collaborative teams for students with severe disabilities: Integrating therapy and educational services* (pp. 37–56). Baltimore, MD: Paul Brookes.

Santelli, B., Turnbull, A., Lerner, J., & Marquis, J. (1993). Parent to parent programs: A unique form of mutual support for families of persons with disabilities. In G. Singer & L. Powers (1993), *Families, disability, and empowerment: Active coping skills and strategies for family interventions* (pp. 27–66). Baltimore, MD: Paul Brookes.

Seed, P. (1988). *Children with profound handicaps: Parents' views and integration.* Philadelphia, PA: Falmer Press.

Singer, G., Irvin, L., Irvin, B., Hawkins, N., Hegreness, H., & Jackson, R. (1993). Helping families adapt positively to disability: Overcoming demoralization through community supports. In G. Singer & L. Powers (1993), *Families, disability, and empowerment: Active coping skills and strategies for family interventions* (pp. 67–83). Baltimore, MD: Paul Brookes.

Singer, G., & Powers, L. (1993). *Families, disability, and empowerment: Active coping skills and strategies for family interventions.* Baltimore, MD: Paul Brookes.

Statum, S. (1995). Inclusion: One parent's story. In P. Browning (Ed.) (1995), *Transition IV in Alabama: Profile of commitment.* State Conference Proceedings, January 1995 (pp. 65–68). Auburn, AL: Auburn University.

Todis, B., Irvin, L., Singer, G., & Yovanoff, P. (1993). The self-esteem parent program: Quantitative and qualitative evaluation of a cognitive-behavioral intervention. In G. Singer & L. Powers (1993), *Families, disability, and empowerment: Active coping skills and strategies for family interventions* (pp. 203–229). Baltimore, MD: Paul Brookes.

Turnbull, A. P., & Turnbull, H. R. (1990). *Families, professionals, and exceptionality: A special partnership* (2nd ed.). New York: Merrill Publishing Company.

Turnbull, A. P., Brotherson, M. J., & Summers, J. A. (1985). The impact of deinstitutionalization on families: A family systems approach. In R. H. Bruininks (Ed.), *Living and learning in the least restrictive environment* (pp. 115–152). Baltimore, MD: Paul Brookes.

Turnbull, H. R., Turnbull, A. P., & Wheat, M. (1982). Assumptions about parental participation: A legislative history. *Exceptional Education Quarterly, 3*(2), 1–8.

U.S. Department of Education. (1993). *Fifteenth annual report to Congress on the implementation of the Individuals with Disabilities Education Act.* Washington, DC: Government Printing Office.

Young, D., & Roopnarnine, J. (1994). Fathers' childcare involvement with children with and without disabilities. *Topics in Early Childhood Special Education, 14*(4), 488–502.

Family Involvement Models

In this chapter, three writers will identify different models of family/parent involvement in the schools. The models will cover programs that serve children from infant to fifteen years of age. The authors (McLean and Sandell) will identify national models or identify a model that can be used at any middle or secondary level (Johnston). Please keep in mind that these are only representatives of many models that are available for discussion. After reading the chapter, you should be able to:

- Identify various parent/family involvement models at the preschool, elementary, middle, and special education level
- Compare and contrast models in and between levels
- Recognize the components of successful parent/family involvement models
- Comprehend why one model may work at one level and not at another level

Family Involvement in Special Education

MARY MCLEAN

Cardinal Stritch College

Inclusion has made all children the concern of the "regular" classroom teacher. Unfortunately, most classroom teachers are not prepared to work with the parents of special needs children. The special education segment of this chapter shares a successful parent involvement model and other information that will be most helpful to educators.

Models of family involvement in Special Education have been strongly influenced by the legal system established by federal law, which regulates the education of students with disabilities. Chapter 10 will provide you with information on special education law and the parental rights which are assured through the law. The Individuals with Disabilities Education Act (IDEA), formerly known as the Education of the Handicapped Act, is the law which has had the greatest impact on the involvement of parents in the education of their children with disabilities. The reauthorization of this law in 1975 (PL 94-142) established the rights of students with disabilities to a free and appropriate public education. Prior to PL 94-142, parents were frequently turned away from public school programs which did not provide educational services for children with disabilities. As described in Chapter 10, this law also established procedural safeguards for parents, such as the right to access their child's educational records (and the right to limit access by others), the requirement of parental consent prior to initial evaluation and initial placement of a child in special education, and the right to written notice in the event that the school proposes to change or refuses to change services. Furthermore, in cases where a disagreement occurs between the parents and the school in relation to the child's educational program, the right to due process of law is assured.

The requirements of the law clearly have a significant impact on the relationship between parents of children with disabilities and school personnel, and, to a great degree, these requirements structure the interactions which occur. However, many programs have gone beyond the requirements of the law in providing services which are not only individualized to meet the needs of the child, but also individualized to meet the needs of the family. These programs see their role as one of providing support as the family undertakes activities necessary for family functioning, including the activities necessary to provide for the child with a disability. Such programs incorporate a *family-centered* philosophy.

Interestingly, two of the most recent amendments to IDEA which authorize services for infants and toddlers with disabilities, PL 99-457 and PL 102-119, incorporated aspects of a family-centered philosophy into the law. This law requires a "family-directed" assessment and the development of an Individualized Family Service Plan which identifies outcomes for the child *and* family as well as the services to be provided in order to facilitate these outcomes.

A Family Systems Conceptual Framework

During the late 1970s and early 1980s, family systems theory emerged as a foundation for intervention in the helping professions. Family systems theory views the family as a social system wherein all members have an impact on each other (Minuchin, 1974). When applied to special education, this theory emphasizes the idea that intervention with one family member will affect all members. In other words, professionals should recognize that the provision of special education services to a child not only affects the child, but will also affect family functioning in a manner which may be beneficial or detrimental.

Turnbull and Turnbull (1990) presented a family systems conceptual framework which incorporates information from family systems theory and the special education literature in order to provide a framework for evaluating the impact of special education services on family functioning. Applying this framework to the provision of educational services to children with disabilities leads the educator to consider the impact of educational activities on the family and to attempt to see the world from the family's perspective. The framework requires us to consider input variables, characteristics of family interactions, and life-cycle changes. It becomes apparent that each family is unique and complex; there will be considerable diversity among families in beliefs and values, in resources, in the challenges they face and in coping and interaction patterns of the family members. Furthermore, educational intervention will have an impact on the entire family system and will not be confined to the member with a disability. Families also change over time. Intervention systems will need to be able to accommodate changes in the family system which will impact the child with a disability. The reader is referred to Turnbull and Turnbull (1990) for more information on the family systems framework.

Family-Centered Intervention

As educators have become more aware of how families function and the impact of the family on the success of intervention efforts, a philosophy of intervention has emerged which is known as family-centered intervention. Family-centered philosophy moves intervention efforts from an agency-oriented approach to a family-oriented approach. It is eloquently described by the following passage from Turnbull and Summers (1985):

> *Copernicus came along and made a startling reversal—he put the sun in the center of the universe rather than the Earth. His declaration caused profound shock. The earth was not the epitome of creation; it was a planet like all other planets. The successful challenge to the entire system of ancient authority required a complete change in philosophical conception of the universe. This is rightly termed the "Copernican Revolution." Let's pause to consider what would happen if we had a Copernican Revolution in the field of disability. Visualize the concept: the family is the center of the universe and the service delivery system is one of the many planets revolving around it. Now visualize the service delivery system at the center and the family in orbit around it. Do you recognize the revolutionary change in perspective? We would move from an emphasis on parent involvement (i.e., parents participating in the program) to family support (i.e., programs providing a range of support services for families). This is not a semantic exercise—such a revolution leads us to a new set of assumptions and a new vista of options for service. (p.12)*

Within early intervention, many different terms have been used to describe this philosophy of family-centeredness: family-guided (Slentz & Bricker, 1992), family-focused (Bailey et al., 1986), and parent empowerment (Dunst, 1985; Dunst, Trivette, & Deal, 1988) are a few examples. Regardless of the terminology used, these philosophies have in common the idea that intervention should be provided in collaboration with family members, in a manner that facilitates the family's decision-making role, and in a manner that is in line with the family's priorities. To incorporate a family-centered philosophy, a paradigm shift must occur. Intervention must move away from being child-focused and agency-directed to being family-focused and, to a large extent, also family-directed. The following three programs exemplify a family-centered philosophy.

Models of Family-Centered Intervention

Project DAKOTA

Project DAKOTA began as a federally funded demonstration program in 1983 and currently is a private, non-profit agency serving children from birth to age three with delayed development or a disability in Dakota County, Minnesota. The stated mission of this project is to assist the family and community to promote optimal development of the child and reduce the negative effects of delay or disability.

A family-centered philosophy is evident throughout all aspects of assessment and intervention provided by Project DAKOTA. The following list of goals is taken from the final report for the project's federal funding (Kovach & Kjerland, 1986). The family-centered philosophy which forms the basis for this project is clearly evident in these goals.

- Parents should be provided opportunities for direct and meaningful participation throughout assessment and program planning. Staff act as consultants and collaborators with parents in order to promote parents' acquisition of knowledge, skill, and confidence.
- Staff resources and skills should supplement, not supplant, family and community resources.
- Intervention goals and strategies are to focus on child *and* family needs considered essential by parents.
- Families are to govern their investment of time and energy; the intervention program is shaped to fit the families' changing schedules, priorities, and energy level. *Families choose options for services from a service menu.*
- Intervention strategies should be a natural part of families' daily routines and fit comfortably into the routine interaction and style of the family.
- Community settings used by nondelayed peers are to be used in preference to specialized or segregated settings in order to increase the child's ability to function in less restrictive environments.
- Families are offered on-going information and assistance in using community resources to supplement their efforts.
- Consultation and assistance to parents, children, and community service providers is given in the settings where the skills are used or practiced.
- Optimal development of the child should be directed by parents' informed priorities following developmental assessments.

COACH

Choosing Options and Accommodations for Children (COACH) (Giangreco, Cloninger, & Iverson, 1993) is actually an assessment and planning tool for developing and implementing educational plans that meet the needs of students with moderate to severe disabilities in inclusive environments. COACH assists in planning for special education services to be provided in general education classrooms. It is chosen here as an example of family-centered special education services because of the emphasis placed on the family as "the cornerstone of relevant and longitudinal educational planning" (p. 6). One goal of COACH is to assist families in becoming partners with professionals in the educational process as well as becoming better consumers of the services provided to their children. The following five beliefs are specified as the basis for establishing partnerships between parents and professionals.

- Families know certain aspects of their children better than anyone else.
- Families have the greatest vested interest in seeing their children learn.
- The family is likely to be the only group of adults involved with a child's educational program throughout his or her entire school career.
- Families have the ability to influence positively the quality of educational services provided in their community.
- Families must live with the outcomes of decisions made by educational teams all day, everyday.

The COACH system begins with a Family Prioritization Interview which identifies family-chosen priorities for the students' educational program. This aspect of COACH establishes the role of the family as co-designer of the educational program rather than simply being asked to approve a program which was predetermined by professionals. COACH then utilizes collaborative teamwork, coordinated planning, and problem-solving strategies in the process of developing goals and objectives and determining options for addressing these goals and objectives in the general education setting.

Co-Instruction

As indicated above, the implementation of family-centered services requires professionals to make a shift from involving families in the approval of professionally-determined intervention plans to family involvement as partners throughout the entire assessment and intervention process. This shift has been difficult for some professionals since it may be very different in orientation from their preservice training and experience (Bailey, Buysse, Edmonson, & Smith, 1992).

One strategy for enhancing the ability of professionals to form partnerships with the families they serve is co-instruction in higher education. According to Whitehead and Sontag (1993), the primary purpose of co-instruction is to give students the consumer's perspective on intervention efforts. This broader perspective should result in increased sensitivity to the impact of their actions on families.

The participation of family members in the professional development of special education personnel is not particularly new; however, it has traditionally been accomplished through rather limited means such as a guest speaker or panel of parents; videotape or film portraying a family's story; or articles, poems, or books written by families (Featherstone, 1980; Fialka, 1994). There has been a recent increase in efforts, particularly in early intervention, to include family members much more extensively in the planning and implementation of both preservice and inservice training (Bailey, McWilliam, & Winton, 1992; Gilkerson, 1994; McBride, Sharp, Hains, & Whitehead, in press). *Recommended Practices,* published by the Division for Early Childhood of the Council for Exceptional Children, suggests that family members be involved in planning, implementing, and evaluating preservice curriculum and that families participate in the delivery of inservice training (Stayton & Miller, 1993). This trend toward family involvement in the training of professionals has brought about new meaning to the term *parent trainer* which, in the 1960s and 1970s, referred to a professional who taught parents how to teach their child. In the 1990s, *parent trainer* refers to a parent who has agreed to teach professionals about working with families.

According to McBride et al. (in press), approaches to co-instruction vary widely across personnel development programs. They suggest thinking of the various possible co-instruction roles as points on a continuum. Parents are frequently involved in courses related to working with families, but may also participate in coursework addressing assessment and curriculum. Parents may participate in limited activities or in every class session. Parents may provide only the family perspective or may also teach core content. Each situation will be different depending on the parent's experience and desire to participate, the content for instruction, and the strength and comfort level of the parent–faculty team.

Parents who are providing the family perspective may be asked to share their family's experience relative to a particular topic, such as receiving the initial diagnosis of disability, participating in assessment experiences, choosing intervention services, and so forth. This can be done in many ways—by using prepared speeches, slides or overheads, or informal conversation. Faculty can help family members determine their preferred mode of sharing experiences. An instructional videotape is now available to help parents in telling their stories (King, 1994).

REFLECTION...

Is co-instruction being used at your college or university? If not, describe the benefits of this model for your college or university. If yes, how could the model be strengthened at your school or university?

Some parents will gain a good deal of expertise as a result of their experience in parenting a child with a disability. These parents will have information to present on topics such as particular diagnoses and disabilities, medical procedures, aspects of the law, particular intervention strategies, funding mechanisms, and advocacy efforts. Demonstrating the expertise parents have to offer can be a very valuable lesson for professionals as they learn to work in partnership with families.

Co-instruction is a model of personnel development which has only recently begun to be utilized in preservice and inservice training. It occurs in many different forms and has the potential to impart the family's perspective to professionals who work with children. This ability to understand the world from the perspective of family members is critical to providing educational services to children and families that reflect a family-centered philosophy.

Summary

The three models described in this section reflect the family-centered approach. The models are attempts to improve the family's role in providing educational services for their children. It is important for all of us to continue to discover programs that work and look at ways to improve those programs or incorporate them into our own educational systems.

Family Involvement Models in Early Childhood Education

ELIZABETH J. SANDELL

Meld Director, Minneapolis, Minnesota

Early Childhood has long been the leader in parent involvement. They have long understood the importance of involving parents in their children's education.

Parent involvement in early childhood education programs is based on the importance of the parent's influence on the child's growth and development. Currently, there is an increase in the number and diversity of parent-involvement programs for the early years. In theory, most school staff members recognize the importance of home and school cooperation. In practice, there are a variety of programs that are implemented, but the long-term effectiveness of such programs is still being researched.

An examination of efforts which have demonstrated parent-involvement effectiveness reveals at least six qualities shared by successful family programs for the early childhood years:

1. Staff and sponsors take responsibility for providing comprehensive, flexible, and responsive programs.
2. Programs are marketed creatively and intentionally to their community. Service providers persevere in their outreach efforts.
3. Programs have strong theoretical foundations which organize their activities toward long-term prevention and empowerment.
4. Participants and staff trust and respect each other. Sponsors create accepting environments and build relationships with families.
5. Staff members deal with the child in the context of the family, neighborhood, and community. Several generations are involved with responding to the concerns of different individuals and populations.

6. Highly competent, energetic, committed, and responsible individuals are involved on the staff and as volunteers. Workers are allowed to make flexible, individualized decisions (Schorr, 1989).

Let's look at some of the model programs that connect families and schools.

AVANCE

AVANCE Family Support and Education Program is a private, non-profit organization whose main goal is to strengthen and support families. It was established in 1973 with funding from the Zale Foundation, as a comprehensive, community-based family-support program targeted for Latino populations. AVANCE is open to all families residing within designated boundaries of each project. In 1993–94, more than 6,000 adults and children received AVANCE services at more than forty-five sites. The program has expanded into twenty-four schools nationwide through the federal Even Start and Project First programs (Cohen, 1994).

Parents' and children's educational programs are usually offered in English and Spanish once a week for three hours for nine months. Bilingual parent educators explain topics in the parenting program, such as child growth and development, nutrition, health, language, and basic needs. During parent classes, children between birth and age four participate in early childhood education programming. Home visits are videotaped for parent self-observation. Other components of AVANCE offer social support, adult basic education, youth programs, and community empowerment. Families which complete the parenting education program can enroll in a family literacy program.

Evaluation of AVANCE has shown that parents demonstrated an increased knowledge and application of positive parenting skills. Parents were more likely to consider themselves teachers of their children. Parents indicated increased nurturing feelings toward their children and increased value of education for themselves and their children. They were less likely to express strict attitudes about discipline (Rodriguez & Cortez, 1988).

The AVANCE National Family Resource Center has disseminated information and provided training to people in more than forty states and in other parts of the world. Curriculum resources have been sold in fifteen states, and training has reached people from twenty-four states.

MELD

Since MELD (formerly Minnesota Early Learning Design) began in 1973 with a grant from the Lilly Endowment Fund, it has been committed to strengthening families. The goal of this non-profit corporation is to enhance the confidence and competence of parents by providing relevant information that is easily understood in a supportive atmosphere.

Parent facilitators have been trained to deliver MELD's program in more than one hundred agencies across the United States, Canada, Europe, and Australia. Sponsoring organizations include public agencies, hospitals and clinics, family service agencies, school-based programs, and others. Currently MELD and its partners serve over 4,000 parents each year. Over 40,000 parents have been served by the MELD network since 1975.

MELD programs bring together groups of parents with common needs. Most of MELD's programs focus on the child's first years. Groups meet either weekly or bi-weekly for two or more hours. The program lasts two years and is divided into four- or six-month phases. The long-term participation gives parents time to learn, grow, and become friends while solving problems and creating a healthy family.

The MELD philosophy suggests that parents can learn from each other, support each other, cooperate while maintaining their individuality, and make informed decisions. Respect and appreciation for the uniqueness of each individual is encouraged. MELD resources are designed to use the "peer self-help" group model of "parents helping parents." Experienced parents volunteer to facilitate groups and receive extensive training and support from MELD. Comprehensive curriculum materials include health, child guidance, child development, family management, and parent development. Materials are available specifically for (1) young, single parents (adolescent and other single mothers of children aged birth to five years); (2) young fathers; (3) adult parents in critical periods of transition (parents of children with special needs between birth and three years, parents who are deaf, first-time adult parents); and (4) recently immigrated populations (Southeast Asian Hmong and Latino populations). Many MELD programs are held in high school settings for adolescent parents.

MELD helps each affiliate site evaluate the program implementation and outcomes. Participation in the MELD New Parent program has enhanced parent attitudes and beliefs in authoritative child-rearing attitudes. Such attitudes have been associated with positive social and academic outcomes for children in other studies (Powell, 1990). In one study, teen mothers in MELD groups scored higher on an inventory of knowledge of child development and tended to continue enrollment in high school, compared to non-participating teen mothers (Rossmann & McCubbin, 1982; Miller, 1985).

Early Childhood Family Education

Minnesota Early Childhood Family Education (ECFE) is a program for any family with a child between birth and enrollment in kindergarten. The mission of ECFE is to strengthen families and support the ability of all parents to provide the best possible environment for the healthy growth and development of their children.

ECFE was developed through a series of pilot programs funded by the Minnesota Legislature from 1974 to 1983. In 1984, the Legislature made it possible for any school district to establish an ECFE program. During the 1993–94 school year, more than 258,000 children and parents participated in ECFE through programs in 369 school districts and the four tribal schools. More than 99 percent of the birth to four population in Minnesota had access to an ECFE program. ECFE programs are sponsored by a local school district's community education program. Participation by families is voluntary, and there are no eligibility guidelines (Goodson, Swartz, & Millsap, 1991). Trained staff including licensed teachers work

The typical ECFE schedule includes parent-child interaction, parenting education, and early child-hood education.

Parent–child interaction includes approximately 30 to 45 minutes for children and parents to participate together in activities. The experiences are designed to help children develop and to help parents understand their children's interests and abilities.

Parenting education is planned for a time between 60 to 90 minutes to provide an opportunity for adults to discuss family concerns, such as self-esteem, sibling rivalry, and nutrition. A licensed Parent Educator guides discussions and offers current information. Support and encouragement from other parents is an important part of this component.

Early childhood education is provided for children to have learning experiences with other children while their parents are in the parent education group. A licensed Early Childhood Teacher plans and supervises activities such as painting, block and truck play, reading, and puzzles.

FIGURE 9-1   Typical Components in an Early Childhood Family Education Session

Reprinted with permission from the Minnesota Department of Children, Families, & Learning, St. Paul.

with both children and parents. The general school-based program involves classes for both parent and child. Classes include parent–child interaction activities, early childhood educa-tion, and parent education groups. Some sessions are for specific audiences, such as hearing-impaired adults, single parents, fathers, or families from a variety of cultures. Other groups may have a specific focus, such as parenting infants, toddlers, or three- and four-year-olds.

Other features which may be available in many programs include educational home visits, sibling care, field trips, special family events, information and referral, and resource lending libraries for children and parents. Programs work closely with local agencies in-volved in education, health, and human services to assist parents and children in obtaining other needed services (Harvard Family Research Project, 1992).

Every program is required to have an advisory council, composed of a majority of par-ents who participate in the program. The councils assist in developing, planning, and mon-itoring the ECFE programs. The programs are funded with a combined local levy and state aid formula, which may be supplemented with registration fees and other sources. Services are offered free or for a nominal fee (Goodson et al., 1991).

Evaluation data for ECFE have shown that parents change perceptions and expecta-tions for themselves as parents and for their children as a result of participation in ECFE. Parents reported increased satisfaction with their parent roles resulting from the support of other parents and the increased skills and understandings acquired. Both children and schools benefit from a higher level of parental involvement that continues throughout the school years (Cooke, 1991, 1992). Current evaluation efforts focus on identification of strategies that work best with low-income, disadvantaged children within a universal ac-cess, collaborative program model.

> **REFLECTION...**
>
> ECFE is a Minnesota program. Although the program is acknowledged as an excellent state program, why do you think it has not been developed in other states? Are there parts of the program that limit its applicability across the country?

Parents as Teachers

The Parents as Teachers (PAT) program originated in Missouri. The program sends certified parent educators to visit expectant families at home and teach them how to be "their child's first teacher." The program is available to all first-time parents beginning during pregnancy and continuing until the child reaches age three years, regardless of socioeconomic or educational level.

PAT began with four pilot sites in Missouri in 1981 with funding from the Missouri Department of Elementary and Secondary Education and The Danforth Foundation, along with federal and local support. In 1984, PAT was adopted by the Missouri Legislature for use by 543 school districts throughout the state. School districts are mandated to offer PAT; however, family participation is voluntary. Funding is received from the State of Missouri based on the number of participants. PAT grew beyond Missouri to serve more than 250,000 families each year at 1,560 program sites in forty-three states, the District of Columbia, and four foreign countries in 1993. The program has been adapted for families in various circumstances, such as teen parents, Even Start and Head Start, child care centers, parents in the workplace, and Native American families.

The average private home-based contact with families is once a month for about an hour. PAT staff members also set up group parent group meetings, screen children for developmental and health problems, and link parents with other community resources. Information on child development is provided for each of five phases of development: birth to 6 weeks, 6 weeks to 8 months, 8 to 14 months, 14 to 24 months, 24 to 36 months (White, 1980).

Evaluations have indicated that parents like the program and that PAT children scored well above national norms on measures of school-related achievement: verbal ability, intelligence, language ability, achievement, and auditory comprehension. Parents who were involved in the PAT program continued to be more involved with their child's education after they began attending grade school. Parents of PAT children were significantly more likely than others to initiate requests for parent–teacher conferences during grade one. Areas most influenced by PAT participation and services were poor parent–child communication and developmental delays (Meyerhoff & White, 1986; Winter, 1991).

In 1987, a National Center on Parents as Teachers was established in Saint Louis, Missouri. Technical assistance and training is required to replicate the program. Parent educators who work in PAT sites are expected to complete PAT certification. Training includes parent empowerment, building on parent strengths, ways to observe and respond to parent–child interaction, and program evaluation.

Parent and Child Education

The Kentucky Parent and Child Education (PACE) program was started with legislation in 1986 as the first family literacy program in the United States funded entirely with state funds. Family literacy programs view the family as a unit and seek to address educational, social, health, and employment issues in a comprehensive manner. The program expanded from six pilot sites during the 1986–87 school year to thirty-six sites during 1994–95. It has been replicated by several states and served as one of the models for the federally-funded Even Start program (State of Kentucky, 1995).

PACE provides remediation for undereducated parents and quality early childhood education programming for their young children at the same time. The program's goals include raising the educational level of parents, enhancing parenting skills, preparing young children for school success, and demonstrating to parents their power to affect their child's ability to learn.

Parents and children attend the program at least three days a week. The four program components actively engage learners in (1) adult education, (2) early childhood education, (3) parent and child time, and (4) parent education time.

The adult education component encompasses basic skills or preparation for the GED, in addition to critical thinking, problem solving, and acquiring interpersonal skills. The early childhood education component focuses on the child's broad developmental skills. The parent and child time is a time when family members work and play together as a family unit. Parents and children become partners in education. The parent education time is a blend of parent support and parent education to meet the needs of the participating families.

PACE teachers are required to participate in ten to fifteen days of training each school year. Teacher certification is not a state requirement for PACE teachers; however, local school districts have the option of requiring certification.

All local school districts are eligible to apply for funds through a competitive grants process. Priority is based on the educational need of the adult population, the incidence of unemployment, and the percentage of school children eligible for free or reduced-priced meals. The total enrollment for the school year 1992–93 was 531 adults and 517 children, representing 512 families.

REFLECTION...

These five models generally have been or could be replicated nationally. What do all these models have in common?

In a study which included twelve PACE programs, several conclusions were reached. Parents gain confidence in their own abilities, their children's abilities, and in the operations of the schools. This confidence translates into parents becoming more involved in their children's school activities and more intent on pursuing their own work-related goals. Parents in family literacy programs learn the value of education along with their children and, in turn, the family becomes mutually supportive in their educational efforts. Children in fam-

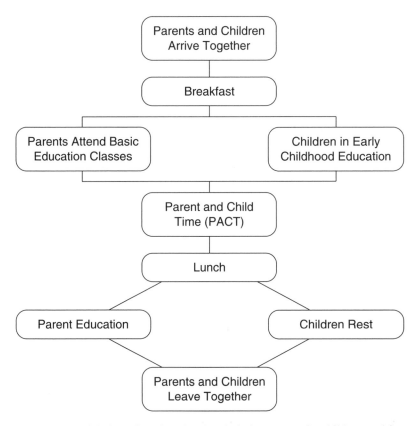

The Pace schedule includes educational periods for parents, for children, and for families together.

**FIGURE 9-2   Typical Schedule for a Day at Parent and Child
            Education Family Literacy Programs**

From: The Kentucky Department for Adult Education and Literacy, Workforce Development Cabinet.

ily literacy programs have more success in school than their older siblings who do not participate in family literacy programs (Seaman, Popp, & Darling, 1991).

Summary

The five models discussed in this chapter represent some ways to involve parents in early childhood education settings. There are many other program models that could be identified, but space limits our discussion of them. However, in closing, there are two important points to remember: (1) These are critical years for a child's development and the more parents can be involved, the better for both parent and child, and (2) Most, if not all, programs offer an environment where parents and children can play or interact together. The models may give you additional ideas that teachers and administrators can use in their programs to help parents feel they are a part of their child's life at school.

Family Involvement Models in Elementary Education

ELIZABETH J. SANDELL

Elementary educators have long understood the importance of parent involvement in the success of children. What we have sometimes forgotten is that parent involvement also means the improvement of the entire system.

Parent involvement in education has repeatedly been linked to higher achievement and many other positive outcomes for students and their families. There are many families and schools that are working to achieve meaningful parent involvement in education. A variety of models are available that encourage families to get involved in different ways in their children's education.

MegaSkills®

The MegaSkills® program is a teacher training program created by the Home and School Institute, which began in 1964. It develops the educational relationship between school and home in support of children's achievement (Rich, 1992).

The home–school learning materials are designed to increase positive parent–child interaction through activities that take fifteen to twenty minutes and cost little money. Materials are available for pre-kindergarten through secondary school children and families.

MegaSkills® is conducted in forty-eight states and reaches more than 110,000 parents from diverse cultural, social, and economic backgrounds. Materials are also available in Spanish. The leaders training program can be delivered to the school district location and is designed to prepare for a series of parent-involvement workshops. Participants are certified as MegaSkills® leaders after conducting five field workshops.

Evaluation data indicate that the MegaSkills® program results in higher student interest in school, higher attendance, more student time spent on homework, higher academic achievement, higher scores on statewide achievement tests, improved student school behavior, and increased parent involvement in education (Austin Independent School District, 1993; Bond, 1990; Edge, 1994).

The basic values, attitudes and behaviors that determine a child's achievement in school:

Confidence	feeling able to do it
Motivation	wanting to do it
Effort	being willing to work hard
Responsibility	doing what's right
Initiative	moving into action
Perseverance	completing what you start
Caring	showing concern for others
Teamwork	working with others
Common sense	using good judgment
Problem solving	putting what you know and what you can do into action
Focus	concentrating with a goal in mind

FIGURE 9-3   MegaSkills® List

From MegaSkills® Education Center of Home and School Institute, Inc., 1500 Massachusetts Avenue, NW, Washington, DC 20005.

The School Development Program

Founded by James Comer in 1968 at two elementary schools in New Haven, Connecticut, the School Development Program (SDP) is based on the belief that the relationship between the school and the family is the critical factor in the school success of children (Comer, 1988). The model emphasizes a comprehensive, collaborative, consensus-based, no-fault approach to problem solving. Teams of stakeholders create comprehensive school plans, including specific goals, periodic assessment and modification, and staff development. The framework includes three governance strategies for running schools: (1) the School Development Team represents parents, teachers, administrators, and support staff as it coordinates the school's program; (2) Parent Program members coordinate parent involvement programs at every level of school activity; and (3) the Mental Health Team addresses issues regarding social services problems. Often, home–school coordinators are employed to bridge the gap between the school and community (Comer, 1993).

The SDP has been replicated specifically in more than 150 schools in fourteen school districts in twelve states and in the District of Columbia. The current SDP expansion plan includes five major components: (1) direct training of school districts, (2) teacher training model, (3) school administrator training model, (4) partnerships with schools of education and state departments of education, and (5) training via telecommunications.

Statistically significant gains were found in targeted academic and social areas—language arts, reading, mathematics, attendance, and school behavior—compared to similar schools not using the model. Furthermore, Comer (1993) found about 1 percent to 5 percent of a school's parents are likely to be engaged as active decision-makers; 10 percent to 25 percent are likely to serve as volunteers in school buildings; and 50 percent to 100 percent are likely to simply participate in parent–teacher conferences and social events.

Center for the Improvement of Child Caring (CICC)

Since the Center for the Improvement of Child Caring (CICC) began in 1974, it has been committed to building the capacities of local communities to train, educate, and support parents. The goal of this non-profit community service, research, and training organization is to assist parents in becoming more effective and humane and to support the instructors who work with families. Parent education staff have been trained to deliver CICC's programs in more than 2000 agencies across the United States (Alvy, 1994).

Most of CICC's focus is on the parent–child relationship. The Effective Black Parenting Program is one of several programs that CICC created. The Effective Black Parenting Program helps African-American parents face the challenges of raising proud and achieving children in a healthy, balanced family environment. Authoritative family leadership is encouraged. In group settings, parents are taught to use basic child behavior management skills, such as effective praise, verbal confrontation, time-out, and a point-system reward method. The program is taught as a fifteen-week, three hours-per-session class for groups of parents. There is a special one-day seminar version of the program for large numbers of parents (between 50 and 500). The Effective Black Parenting Program is used in communities in more than forty states.

In field testing for the past ten years, Effective Black Parenting has been shown to enhance family relationships, reduce child behavior problems, decrease harsh disciplinary practices, and improve parents' mental well-being (Alvy et al., 1988).

CICC delivers a variety of parenting skill-building programs and instructor training workshops, and distributes a wide array of parent and family life training materials. It also sponsors the National Parenting Instructors Association to provide networking, communication, advocacy, and training.

Families Together with Schools (FT)

Families Together with Schools (FT) (formerly FAST: Families and Schools Together) was established in 1988 in Madison, Wisconsin, as a substance-abuse prevention program in collaboration with elementary schools, mental health agencies, substance-abuse prevention agencies, and families. In 1993, Family Service America began a national replication effort under its new name. The main goals are: (1) to enhance family functioning by strengthening the parent and child relationship and by empowering parents as primary prevention agents for their own children; (2) to prevent the child from experiencing school failure by improving the child's behavior and performance in school, making parents partners in the educa-

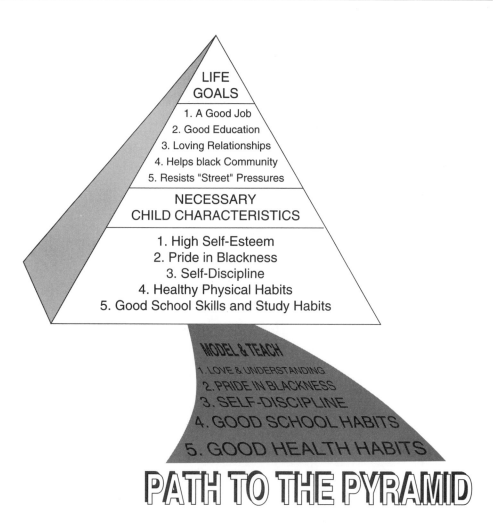

FIGURE 9-4   CICC's "Path to the Pyramid" encourages parents to model and teach in order to develop necessary child characteristics which lead to fulfilling life goals.

Reprinted with permission from The Center for the Improvement of Child Caring.

tional process, and increasing the family's sense of affiliation with the school; (3) to prevent substance abuse by the child and the family by increasing knowledge and awareness of alcohol and other drugs and their impact on child development, and by linking families to assessment and treatment services; and (4) to reduce stress experienced by parents and children in daily situations by developing a support group for parents of at-risk children, linking families to community resources and services, and building the self-esteem of each family member.

Participation in the Families Together program is voluntary. The program is designed for education and community agency professionals from collaborating organizations to meet for eight weeks with eight to twelve entire families together for these components: (1) family meal time, (2) family recreation time, (3) quality one-to-one parent–child time, and (4) parent support meeting. After the two months of weekly meetings, family teams meet monthly for two years in a parent-led follow up program (McDonald et al., 1991).

As a school-based program which targets children in kindergarten through grade three, the neighborhood of the school determines its community and the school staff select its participants. FT has trained staff from approximately 100 agencies and 113 schools. FT is developing adaptations of the program for pre-kindergarten children and for middle-school students and their families. Replication programs have involved families from diverse backgrounds, including Native American families, Spanish-speaking families, African-American families, and rural white families.

Evaluation of FT involving more than 1,000 families has indicated improvements in self-esteem, attention span, family closeness, and family–school involvement. Consumer satisfaction feedback from parents has been positive (McDonald & Billingham, 1993). Technical assistance training and consultants are available from the Family Service America office. The formal training program, held at the local program site, is required in order to replicate FT because of its foundation in family therapy principles.

Teachers Involve Parents in Schoolwork (TIPS)

Epstein developed the Teachers Involve Parents in Schoolwork (TIPS) program for the elementary grades at Johns Hopkins University, Baltimore, Maryland, in 1987. In 1992, the program expanded to the middle grades in collaboration with the Fund for Educational Excellence. Two Baltimore schools served as test sites from 1990 to 1994, with grants from the U.S. Department of Education, Office of Educational Research and Improvement, and the Edna McConnell Clark Foundation. The goals of the TIPS process are: (1) to increase parent awareness of their children's schoolwork, (2) to increase parent involvement in their children's learning activities at home that are linked to classwork, (3) to increase students' ability and willingness to talk about schoolwork at home and the frequency of this happening, and (4) to improve students' skills and homework completion in specific subjects (Epstein, 1993).

The TIPS program is organized to establish regular communication between school and home concerning language arts and science/health (developed in 1993) and math (developed in 1994). The interactive homework process keeps families involved in their children's learning and progress in school. TIPS' interactive activities require students to show, share, demonstrate, interview, gather reactions, and interact in other ways with their family members (Epstein, 1992).

TIPS is not a "canned curriculum." The TIPS activities are assigned by teachers; students conduct them with their families once a week or twice a month. The program may be adopted by one teacher, an entire school, or an entire district. Any teacher may obtain the TIPS manuals and adopt or adapt TIPS. Training by outsiders is not necessary, although the co-authors of the TIPS program are available occasionally as consultants. However, the au-

Name: _____ Date: _____

Grouping ABC's and Animals

Dear Parent/Guardian:

In science we are learning about systems of classification. This activity asks me to develop a classification system. I hope that you enjoy completing this activity with me. This assignment is due: _____

Sincerely, _____ (student's signature)

- -

PROCEDURE

1. Print the entire alphabet in capital letters here:

2. Make up a rule for separating all the letters of the alphabet into three groups. Write your rule here:

3. Below, give each group a title, then list the letters in each group under the title.

Group 1: _____	Group 2: _____	Group 3: _____

- -

FAMILY INTERVIEW   Who are you interviewing?   _____

Explain your system of alphabet classification to a family member, then ask: Can you think of a different rule to make three groups out of all letters of the alphabet?

Group 1: _____	Group 2: _____	Group 3: _____

- -

TRY THIS!

You are a scientist who has been asked to classify a dog, a cat, a fish, a butterfly, a moth, and a turtle. Would you put them all in the same group or in different groups?

1. Explain your classification system for these animals.

I would group these animals into _____ (how many?) groups called:

My reasons are:

FIGURE 9-5   The TIPS process includes interactive homework assignments for students and parents together.

From: J. Epstein, V. Jackson, and K. Salinas. (1992). *Teachers Involve Parents in Schoolwork (TIPS) Interactive Homework.* Baltimore, MD: Johns Hopkins University, Center on Families, Communities, Schools, and Children's Learning. Adapted for *Instructor* magazine, Nov/Dec 1993, pp. 16–18.

SCHOOL-HOME CONNECTION

	Group	Reason
dog		
cat		
fish		
butterfly		
moth		
turtle		

- -

FAMILY INTERVIEW   Who are you interviewing? _____

Ask your family to name six other animals. Will the animals work in the classification system you used above or do you need new categories? Fill in the chart to show your answer.

Animal	Group	Reason

- -

HOME-TO-SCHOOL COMMUNICATION

Dear Family Member:

Please record your reactions to your child's work with this activity. Write *yes* or *no* for each statement.

_____ My child understood the assignment and was able to discuss it.

_____ My child and I enjoyed this activity.

_____ This assignment helped me know what my child is learning in science.

Other comments:

_____
(parent/guardian's signature)

Instructor Reproducible • Permission Granted to Duplicate

FIGURE 9-5   *Continued*

thors suggest that funds for staff development be used to support teachers to select, design, and print TIPS activities for their own schools (Epstein, Jackson, & Salinas, 1992).

Resource materials include the manuals for teachers in the elementary and middle grades and packets of prototype interactive homework assignments in the three subject areas. Packets include prototype math activities for kindergarten through grade eight, basic skills for the middle grades, science for elementary grade three, 120 science examples for grades six through eight, and 120 language arts activities for grades six through eight. Computer disk forms of TIPS are available.

Evaluations of the TIPS program indicate that students, parents, and teachers find TIPS activities stimulating. Teachers report that more students completed TIPS homework than other homework. Parents and students reported positive interactions and learning (Rioux & Berla, 1993).

REFLECTION...

Compare these program models to the early childhood program models. What are the similarities? What are the differences? Try to take components of all the programs (early childhood education and elementary) and develop a program for ages 6 weeks to 12 years.

Summary

These five models are representative of attempts by educators, parents, and other community people to involve parents with the schools. The elementary years are critical times when parents should be and are very involved in their child's education. It is important to have different options available to help parents be involved.

Family Involvement Models in Middle Schools

J. HOWARD JOHNSTON

University of South Florida

Middle schools are based on a student-centered concept. It is a team approach and parent involvement is a logical extension of the team concept. In the past, parent involvement has dropped significantly as the children get older, and by the time they reach the middle grades, those parents who appeared in great numbers in first grade have dwindled to a few. These developmentally sensitive years demand the team effort of educators and parents.

There is one irrefutable truth in education: parent involvement in the schools promotes student success and achievement. This involvement is at the very heart of most school reform efforts and is advocated directly by local, state, and national policy makers. Indeed, one of the national educational goals states explicitly that, "By the year 2000, all schools will promote partnerships that will increase parent involvement and participation in promoting the social, emotional and academic growth of children" (*Goals 2000,* 1994).

For middle school educators, however, it is also widely believed that securing parent involvement is extraordinarily difficult, largely because students would prefer that their parents *not* exert a strong influence on their educational or social lives. While there may be a grain of truth in that belief, the positive effect of parent involvement at the middle school level is so clear that schools and communities should work diligently to overcome impediments to parental involvement and promote significant, important parental participation in the school life of their children.

The Outcomes of Involvement

Although less research has been done at the middle level than the elementary level, the results are clear: family and parent involvement in the educational process has a profound and positive effect on students' achievement, school adjustment, and behavior. Conversely, students whose families do not collaborate with schools are likely to exhibit more behavior problems, experience achievement difficulties, and drop out of school. For those families that establish strong partnerships with the school, the benefits are obvious and enduring.

Higher Aspirations and Stronger Commitment to Life-Long Education

Students whose families are involved in school tend to express higher aspirations for their careers and educational attainment. Such students are inclined to set career goals in scientific, technical, and professional areas and to aspire to higher levels of education and training than students who see their parents as uncommitted to the school. Students with involved parents are much more likely to be motivated to continue their education beyond high school. At the middle level, students of involved parents are more likely to select advanced courses in high school and engage in more academically rigorous programs of study. These students also tend to use terms such as *learners* or *students* when asked to describe themselves and their strengths.

Avoidance of High-Risk Behaviors

Alcohol use, drug use, crime, and other anti-social behavior decreases among adolescents as the amount of family participation in schooling increases. Students of involved parents tend to avoid high-risk and other dangerous behavior at the same time they form relations with peers who also avoid problematic situations and behavior. When students of involved parents do encounter difficulty in school or in the community, it is likely to be a single incident rather than part of a pattern of disruptive or delinquent behavior. These encounters, if handled in a supportive way by the parents, are treated as learning experiences by the student and are unlikely to be repeated.

Increased School/Community Participation

Students with involved parents are nearly three times more likely than young people with uninvolved parents to engage in school-sponsored activities in athletics, the arts, academics, or service clubs and projects. Because these activities tend to help the student bond more closely to the school, this type of engagement virtually ensures that students will become supportive, contributing members of the school community. Typically, students who feel "connected" to the school exhibit higher achievement, better social adaptability, and high levels of self-esteem.

Avoidance of School Problems

As might be expected, students with involved parents are much less likely than those with non-involved parents to have problems in school. Students whose parents are uninvolved are twice as likely as those with involved parents to be in the bottom half of their class or repeat a grade. In fact, there is some indication that the degree of parent involvement is more significant in the school success of students than virtually any other variable, including race, social class, or native language.

> ### REFLECTION...
>
> The middle school population is young adolescents. How do parents get involved, yet give this age some autonomy, without "embarrassing" their adolescents? Given what you know about adolescent development, how do parents walk this fine line compared to elementary school involvement?

Impediments to Family Involvement

With such compelling evidence of its positive effects, it seems that every parent would want to work diligently to become involved in his or her child's education program, and that every school would make meaningful parent participation its first priority goal. Unfortunately, the impediments to parent engagement are just as clear as the benefits of that involvement.

Low Involvement and Declining Involvement

Less than half of most young people in middle schools report that their parents are actively engaged in their school programs. In a recent survey by the Search Institute, only 42 percent of 6–12th grade students report that their parents assist with homework. Similarly, 39 percent say their parents seldom or never attend parent meetings at their school.

As students get older, that involvement declines dramatically. All types of parent involvement decline between the sixth and twelfth grade, by which time a relatively small minority of students benefit from active parent involvement, ranging from simply inquiring about the student's school work to actually helping with that work and participating in parent functions at the school.

Because students with high participating parents tend to have fewer school problems, most parent contact with the school is among parents whose students are doing well. The parents most disinclined to become involved with the school are those whose children are having academic or behavioral difficulty. Thus, the students who need the strongest collaboration between home and school are often those least likely to have it.

Poor Communication between Home and School

Often, parents who are not involved in their child's education avoid contact with the school because their prior contacts have been unproductive, frustrating, or hostile. If parents believe that contacts with the school will result in their being blamed for problems, judged as inept or incompetent as parents, or confronted with demands that they simply cannot meet, they can hardly be expected to seek such contacts with any enthusiasm.

Destructive patterns can evolve in a number of ways, but, typically, they begin when parents are poorly informed about ways they can help their children be successful. If the child is not successful, and the parent does not know what to do to support success, the parent feels helpless and powerless. When the school continues to convey messages about their child's problems without offering concrete ways for the parents to support the child's achievement, parents often become withdrawn, defensive, resentful, and hostile.

Different Expectations Regarding Norms and Behaviors

Often, parents and schools disagree markedly on what is best for students. In most instances, these differences arise because of beliefs, values, and norms that are held by the parents and the teachers involved. Behavior that may be perfectly normal or acceptable to one person may be viewed as inappropriate, irresponsible, or immoral by someone who holds a different value perspective. Attempts to solve problems between the home and the school are often thwarted by the clash of two essentially reasonable but contradictory value positions.

A common example is found when students have obligations outside school which conflict with school requirements. Many young people, particularly those from impoverished backgrounds, are expected to contribute to the family's economic resources in very material ways. This might take an indirect form, such as providing child care for a younger brother or sister, or very direct forms, such as contributing income from a job.

If a student arrives at school late every morning because he must provide before-school child care for younger siblings, or a student fails to complete homework because she must work after school and in the evenings, school personnel can easily interpret these actions as indicators that the parents lack interest in their child's school program or are not supportive of school achievement. The parents, on the other hand, might see the school's efforts to compel on-time attendance or punish the student for lack of homework as unfair and unnecessary intrusions into the family's economic life. Resolution of these kinds of conflicts are made even more difficult because each party in the disagreement sees their position, quite accurately, as reasonable and right.

Trivialization of the Parent's Role

As students progress through the curriculum, the nature of the subject matter becomes more specialized and more difficult. Parents who were able to provide academic assistance for their children throughout the elementary grades may suddenly, despite their best intentions, find themselves unprepared to help their children with their school work. These conditions are particularly prevalent among parents who were not themselves successful in school, especially those who are impoverished, are limited in English proficiency, or have dropped out of school.

Even among well-educated parents, the increasing complexity of the curriculum, especially in mathematics and science, may make their direct assistance impossible. For virtually all parents, skill deficiencies associated with sophisticated technology use may render them helpless to provide their child with direct assistance in fields which make heavy use of technology.

For other parents, though, especially those with few resources or little personal success with schooling, the potential for such direct assistance may be even more limited. The frustrations produced by their own difficulties with school are reinforced by their inability to help their children be successful.

Despite the best of intentions, schools often reinforce this sense of powerlessness by the nature of the tasks they ask parents to perform in support of their child's education. Volunteering in the library, or sponsoring fund-raising events, or serving on the PTA council, while important for the overall functioning of the school, may be seen as trivial by parents because, while these activities support the *school* and its programs, they do little to support, directly, the success of a parent's individual child. Rather than volunteering for an activity that is seen as having a relatively low pay-off for the success of their own child, many parents simply withdraw from school participation by the middle school years.

Conflict between Family Resources and School Requirements

Often, schools require parents to become involved in their child's educational program in ways that are beyond their personal or material resources. The parents' inability to provide such resources may result in a student failing to meet course requirements or to engage in the kind of co-curricular activity that is clearly associated with school success. While it is patently unfair for a student to be punished with poor grades or lack of access to school, such occurrences may be quite inadvertent on the part of the school.

One common example of these conflicts may be found in project assignments. Students who come from families with sufficient resources may have access to both the money and the parental assistance that will enhance their likelihood of success. Most educators have seen professional-quality projects submitted for science fairs, social studies courses, or other academic competitions and have harbored the vague hunch that the student submitting the work received more than a reasonable amount of adult assistance in completing the assignment.

Other examples are not so obvious. Simple assignments which assume the presence of certain resources (books, a TV, newspapers in the home, an employed parent, transportation) may be impossible for a student to complete. If the student is embarrassed by his family circumstances, a teacher may never know what is preventing the successful completion of assigned work. All the teacher sees is a consistent pattern of non-compliance with respect to out-of-class assignments.

REFLECTION...

We, as educators, often hear the comment by teachers, "The parents whose children are not a problem show up for open house, parent-teacher conferences, etc. Why can't we get the "other" parents involved? We could really 'help' them, and they could help us with their child."

A Model for Family Involvement

As with all levels of schooling, it is no longer sufficient to provide opportunities for parent participation in the education of their children, or to admonish parents about its importance and their responsibility to provide it. Instead, schools must *actively support* parent participation in tangible ways. First, they must work to mediate the barriers to home–school collaboration outlined above; then, they must take a proactive stance in helping families to become major participants in the education and school lives of middle school students.

A model proposed by Shea and Bauer (1991) for the support of special education parents can easily be adapted to support parent involvement in middle schools. The model is hierarchical, requiring that conditions at each level be satisfied before parental participation at the next level can be expected.

1. *Crisis assistance.* Among the families of middle school students, crises often arise that prevent either the parents or the student from focusing their attention on school or academic matters. For many students, divorce, substance abuse, legal troubles, family financial difficulties, and a host of other problems make school-related problems appear trivial indeed. While schools can often do little to resolve specific crises that exist outside of their domains of influence, they can do several things which help solve problems, or at least keep them from becoming worse.

   a. *Referrals.* Often, when families confront a crisis, they are not sure what resources are available for help. Schools which support parental participation keep themselves well-informed about the support services that are available in a community to assist families in crisis. Since family crises are often first noticed in school, or even reported to a child's teacher or counselor, it is important that everyone in the school be aware of the range of social services available and be equipped with information about contacting those services. Spouse abuse, arrests of older siblings, drug-related crime, pregnancy, forced eviction, and a host of other problems seem far removed from the purview of the school, but it is essential that school personnel be able to direct families to the available support and assistance in their community. Without the resolution of these crises, students affected by them are likely to remain unsuccessful in school.

b. *Do no harm.* The physician's Hippocratic oath stipulates that the first criterion to be applied in selecting a treatment for a patient is that it "do no harm." Schools would be well advised to follow the same policy for students in crisis. Often, school policies or practices exacerbate family crises, sometimes to the point of overwhelming a student so that he or she drops out of school. An attendance policy which punishes a student for staying home to care for a seriously ill parent or sibling, a grading policy which does not permit make-up work for a student who has been in foster care or some other emergency care facility, a teacher who makes insensitive jokes about jails and convicts in front of students with an incarcerated parent or sibling may be sufficient to convince a student that the school is "part of the problem" and needs to be avoided.

To avoid doing harm, teachers must be alert to the signals students may give that they are in distress: excessive absence, extreme fatigue, changes in mood or disposition, extreme irritability, dramatic physical changes such as sudden weight gain or loss, or evidence of abuse. Then, in a gentle and sympathetic way, teachers must be able to express their concern to the student and offer to secure help if it is needed. Although specific assistance needs to be provided by specially trained professionals in accordance with district policy and state law, initial training in sensitive observation and first-line interviewing skills should be a fundamental part of every teacher's inservice development.

Fortunately, genuine crises are rare among most students, so teachers are not often called upon to confront them. Sensitivity and commitment to the success of every student, however, will help assure that the school is seen as a helpful resource in a crisis rather than an aggravating factor.

2. *Information and resources.* For most parents, the most important form of support a school can provide is in the form of information. The nature of that information is crucial, though, in supporting parent participation. Information should be specifically related to the child, his or her program, and his or her performance in it. General information about the school is not particularly interesting to most parents. If their child is not involved in the new physical science program, for example, they are not especially keen to receive a lot of information about it. At the same time, they are vitally interested in the programs their children are participating in, the services that are available to him or her, and the way the child is performing in school. Many parents find traditional "open house" a waste of time; the school showcases *its* achievements without providing specific information to parents about *their child's* achievement.

Information shared with parents should be routine, balanced, and specific. Advances in technology now permit teachers to select comments from extensive menus to produce detailed progress reports for parents; report cards can now carry extensive comments about a student's work and achievement. Informal notes can supplement routine communication in order to note a special achievement or a special problem the child is facing.

In each type of communication, parents should be told what they can do to help their child perform more effectively in school. A problem should not be identified without providing the parent with direction on how to correct it. Once again, the use of technology makes it possible for teachers to select from a menu of suggestions that will provide specific guidance as they promote school success at home.

3. *Supporting parent engagement.* Beyond information, it is important to help parents develop skills of effective parenting and support for their children. These skills not only help parents work more effectively to resolve the problems of adolescence, which often divert attention from school achievement, but also provide them with the support and encouragement they need to parent their children in these demanding times.

   a. *Parenting and supportive skills.* Parent training can be offered by the school not only to enhance the overall effectiveness of the parents, but to help them develop the skills which will support their child's success and achievement. This training may be general (such as effective parenting skills) or quite specific, focusing on a specific need in the school (such as helping SLD students with homework, or how to start planning for high school course selection).

   The most effective parent training is provided when it is planned by parents and professionals who are committed to the success of the community's children. When parents are involved in planning and delivering the training, the school can be sure it is topical, relevant, and interesting to parents. The use of parents also broadens the scope of community resources that can be used, including other community agencies or individual experts on specific topics.

   b. *Social/emotional support systems.* Parenting in modern America can be a lonely and difficult job. Many parents are single and are solely responsible for their children. Most Americans no longer live in tightly knit communities where extended family and kin provide support and assistance in raising children. All parents are coping with new influences and demands on their children which are often beyond the parents' control.

   The school can play a valuable role in providing a center for social and emotional support of parents. Schools can help parents organize support groups where individual parents can receive help from a group of people who share common interests and concerns. Although these groups work best when they are organized by parents themselves, the school might begin the process by inviting parents to consider forming such a group to help each other through the tumultuous times of adolescence and early adulthood.

   c. *Enabling activities.* It is essential that the school not only encourage parent involvement, but remove barriers and impediments to parent participation. Scheduling meetings that respect parents' work schedules, or providing phone access to teachers or counselors at predictable times enable parents to remain in touch with the school. Some districts have even run the school buses on "back to school" night in order to serve poor parents who do not have access to transportation. Similarly, a child-care service at the school during parent meeting times may allow parents with younger children to attend events they might otherwise miss. Other districts where students are bused great distances may conduct parent conferences in the churches and community centers in the school's community, rather than trying to get parents to travel to attend school functions. In short, it is essential for schools to assess all of their practices, identify those which stand in the way of meaningful parent participation and work to change or eliminate them. Most importantly, though, the school must demonstrate a genuine commitment to securing parent involvement.

4. *Securing support for school programs and operations.* When crises have been resolved, parents are well informed, and they feel supported by the school with the monumental job of raising adolescent children, *then* they are ready to support the school's programs and operations by volunteering their time and effort, sharing their resources, and participating in the governance of the school. Once again, schools must work carefully to provide opportunities for parent involvement and service that do not discriminate against any particular parent or group. As a beginning, parents should be surveyed to determine what their strengths are and what kinds of contributions they can make to support the school. Often, parents, particularly those who are poorly educated, are reluctant to volunteer because they are not certain what they could possibly do to enhance the school's program. However, many of them possess skills and strengths which can contribute much to the school if they were asked to do so.

In one school, a group of parents with limited English proficiency might work with a teacher after school to provide Spanish language tutorials for students studying that language. The parents benefit from interaction with English-speaking students, and the school benefits from a rich instructional resource. In another setting, recent immigrants might stage a "culture festival" which raises money for the school's library; still another school could recruit retirees to teach craft courses in sewing and carpentry; yet another may use the Internet to put students in touch with parents who work in specialized and advanced technical fields and who are willing to serve as mentors to students who share a common interest. Imagination and commitment to securing meaningful participation will lead schools to create numerous opportunities that are mutually beneficial and which enhance student success.

Contextual Considerations

In planning any parent involvement program, it is very important to consider the environment and context in which the school operates. It may not be necessary to provide transportation and child care to secure parent attendance in an affluent school, but it may be necessary to plan conference dates and school activities far ahead of time to accommodate busy professional calendars. In some communities, particularly those populated heavily by recent immigrants from Third World countries or by adults with low rates of literacy, communication with the home may have to proceed through informal means: a network of parents who speak the native language of the other parents, a church, or a social group. Many schools produce and duplicate tapes and videos regarding parent involvement, ensuring that parents who are not literate in English are not excluded from meaningful school participation.

The most important consideration, though, is that the school understand its community, its culture, and its needs in order to provide opportunities and support for parent involvement. No single set of practices works equally well for all parents and all communities. Each school community, indeed each family, is unique, with special needs, interests, resources, and commitments. Part of a school's commitment to the diversity which has come to characterize the American school system must be a strong, explicit, and sincere commitment to supporting families and students, regardless of their economic, social, or educational circumstances.

The Model in Operation

The model outlined above looks quite different in each school setting. However, in a successful parent involvement program, it is essential that each component of the model be in place for the community served by that school. The following example shows how one middle level school, located on the suburban fringe of a large city, supports significant parent involvement.

Lee Junior High School serves eleven hundred students in grades seven through nine. Located in an older suburb near a large midwestern city, Lee's student population reflects the diversity of its community. Nearly a third of its students are African American, 20 percent are Hispanic, 40 percent Caucasian, and 10 percent Asian and Pacific Islander. Virtually all of its Hispanic and Asian students are recent refugees and immigrants from Central America and Southeast Asia. Just under a third of the students qualify for free or reduced-price lunch; ESOL programs are provided for approximately 15 percent of the students. Lee provides a comprehensive parent involvement program which is designed to accommodate the need of diverse groups in the community and support student achievement.

Crisis Assistance

Lee's "Assistance Line" is staffed by parent volunteers who have a directory of community services available for virtually any kind of family difficulty. The line's volunteers, parents and retirees from the surrounding area, are trained to make referrals, but not to engage in counseling or other direct assistance. For times when the assistance line is not covered, a recording device allows parents to leave questions which can be answered when a volunteer is present. The line is not used in the case of emergencies.

In addition, Lee's staff and faculty are provided with directories and contact numbers of social service agencies, clinics, shelters, and a variety of other community resources which can guide them if a parent seeks help during a conference or phone call. Under the laws of the state in which Lee is located, teachers are protected from liability in making such recommendations, and they are required by law to report suspected child abuse to a specific governmental authority for investigation.

Lee's faculty has also conducted a "family impact assessment" of the policies and practices in their school, particularly those affecting attendance and grading. They attempted to identify those practices which might have a substantially negative impact on families who are coping with other difficulties, and have either modified those policies and practices or developed procedures whereby a student can be granted relief from punitive policies while involved in a family crisis. Faculty have also been trained by the counselors to conduct interviews of students who appear to be experiencing some form of stress or difficulty. Normally, these students are referred to a counselor for additional consultation and assistance.

Information

Lee's information plan is comprehensive, systematic, and responsive to changing conditions in a student's performance or program. It is designed to share important information and provide opportunities for parents to contact teachers and administrators who work with their child.

Each year, an orientation packet is sent to each parent in the school. It includes a school-year calendar which lists meetings, significant dates, and tips to parents for remaining engaged in the education of their child. This calendar includes a description of school policies, rules, and expectations. It also contains course descriptions; information about the school's support services, such as counseling and special education; and its co-curricular and arts programs. Every significant parent meeting is listed for the entire year, as are special training sessions, parent support/social groups, and special "booster" activities, such as band parents or math club parents. The calendar is a comprehensive planning resource for parents and includes significant dates for each grade level. Eighth grade parents are advised that the grade level dance is from 6:00 until 9:00 P.M.; ninth grade parents are informed about "moving-up" ceremonies. In this way, information is not distributed haphazardly throughout the year, nor does the school depend on students to keep parents informed of special school events.

Also in the orientation packet, parents will find a print-out of their child's schedule and the name of each of his or her teachers. In addition, the teacher's planning period and the school's phone number is listed so that parents know when it is best to contact them. Each teacher also posts "phone conference appointment hours" in the school office so that student assistants can schedule parent calls at times other than the planning period.

Progress reports are very detailed, with the aid of a computer program designed specifically for the task. Teachers can select from hundreds of descriptive comments in all areas of student performance, behavior, or social adjustment. After selecting a descriptive comment, they are given another menu of recommended actions for parents to take in order to correct a problem or support a student's strength. Progress reports end with an invitation to contact the teachers with questions, and a reminder about the teacher's conference hours and phone number.

Report cards also provide for extensive comments, and both report card and midterm progress reports are kept in a cumulative computer file so that parents and teachers can review student progress at any time.

Parent conferences are held twice each year, early in the fall and in the middle of the spring semester. They are scheduled between 3:00 and 9:00 P.M. so that working parents may attend. At the beginning of each year, every teacher is provided with a print-out of computer labels for each student, bearing their parents' names and home address. This allows teachers to write informal notes to parents quickly and easily without having to look up an address.

Recently, Lee has begun experimenting with technologically enhanced communication, including a computerized bulletin board, which may be accessed through one of the popular on-line computer services. Information about the school, its programs, calendar, events, and services is available twenty-four hours a day to parents or students who need it for planning or decision making. It has also begun producing a weekly show called "Focus on Lee," which is aired over the community's cable TV, public access channels. This show replaces much of the "show and tell" about the school that is normally conducted at open houses. Videos may be borrowed for home viewing or for use by community groups. All of Lee's publications are available in Spanish and Vietnamese, translated by parent volunteers, and special editions of its videos are translated into each language as well. Anticipating an upgrade of its phone system, Lee is also planning to provide "voice mail" boxes for each of its teachers which will allow them to leave or receive messages from parents and students without going through the school's cumbersome switchboard.

Supporting Parent Involvement and Securing Assistance for the School

Lee seeks to provide opportunities for all forms of parent involvement. To that end, its parent council has provided a large array of opportunities and services for parents.

In addition to a host of specialized "booster" groups, which support everything from band to basketball and computer club, the school invites parent participation in its Foundation, an independently chartered organization devoted to supporting the school through fund raising and sponsorship of specific activities. The Foundation provides specialized equipment for the computer and video facilities, offers mini-grants to teachers to encourage innovation and advanced training, and provides financial support for students who may not be able to afford specific school activities, such as the purchase of a yearbook or the expense of a class trip.

The parent council also organizes orientation meetings for parents of incoming seventh graders, parent-training sessions, support groups, and numerous other opportunities based on a needs assessment conducted by the group. Every parent in the school is asked to volunteer ten hours of service per year, although some are not able to do any and some do much more. These volunteer resources are used to support telephone trees to disseminate information about upcoming meetings, translation services, and a variety of other activities.

For all school-sponsored activities, parents organize a ride share program for parents who lack transportation, and the student council provides child care at the school site for parents who are unable to find or afford babysitters.

The school also supports parents indirectly by providing academic support for students whose families may not be able to do so. An after-school "homework club" is available for all students, staffed by parent volunteers, teachers, and students who use it as an opportunity to fulfill a community service requirement for graduation. In addition, the after-school latch-key program, sponsored in conjunction with a local community agency, is operated in the school building. This program offers tutorial assistance, service opportunities, and educational programs in technology, sports, and the arts.

In conclusion, by studying carefully the needs of its community, mobilizing committed parents who are willing to serve in leadership capacities, and creating both opportunities for and the expectation of parent participation, Lee has established a comprehensive, effective parent engagement program. Most important, it is a dynamic program; it changes constantly to adjust to new needs and opportunities in the community. Such a comprehensive program obviously requires the attention, commitment, and support of school personnel, but by creating a school culture which nurtures parent involvement, the school is able to provide high quality service to parents and students without additional money—just a deeply committed *human* resource.

Conclusion

The models of parent involvement for special educators, early childhood, elementary, and middle school are just that—models. In schools today, there are variations on the models, other models, and teachers, parents, administrators, students, and other community members trying to get families involved in schools in a variety of ways. The ultimate reason, obviously, is that students do better in school when their parents and/or families are involved.

Recommended Activities

1. We know there are more models or examples of programs that involve parents/families in the school. Identify two other models or examples currently being used in your state or region.
2. Identify schools or programs that are using any of the models presented in this chapter. Have teachers or administrators that are using those models come into the class to discuss the model presented and how it is being specifically used.
3. Develop your own model(s) of what you think a successful parent/family involvement program should look like in the schools.
4. Write to the organizations that have developed the various models to obtain detailed information about how the models work.
5. Discuss family system theory. Is the theory identified in other parts of this book? What is it and how do psychiatrists or psychologists use it?

Additional Resources

Family Involvement: Special Education, Early Childhood, Elementary and Middle School

Organizations:

AVANCE-Hasbro National Family Resource Center
Suite 310, 301 South Frio
San Antonio, TX 78207
Phone: 210-270-4630
FAX: 210-270-4612

Center on Families, Schools
  and Children's Learning
Johns Hopkins University
3505 N. Charles Street
Baltimore, MD 21218
Phone: 410-332-4575

ECFE
Minnesota Department of Education
992 Capitol Square Building
550 Cedar Street
Saint Paul, MN 55101
Phone: 612-296-6130
FAX: 612-297-5695

Family Literacy Branch Department for
  Adult Education and Literacy
Third floor, Capital Plaza Tower
500 Mero Street
Frankfort, KY 40601
Phone: 502-564-5114
FAX: 502-564-5436

Home and School Institute MegaSkills Center
1500 Massachusetts Avenue, NW
Washington, DC 20009
Phone: 202-466-3633

MELD
123 North Third Street, Suite 507
Minneapolis, MN, 55401
Phone: 612-332-7562
FAX: 612-344-1959
Email: MELDCTRL@aol.com.

National Committee for Citizens in Education Center
  for Law and Education
1875 Connecticut Avenue, NW, Suite 510
Washington, DC 20009
Phone: 202-462-7688

National Middle School Association
2600 Corporate Exchange Drive, Suite 370
Columbus, OH 43231
Phone: 614-895-4730

Parents as Teachers National Center, Inc.
10176 Corporate Square Drive
Saint Louis, MO 63146
Phone: 314/432-4330
FAX: 314-432-8963

The Search Institute
Suite 210, 700 South Third Street
Minneapolis, MN 55415
Phone: 612-376-8955

References

Alvy, K. T. (1994). *Parent training today: A social necessity.* Studio City, CA: Center for the Improvement of Child Caring.

Alvy, K. T., & M. Marigna. (1985). *CICC's effective black parenting program: Instructor's manual.* Studio City, CA: Center for the Improvement of Child Caring.

Alvy, K. T., et al. (1988). *Effects of a culturally-appropriate black parent training program on parental attitudes and practices, parental mental health, and child behavior outcomes in inner-city Black families.* Studio City, CA: Center for the Improvement of Child Caring.

Austin Independent School District, Office of Research and Evaluation. (1993). *Megaskills.* Austin, TX: Austin Independent School District.

Bailey, D. B., Buysse, V., Edmonson, R., & Smith, T. M. (1992). Creating family-centered services in early intervention: Perceptions of professionals in four states. *Exceptional Children, 58,* 298–308.

Bailey, D. B., McWilliam, P. J., & Winton, P. J. (1992). Building family-centered practices in early intervention: A team-based model for change. *Infants and Young Children, 5,* 73–82.

Bailey, D. B., Simeonsson, R. J., Winton, P. J., Huntington, G. S., Comfort, M., Isbell, P. (1986). Family-focused intervention: A functional model for planning, implementing and evaluating individual family services in early intervention. *Journal of the Division for Early Childhood, 10,* 156–171.

Bond, C. L., and others. (1990). *Evaluation report: Learning is homegrown workshop series.* Memphis, TN: Center for Research in Educational Policy, College of Education, Memphis State University.

Clark, R. E. (1983). *Family life and school achievement.* Chicago: University of Chicago Press.

Cohen, D. L. (1994, October 19). Teach their parents well. *Education Week, 14*(7), 30–32.

Comer, J. P. (1988). Educating poor minority children. *Scientific American, 259*(5), 42–48.

Comer, J. P. (1991). *A brief history and summary of the school development program.* New Haven, CT: Yale Child Study Center.

Comer, J. P. (1993). *School power: Implications of an intervention project.* New York, NY: Free Press.

Cooke, B. L. (1991). *Does participation in early childhood family education impact parent involvement in the elementary years?* Saint Paul, MN: State of Minnesota, Minnesota Department of Education.

Cooke, B. L. (1992). *Changing times, changing families: Minnesota early childhood family education parent outcome interview study.* Saint Paul, MN: State of Minnesota, Minnesota Department of Education.

Dunst, C. J. (1985). Rethinking early intervention. *Analysis and Intervention in Developmental Disabilities, 5,* 165–201.

Dunst, C. J., Trivette, C. M., & Deal, A. G. (1988). *Enabling and empowering families: Principles and guidelines for practice.* Cambridge, MA: Brookline Books.

Edge, D. (1994). *Executive summary: Evaluation results of the Maupin MegaSkills program.* Louisville, KY: University of Louisville.

Epstein, J. L. (1992). In Hyman, C. S. (Ed.), *The school–community cookbook: Recipes for success-*

ful projects in the schools. Baltimore, MD: Fund for Educational Excellence.

Epstein, J. L. (1993). School and family partnerships. *Instructor, 103*(2), 73–76.

Epstein, J. L., Jackson, V. E., & Salinas, K. C. (1992). *The TIPS manual for teachers: Language arts and science/health interactive homework in the middle grades.* Baltimore, MD: Center on Families, Communities, Schools, and Children's Learning, The Johns Hopkins University.

Featherstone, H. (1980). *A difference in the family: Living with a disabled child.* New York: Penguin Books.

Fialka, J. (1994). You can make a difference in our lives. *Early-On Michigan, 3*(4), 6–11.

Giangreco, M. F., Cloninger, C. J., & Iverson, V. S. (1993). *Choosing options and accommodations for children: A guide to planning inclusive education.* Baltimore, MD: Paul H. Brookes.

Gilkerson, L. (1994). Supporting parents in leadership roles. *Zero to Three, 14*(4), 23–24.

Goodson, B. D., Swartz, J. P., & Millsap, M. A. (1991). Working with families: Promising programs to help parents support children's learning. *Equity and Choice, 7*(2/3), 97–107.

Harvard Family Research Project. (1992). *Pioneering states: Innovative family support and education programs.* Cambridge, MA: Harvard Graduate School of Education.

Johnston, J. H. (1990). *The new American family and the school.* Columbus, OH: National Middle School Association.

King, S. (1994). *Telling your family story: Parents as presenters.* Madison, WI: Wisconsin Personnel Development Project, Waisman Center, University of Wisconsin–Madison.

Kovach, J., & Kjerland, L. (1986). *Final report: Project DAKOTA 1983–1986.* Fagan, MN: DAKOTA, Inc.

Kristensen, N. (1989). *A guide for developing early childhood family education programs.* Saint Paul, MN: State of Minnesota, Department of Education.

McBride, S. L., Sharp, L., Hains, A. H., & Whitehead, A. (in press). Parents as co-instructors in preservice training: A pathway to family-centered practice. *Journal of Early Intervention.*

McDonald, L., & Billingham, S. (1993). *Families and schools together: Final report.* Washington, DC: U.S. Office of Human Development, Administration on Children and Families.

McDonald, L., et al. (1991). Families and schools together: An innovative substance abuse prevention program. *Social Work in Education, 13*(2), 118–128.

Meyerhoff, M. K., & White, B. L. (1986). New parents as teachers. *Educational Leadership, 44*(3), 42–46.

Miller, S. (1985). *Report to the Ford Foundation.* New York, NY: Ford Foundation.

Minuchin, S. (1974). *Families and family therapy.* Cambridge, MA: Harvard University Press.

Powell, D. R. (1990). *The role of information and social support in the transition to parenthood: A study of MELD.* Speech given for the 1990 Family Resource Coalition Conference, Chicago, IL.

Rich, D. (1992). *MegaSkills.* New York, NY: Houghton Mifflin.

Rioux, W., & Berla, N. (Eds.). (1993). *Innovations in parent and family involvement.* Princeton Junction, NJ: Eye on Education.

Rodriguez, G. G., & Cortez, C. P. (1988). The evaluation experience of the AVANCE parent–child education program. In H. B. Weiss & F. H. Jacobs (1988), *Evaluating family programs.* New York: Aldine de Gruyter.

Rossmann, M. M., & McCubbin, H. I. (1982). *Report to Minnesota early learning design: Young moms groups* (Pilot Study and Evaluation Design). Minneapolis, MN: Minnesota Early Learning Design.

Schorr, L. (1989). *Within our reach: Breaking the cycle of disadvantage.* New York: Achor Books, Doubleday.

Seaman, D., Popp, B., & Darling, S. (1991). *Follow-up study of the impact of the Kenan Trust model for family literacy.* Louisville, KY: National Center for Family Literacy.

Shea, T. M., & Bauer, A. M. (1991). *Parents and teachers of children with disabilities* (2nd ed.). Boston: Allyn and Bacon.

Slentz, K. L., & Bricker, D. B. (1992). Family-guided assessment for IFSP development: Jumping off the family assessment bandwagon. *Journal of Early Intervention, 16*, 11–19.

State of Kentucky. (1995). *PACE: Parent and child education handbook.* Frankfort, KY: State of Kentucky, Department for Adult Education and Literacy.

Stayton, V., & Miller, P. (1993). Personnel competence. In DEC Task Force on Recommended Practices, *DEC recommended practices: Indicators of quality in programs for infants and young children with special needs and their families.* Reston, VA: Council for Exceptional Children.

The Goals 2000: Educate America Act. (1994, April 11). *Washington Social Legislation Bulletin, 33,* 31.

Turnbull, A. P., & Summers, J. A. (1985). *From parent involvement to family support: Evolution to revolution.* Paper presented at the Down Syndrome State-of-the-Art Conference, Boston, MA.

Turnbull, A. P., & Turnbull, H. R. (1990). *Families, professionals, and exceptionality: A special partnership.* Columbus, OH: Merrill.

White, B. L. (1980). *A parent's guide to the first three years.* Englewood Cliffs, NJ: Prentice-Hall.

Whitehead, A., & Sontag, J. (1993). *Co-instruction: A case study.* Madison, WI: Wisconsin Personnel Development Project, Waisman Center, University of Wisconsin-Madison.

Winter, M. (1991, February). *An overview and discussion of parents as teachers: A parent education project for the state of Missouri.* Speech given for First Impressions, Denver, CO.

Chapter *10*

Education Law and Parental Rights

GLORIA JEAN THOMAS
University of North Dakota

In this chapter, the author will present information on the legal rights and responsibilities of parents and schools. The author will describe the history of the legislation
between the home and the school. Actual court cases, as well as case studies, will be
cited as they relate to issues such as curriculum, special education, students' rights,
harassment, and liability.

After reading the chapter, the student should be able to:

- Discuss the history of the legal relationship between parents and schools
- Identify the origins of local taxes for schools, compulsory attendance laws, aca-
demic standards for schools, and state credentials for teachers
- Understand how the issue of religion has been a constant source of tension be-
tween parents and schools
- Recognize the significance of sexual harassment lawsuits in the K–12 school
system today
- Comprehend the significance of *Brown* v. *Board of Education of Topeka, Kansas*
(1954) in relation to school and parents, then and now
- Distinguish between school rights and student rights
- Understand the effect Title IX has had on extracurricular issues
- Differentiate between discrimination and harassment

Parents have always been a child's first teachers. Only in recent history have governments
assumed responsibility for much of a child's formal education. Even when schools are organized, however, parents retain their rights to influence and guide a child's upbringing.
This chapter discusses the legal rights and responsibilities of parents and schools in today's
litigious society. The history of the legal relationship between parents and schools will first
be explained, followed by a discussion of the legal role of the states in the education of their
citizens. Court cases will be used to demonstrate the role of the federal and state courts in
resolving disputes between parents and schools. Issues to be discussed include compulsory
attendance, vaccinations, the curriculum, religious exercises, school fees, special education, student rights, liability, and discrimination. A sample case will conclude each section.

History of the Legal Relationship between Parents and Schools

In 1642 the colonial legislature of Massachusetts Bay became concerned that parents were
so busy eking out a survival in the harsh New World that they were shirking their responsibilities to educate their children. Children who were not taught to read the Bible were sure
to fall prey to "ye olde deluder Satan." Therefore, the legislature passed a statute charging
all parents to see to the education of their children. In 1647 the legislature required towns
of fifty households to appoint a teacher and towns of one hundred households to build a

school. Taxes could be levied to support these schools, which were not only to ensure that children could read the scriptures but to facilitate a literate society for the good of the colony. Thus, these laws became the first compulsory education laws, the first school funding laws, and the first official recognition of a legal relationship between schools and parents.

However, the legal rights of parents for the education of their children predate any written law. From the beginning of time, parents have been a child's first teachers, assuming responsibility for instructing the child in survival skills and tribal or community ethics to enable society to exist and perpetuate. Because the right of parents to guide the upbringing and education of their children is recognized as natural and inherent, that right is regarded as fundamental for citizens of the United States.

Fundamental rights are those rights that citizens of this country take for granted because they have always existed in a free society. Other fundamental rights include the right to marry whomever one chooses (or not to marry), the right to have children (or not to have children), and the right to choose one's job, career, or profession. These rights are not written down in any federal or state constitution or statute. Yet, they are protected as if written into the United States Constitution, the supreme law of the land. Therefore, the right of parents to guide the upbringing and education of their children is a protected right.

The legal status of children as minors means that children under the age of majority (age 18 for most purposes in the United States) are not expected to have adult judgment to determine what is best for their own welfare. Because minors are not considered capable under the law of exercising responsibility for their own decisions, laws prohibit them from signing binding contracts, from buying harmful substances (such as alcohol and tobacco products), and from being held to the criminal and civil codes of law as adults. Children are under the protection of their parents, who are charged with ensuring the safety and welfare, including the education, of their minor children.

Because parents have the ultimate legal authority for the education of children, the role of schools is *in loco parentis* (in place of the parent). The concept of *in loco parentis* dates back to old English law that allowed schoolmasters to have power over pupil conduct. However, the schoolmaster had only that portion of parental powers necessary for the conduct of the school. Parents could never give up all authority over their child because of the "natural relation of parent and child…the tenderness which the parent feels for his offspring, an affection ever on the alert, and acting rather by instinct than reasoning" (*Lander* v. *Seaver,* 1859).

Therefore, when children go to school, the school as an entity and teachers as individuals are *in loco parentis* to them. They are responsible for the safety, welfare, and education of the child in place of the parents. However, parents do not abdicate their ultimate authority over the upbringing of their children simply because they comply with state compulsory attendance laws by sending their children to school.

The issue becomes one of finding the balance between the school's right and responsibility, delegated to it by the state, to prepare children to be knowledgeable, productive citizens of a democratic society and the parents' right and responsibility, inherent because of their being parents, to guide the upbringing of their children. All legal issues involving parents and schools are based on the tension between these two sets of rights and responsibilities. However, the states have delegated these rights and responsibilities to the schools.

> **REFLECTION...**
>
> Should the rights of parents or the rights of schools weigh more heavily when a dispute reaches the courts? What else needs to be considered?

State Constitutions and Education

Education is not mentioned in the United States Constitution, perhaps by conscious design but more probably because the writers of the Constitution had themselves been educated in private schools, by tutors, and by self learning. The idea of public schools, even though in existence since the Massachusetts Bay Colony time, had not become universally accepted. In the late 1700s, a few pauper schools existed for the children of the poor, orphans, and other wards of the colonies, but education was generally a private concern of parents.

However, interpretation of the Tenth Amendment gradually resulted in education becoming the responsibility of the states. The Reserved Powers Clause of the Tenth Amendment meant that education would come under the authority of the states:

> *The powers not delegated to the United States by the Constitution, nor prohibited by it to the States, are reserved to the States respectively, or to the people.*

Over time, the states recognized the importance of education for all children if the experiment in democracy was to succeed. Colonial legislatures wrote education into their state constitutions. Later, territorial legislatures were required to include provisions for education in their constitutions prior to applying for statehood. Most territorial authorities followed the lead of older states, resulting in the education clauses in many state constitutions being worded very similarly. The North Dakota Constitution, written in 1889, is similar to that of many states admitted to the Union after the Civil War. Article VIII, with variations, could be found in the constitutions of many states:

> *Section 1. A high degree of intelligence, patriotism, integrity and morality on the part of every voter in a government by the people being necessary in order to insure the continuance of that government and the prosperity and happiness of the people, the legislative assembly shall make provision for the establishment and maintenance of a system of public schools which shall be open to all children of the state of North Dakota and free from sectarian control. This legislative requirement shall be irrevocable without the consent of the United States and the people of North Dakota.*
>
> *Section 2. The legislative assembly shall provide for a uniform system of free public schools throughout the state, beginning with the primary and extending through all grades up to and including schools of higher education, except that the legislative assembly may authorize tuition, fees and service charges to assist in the financing of public schools of higher education.*

After writing lofty ideals into their constitutions, most states did not get involved in the local control of schools for many years. Frontier villages were so isolated that parents were the only teachers, fundraisers, architects, builders, administrators, and evaluators for tiny, one-room schoolhouses. As communities grew and state governments became more organized and stable, the role of the states, as defined in state constitutions, became important.

State Legislatures and Education

From the days of the Massachusetts Bay Colony, state legislatures assumed limited responsibility for the schools. As populations of cities grew, the problems of low educational standards, inconsistency in curricula, lack of training for teachers, inconsistent school funding, and lack of school governance structure became apparent. Relying on state constitutions that indicated state responsibility for schools, state legislatures slowly became involved in schools.

In the 1800s, reformers such as Horace Mann and Charles Barnard took their causes to state legislatures and encouraged laws to be passed to improve the physical facilities of schools, to mandate compulsory attendance of children, to require local tax support for schools, to require state credentialing of teachers, and to establish minimal academic standards for schools. Other state legislatures followed the lead of Massachusetts, Connecticut, and other progressive states of the nineteenth century.

As the nation's population grew, school districts were formed with school boards elected from the citizenry of the district in accordance with state laws. School board members were officers of the state, charged with implementing state statutes in the local schools. As schools became more and more complex, state legislatures became more and more involved in the day-to-day operation of the schools, passing laws regulating teacher qualifications, the curriculum, teacher evaluation, high school graduation requirements, the school calendar, extracurricular activities, school consolidation, bond elections, personnel records, student records, disciplinary procedures, fees, bus service, textbooks, vaccinations, and religious exercises. To enforce the myriad of laws being passed, state departments of education evolved from advisory to regulatory bodies and assumed responsibility for enforcement of state statutes.

As education became accepted as one of the primary responsibilities of the state, responsibility for the funding of schools shifted from the local community to the state. Prior to this shift, the funding for schools had depended on the goodwill of local tax assessors and city councils because the school tax was usually a tax on local property.

In the 1990s, state responsibility for schools is an accepted fact. As that responsibility for the funding of schools shifted from the local community to the state, the control of decision making for the schools also shifted from the local community to the state education agencies. The result has been a loss of control and sense of responsibility for schools at the local level for all persons involved in the school, but especially parents. Where once they hired, evaluated, and fired the teachers; chose the textbooks and the curriculum; held box lunch auctions, passed the hat at school concerts, and donated land to finance the equipment, supplies, books, furniture, and teacher's salary; and designed and built the school building, parents now pay state taxes and are asked to adhere to their elected state legislators' decisions about their schools. The legal distance between parents and schools has increased as the state has exercised its legal authority over the educational system.

> ***REFLECTION...***
>
> Why are school boards comprised of lay persons, not professional educators?

State and Federal Courts and Education

Although most disputes between parents and the schools never go beyond discussions before the local school board, the courts have long been involved when disputes cannot be resolved easily. Because education is a state responsibility, most disputes arise over state laws or policies passed by school boards acting as agents of the state. Therefore, the majority of court cases involving schools are brought in state courts. Only when the dispute involves the federal Constitution or a federal law can a case be heard in federal court. Involvement of the federal courts to any great extent has arisen only since the conflicts over desegregation of the schools began in the 1950s.

When a dispute arises between parents and the schools, generally the courts are asked to balance the fundamental rights of the parents to guide the upbringing of their children against the delegated rights of the school to educate productive citizens for the democratic state. Figure 10-1 illustrates the historic role of the courts in weighing the rights of one party (the parents) against the rights of the other party (the school).

The question of whose rights weigh more heavily, those of the parent or those of the state, has been the subject of court cases that have been appealed all the way to the United States Supreme Court, the highest court of the country. This fundamental right of parents to guide the upbringing of their children was the core issue of a case brought before the United States Supreme Court in 1925. In *Pierce* v. *Society of Sisters* (1925), an Oregon law requiring all parents to send their children between the ages of eight and sixteen years to only public schools was challenged successfully. This decision allowed parents the right to

Rights of School   Rights of Parents

FIGURE 10-1

send their children to parochial or other types of private schools. The Supreme Court quoted *Meyer* v. *Nebraska:*

> *Under the doctrine of Meyer v. Nebraska, we think it entirely plain that the Act of 1922 unreasonably interferes with the liberty of parents and guardians to direct the upbringing and education of children under their control.... The child is not the mere creature of the state; those who nurture him and direct his destiny have the right, coupled with the high duty, to recognize and prepare him for additional obligations.* Pierce v. Society of Sisters *(1925)*

In resolving disputes between parents and the school, the courts almost always must interpret state laws or school board policies. Fundamental rights of parents will weigh very heavily in these cases, but reasonable laws and policies of the school will be upheld if parents' fundamental rights are not in jeopardy.

Court Involvement to 1940

The federal courts were seldom involved in the schools prior to the desegregation cases of the 1950s. Therefore, court cases prior to the 1950s were almost all heard in state courts because usually state laws or school board policies were the subject of disputes. Prior to 1954, the courts heard cases dealing with issues such as vaccinations, the curriculum, and religion.

In spite of the fundamental rights of parents to guide the upbringing of their children, parental requests are not always honored by the courts. When parental desires or requests endanger the health, safety, or welfare of their child or others, the courts rule against the rights of parents. In an era before medical science stopped deadly diseases from causing epidemics in communities, schools were often closed when smallpox, tuberculosis, diphtheria, influenza, and other contagious diseases struck. When vaccinations were developed against some of these diseases, schools often required students to be immunized before they were allowed to go to school. However, some parents were against vaccinations, often citing religious reasons. The school's right to require vaccinations has been upheld (see *Viemeister* v. *White,* 1904), and the parent's right to circumvent compulsory attendance laws by not complying with vaccination requirements has been denied (see *People* v. *Ekerold,* 1914). In later cases, the court ruled against parents even when smallpox and diphtheria were on a decline, stating, "A local board of education need not await an epidemic, or even a single sickness or death, before it decides to protect the public. To hold otherwise would be to destroy prevention as a means of combating the spread of disease" (*Board of Education of Mountain Lakes* v. *Maas,* 1959).

Court Involvement 1940–1954

When disputes about the school curriculum involve religion, the federal courts have long been involved because these disputes always involve the First Amendment to the United States Constitution. Questions related to the relationship between church and state, as defined by the First Amendment, can be brought before the federal courts. The key clauses of the First Amendment are the Establishment and Free Exercise Clauses:

> *Congress shall make no law respecting an establishment of religion, or prohibiting the free exercise thereof.*

In 1943 the Supreme Court handed down the first of its many controversial decisions dealing with religious exercises in the schools. A West Virginia school board had adopted a resolution ordering that the salute to the flag become a regular part of the curriculum of the schools. The children of parents who were Jehovah's Witnesses refused to participate because the flag salute is against their religion. Jehovah's Witnesses literally interpret the second of the Ten Commandments from the Bible:

> *Thou shalt not make unto thee any graven image, or any likeness of anything that is in heaven above or that is in the earth beneath, or that is in the water under the earth; thou shalt not bow down thyself to them nor serve them. (Exodus 20:4–5)*

The parents brought suit in United States District Court, asking for an injunction to stop enforcement of the policy. In ruling for the parents, the United States Supreme Court noted that "the refusal of these persons to participate in the ceremony does not interfere with or deny rights of others to do so" (*West Virginia State Board of Education* v. *Barnette,* 1943).

The flag salute case was brought in the patriotic heat of World War II, and the conclusion of that war brought a cry for a return to values of the past. Attempts were made by many parents and religious organizations to bring religious instruction into the schools. In Illinois, parents and clergy of Jewish, Roman Catholic, and a few Protestant faiths formed an association and obtained permission from the school board to offer religious instruction in school. The classes were voluntary in that parents signed cards requesting that their children be permitted to attend the religion classes. However, those students who did not enroll had no other class option but merely were sent to another room to study. Parents and others who believed that bringing in rabbis, priests, and ministers to teach religion classes was a violation of the Establishment Clause brought suit. The United States Supreme Court agreed that these classes fell "squarely under the ban of the First Amendment" (*McCollum* v. *Board of Education,* 1948).

However, in 1952, the Supreme Court upheld a released time program in which students were released by their parents from school to attend religion classes held at nearby churches. The court ruled that schools may accommodate religion because there is "no constitutional requirement which makes it necessary for government to be hostile to religion" (*Zorach* v. *Clauson,* 1952). Thus, the stage was set for the battle over the separation of church and state to be waged in the public schools.

These early cases all set precedents for the many cases which would soon follow as society became more complex after World War II. Very few cases against the schools were brought by parents before the 1950s, for several reasons. Before World War II, local communities were still in control of their schools, with parents feeling that they knew the school personnel and the activities going on at the school. People did not leave their small towns, and the teachers, administrators, and board members were their next door neighbors and would be their children's next door neighbors. The curriculum had not changed drastically since parents had been in school. Radio brought the world closer to the hometown, but national and international news was of places that had little to do with the local community.

With the end of World War II, the nation grew rapidly, not only in numbers but in diversity and complexity. Immigrants were no longer from primarily Judeo-Christian, European countries, and they brought their own cultural and religious beliefs, plus the memory of traumatic experiences during the war. Farming became mechanized, forcing small farmers out of business and requiring fewer farmers' children to remain on the farm. Immigrants, farmers, and others looking for a better life flooded the cities, multiplying urban problems for the first time. People became mobile, not staying in one place long enough to know their neighbors. Communication systems improved, and people became aware of changes and trends in other states and cities across the country. Compulsory attendance laws began to be enforced by the states, and parents realized that the only way their children could get jobs and improve their lives was by staying in school through high school. The United States took center stage in world affairs, and the schools were pressured to revise and expand the curriculum to ensure that the nation was the best in everything from military armaments to space travel to industrial output. The casual, informal, neighborly relationship between parents and the schools changed to a formal, legal relationship because of the changing world. However, much of this was to change with the issue of desegregation.

REFLECTION...

What changes did the end of World War II bring to your community, including the schools?

Court Involvement after 1954

The year 1954 is often used as the watershed year for school law and the relationship of parents and schools. In the 1950s the National Association for the Advancement of Colored People (NCAAP) along with many other organizations and individuals began a campaign to end segregation of the schools on the grounds that separation of the races forever branded minority people as second class citizens. In Topeka, Kansas, the case of Linda Brown and several other black children who were forced by Kansas state law to attend all-black schools provided an appropriate test case. With Thurgood Marshall as the attorney, *Brown* v. *Board of Education of Topeka, Kansas* (1954) became the most important school law case ever brought before the courts. Declaring that the doctrine of "separate but equal" has no place in the field of public education, the United States Supreme Court changed forever the relationship between the schools and the federal government and, hence, the relationship between parents and the schools. The Brown case officially desegregated the schools, but it also brought the federal court system into the schools to a degree never before known. Because of continual resistance to desegregation, the federal courts took on the role of overseers of some school districts, imposing mandates on hiring of teachers and administrators, enrollment systems, district boundaries, busing, and school board elections. The 9–0 vote of the

Supreme Court in Brown signaled to the nation that the time had come for society to change, for the civil rights of all people to be recognized and protected, and for the schools to provide an education for all children. That decision also indicated that the courts would be used to enforce the mandated changes because society was refusing to make the changes voluntarily.

REFLECTION...

Why is *Brown* v. *the Board of Education* often considered the most important school law case ever heard by the United States Supreme Court? Did the case have any effect on your local school district?

Parents were often the ones reluctant to accept court mandates for change. The images of adults screaming at black children walking to school under the protection of federal marshals have been imprinted on the national conscience. As one group's rights came to the forefront in the media, other minority groups began seeking their children's rights. Individual rights became important to persons who had previously given little or no thought to their fundamental or constitutional rights. As society became more complex, as awareness of rights grew, as disenchantment with the public schools increased, and as local communities lost control of their schools, parents turned to the courts to resolve their problems and to reclaim their right to guide the upbringing of their children. Educators became threatened when parents wanted to become more involved in the schools than school personnel desired, and an adversarial relationship was established. Controversies led to court cases dealing with compulsory attendance, school fees, special education, student rights, the curriculum, liability, and discrimination. All of these issues raise questions that are still debated by school personnel and parents today.

Compulsory Attendance

Although some southern states attempted to circumvent desegregation orders by repealing their compulsory attendance laws, all states had such laws in place by the 1970s and started enforcing the laws even for groups that had previously been exempt. In Wisconsin, the Amish had traditionally allowed their children to attend public schools through only the eighth grade. Fearing a threat to their lifestyle and their religion if their children were exposed to worldly values, several Amish parents did not enroll their children in high school and were convicted of violating the state compulsory attendance law. The United States Supreme Court in *Wisconsin* v. *Yoder* (1972) once again upheld the fundamental right of parents to guide the upbringing of their children:

> *Thus, a State's interest in universal education, however highly we rank it, is not totally free from a balancing process when it impinges on fundamental rights and interests, such as those specifically protected by the Free Exercise Clause of the First Amendment, and the traditional interest of parents with respect to the religious upbringing of their children.... The primary role of the parents in the upbringing of their children is now established beyond debate as an enduring American tradition. (Wisconsin v. Yoder, 1972)*

The United States Supreme Court carefully stated that the Yoder decision applied only to the Amish or other religious groups with a similar history. However, many other religious sects, private schools, and home schools have used the rationale in the Yoder decision as a basis for challenging compulsory attendance laws.

Compulsory attendance laws continue to be challenged by parents who do not wish to comply with vaccination rules. Although many contagious diseases have been eradicated or at least controlled in the United States, the courts still uphold reasonable requirements for vaccinations for smallpox, tuberculosis, and other diseases. When the argument is forwarded that vaccinations are against the parents' religion, the courts often respond with statements such as the following made by the Arkansas Supreme Court:

> *Anyone has the right to worship God in the manner of his own choice, but it does not mean that he can engage in religious practices inconsistent with the peace, safety and health of the inhabitants of the State, and it does not mean that parents, on religious grounds, have the right to deny their children an education.... A person's right to exhibit religious freedom ceases where it overlaps and transgresses the rights of others.* (Cude v. Arkansas, *1964)*

As new contagious diseases proliferate (AIDS and Ebola) and previously controlled diseases emerge with new deadly strains (hepatitis, meningitis, and tuberculosis), debates over vaccination (if available), quarantine, and school attendance by stricken children will arise as parents feel their children's lives are threatened. Although many persons in this nation may have felt at one time that deadly diseases would soon no longer threaten lives in the United States, the courts are likely going to be asked to continue to weigh the rights of parents to exercise their personal and religious beliefs about disease and vaccination against the right of schools to protect the health and welfare of all children and personnel.

As HIV and other sexually transmitted diseases become rampant among students, the issue of how to deal with sex education in the curriculum arises. Until the 1970s, some teachers may have dealt with topics related to human sexuality in health classes, but when those topics became labeled "sex education," many parents became concerned about the content of such courses. The parents' right to guide the upbringing of their children certainly includes the right to teach them about sex according to family or religious values. Sex education was purported to be a solution to the explosion in number of teen pregnancies. However, when parents questioned the information taught in the classes, many schools allowed a waiver system whereby parents could have their child excused from the classes. With the susceptibility of the teenage population to the still fatal effects of HIV and the harmful, disfiguring effects of other sexually transmitted diseases, schools argue that sex education must be compulsory because all students are at risk and parents may not have the knowledge to teach their children about the new dangers that accompany sexual behavior. The courts are divided in their rulings about sex education courses, upholding those that include an excusal system (see *Medeiros* v. *Kiyosaki,* 1970; *Smith* v. *Ricci,* 1982) as well as those that mandate the course for all students (see *Cornwell* v. *State Board of Education,* 1969).

As parents become disillusioned about public schools, more challenges to compulsory education laws may be anticipated. Private schools, including parochial, for-profit, and home schooling, will be established, some adhering to state guidelines for licensure and some claiming that such guidelines merely perpetuate the problems the new schools are attempting to combat. Mandatory parts of the curriculum, such as sex education, will continue to be challenged by parents who want more control over what their children are being taught at school. When parents feel that the schools are failing in their responsibility to prepare students for productive lives, then parents will challenge the validity of compulsory attendance laws. Teachers will have to deal with parents who question the purpose of schools and at least some parts of the curriculum. The courts will continue to be faced with the task of balancing the rights of parents to guide the upbringing of their children and the right of states to require school attendance. School personnel will want to ensure that district policies about controversial topics such as home schooling, vaccinations, and sex education are in place prior to questions arising about compulsory attendance laws. Teachers and administrators will need to be prepared to defend the role of public schools in society and how the curriculum will aid in preparing a child for the future.

REFLECTION...

Why should children be compelled to attend school?

Besides being compelled to attend school, children and their parents are often assessed school fees. These fees can be a source of conflict.

School Fees

Public school education in the United States has always been free, that is, no tuition is charged when a student enrolls in the school. However, the charging of fees has a long history, dating back to when every student took a turn bringing a bucket of coal for the potbellied stove. In today's more sophisticated world, fees are charged for everything from the school yearbook to towels for physical education classes to anticipated breakage in laboratory classes to participation in extracurricular activities to textbook rental. When a state constitution guarantees a free, public education for every child in the state but then fees are assessed, some parents have challenged the legality of such fees. Courts are then faced with having to interpret what the state constitution writers meant when they included the word *free* in the description of public schools.

A North Dakota school district's authority to charge rental fees for textbooks was challenged by a group of parents in 1978. The state supreme court ruled in favor of the parents:

> *The term "free public schools" without any other modification must necessarily mean and include those items which are essential to education. It is difficult to envision a meaningful educational system without textbooks. No education of any value is possible without school books. (Cardiff v. Bismarck Public School District, 1978)*

However, other state courts have ruled that "free" applies only to the lack of tuition and that charging for essentials like textbooks is legally tenable.

Other fees have been challenged in other states. In California, for example, the charging of fees for extracurricular activities was ruled unconstitutional under their state law that requires the Legislature to "provide for a system of common schools by which a free school shall be kept up and supported in each district" (*Hartzell* v. *Connell,* 1984). Extracurricular activities were shown to be a vital part of public schooling in California, and fees were not allowed.

Court challenges by parents against school fees will likely continue as the resources of school districts diminish, costs of educating students increase, and parents are called upon to bear more and more of the cost of their children's "free" education. Teachers will have to be careful not to waste any of the district's resources or expect parents to provide too many expensive items, such as elaborate treats, costumes, or supplies, to replace what the school may have once been expected to provide. School administrators may want to consider including parents as members of committees that develop fee levels and structures and that determine which activities may have to be dropped in the face of rising costs.

REFLECTION...

With three children in middle school, Kathy and Robbie are facing having to pay substantial school fees. Jack and Jim both want to play basketball, and Amanda wants to play soccer and volleyball as well as audition for the school play. The school charges a fee for each extracurricular activity plus towel fees for each sport and for the required physical education classes. In addition, there are fees for a card to get admitted to school activities (games, plays, concerts, etc.), for the school newspaper, for the yearbook, for having one's picture taken for the yearbook, and for class expendables (workbooks, paper, etc.). Kathy and Robbie do not see how they can afford the fees; yet, they understand the value of their children participating in and attending school activities.

- What legal questions should Kathy and Robbie ask?
- What does your state law and case precedent say about school fees?
- What questions should they ask of the school district? of their building principal?

As previously mentioned, school fees can have an effect on curriculum depending on the type of fees charged. However, the curriculum and law has its own place in the schools

Curriculum

The curriculum has long been considered the province of professional educators, and those who challenge the curriculum have been considered trouble makers. Yet, parents have a right to know what their children are learning from the teachers acting *in loco parentis* and even should have a voice in the curriculum. Too often, school personnel forget that parents need to be allies of the school in assisting children to learn; therefore, the parents need to know what is being taught. The curriculum is becoming too complex and too fragmented for parents to be left out of the teaching–learning process. Today's parents would have a difficult time guiding the upbringing of their children if they have no idea what the schools are teaching their children.

Challenges to the curriculum are made for many reasons, but the majority of those that reach the courts are made on the basis of religious arguments. These cases are often brought by parents who believe that the schools are fostering secular humanism (usually defined as a belief in the supremacy of man instead of supernatural beings) instead of a belief in God, or teaching values antithetical to family values. On the other hand, our nation, as a haven for persons of all religious creeds, has led to an increasing number of diverse religious backgrounds and beliefs being represented in the schools. The school has been called the battleground for the struggle to define the separation of church and state. The conflict becomes especially difficult when the two religion clauses of the First Amendment become pitted against each other, as so often happens when the school claims that allowing a religious practice to occur on school property would be a violation of the Establishment Clause but parents claim that not allowing that religious practice to occur on school property would be a violation of the Free Exercise Clause.

In 1963 the United States Supreme Court unleashed a furor when it ruled in *Abington School District* v. *Schemmp* that vocal prayers in school were in violation of the Establishment Clause of the First Amendment. Many accused the Supreme Court of being atheist when the ruling went in favor of arguments made by the "professed atheist," Madeline Murray, on behalf of her son in the companion case, *Murray* v. *Curlett* (1963). Church–state cases are the school-related issue on which the United States Supreme Court has made the second greatest number of rulings (the first being desegregation).

In 1985 a Mobile, Alabama, attorney, Jaffree, sued the state of Alabama (represented in the title of the court case by its governor, George Wallace) in an attempt to get two state statutes declared unconstitutional because of violating the Establishment Clause. One state statute authorized a one-minute period of silence for meditation or voluntary prayer, and the second authorized teachers to lead "willing students in a prescribed prayer to Almighty God…the Creator and Supreme Judge of the world." The federal district court ruled that the two statutes were constitutional because "Alabama has the power to establish a state religion if it chooses to do so." However, the United States Court of Appeals, Eleventh Circuit, held the two statutes to be unconstitutional, and the United States Supreme Court agreed, stating that "the individual freedom of conscience protected by the First Amendment embraces the right to select any religious faith or none at all" (*Wallace* v. *Jaffree*, 1985).

Thus, vocal prayers in the classroom as well as moments of silence for the specified purpose of prayer have been ruled unconstitutional. The focus then turned to prayers and other religious exercises at school-related activities. In the early 1990s, the issue of prayer at public school graduation ceremonies arose when Daniel Weisman went to court to get a permanent injunction to prevent prayers at his daughter Deborah's middle-school graduation. The court did not act quickly enough to stop the school from inviting a rabbi to offer a prayer that was in accordance with the guidelines in a pamphlet provided by the school. Eventually, the United States Supreme Court in *Lee* v. *Weisman* (1991) ruled that clergy-led prayers at public school graduation ceremonies do violate the Establishment Clause of the First Amendment even though attendance at graduation is voluntary and even though the prayers are short and nonsectarian.

In the 1980s, the number of challenges to textbooks and curriculum materials increased rapidly as several organizations began sponsoring conferences about and publishing lists of books that should not be found in schools. A New York school board took action to remove several of these books from the school library, and a group of students, parents, and teachers went to court, claiming censorship. Asserting that "the State may not, consistently with the spirit of the First Amendment, contract the spectrum of available knowledge," the United States Supreme Court in *Board of Education, Island Trees Union Free School District* v. *Pico* (1982) settled the question about school library books. Once books are on the shelf, they may not be removed.

Two well-publicized cases related to textbook censorship were heard in 1987 by the circuit courts of appeal. A Tennessee case involved several parents who argued that the Holt, Rinehart and Winston reading series contained stories that violated the religious beliefs of the parents. Because the reading series was required of all students, the parents claimed that their Free Exercise rights and those of their children were being violated. In an Alabama case, parents wanted forty-four textbooks banned because of their secular humanism teachings. In both cases, the parents prevailed at the federal district court level. However, the United States Courts of Appeal, Sixth and Eleventh Circuits, overturned the lower court decisions. The Sixth Circuit Court decision noted that the parents "testified that reading the Holt series 'could' or 'might' lead the students to come to conclusions that were contrary to teachings of their and their parents' religious beliefs. This is not sufficient to establish an unconstitutional burden…" (*Mozert* v. *Hawkins County Board of Education,* 1987). The Eleventh Circuit Court stated the following:

> *There simply is nothing in this record to indicate that omission of certain facts regarding religion from these textbooks of itself constituted an advancement of secular humanism or an active hostility towards theistic religion prohibited by the establishment clause. (*Smith v. Board of School Commissioners of Mobile County, *1987)*

Parents are going to continue to challenge the school curriculum. Instead of such challenges becoming a threat to the autonomy of the schools or the academic freedom of the teachers, parents should be welcomed as part of the curriculum development and textbook selection processes, especially as members of textbook selection and curriculum evaluation committees. Their suggestions and criticisms should be taken seriously, but school administrators must ensure that representative of all segments of the community are heard, not just the loudest or most articulate. Parental input must be balanced against the professional expertise of teachers and administrators. Schools should have a coherent curriculum revision process to ensure that all textbooks, activities, and instructional methods are meeting educational objectives. Teachers must be sure that their textbooks, supplemental materials, lessons, and activities are based on sound educational principles and are meeting district and state educational objectives. Processes for handling challenges to textbooks, methods, and materials should be developed and followed. Reasonable exceptions should be allowed, but policies defining exceptions to the standard required curriculum should be established before the first request is made. Welcoming parents as partners in the teaching–learning process, even in the building of the curriculum, may encourage parents to view the schools as their allies in guiding the upbringing of their children.

The curriculum war was also obviously affected by special needs children. As inclusion has become the mode of teaching special needs children, the teacher had to respond to those students' curriculum needs.

REFLECTION...

Kenneth and Grace are becoming concerned about how African Americans are portrayed in the literature taught in their children's English classes. They know *Huckleberry Finn* and *Gone with the Wind* are required reading, but students are not required to read anything that portrays African Americans in other than slave roles or anything written by African American authors. They do not want any books removed from the curriculum, but they would like to request that books such as the *Autobiography of Malcolm X* and *Why the Caged Bird Sings* be added to the required reading.

- What legal questions should Kenneth and Grace ask?
- What does your state law and case precedent state about textbook selection?
- What questions should Kenneth and Grace ask of the school district? of the English teachers?

Special Education

When the writers of state constitutions provided for systems of public schools that were to be open to all children, they often did not consider children with disabilities. Most children with disabilities were not in public schools at the time state constitutions were written, and few persons would have thought that they ever would be. The history of most states in regard to the education of children with various mental and physical disabilities is shameful. Either the children were excluded from any type of education at all or were in settings where they received few, if any, educational benefits. Many states felt they had met the needs of children with disabilities by providing residential state schools for the deaf, blind, and "trainable," and quasi-hospital settings for those with severe or multiple mental and physical disabilities.

By the early 1970s, advocacy groups for veterans and other handicapped persons organized their efforts to secure the civil rights of a formerly silent minority group—the disabled. The result was legislation at the federal level that banned discrimination on the basis of disability (the Rehabilitation Act of 1973) and that provided funding for schools which provided an individualized, free, appropriate public education in the least restrictive environment for children with disabilities (the Education for All Handicapped Children Act of 1975 or PL 94-142). Changed to the Individuals with Disabilities Education Act (IDEA) in 1991, this latter special education law impacted the rights of parents in relation to the schools as no previous legislation, at either the state or national level, had done. Because children with disabilities are the least able to serve as their own advocates, the rights of parents as advocates for the rights of their children are safeguarded in this law. In fact, parents are required to be involved in their child's education as they must be active members of the child's Individual Education Plan (IEP) team. The IEP team is the group that determines the special education and related services the child will receive during the school year.

IDEA is a very complex law, but major parental rights which are defined in the law and which impact the relationship between parents and the school include the following:

- the right to be informed of parental rights under IDEA
- the right to be informed in the parents' native language or other appropriate means
- the right to be informed prior to assessment being done if placement in special education may be the outcome of the assessment
- the right to be informed of outside evaluators and no- or low-cost legal services
- the right to be involved in determining educational goals, services, and placement through membership on the IEP team
- the right to be informed prior to any change in placement or services
- the right to see the child's records
- the right to initiate a due process hearing
- the right to receive a transcript of the hearing and the decision
- the right to appeal through the court system

Although the major laws governing special education at the national level have been in effect for a relatively short time, much case law has resulted from them. In fact, special education is likely to become the greatest subject of school-related litigation in the next decade unless states and school districts initiate mediation as a process for resolving conflicts before going to court. The number of children who qualify for special education is increasing each year as medical science improves the survival rate of at-risk babies and accident victims, as assessment measures become more sophisticated and better able to identify children with special needs earlier, and as more physical and mental conditions are categorized as qualifying for some type of special education service. Advocacy groups for children with disabilities are very strong, and both parents and school personnel need to become more aware of the legal rights of these once forgotten children and work together to facilitate their special education. Otherwise, lawsuits will proliferate.

REFLECTION...

Can all children be educated? Should all children be educated at public expense?

The first special education case that reached the United States Supreme Court involved a hearing-impaired child whose parents wanted the school to provide a full-time sign language interpreter in the classroom. Noting that "this very case demonstrates [that] parents and guardians will not lack ardor in seeking to ensure that handicapped children receive all of the benefits to which they are entitled by the Act," the Supreme Court, nevertheless, ruled against the parents in *Board of Education of Hendrick Hudson Central School District Board of Education* v. *Rowley* (1982) because of the efforts the school had made to assist Amy Rowley to benefit from her education. The court said that a school district does not have to "maximize the potential of each handicapped child commensurate with the opportunity provided nonhandicapped children." Amy was advancing at grade level academically and socially, and even the sign language interpreter testified that her services were superfluous.

In 1984 the United States Supreme Court was asked to determine the definition of "*related services*" as provided in the law. Amber Tatro needed clean intermittent catheterization every three or four hours, which the school argued was a medical service that should not be required of school personnel. The parents argued that the service was merely a procedure that would enable Amber to benefit from special education and could be performed by a layperson with minimal training. In ruling in favor of the parents in *Irving Independent School District* v. *Tatro* (1984), the Supreme Court impacted the relationship between parents and the school by requiring the school to provide services once provided only by parents or nurses.

Placement of students with disabilities is probably the most controversial topic dividing parents and the schools. Unfortunately, IDEA has never been fully funded by Congress, leaving the states and local districts with much of the cost of compliance. When parents and school personnel disagree over the services or placement of a child with a disability, the issue almost always involves the cost. The parents are interested in getting the best services possible for their child, and the school personnel are interested in containing costs. The result is a growing number of special education lawsuits.

In 1989 a New Hampshire school district attempted to get the courts to rule that some children with very severe disabilities could not benefit from any type of education and so would be excluded from coverage by the law. Timothy W. was multiply and profoundly mentally and physically disabled, but the United States Court of Appeals, First Circuit, ruled that a child does not have to demonstrate the ability to benefit from education in order to qualify for services, no matter how minimal:

> *The law explicitly recognizes that education for the severely handicapped is to be broadly defined, to include not only traditional academic skills, but also basic functional life skills, and that educational methodologies in these areas are not static, but are constantly evolving and improving. It is the school district's responsibility to avail itself of these new approaches in providing an education program geared to each child's individual needs. The only question for the school district to determine, in conjunction with the child's parents, is what constitutes an appropriate individualized education program (IEP) for the handicapped child. We emphasize that the phrase "appropriate individual education program" cannot be interpreted, as the school district has done, to mean "no educational program."*
> (Timothy W. v. Rochester, New Hampshire School District, *1989*)

The *Timothy W.* decision meant that all children with disabilities are to be served by special education, no matter how severe their disabilities. The United States Supreme Court merely confirmed this decision without comment, and so it is used as precedent for lower court cases.

Another case that involved the cost of placement was *Florence County School District Four* v. *Carter* (1993). This case resulted from a dispute between a school district and parents over services for a child with learning disabilities. Frustrated by the school district's lack of attention to their requests, the parents removed their daughter Shannon from the public school and placed her in a private school that specialized in services for children with learning disabilities. After Shannon completed her schooling, the parents sued the school district for reimbursement of the tuition charged by the private school. Ruling in favor of the parents, the United States Supreme Court commented on the cost argument of the school district:

> There is no doubt that Congress has imposed a significant financial burden on States and school districts that participate in IDEA. Yet public educational authorities who want to avoid reimbursing parents for the private education of a disabled child can do one of two things: give the child a free appropriate public education in a public setting, or place the child in an appropriate private setting of the State's choice. This is IDEA's mandate, and school officials who conform to it need not worry about reimbursement claims. (Florence County School District Four *v.* Carter, *1993)*

Attempting to stay abreast of case law plus the continually changing regulations in Section 504 of the Rehabilitation Act, the Individuals with Disabilities Education Act, and the Americans with Disabilities Act will be a challenge for parents of children with disabilities and the schools that must provide special education and related services. All teachers, not just special education teachers, will have an opportunity to work with children with various disabilities. Teachers must learn about special needs and how to meet them. Because of the involvement of parents in the education of their children with disabilities, many parents are becoming more and more involved in the education of all children, sometimes to a degree not known by the schools previously. Some parents question why every child's education cannot be individualized and why more services are not available for all children. For school personnel, the increased interest of parents in their children's education can be an opportunity to set a tone of cooperation and partnership in striving to meet the needs of all children. Parents can become the greatest advocates for the schools if they know the schools are working to assist their child in gaining an education. Then the adversarial relationship between parents and the schools will not exist, and costly, time-consuming lawsuits can be avoided.

Student Rights

With all the emphasis on special education, sometimes the rights of students in general seem to take second place. Actually, the rights of students with disabilities were recognized only because of the Brown (1954) case that led to the conclusion that all children had a right to an equal education, and because of a historic student rights case in 1969. In *Tinker* v. *Des Moines Independent Community School District* (1969), the United States Supreme Court declared that "it can hardly be argued that…students…shed their constitutional rights to freedom of speech or expression at the schoolhouse gate." Thus, the constitutional rights of students were legally recognized for the first time, and the relationship between the school and parents and their students subtly changed. Although *in loco parentis* still governs that relationship, Tinker and successive court decisions determined that students have a legal

> ### REFLECTION...
>
> Joyce has been notified that her daughter, Beth, is going to be assessed for a possible learning disability. Joyce is to sign a card, indicating her approval for the tests, and return it to the school. Because she had no idea that Beth was having any difficulty in school, Joyce is upset and does not want to sign the card.
>
> - What legal questions should Joyce ask? What are her rights as a parent?
> - What does your state law and federal law say about assessment and parents' rights?
> - What questions should Joyce ask of the school district? of the classroom teacher? of the special education teacher?

right to an education. That right cannot be denied without due process. When that right to an education is in jeopardy, parents become involved in working with the school's disciplinary procedures and sometimes taking their child's case to court. In most court cases involving student rights, whether the issue is expulsion of a student because of fighting or a student being sent home to change a T-shirt with a vulgar message, the parents bring the lawsuits because of the minor status of almost all students.

The question often arises of "what process is due" when a student claims his or her rights have been violated. Unless school officials know about due process, often a student's claim will prevail because the school official will back off in fear of violating a student's rights. Then the rights of other students and school personnel to an orderly, educational atmosphere may be jeopardized. Generally, as long as rules allow a student to tell his or her side of the story, are fairly and consistently enforced, and provide for fair and consistent sanctions, due process is satisfied. Students and teachers must know what the rules are. The role of student handbooks in due process is to serve as notice of the rules and the applicable punishments. The more serious the infraction, the more serious the sanction should be.

More student rights cases are going to court for resolution because of the awareness of individual rights by students and their parents and because many school personnel are not sure of the status of student claims to rights. When school personnel fail to follow due process as outlined in the student handbook or, worse, fail to have a process established, a student's rights could be jeopardized, and the courts will be willing to hear the student's case. Generally, the courts do not desire to become involved in the disciplinary procedures of the schools; they prefer leaving those decisions to the educational experts. However, when a student's constitutional rights are violated, the courts will step in.

One of the areas of student and parent rights that has a long history of violation prior to the passage of a federal law is student records. Before the Family Education Rights and Privacy Act (FERPA) was passed in 1974, school records policies were generally nonexistent. Parents had little or no access to student records; yet, third parties (college recruiters, military recruiters, police officers) had only to make a request, and a student's file was made available. Few processes were in place to ensure accuracy of records, and the result was blatant violation of the privacy of a student and often the family. FERPA specifies that only parents and educators (who have a need to know) should have access to a student's educational file. That file should contain only official transcripts and other official school documents, not anecdotal notes. The parents have the right to question the information in the file and to write responses to what they perceive as inaccurate data. These requests to see files, to get copies, and to get test scores interpreted do not have to be met on demand; the school cannot be expected to produce records, especially archival records, without notice. Only parents can give permission for third parties to see a student's records. Schools cannot keep secondary or secret files that are used for any decision making about the student's education. Teachers should be aware of records policies and follow them, realizing that parents have rights to see the records of their child but not those of other children. Only one official educational file should exist for each student; a teacher's personal notes are not official records so do not have to be shown to parents. However, those notes should not be used for informing decisions about the child nor kept in any permanent file. The school can facilitate good relations with parents by informing them of their rights under FERPA, having good records policies in place, and following them.

To encourage good relations between parents and the school should be the goal of all teachers and administrators. Parents who feel comfortable coming to the school, calling teachers, or visiting with administrators over school-related issues will be less likely to take their child's side without checking the school's side of the story. Communication channels with parents should be open so that parents know of the school rules and expectations and will be less likely to defend their child when the child breaks the rules. Students and their parents have constitutional rights that cannot be arbitrarily or capriciously violated by the schools, as may have happened in the days prior to Tinker. Teachers must be prepared to know the rules, enforce the rules fairly and consistently, and follow the due process outlined in handbooks. Focusing on the student's education and the partnership with parents that can enhance that education may preclude legal resolution to problems that may arise over a student's claim to individual rights.

Liability

This is a litigious age in the United States, and tort law is where much of the litigation is occurring because when a suit is brought under tort law, the plaintiff is looking for monetary awards for damages. Anyone can sue anybody for almost anything under tort law. Schools in states that no longer have the policy of governmental immunity (governmental immunity means one cannot sue the government) can be held liable for injuries to anyone in the school or at school-related activities if the injuries are shown to have been caused by intent to injure or negligence. More and more people are willing to sue government entities such as schools because they believe that nobody is really being hurt by a damage award. However, the cost of litigation is very high, regardless of the outcome. Time spent preparing for the case, emotional energy expended on attempting to settle the issue amicably, and actual money damages or increase in insurance premiums are some of the indirect and direct costs associated with every lawsuit filed against a school. School personnel must take all reasonable precautions to prevent students, employees, and guests from being injured while at school, recognizing that lawsuits claiming negligence are all too frequent.

Parents believe that their children will be safe at school and are becoming more willing to sue for damages when a child is injured. Yet, most injuries are the result of accidents, not willful, malicious, or negligent actions by teachers or administrators. Schools are held to a very high standard of care for students, and when that standard of care is breached, the courts will award damages. Every teacher and administrator must remember that the standard of behavior the courts will use is the ordinary, reasonable, prudent person standard but adapted to allow for the professional training and experience of educators. If a teacher does not do what the ordinary, reasonable, prudent teacher would have done when in the same situation and a student is injured, negligence may have been the cause of the injury and the teacher and school district may be found liable for damages. Injuries will happen at school, but parents should be immediately informed and every reasonable action taken to care for the child. Guidelines for all school activities should include provisions for preventing injuries and procedures to follow should injuries occur. All educators should know and follow such guidelines in order to prevent claims of negligence or intent to injure.

In the legal relationship between parents and the school, liability can become an issue when parents are in the school as visitors, but a related issue is the parent who is working in the school or at school-related activities as a volunteer or paraprofessional. Teachers and staff are generally covered by liability policies of the school when they are acting in the course of their employment. However, insurance policies may or may not cover persons acting under the supervision of an employee, and school personnel should check their district liability policies before asking parents to drive students to activities, to chaperon field trips or other off-campus activities, to supervise classroom activities such as reading groups or art projects, to work as volunteer coaches, to supervise playgrounds or lunchrooms, or to perform any of the dozens of tasks which many parents welcome as opportunities to become involved in their child's school. Everything goes smoothly when parents are involved in the school's activities until either the parent or a student under the parent's supervision is injured. Then lawsuits may arise if malice, intent, or negligence can be shown.

Teachers and administrators cannot delegate their responsibility, which means that if a child or the parent is injured when the teacher or administrator is the person in the supervisory role, the ultimate responsibility for the injury will rest with the employee, not with the volunteer. Therefore, it becomes critical for teachers and administrators to train parent volunteers adequately for their roles, whatever they may be. The professional teaching certificate indicates that the teacher or administrator is experienced in the supervision of large numbers of children and can foretell what types of behavior may occur. The parent volunteer may have no such experience in the school setting and cannot be held liable for being unable to foretell that an action may lead to an injury. Schools should develop guidelines for the use of parent volunteers and follow the guidelines in the selection, training, and supervision of such volunteers. There is some irony to the fact that just at a time when the schools need all the help they can get and want to encourage involvement of parents in the schools, the threat of litigation might deter involving parents. The standard to use always is to do what the reasonable, prudent teacher or administrator would do in similar circumstances.

One of the areas of liability where the relationship between parents and schools can become most strained is in the reporting of suspected child abuse. The role of educators in reporting suspected child abuse is mandated by law; teachers and administrators must report abuse to the state social services agency or other designated authority. Schools should have guidelines in place about identifying child abuse, verifying reports of abuse, and the actual reporting process. Failure to report can lead to civil or possibly criminal recriminations against the teacher or administrator.

Reporting a parent for suspected child abuse sets up the potential for a very bad relationship with the parents, but the welfare of the child must be the top priority in all cases. This situation is where *in loco parentis* is probably most critical; the school is acting in place of the parent when the parent has abdicated his or her rights by violating the rights of the child. State laws always provide a good faith clause so that teachers who follow the mandate to report suspected abuse are protected should the report turn out to be false but was made in good faith.

One of the worst situations that may arise to destroy good school–parent relationships is when a school employee is suspected of sexually molesting or abusing students and parents learn that other school personnel knew and did nothing about the actions of the abuser. In *Franklin* v. *Gwinnett County Public Schools* (1992), parents reported to school officials that a teacher was having sexual contact with their daughter, and the school officials did not take the report seriously. Only minimal investigation was conducted, and nothing was done to stop the abuse or remove the teacher from the school. The United States Supreme Court ruled that Title IX could be applied to this case, setting the stage for federal court involvement in the violation of student civil rights in these cases when educators, in their official role as government employees, are guilty of abusing students and administrators reasonably knew or should have known the abuse was occurring and did nothing to stop it.

Schools are liable for injuries that occur on the school grounds, whether those injuries are physical or emotional. Developing good relationships with parents so that school personnel and parents can work together when injuries to students occur can prevent the bitterness that sometimes leads to punitive lawsuits. Schools must work to prevent injuries to students and parents when they are on school property or at school-sponsored events. Teachers must realize how vulnerable they are to being held liable for student injuries and take every precaution to prevent injuries. Even though parents can not sign away their own or their child's rights, permission slips for out-of-school activities are necessary to give parents notice about an event and an opportunity to give or deny permission for their child to participate. No one can prevent a lawsuit from being filed, but doing what the reasonable, prudent educator would do in similar circumstances may prevent a lawsuit from going to trial or excessive damage awards being made.

Discrimination and Harassment

With our nation becoming more diverse, claims of discrimination by members of various minority groups are on the rise as well as claims of reverse discrimination by members of majority groups. Not all claims are valid because not all minority groups are protected under federal and state laws. Discrimination against protected classes of people is illegal. Members of religious minority groups are protected by the First Amendment. Members of racial and ethnic minority groups are protected by the Fourteenth Amendment and various federal civil rights laws, such as Title VI and Title VII of the Civil Rights Act of 1964. Women (and sometimes men, depending on which gender has historically been the majority group in a setting) are protected by various federal laws, including Title IX of the Education Amendments of 1978. Persons with disabilities are protected by the Rehabilitation Act of 1973 and the Americans with Disabilities Act of 1991. The claims of these and other groups also may be protected by state or municipal laws. In addition, all children are to receive an equal opportunity for an education under various federal and state statutes.

REFLECTION...

Joyce has begun volunteering at Beth's school for one afternoon per week. She helps with reading groups, assists the classroom teacher with supervising the playground during afternoon recess, and tutors individual children with spelling, writing, and reading. During one afternoon recess, the classroom teacher was called to the office for an emergency phone call, leaving Joyce as the only adult on the playground. The teacher had been gone only a couple of minutes when a small girl fell out of a swing and broke her arm. When running over to the swingset, Joyce tripped over a rolling basketball and fell, spraining her ankle badly. Angry at the teacher for leaving her alone, Joyce is also worried because she is not sure her health insurance will cover her injury.

- What legal questions should Joyce ask?
- Generally, do school insurance policies cover volunteers and children?
- What questions should Joyce ask of the school district?

For educators, students, and parents, these anti-discrimination laws mean that all children are entitled to an equal opportunity for an education in the nation's public schools. Policies separating students because of race, color, ethnicity, religion, gender, and disability are almost impossible to justify. School districts that are found to discriminate on the basis of these usually unchangeable characteristics risk losing their federal funding.

One area related to discrimination that has received much publicity is athletics. Title IX is very definite in specifying equal opportunity for girls and boys in athletics, and school districts found not to be in compliance with Title IX risk losing all their federal funding, not just funding for athletics. However, Title IX applies much more broadly than just to athletics. School districts must provide equal opportunities for girls and boys in all areas, including curriculum, extracurricular organizations, and facilities.

Official discrimination by school districts or school employees is usually brought to public notice quickly and handled through formal channels. More difficult to handle are claims of harassment, which has been defined by the courts as a form of discrimination. Claims of sexual and racial harassment are increasing, whether because of awareness of the problem, media attention to the problem, or intolerant attitudes toward growing diversity in our population. Harassment is difficult to define because every person's tolerance for jokes, comments, teasing, touching, graffiti, and threats differs. However, the relative position of the perpetrator and the victim often determines if harassment has occurred. Persons in higher positions (employers, supervisors, administrators, teachers) should be very careful that persons in subordinate positions (employees, trainees, students) will not be able to interpret the superordinate's words or actions as harassment.

Teachers and other school personnel must never be involved in any type of harassment of students and should not allow students under their supervision to harass other students. One of the latest issues to come before the courts involves sexual and racial harassment of students by students. In several leading Minnesota cases, parents informed school officials that their children were being harassed by other children, and the school officials did little, if anything, to stop the harassment. When the courts have become involved in harassment cases, whether teacher-to-student or student-to-student, generally the rulings have been in favor of the victims and their parents, especially when documentation exists that the parents complained to the school officials but the harassment continued.

REFLECTION...

Kathy and Robbie are becoming very concerned about stories Amy and Fred are bringing home from school. On the playground at noon, several boys in the fifth grade have started "picking on" some of the younger boys in the first and second grades. The older boys taunt the younger ones, steal their frisbees, balls, and other toys, and sometimes even pull down the jeans of the younger boys. Fred has become afraid to go outside at noon, but the school rules allow students to stay inside only during bad weather.

- What legal questions should Kathy and Robbie ask?
- What does your state law and case precedent state about harassment?
- What questions should Kathy and Robbie ask of the school district? of the principal?

As our nation's complex diversity increases so will the potential for discrimination and harassment. Schools will help solve this national problem when discrimination and harassment are not tolerated in schools and students are educated about tolerance for persons who are not like them in every way. Parents will protect their children from the mental and physical harm of discrimination and harassment, even if they have to go to court. Therefore, teachers and administrators must do all they can to stop discrimination and harassment in schools.

Conclusion

The legal relationship between parents and the schools is becoming more complex every day as more federal and state laws are passed and more court decisions are handed down. Yet, the courts do not want to become involved in school issues; they would prefer if parents and school personnel would work out their differences outside of the courtroom. School personnel set the tone for parental involvement in schools. If schools refuse to recognize the fundamental right of parents to guide the upbringing of their children, the relationships between parents and the schools may become adversarial. If school personnel fear lawsuits and are always looking for an attorney behind the parent who wants to be involved in his or her child's education, they probably will find one because they will always be on the defensive. If teachers fail to respect the rights of students and parents and fail to maintain an orderly, educational atmosphere in their classrooms, all students suffer and parents will be disillusioned about the value of public schools. If schools genuinely welcome parents' involvement in their child's education because it will further the teaching and learning process, then schools and parents can become partners in educating children, not parties to lawsuits where no one wins.

Recommended Activities

1. Read the sections in your state constitution that deal with education. How are they similar to or different from the sample North Dakota Constitution?
2. After the next legislative session in your state, get a copy of all the new laws dealing with schools. How will these laws affect your local schools? the parents in your district?
3. How do the schools in your district "accommodate" religion? Do you agree or disagree with these practices?
4. Interview teachers who were teaching prior to 1969 about their perceptions of student rights. What changes did they observe in schools and students from the early 1960s to the 1980s? What changes did they observe in parents' rights and involvement in schools during that time?
5. How would you answer parents' arguments that sex education is a family or religious issue that has no place in schools?
6. What student fees are charged in your school district? Why are fees charged?
7. What do regular education teachers need to know about special education? and what related services are provided students with disabilities in your school district?
8. What rules govern student behavior in the schools in your district? Where are these rules printed?
9. How can school personnel control drugs, alcohol, gangs, and weapons in the schools and not violate student rights?
10. What textbooks or other education materials have been challenged in your school district? by whom? for what reasons?
11. Follow a teacher for a day and note how many potential lawsuits occur. Did you see any negligence? Were any students injured? What could be done to prevent liability in these instances?
12. What do you think will be the role of the courts in parent–school conflicts in the future?

Additional Resources

Educational Law and Parental Rights

Websites:

American Bar Association
http://www.abannett.org/

American Civil Liberties Union
http://www.aclu.org/

Children's Defense Fund
http://www.tmn.com/cdf/index.html

Children Now
http://www.dnai.com/~children/

Gender Equity in Sports
http://www.arcade.uiowa.edu/proj/gel

National Child Rights Alliance
http://www.ai.mit.edu/people/ellens/NCRA/ncra.html

Native American Bar Association
http://www.free.websight.com/10/

Case References

Abington School District v. Schemmp and Murray v. Curlett, 374 U.S. 203, 83 S.Ct. 1560 (1963).

Board of Education, Island Trees Union Free School District No. 26 v. Pico, 457 U.S. 853, 102 S.Ct. 2799 (1982).

Board of Education of Hendrick Hudson Central School District Board of Education v. Rowley, 458 U.S. 176, 102 S.Ct. 3034 (1982).

Board of Education of Mountain Lakes v. Maas, 152 A.2d 394 (App. Div. 1959).

Brown v. Board of Education of Topeka, Kansas, 347 U.S. 483, 74 S.Ct. 686 (1954).

Cardiff v. Bismarck Public School District, 263 N.W.2d 105 (ND 1978).

Cornwell v. State Board of Education, 314 F. Supp. 340 (D. Md. 1969), affirmed 428 F.2d 417 (4th Cir. 1970), cert. denied 400 U.S. 942, 91 S.Ct. 240 (1970).

Cude v. Arkansas, 377 S. W.2d 816 (Ark. 1964).

Florence County School District Four v. Carter, 114 S.Ct. 361 (1993).

Flory v. Smith, 134 S.E. 360 (Ct. of Appeals, Vir. 1926).

Franklin v. Gwinnett County Public Schools, 112 S.Ct. 1028 (1992).

Hartzell v. Connell, 679 P.2d 35 (Cal. 1984).

Irving Independent School District v. Tatro, 468 U.S. 883, 104 S.Ct. 3371 (1984).

Lander v. Seaver, 32 Vt. 114 (Vermont, 1859).

Lee v. Weisman, 112 S.Ct. 2649 (1992)

Medeiros v. Kiyosaki, 478 P.2d 314 (1970).

Meyer v. Nebraska, 262 U.S. 390, 43 S.Ct. 625 (1923).

Mozert v. Hawkins County Board of Education, 827 F.2d 1058 (6th Cir. 1987).

People v. Ekerold, 105 N.E. 670 (1914).

People of State of Illinois ex rel. McCollum v. Board of Education of School District No. 71, Champaign County, Illinois, 333 U.S. 203, 68 S.Ct. 461 (1948).

Pierce v. Society of the Sisters of the Holy Names of Jesus and Mary, 268 U.S. 510, 45 S.Ct. 571 (1925).

Smith v. Board of School Commissioners of Mobile County, 827 F.2d 684 (11th Cir. 1987).

Smith v. Ricci, 446 A.2d 501 (1982).

State ex rel. Andrews v. Webber, 8 N.E. 708 (Ind. 1886).

State ex rel. Kelley v. Ferguson, 144 N.W. 1030 (Neb. 1914).

Timothy W. v. Rochester, New Hampshire School District, 875 F.2d 954 (1st Cir., 1989).

Tinker v. Des Moines Independent Community School District, 393 U.S. 503, 89 S.Ct. 733 (1969).

Veimeister v. White, 72 N.E. 97 (New York, 1904).

Wallace v. Jaffree, 472 U.S. 38, 105 S.Ct. 2479 (1985).

West Virginia State Board of Education v. Barnette, 319 U.S. 624, 63 S.Ct. 1178 (1943).

Wisconsin v. Yoder, 406 U.S. 205, 92 S.Ct. 1526 (1972).

Chapter *11*

Family Violence

The Effect on Teachers, Parents, and Children

DOUGLAS D. KNOWLTON, PH.D.
University of North Dakota

TARA LEA MUHLHAUSER, J.D.
University of North Dakota

To understand the impact of family violence it is important to be aware of the dynamics of child abuse and neglect and domestic violence. This chapter will prepare teachers by providing general information about the characteristics of child victims, abusive and neglectful parents, and the impact of violent homes. Specific recommendations for action and decision making are found throughout the chapter. The purpose of this chapter is to help readers:

- Understand the educational and developmental implications of child abuse and domestic violence
- Grasp the severity of the problem of family violence
- Gain applicable skills for communicating with children and parents when high risk indicators for violence are present
- Understand the role of teachers in reporting and identifying high risk situations
- Have access to information on resources available at the county, state, and national level
- Understand the family dynamics of, and nexus between, child abuse and domestic violence

Every teacher envisions a classroom of energetic, enthusiastic, and responsive students; students who come to school nurtured, nourished, and without worries that might intrude on their engagement in the learning process. This vision is now tempered by our growing realization of the fact that "it is not always happy at our house," (the title of an instructional videotape on domestic violence). Students are instead coming to school encumbered by the anxieties, fears, and diminished self-esteem typical of children who have been victims of abusive and neglectful situations (Becker et al., 1995). The following statistics regarding these children are presented to alert us to the magnitude of this problem:

- In 1994, over one million children were the victims of substantiated or indicated child abuse and neglect, an increase of 27 percent since 1990.
- Two million reports of alleged child abuse and neglect were received by child protective service agencies.
- More than half of all reports of maltreatment (53%) came from professionals, including educators, law enforcement officials, medical professionals, and child care providers (Child Maltreatment, 1996, p. 2–1).

While these data on children as direct victims of violence are sobering, it is clear that just being in the presence of one family member perpetrating violence such as spouse abuse also has a significant negative impact. In the past, spouse abuse and child abuse had traditionally been treated as separate issues. As the American Humane Association's publication, *Domestic Violence and Child Abuse: Double Jeopardy for Families* (1995), points out, violence between partners frequently occurs in the same homes where violence is perpetrated against children.

Any child who is living in a home situation that is threatening or assaultive will expend energy coping with that probability. Whether it is devising plans for avoiding the threat or obsessively thinking about what might happen after school, the student will not have their full resources available for functioning in the classroom.

Studies estimate that anywhere from 45 to 70 percent of men who batter their female partners also abuse the children in the home. Stark and Flitcraft (1988) found that as many as two-thirds of abused children had mothers who were being beaten. This abuse might be from direct physical aggression or by being "in the wrong place at the wrong time"; for example, the children may try to protect the parent or they simply get in the way. Given that these child witnesses are also victims, it becomes important to have an appreciation of the level of domestic violence occurring in our homes. It is currently estimated that four million women are battered every year, one every nine seconds. Two million are beaten severely, and the FBI estimates that between 1,400 and 1,500 women are murdered every year by former husbands or boyfriends. The U.S. Department of Justice estimates that 95 percent of assaults on spouses/partners or ex-partners are committed by men against women (Alsop, 1995).

In addition, we cannot overlook our national concern about the increase of violent and antisocial behaviors on the part of our children. If we are to understand the root causes of this antisocial behavior and particularly the increase in adolescents' school and community violence, the need for information regarding possible explanations becomes a high priority. Over the span of two decades a significant body of information has pointed to child maltreatment as a causative factor for this aggression (Hoffman-Plotkin & Twentyman, 1984; Wodarski, Kurtz, Gaudin, & Howing, 1990). While our national attention has been on this aggressive behavior, other very important developmental consequences for children have also been found: increased anxiety (Wolfe & Mosk, 1983), depression (Kaufman & Cicchetti, 1989), attachment and social interaction deficits (Crittenden, 1992), academic difficulties (Salinger et al., 1984), and decreased self-esteem (Fantuzzo, 1990). Any one of these consequences has implications for a child's school performance, and all of them have been tied to school success and/or failure.

From this data we know that children are arriving for their busy school day having experienced traumas that clearly influence their responsiveness in the classroom. If we are to serve these children well, we will need to understand some of the theories about family violence, as well as the characteristics of children who are victims, characteristics of parents who are victims, and the characteristics of parents who may engage in this violent behavior. In addition, there are societal issues that have frequently been cited for creating an environment that is conducive to child maltreatment. Economic factors such as high unemployment and poverty are associated with increased incidents of abuse. More recently we have seen an increase in homeless families and the children in these families are vulnerable to a variety of maltreatment issues.

- What has led to an environment in which children are routinely maltreated in our society?
- What attitudes and beliefs support this type of interaction with children?
- When does appropriate discipline become abuse?

All of these questions are relevant to the relationships between families and teachers because the answers may have an impact on a child's capacity to learn. Once we understand some of these dynamics and can recognize their impact on our students, we then need to know what we can do to support and, if necessary, intervene with these families. It is clear that children who are physically and/or emotionally maltreated are going to present significant challenges for our schools and communities. While some educators might find it tempting to try and ignore this problem or perceive it as just a family issue, our students' needs and their cries for help will continue to push us toward a more active approach.

Child Abuse and Neglect

Child abuse and neglect is a very widespread social phenomenon. The dynamics of abuse and neglect can be found in all settings within the community. Income, race, gender, and family structure aside, the dynamics of adult-to-child violence and the effects of such violence cut across many strata in our classrooms. While the risk factors may be more obvious with certain groups of children, all children remain at risk from abuse and neglect in every home represented in our classrooms.

Child abuse is widely defined as an act of power and control over a child by use of corporal punishment, exploitation (sexual and physical), or emotional or psychological maltreatment. Abuse is often categorized as physical, emotional, or sexual maltreatment (Tower, 1996). *Neglect* is often defined as the deprivation of the child's needs that in turn leaves the child vulnerable to a variety of conditions, harm, or emotional strain. Neglect is categorized as physical, emotional, or medical neglect and includes "lack of supervision" (Tower, 1996).

While defining the terms is not difficult, identifying individual acts or situations as abusive or neglectful can be problematic. Many times the categorization or identification of an act as abusive or neglectful depends on factors such as severity, frequency, and pervasiveness of the action as well as the age and vulnerability of the child.

Generally we hold those in caretaking positions responsible for meeting the child's needs and protecting the child from exploitation; those caretakers may not always be the child's parents. A diverse group of adult caretakers (e.g., child care providers, relatives, live-in partners, grandparents) and the abusive or neglectful caretakers' access to the child can complicate the child abuse and neglect dimension.

Characterizing of the home life of abused and neglected children requires the examination of three separate areas: the caretakers, the child, and the environment where abuse and neglect is found. The dynamics are often described as either *conduct*—what the parent/ caretaker does (e.g., striking the child), or *conditions*—the issues a parent/caretaker may be faced with (e.g., mental illness).

Parental Factors in Child Abuse and Neglect

Caretakers who resort to violence in their interactions with children frequently are described as making poor decisions in a time of stress, that is, using corporal punishment out of anger and to exert control over a difficult situation. Their reaction may be intensified by

---

> ### *REFLECTION...*
>
> Corporal punishment in schools and spanking as a form of discipline are much debated issues. The Swedish government has banned all spanking. Should the U.S. government take similar steps to ban spanking or corporal punishment? Should there be specific limitations on physical discipline?

the lingering presence of drugs or alcohol (or the effects of an addiction), the effects of mental illness, the presence of physical illness or depression, or unhappiness about their life situation. All of these factors can trigger a stress response. In addition, research has identified two other very important variables in predicting the risk of child maltreatment: caretakers for whom violence is a learned response (often because of violent family histories and relationships) and caretakers who lack basic parenting skills. In this latter group, the lack of skills can mean a deficit in understanding a child's developmental needs and vulnerabilities as well as a lack of skills to respond to a child's misbehavior.

For example, an unskilled and stressed parent may resort to shaking a baby because the parent is frustrated and thinks the act will provide a signal to the baby that it is time to quit crying and resume sleep. In doing so, the parent exposes the infant to a developmental vulnerability (head injury by shaking the baby) and misjudges the child's developmental readiness to understand both act and consequence. Frequently, abusive parents simply don't understand how damaging certain attempts to discipline or punish younger children can be. Lack of skills also plays a part in the abuse of older children. With younger children, parents frequently reach a threshold of frustration and strike out. These parents think that the child will then heed their request or understand and learn their point of view.

Children who are sexually exploited by family members (often called intra-familial child sexual abuse) also have caretakers who fall into the above dynamic, but in a slightly different way. In these families it is common to see a blur of boundaries among the generations (for example, between parent and child). The expectations of family members follow that pattern, and the children are expected to step into the shoes of an adult member for some of the family functions (i.e., sexual partner). This creates great chaos and confusion in the family which compounds the secret being kept between the adult and child in regard to the sexual relationship (Faller, 1990).

The caretaker's available cognitive and emotional skills have a significant impact on the choices they make, particularly when stressed. The lack of such skills or compromised skills can contribute to a condition which makes children in their care more vulnerable to abuse.

Many of the same characteristics are seen in neglectful situations. Often the scenario of a child's life includes both neglect and abuse. Neglect dynamics are also inextricably bound to environmental characteristics. These conditions frequently set the stage for a situation of child neglect to occur.

Chronic neglect can be one of the most difficult situations for us to work with in the classroom. It is not uncommon to find conditions of physical neglect creating a dynamic of emotional neglect for a child in class. Even with intervention, sometimes the condition and conduct are so pervasive and deeply ingrained in the family structure that successes are small and take time. In these situations, it is important not to underestimate the impact a positive school relationship can have on a child. We may be meeting, or have an opportunity to meet, some very basic self-esteem, emotional, and developmental needs that are not being met in the home.

As we work to build relationships with parents or caretakers who may arouse our concerns, remember that they often are very isolated physically, emotionally, or psychologically from the needs of their children because they are frequently overwhelmed with other issues in life. Isolation, in combination with a lack of parenting or social/emotional skills and any conditioning factors (such as alcohol abuse, mental illness), can be very difficult to work with, and you may benefit from working with others as a team to build and maintain personal relationships.

Environmental Factors in Abuse and Neglect

While child abuse and neglect is widespread in all communities, we should be aware of the important environmental indicators of risk. Poverty and the surrounding conditions (unemployment, poor housing and diet, etc.), social isolation, and the stress of single-parenting, or a combination of these factors, are widely accepted as environmental risk factors. Certainly the lack of income contributes in direct and indirect ways to the child abuse and neglect dimension (Tower, 1996). For instance, a parent may not have the ability to afford after-school child care, which places the child in an unsupervised situation everyday for several hours. This may not be a true reflection of the parent's decision-making capability; it may instead reflect the financial reality the parent faces and how the parent may have to balance and weigh risk factors (e.g., a job that will bring in money versus supervising their eight-year-old child after school). If a parent is not socially isolated in this scenario, they may have the ability to leverage available resources to provide care for their child in the form of a neighbor or a play/recreation group with revolving parental supervision. If the parent is socially isolated, their choices and alternatives narrow and this may create undue stress on the parent–child relationship.

This scenario creates a good opportunity for home–school partnerships with an emphasis on a win–win outcome. If the school or community provides some alternatives for working parents in these situations, the child stays in a safe after-school environment where he or she is supervised. In this setting, the child is given the chance to build peer relationships or enhance a variety of skills. The parent can then complete a full day of work with assurance that their child is safe. This can provide that layer of support that can make tremendous difference in the parent–child relationship.

Characteristics of Child Victims

It is clear that virtually all of us will at some time be involved with a child who has been a victim of physical or emotional abuse, sexual abuse, neglect, or a witness to violent behavior. Therefore, it is important that we are familiar with the characteristics of these children. While each child is an individual and will have a different configuration of symptoms or classroom problems, there are some commonalities to their psychological and behavioral status. Sometimes children will give us very simple clues that indicate they are uncomfortable in certain situations or appear to be different than other children in the classroom. At other times, they may be very hostile and angry and may tend to alienate other children as well as alienating teachers or other adults in the school setting. Perhaps one of the most striking symptoms is the dramatic change in a child's demeanor or personality. These changes are often very sudden; for example, a child who has been very outgoing and involved with other children may suddenly become isolated and avoidant. These changes are often reflected in a student's performance or grades. A sudden drop in responsiveness or accomplishment in the classroom can be a cue that something significant is going on in the child's life. Listed below are some of the typical distressful emotions that a child victim may experience and explanations of how they might affect children at different developmental points.

Anxiety

One of the child's very early developmental needs is for security and safety. A young child who does not feel safe may have significantly elevated anxiety. This might show up in simple nervous behaviors (habits such as twirling hair or biting nails) or actually be seen in the development of phobias, panic disorders, obsessive/compulsive disorders, and so forth. At times this anxiety may be associated with a particular person or environment, or it may be more generalized with the child constantly feeling on edge or irritable. Young children often use avoidance to cope with this kind of anxiety or develop other symptoms such as nightmares, bed wetting, or physiological symptoms such as headaches or stomach distress.

As the child gets older, the anxiety may take on other behavioral manifestations. In adolescence these young people may cope with their anxieties by becoming aggressive or resorting to the use of alcohol and drugs to numb some of the agitation or irritability they may experience.

Depression

Depression can be seen in children through classical symptoms (i.e., change in appetite, change in sleep patterns, overall mood problems, etc.). It is important to note that in young people, depression can also look like an agitated state with increased activity and inattention. There have even been children diagnosed with Attention Deficit Disorder (ADD) or Attention Deficit Hyperactivity Disorder (ADHD) who may very well have been depressed, but their activity levels were significantly increased due to agitation. While the diagnosis of depression is not often made for very young children, these symptoms could clearly be manifestations of a child who is in an abusive situation.

In the area of adolescent development, depression may take on a more serious note, particularly as it is paired with an increase in adolescent impulsive behavior. This impulsiveness can add to the potential for drug and alcohol abuse and the risk of adolescent suicide.

Anger

It is important to note that anger, when expressed by a young child, may simply be increased irritability or uncontrollable behavior; it may be a result of their difficulty understanding and/or expressing feelings of anger. Sometimes this anger can become self-directed and contributes to depression or high-risk behavior. At other times, these children may display behavioral difficulties and become more aggressive, particularly toward other children. This behavior is often difficult to manage in the classroom and if we don't see this behavior as a cry for help, we may take a very destructive approach with the child. Anger expressed by adolescents tends to be more hostile and can be seen in aggressive behaviors with the increased possibility of sexually aggressive behavior.

Self-Concept

It is becoming increasingly clear that a child's sense of self is negatively impacted by involvement in any abusive situation. Levels of self-esteem (a child's positive view of him/herself) and appropriate self-concept (a child's realistic view of their capabilities) are crucial to the on-going psychological development and well-being of children. An assault on this self-esteem can negatively impact the child's developmental progress. When children have an impaired sense of self or a reduced sense of self-esteem, they are often unable to control their own emotions. They may not be able to calm or soothe themselves when they are in a situation in which there is a lot of stress. This can also have an impact when children need to separate or become independent from others; a diagnosis of separation anxiety disorder may be associated with these particular times. Later in the child's development, there may be difficulties defining one's own boundaries or appreciating the needs and desires of others in their environments. In addition, there are reports of increased suggestibility or gullibility, inadequate self-protectiveness and a greater likelihood of being victimized or exploited by others.

Post-Traumatic Stress Disorder (PTSD)

Highly distressing or threatening environmental situations can cause a reaction that has been called post-traumatic stress and diagnosed as post-traumatic stress disorder (PTSD). This disorder is evidenced by: (a) a numbing of emotions or responsiveness to events; (b) frequent reexperiencing of events sometimes through intrusive thoughts or nightmares; and (c) increased irritability, sleep disturbance, poor concentration. Children who have been abused tend to exhibit more post-traumatic fear, concentration problems, and anxiety than do children who have not been abused.

While these symptoms are most common in children who have been exposed to high levels of violent or abusive behavior, there are other symptoms that are sometimes problematic and indicative of this type of exposure. These include the potential for suicide, high-risk sexual behavior, and a higher incidence of suicidal thinking and behavior in children. Some children, particularly adolescents, might engage in indiscriminate sexual behavior as an expression of the need for acceptance and self-worth. It is also not uncommon to see eating disorders such as anorexia or bulimia. Bulimia is evidenced primarily by binging and purging behaviors and these symptoms have been associated with higher incidents of abuse, particularly sexual abuse.

One of the most obvious characteristics of these children is their difficulty negotiating within their personal relationships. A sudden change in the child's relationship with other children can be a clue that there is a source of additional stress in their life. These children may engage in avoidance behaviors (withdrawal, isolation) which create problems with their interpersonal activities. These children may actually perceive themselves as less worthy of appropriate relationships. In general, abused children have been found to be socially less competent, more aggressive, and more withdrawn than their non-abused counterparts. In later life, it becomes very difficult for these children to develop intimate relationships, and if they do develop, the relationships often center on some type of ambivalence or fear about becoming vulnerable.

REFLECTION ...

Consider the characteristics of abused children and how each would appear in a classroom environment. How will you be able to recognize these behaviors?

Intervention and Treatment

Obviously, the intervention and treatment process cannot begin until the children and families at risk of further abuse and neglect have been identified. That is why it is so crucial for us to identify and report abusive and neglectful situations and incidents to the local child protection agency. Once identified, an assessment process is conducted by social workers to determine the safety of the child in their present environment and to recommend a treatment service. Usually this process will include some determination, by the child protection services agency or multi-disciplinary child protection team, of whether the reported act or situation is recognized as abusive or neglectful.

If the child is in need of immediate protection from further abuse or harm, the child protection agency will seek the authority of the court to remove the child from a harmful environment. Taking temporary or emergency custody of a child generally means that the child will be placed with a nurturing relative or in a foster home or facility until it is safe for the child to return home. If it is found that the abuse or neglect did occur, the court will usually mandate parents/caretakers to participate in some kind of recommended treatment before the child will be returned home. In child sexual abuse cases, the child protection agency may require that the abusive adult leave the home and cease to have contact with the child. In this situation, the child can remain at home with the supervision of a supportive parent while the abusive adult is monitored and allowed to return home after completing the sex offender treatment process.

Treatment recommended by the child protection agency is generally part of a plan for the child and/or family. Many different treatment options are available and can vary greatly in each community. Often the family is involved in some educational process to assist the parents/caretakers with the enhancement of parenting skills. Support groups, individual therapy, family therapy, and in-home, family-based services (with a specific set of goals and a case worker in the home) are used. If there are conditions such as mental illness or alcoholism, the parent/caretaker is referred to the appropriate treatment facility or agency prior to participating in the aforementioned treatment services. Also, social workers frequently work with families to provide or suggest resources in the community to assist with financial issues, feelings of isolation, and domestic violence. In some cases, we may be asked to be involved in a team process to monitor, recommend, and assist agency treatment providers with assessment and development of a treatment plan for a child and/or family.

Long-Term Effects of Abuse on Children

Significant research and pages of popular media have been devoted to the long-term effects of abuse and neglect on children. There are so many possible effects that it is difficult to predict an outcome. Some individuals even claim a sense of strength from the early maltreatment. Much of the current research on resiliency indicates that positive forces in a child's life may be able to mitigate the harm of abuse and neglect, although nothing will completely obliterate the harm from a child victim's life or memory (Wolin & Wolin, 1993). It is clear that the maltreatment does have a diminishing effect on a child's abilities, although which abilities and to what degree seem to vary on a case-by-case basis.

Research has documented neurological, cognitive, behavioral, psychological, emotional, and intellectual effects. Educationally, effects of child abuse and neglect have been linked to academic outcomes and lower test scores, indicating that maltreatment may diminish a child's ability to fully participate and advance (Tower, 1992).

Domestic Violence

Domestic violence is defined as a pattern of assaultive and controlling behaviors in the context of an intimate adult relationship. While domestic violence is often referred to as spouse abuse, that term is not inclusive enough to apply to the violence that happens between adult intimates outside of marriage. The pattern of assaults and control frequently takes the form of coercion, terrorism, degradation, exploitation, and actual violence in the form of physical assault (Peled, Jaffe, & Edelson, 1995). One author (Ganley, 1993) describes domestic violence as "hands-on" (meaning the physical assaults) and "hands-off" (meaning the psychological pattern of terrorism that leaves no visible scars). According to the FBI in their 1990 Uniform Crime Report, battering is the establishment of control and fear in a relationship through violence and other forms of abuse. The batterer uses acts of violence and a series of behaviors, including intimidation, threats, psychological abuse, isolation, and so forth, to coerce and control the other person. The violence may not happen often, but it remains as a hidden (and constant) terrorizing factor.

When research tells us that 30 percent of all women will suffer from some form of abuse in an adult relationship (Peled, Jaffe, & Edelson, 1995), it is clear that the effects of domestic violence are far reaching in any community, including the classroom. The pattern of adult violence usually has ebbs and flows; there are periods of chaos and immediate fear interrupted by periods of controlled calm, apology, and remorse. The violence usually escalates with each new onset and in the latter stages often involves weapons. As domestic survivors will tell you, they must spend tremendous energy "keeping a lid" on everything so that an episode of violence does not erupt. Why do they stay in such situations? Aside from the obvious issue of parenting, there are financial concerns, family issues, and practical issues of where to live, how to provide for children if one leaves a relationship, and danger. Also, research confirms that women who leave their batterers are at a 75 percent greater risk of being killed by the batterer than those who stay (Hart, 1988).

Characteristics of Violent Households

While the great majority of reported incidents of battering involve male batterers, there is a small percentage of reported battering by women. Because domestic violence is a crime, the report of an incident can be a very difficult time for a family and a confusing time for the children. While many once thought that the effects on children living in a violent home

> *REFLECTION...*
>
> Isn't it difficult to understand why someone who is being battered or exploited doesn't leave the relationship? Why might it be very difficult or dangerous for someone to leave a violent relationship? What might be some of the early characteristics or signals in our own relationships that might include the potential for violent interactions?

were minimal, research is strongly confirming that the effects are clearly damaging, both because children are caught, literally, in the crossfire and because they are passive witnesses to violent and abusive acts (Jaffe et al., 1995; Peled, et al., 1995; Roy, 1988).

Often we hear of violent incidents that children disclose in the classroom long before the incidents are reported to any authority. As classroom teachers, we must be prepared to listen to the children and let them talk about what they have observed and heard at home and give them an opportunity to tell how they feel. How, and if, you then approach the issue with a parent will be a very crucial decision. Consideration must be given to issues of safety, shame and guilt, the stigma of being battered, and fear on the part of both the child and the battered parent. The patterns of control in violent families is so pervasive that it may take a battered parent years before she is ready to take the risk of leaving the violent relationship.

As indicated in Table 11-1, the characteristics of the batterer are similar across the categories of family violence we've discussed in this chapter. This violent interaction creates the same kind of reoccurring crisis and chaos that we see in families where there is abuse and neglect. While conditions such as alcohol use and abuse and mental illness may aggravate the pattern of power and control in a family, the use of power and control to dominate family members is a learned behavior, not a result of the use or misuse of chemical substances or a chemical imbalance. According to researchers and therapists in the field, men who batter minimize or deny the seriousness of their behavior; externalize responsibility for the violence to other situations and people; have a need to control and dominate people,

TABLE 11-1 Commonalities in Family Operations across Violent Families

	Child Maltreatment	Sexual Abuse	Conjugal Violence	Elder Mistreatment
(1) Confused and distorted attachments	X	X	X	X
(2) Unequal power and status distributions	X	X	X	X
(3) Frustration	X	X	X	X
(4) Distorted cognitions and attributions	X	X	X	X
(5) Role incompetence in the face of stress	X	X	X	X

From: Bolton, *Working with Violent Families,* 163. Copyright © 1987. Reprinted by permission of Sage Publications, Inc.

most specifically their partners; and isolate their victims to keep the abuse inside the family (Stordeur & Stille, 1989).

From the other perspective, battered women can be so compromised by fear that their ability to respond to a situation of violence can be diminished. Psychologically, research shows that battered women can be characterized by the following:

> *learned helplessness (i.e., the belief that their best efforts to be effective will produce random results); a diminished perception of alternatives (to the violence, especially); a heightened tolerance for ideas that do not belong together (e.g., I love him and I fear him); and knowledge of the abuser's potential for violence and the range of violent acts which they can perform. (Blackman, 1996)*

These characteristics may also diminish these women's ability to nurture children and provide the necessary encouragements and supports for their children's emotional growth and development and sense of security. Susan Schechter, an expert in the field of domestic violence, is frequently quoted as saying "the best way to protect the children is to protect their mother." Because of the battered woman's response to the violence, they may not be able to fully protect their children while they continue to live in a violent environment (Roy, 1988).

Intervention and Treatment

Because domestic violence is a crime, intervention is available through law enforcement agencies. Most states have a protocol used for domestic violence cases that determines whether the case will proceed on to the criminal justice system once a referral or arrest has been made. Arrest has been shown to be an effective intervention in domestic violence situations. It is important for the intervention process to include a treatment component to assist batterers with "unlearning" the learned behavior. During treatment, the batterer learns new skills and ideas to help replace old behavior with acceptable and appropriate ways of expressing anger and managing power and control in relationships. Many treatment programs are available in community settings; the best programs combine elements of education, therapy, and crisis management. Most comprehensive programs include weekly sessions for at least twenty-four weeks.

Battered women are provided support through formal support group sessions and individual therapy, generally available through a community domestic violence agency. Many programs also provide treatment services for children by using a support group/education process or play therapy to help the child to express and understand feelings.

Many communities currently have efforts of ongoing collaboration to provide a team approach for delivery of services and to enhance the array of services and intervention available to assist families and children living in violence. Because the effects of violence are so far reaching in our communities, it is important for us to be involved with collaborative efforts and understand the issues from the perspectives of domestic violence advocates and law enforcement. Involvement at this level can also assist us in building confidence in how we can respond when one of our students discloses a violent incident at home, when a colleague discloses a violent incident, or when a parent confides in us about a situation. The potential for lethality in these incidents is great, and we must be prepared to use community resources in assisting families and children in finding a safe haven and a way out of the cycle of violence.

Long-Term Effects of Domestic Violence on Family Members

The effects of domestic violence on children, as stated earlier, correlates with the child's developmental stage and the severity and frequency of the abuse. The effects must always be assessed on a case-by-case basis—some children may experience a very traumatic result from witnessing only one act. Generally, research shows that boys who witness violence are three times more likely to grow up to use violence in their intimate relationships than those boys not exposed to family violence (Stark et al., 1996). This same research shows that violence is quite a legacy; sons of violent fathers have an estimated rate of woman abuse 1,000 times higher than the sons of nonviolent fathers. Conversely, girls who witness their mothers being abused may have a greater rate of tolerance for abuse in a relationship (Hotaling & Sugarman, 1986).

According to Jaffe, one third of the children witnessing violence show behavioral and emotional disruptions, anxiety, sleep disruption, and school problems. Approximately 20 to 40 percent of the families of chronically violent delinquent adolescents had family histories of domestic violence (Jaffe, Wolfe, & Wilson, 1990). Other research indicates that depression and reduced verbal, cognitive, and motor abilities are results of witnessing adult violence. Significant volumes of research consistently show that witnessing violence as a youth promotes the use of violence in adulthood to solve problems and as a means of gaining control. Research on the long-term effects on adults show that depression, low self-esteem, emotional trauma and post-traumatic stress, and revictimization are often experienced by survivors of violence (Bolton & Bolton, 1987). All of these factors must be considered before examining a specific situation and creating a plan or opportunity to work on building a relationship with a parent who is living with violence.

The Link between Child Abuse and Domestic Violence

As educators we have been sensitized to the issues of child abuse. We have been trained on the reporting procedures to employ when we suspect abuse, but few of us have been aware of the significant problems caused when children witness violent behaviors in their homes. There is a growing awareness of the link between domestic violence and child abuse in children's lives. The American Humane Association (AHA) highlighted this link in their publication *Protecting Children* (1995).

One of the articles in the AHA publication, written by Schecter and Edleson (1995), cited studies that indicate the link among patterns of response between children who are witnesses and those who are actually abused themselves. Increased aggression and antisocial behaviors, lowered social competence, higher anxiety and depression, and lowered verbal, cognitive, and motor abilities were found to exist when children are exposed to the range of family violence. The cognitive and emotional implication for the educational setting is obvious. If we, as teachers, are to promote and facilitate learning, we must be aware of the negative impact domestic violence has on our students.

When either children or their mothers are at risk they are both at risk. A study of over 6,000 American families (Straus & Gelles, 1990) found that 50 percent of men who frequently assault their wives also frequently abuse their children. This same study found that "the rate of child abuse by those (mothers) who have been beaten is at least double that of mothers whose husbands did not assault them" (p. 409). Thus, many of these children are at risk for harm from both their fathers and their mothers.

Because of the interrelatedness of child abuse and domestic violence, there has been some tension between the Child Protective Services and those services directed at helping victims of domestic violence. For example, child protection social workers might determine that if a woman is not able to protect herself, then she might not be able to protect her children. The domestic violence advocates feel that if the best interests of children are to be protected, their mothers need to be protected first and foremost.

Our vision of a classroom of children who are free from violence in their homes may not be realistic at this time. The problem can be overwhelming and lead to a feeling that nothing can be done to protect our students. The information presented in this chapter is best used as a knowledge base to increase our confidence and empower us to make a difference in our students' lives. The following recommendations provide positive courses of action.

Recommendations for Action

Be Alert to Behavioral Cues

By educating ourselves we can be aware of the kinds of behavioral manifestations that we may see in our classrooms. These are most clearly seen in academic clues, with the primary indicator being sudden changes in academic performance. There may also be indications in achievement test score problems, truancies, suspensions, and infractions of disciplinary codes.

Emotional and psychological cues are also very evident and may include the change from one particular demeanor to another; for example, a child who has been cooperative becoming more hostile, angry, and alienating.

Be Alert to the Cues That Parents May Provide

Your contacts with family members, such as conversations with parents during parent conference time or other contacts, may very well provide some clues as to what may be going on in the family. Be especially alert for the following parental behaviors that may be an indication of potential problems:

- blames or belittles child;
- sees the child as very different from his or her siblings (in a negative way);
- sees the child as bad, evil, or a "monster";
- finds nothing good or attractive in the child;
- seems unconcerned about the child;
- fails to keep appointments or refuses to discuss problems the child may be having in school;
- misuses alcohol or drugs; or
- behaves in bizarre or irrational ways.

By being in contact with the family, we may be able to tell whether there are situations that may be arising which are potentially dangerous to both the child and the family.

Interacting with the Child

When having a conversation with a child in which issues arise that lead to concern, there are some guidelines that can be helpful for speaking with children about these issues. Remember that there is no benefit in conducting an investigation—that is the role of the child protective services staff. When it is necessary to talk to the child about a situation, remember that the child may be very fearful, apprehensive, or actually in pain. It is, therefore, important to make the child as comfortable as possible. The person who talks with the child should be someone who the child trusts and with whom he or she feels safe. There may be an individual in the school who has been trained and is more capable of performing these interviews, such as the school social worker or psychologist. Remember to conduct these kinds of conversations in a very private and non-threatening place. The following suggestions will prove helpful in the interviewing process:

- Children need to know that they are not in trouble and they have not done anything wrong. Children in these situations often feel responsible and blame themselves for the difficulties and there is some potential that a conversation about these issues could increase those feelings. Children need to know very clearly and directly that they are *not* at fault.
- It will be important to assure the child that information they provide will not be shared with other teachers or classmates.
- If we feel that we will have to report the information, we should inform the child while continuing to let the child know that we will be their support and that they can come to us at any time.
- When talking with a child, make sure the language used is at an appropriate developmental level. If the child says something that is confusing or not understandable, ask for clarification.
- Do not press for answers or details a child seems unwilling to give. Again, this should not be an investigation; the child needs to feel that they can protect themselves in terms of the information they might give. Initial interviews in cases like this have sometimes led to the dismissal of legal charges because of problems with the interview process.
- Don't ever insist on seeing a child's injuries; although if they want to show the injuries, don't hesitate to let them do so using good professional judgment. Be sure pieces of clothing are never removed; if for some reason we must remove clothing to view an injury, we must be sure a school nurse or an appropriate school official is present.

Guidelines for Talking with Parents

Sometimes a conversation during a parent conference leads to concerns about abuse or violent behavior. A decision should be made as to whether the teacher is the most appropriate person to meet with the parent or if a principal or some other staff member would be in a better position. Clearly, parents will be apprehensive and may be very angry when first confronted about the existence of violent behavior. It is important to make the parents feel as comfortable as possible. Again, conversations should be in private and parents should be informed immediately as to what action might be taken. Try to be sympathetic and do not display any kind of anger, repugnance, or shock. It is usually best not to give advice but to allow the parent to make some determination of their own course of action. This is particularly true for cases in which there has been some domestic violence and the mother has disclosed information; it will be up to her to make some decisions regarding future action. To force her into some kind of position or to give strong advice may very well be disempowering and create more problems for the family.

Reporting

Educators are mandated, by both state laws and federal standards and regulations, to report concerns or suspicions about child abuse and neglect. These regulations often tell us what is required and expected of us. Many state statutes specifically name educators as mandated reporters; other statutes indicate that any citizen must report. It would be helpful for teachers to have copies of their state's guidelines, laws, and the local regulations regarding this reporting. When reporting incidents or suspicions, most states will require some basic information. This may include:

1. Child's name, age, and address; parent's name and address;
2. Nature and extent of the injury or condition observed;
3. Prior injuries and when observed; and
4. Reporter's name and location (sometimes this is not required but it is often helpful to child protective services staff).

The National Education Association offers a publication entitled *How Schools Can Help Combat Child Abuse and Neglect.* As cited in Tower (1992), it provides an outline to aid schools in preparing appropriate school policy. Such a policy should include answers to the following questions:

1. At what point should the teacher report child abuse? Suspicion? Reasonable cause to believe? (This may be based not only on school policy but also state law.)
2. Who does the teacher notify? Nurse? Principal? School social worker?
3. What specific information does the teacher need to know to report?
4. What other school personnel should be involved?
5. Who makes the report to the appropriate authorities? How?
6. What information should be included in the report? (This may be dictated by state law and protective agency policy.)
7. What follow-up is expected on reported cases?
8. What role will the school play in possible community/child protection teams?
9. What commitment does the school have to in-service training or community programs? (pp. 36–37)

Reporting is often a very difficult and anxiety-provoking process for us. Often personal feelings about parents or a particular child may have an impact on our decisions. It is difficult for people to make decisions that cause others to become angry. Because of this, we sometimes fear for our own safety. At times, we may also feel that we are not appropriately supported by administrators or other school officials and this may have some impact on our decisions. In other cases, previous difficulties or bad experiences with child protective services may make us hesitant about reporting. This hesitancy may involve thoughts that "nothing can be done." Often we feel left out of the "information loop" with regard to what happens to the child after child protective services has become involved. Confidentiality laws and policies at times make that relationship a difficult one. Some state laws will allow release of information from child protective services to other professionals when the individual is the member of a multi-disciplinary team.

Awareness of Community, State, and National Resources

It is important for us to be aware of the various programs in our community which offer services to children and families, particularly those intervening in and providing treatment for violent families. Locate your child protection agency for more information regarding child abuse and neglect issues in your community and contact either the domestic violence program or a law enforcement agency for more information on domestic violence issues. These programs can provide a profile of the needs of families in the community as well as educational resources to assist you and your students, colleagues, and parents in learning more about the issues and the available services.

Several national resources exist that provide information on family violence. The National Resource Center on Domestic Violence (800-537-2238) and the Resource Center on Child Protection and Custody (800-527-3223) are excellent resources and have many fine materials available at no cost. Similarly, the Clearinghouse on Child Abuse and Neglect Information (703-385-7565) and the National Committee for Prevention of Child Abuse at (312-663-3520) also have excellent materials and provide technical assistance. There may be similar state entities or affiliates that provide information specific to your state; the local programs you contact in your community should have names and addresses of those resources.

Recommended Activities

1. Invite Child Protective Services or Domestic Violence staff to provide a staff development in-service on reporting and identifying high risk situations.
2. Access the *Bookfinder: A Guide to Children's Literature about the Needs and Problems of Youth* (Dreyer) which reviews literature and books for children that focus on social issues relevant to abuse and family violence.
3. Participate in child abuse and neglect prevention activities such as wearing a blue ribbon during the month of April to bring attention to the issue.

4. Investigate whether a specific curriculum has been adopted by the school to address family violence or child abuse and neglect issues.

5. Have students design a poster and theme for the class on child abuse/neglect or domestic violence to speak to children living with daily violence in their home.

6. Gather and distribute a list of community resources of agencies/groups that respond to and help families who are violent.

7. Role play a parent conference in which you suspect your student has witnessed significant violence in the home. Identify your feelings as you struggle with the idea of reporting or identifying the violence.

Additional Resources

Child Abuse

Books:

Fontana, V. J. (1989). *Somewhere a child is crying: Maltreatment causes and prevention.*

This is also a classic on various forms of child abuse that has had a number of printings. It has been up-dated and is as timely now as when first printed. 242 pp. ISBN: 451-62429-7.

Penguin
120 Woodbine
Burenfield, NJ 07621
Phone: 800-331-4624

Kempe, C. H., & Helfer, R. E. (Eds.). (1987). *The battered child (4th ed.).*

This is a classic on the subject. It is easy to read, practical, and informative.

Kempe National Center
Division of University Health Science Center
Department of Pediatrics
1205 Oneida Street
Denver, CO 80220
Phone: 303-321-3963

Kempe, C. H., & Kempe, R. (1984). *The common secret: Sexual abuse of children and adolescents.*

Although this book is a few years old, it remains relevant. This book uses case studies to help the reader understand definitions, legal aspects, evaluation, and treatment. It is highly readable. ISBN: 0-7167-1625-9.

W. H. Freeman
41 Madison Avenue
New York, NY 10010
Phone: 800-347-9415

Lew, M. (1988). *Victims no longer: Men recovering from incest and other sexual child abuse.*

For many years there was the assumption that boys were seldom sexually abused. We now know differently. This book is of particular importance because there is so little information for educators about minor males being sexual abused. This is a well written and useful book. 315 pp. ISBN: 0-06-097300-5.

Harper & Collins, Publishers
Perennial Library
East 53rd Street
New York, NY 10022
Phone: 212-207-7000

Nelson, M., & Clark, K. (Eds.). (1986). *The educators guide to preventing child sexual abuse.*

This may be the best single source on the topic of child sexual abuse. It is an important part of every educator's professional library. 208 pp. ISBN: 0-941816-17-6.

Network Publications
1700 Mission Street, Suite 203
PO Box 1830
Santa Cruz, CA 95061-1830
Phone: 408-438-4060

Videos:

Child Abuse

This video deals with the subject of physical and emotional abuse. It identifies common characteristics of the offender, examines therapy for young victims of physical and sexual abuse, and offers tips in selecting day care settings for young children. (19 minutes, color).

Films for the Humanities & Sciences
PO Box 2053
Princeton, NJ 08543
Phone: 800-257-5126

Child Abuse: It Shouldn't Hurt to Be a Kid

Educators and other school personnel are required by law to report suspected child abuse. This video advises these mandated reporters of their responsibilities under the law. It defines child abuse and explains how to recognize it. 1987. (27 minutes, color).

> Insights Media
> 2162 Broadway
> New York, NY 10024
> 212-721-6316

No One Saved David

This is the story of a child who was killed by his adoptive parent. The death was listed as accidental. Twenty years later the case was reexamined and the adoptive mother was found guilty of murder. This video is of special interest to educators because it looks at how a whole community (friends, family, social workers, law enforcement, etc.) contributed to a situation that allowed this to happen. A segment of 60 Minutes, with Diane Sawyer. (14 minutes, color).

> Films for the Humanities & Sciences
> PO Box 2053
> Princeton, NJ 08543
> Phone: 800-257-5126

Organizations:

> C. Henry Kempe National Center for Prevention and Treatment
> of Child Abuse and Neglect
> 1205 Oneida
> Denver, CO 20001
> Phone: 303-321-3963

> Clearing House on Child Abuse and Neglect Information
> PO Box 1182
> Washington, DC 20013
> Phone: 703-385-7565

Curriculum:

Botvin, G. J. (1983). *Life skills training: Teacher's manual* (seventh grade curriculum). New York: Smithfield Press.

Kassees, J. M. (n.d.) *Educators guide to child abuse prevention.* Wilmington, DE: Parents Anonymous of Delaware, Inc.

Nelson, M., & Clark, K. (Eds.). (1986). *The educator's guide to preventing child sexual abuse.* Santa Cruz, CA: Network Publications.

Positive Parenting. (1995). St. Paul, MN: Minnesota Extension Service.

Tower, C. C. (1984). *Child abuse and neglect: NEA multi-media training program.* Washington, DC: National Education Association.

Tower, C. (1992). *The role of educators in the protection and treatment of child abuse and neglect.* U.S. Department of Health and Human Services. DHHS Publication No. (ACF) 92-30172.

Walker, C., Bonner, B., & Kaufman, K. (1988). *The physically and sexually abused child.* New York: Pergamon Press.

Websites:

Abuse and Violence—Social Work
http://www.gwbssw.wustl.edu/%7Egwbhome/websites.html/#abuse

Kids Count Report on Children and Violence
http://www.cait.cpmc.columbia.edu/dept/nccp

National Clearinghouse on Child Abuse and Neglect Information
http://www.calib.com/nccanch

Safety Net—Domestic Violence Resources
http://www.cybergrrl.com/dv.html

References

Alsop, R. (1995). Domestic violence and child abuse: Double jeopardy for families. *Protecting Children, 11*(3), 2.

Becker, J., Alpert, J., Subia Big Foot, D., Bonner, B., Geddie, L., Henggeler, S., Kaufman, K. & Walker, C. (1995). Empirical research on child abuse treatment: Report by the child abuse and neglect treatment working group, American Psychological Association. *Journal of Clinical Child Psychology, 24,* 23–46.

Blackman, J. (1996). "Battered women": What does this phrase really mean? *Domestic Violence Report, 1*(2), pp. 5, 11.

Bolton, F. G., & Bolton, S. R. (1987). *Working with violent families: A guide for clinical and legal practitioners.* Newbury Park: Sage Publications.

Child maltreatment 1994: Reports from the states to the national center on child abuse and neglect. (1996). U.S. Department of Health and Human Services. National Center on Child Abuse and Neglect. Washington, DC: Government Printing Office.

Crittenden, P. (1992). Children's strategies for coping with adverse home environments: An interpretation using attachment theory. *Child Abuse and Neglect, 16,* 329–343.

DePanfilis, D., & Salus, M. K. (1992). *A coordinated response to child abuse and neglect: A basic manual.* U.S. Department of Health and Human Services. NCCAN.

Faller, K. C. (1990). *Understanding child sexual maltreatment.* Newbury Park: Sage Publications.

Fantuzzo, J. (1990). Behavioral treatment of the victims of child abuse and neglect. *Behavior Modification, 14,* 316–339.

Federal Bureau of Investigation (1990). *Uniform Crime Report.* Washington DC: U.S. Printing Office.

Ganley, A. L. (1993). Workshop Notes, "Domestic violence in civil cases," North Dakota Judicial Conference, Bismarck, ND, November, 22, 1993.

Hart, B. (1990). Gentle jeopardy: The further endangerment of battered women and children in custody mediation. *Mediation Quarterly, 7,* 317–330.

Hoffman-Plotkin, D., & Twentyman, C. (1984). A multimodel assessment of behavioral and cognitive deficits in abused and neglected preschoolers. *Child Development, 55,* 794–802.

Hotaling, G. T., & Sugarman, D. B. (1986). An analysis of risk markers in husband and wife violence: The current state of knowledge. *Violence and Victims, 1*(2), 101–124.

Jaffe, P., Wolfe, D., & Wilson, S. (1990). *Children of battered women.* Newbury Park: Sage Publications.

Kaufman, J., & Cicchetti, D. (1989). Effects of maltreatment on school age children's socioemotional development: Assessment in a day camp setting. *Developmental Psychology, 25,* 516–524.

McKay, M. (1994). The link between domestic violence and child abuse: Assessment and treatment considerations. *Child Welfare, 73,* 29.

Peled, G., Jaffe, P. G., & Edelson, J. L. (1995). *Ending the cycle of violence.* Newbury Park: Sage Publications.

Roy, M. (1988). *Children in the crossfire.* Deerfield Beach, FL: Health Communications.

Salinger, S., Kaplan, S., Pelcovitz, D., Samit, C., & Kreiger, R. (1984). Parent and teacher assessment of children's behavior in child maltreating families. *Journal of the American Academy of Child Psychiatry, 23,* 458–464.

Schlecter, S., & Edleson, J. (1995). In the best interest of women and children: A call for collaboration between child welfare and domestic violence constituencies. *Protecting Children, 11*(3), 6–11.

Stark, E., & Flitcraft, A. (1988). Women and children: A feminist perspective on child abuse. *International Journal of Health Services, 18,* 97–118.

Stark, E. & Flitcraft, A. (1996). *Women at risk: Domestic violence and women's health.* Thousand Oaks: Sage Publications.

Stordeur, R. A., & Stille, R. (1989). *Ending men's violence against their partners: One road to peace.* Newbury Park: Sage Publications.

Straus, M., & Gelles, R. (Eds.). (1990). *Physical violence in American families.* New Brunswick, NJ: Transaction Publishers.

Tower, C. (1992). The role of educators in the protection and treatment of child abuse and neglect. U.S. Department of Health and Human Services. DHHS Publication No. (ACF) 92-30172.

Tower, C. (1996). *Understanding child abuse and neglect* (3rd ed.). Boston: Allyn and Bacon.

Wodarski, J., Kurtz, P., Gaudin, J., & Howing, P. (1990). Maltreatment and the school age child: Major academic, socioemotional, and adaptive outcomes. *Social Work, 35,* 506–513.

Wolfe, D., & Mosk, M. (1983). Behavioral comparison of children from abusive and distressed families. *Journal of Consulting and Clinical Psychology, 51,* 702–708.

Wolin, S. J., & Wolin, S. (1993). *The resilient self: How survivors of troubled families rise above adversity.* New York: Villard Books.

C h a p t e r *12*

Poverty

The Enemy of Children and Families

MARY LOU FULLER
University of North Dakota

SANDRA WINN TUTWILER
Hamline University

> The number of children in poverty is growing, and educators must understand the complexities of poverty in the lives of these children and their families. Schools have traditionally been designed for the Euro-American, middle-class student, in order to make the schools a positive learning environment for these children. The purpose of this chapter is to help the reader:
>
> - Understand the demographics of poverty
> - Examine some of the myths about poverty
> - Understand the effects of poverty on the lives of children and their families
> - Explore the school's relationship with these children and their families

Societies must be judged by the way they treat their children, and while an equal chance at life has long been a United States policy goal, that goal is not being met. (Rainwater & Smeeding, 1995)

This chapter examines the influence of poverty on the families of school children. There are obvious differences between the families of those that have, and those that do not, but there are also more subtle differences—both damaging to families generally and children specifically. If, as educators, we are to engage in an effective partnership with families of a lower-income status, we must understand the effects and dynamics of poverty and families.

As an educator, it is imperative that you understand the structures of families and how they function, but it is equally as important to understand how financial resources affect the way families function. The consequences of limited financial resources can be obvious as well as subtle.

Clearly children living below the poverty line may lack adequate diet, sufficient health care, adequate housing, and child care. But poverty also affects the less obvious needs that influence a child's ability to do well academically. Furthermore, as school children get older, clothes become more important for acceptance. The "in crowd" generally wears more expensive, designer clothes that are often out of the reach of low-income families. Who are these victims of poverty?

Twenty-five percent of the children in this country live in poverty. While this in itself is an appalling number, the figure for young families (family head less than 30 years of age) is even worse—42 percent. And, in addition, a frightening 54 percent of children of female-headed households live below the poverty line (U.S. Census Bureau, 1993). Furthermore, if we included all those families who live just above the poverty line, these figures would increase significantly.

What Is Poverty?

The government officially determines what constitutes poverty. The standards are determined by the size of the family, total family income, and an annual adjustment for inflation (e.g., the rising cost of rent, food, utilities, clothing, transportation, etc.). When we talk about the national poverty level, what are we actually talking about? Currently, the poverty level for a family of four is $15,150 (*Federal Register,* 1995). This figure does not mean that a family of four can provide for all of their basic needs with this sum, but the figure represents that on which a family can marginally exist. It often doesn't even mean basic medical and dental care—much less "extras" such as visits to the orthodontist, trips to Disneyland, special lessons, or sports. Parents in poverty lack options. The average poor family with children in 1992 had a total income of $7,541—$5.40 per person per day, $37.80 per person per week. "Every day you face impossible choices about cutting back on food, housing quality and your children's other needs," and to make matters even worse nearly one in two poor live in extreme poverty, with incomes below one-half of the poverty line (Sherman, 1994, p. 3).

> ### *REFLECTION...*
>
> Consider the ways that the life of a child living in poverty is different from the life of a middle-class child. Consider not only the major areas such as nutrition but also the small pleasures and experiences of childhood. What are some of your favorite childhood memories? Do children of poverty have access to these experiences?

To put these numbers into perspective, the cost of rearing a child born in 1990 to age 18 is approximately $150,000 (Outtz, 1993), and this doesn't include the costs of postsecondary education. For a family with three children, the cost would be $450,000 dollars—close to half a million dollars. Compare the resources of families and you can begin to understand the inequality of the experiences between the children of poverty and their middle-class counterparts.

Middle-class families simply have more choices as to how they'll meet the cost of raising their children. Families living in poverty are less able to purchase goods and services that allow them to share in a way of life that is characteristically American (Lichter & Eggebeen, 1993). Currently, the gap between the haves and the have-nots is widening. In addition, the economic gap between minority and majority groups continues to increase as well, with a disproportionate number of minority families living in poverty (Chavkin, 1993). At the same time, based on current demographic shifts, the school age population in the United States is projected to be 33 percent minority children by the year 2000.

It is important to note that there is a difference between being "broke" and being poor—living in poverty. Being broke is a temporary state, while living in poverty is usually seen as a hopeless condition. As college students, many educators have been broke; they barely survived from month to month, but they knew that their financial situation would at some point in time improve. People in poverty generally can't see their situations changing.

In addition, while it is easier to discuss people living below the poverty line (the demographics are more readily available), we must also remember that there are a sizeable number of families who live just above the poverty line and who also struggle to meet the basic needs of their children. The observations in this chapter are also pertinent to this very large population.

Who Lives in Poverty and Why?

Approximately 22 percent of all American children live in poverty. To make matters worse, more than 25 percent of all children under the age of six (the most important years developmentally) live in poverty. The United States ranks eighteenth out of twenty industrialized countries of the world for childhood poverty, and a child is nine times more apt to live in poverty in the United States than in countries such as Britain, France, Italy, Australia, and Finland (Children's Defense Fund, 1996).

One reason for the rise in child poverty in recent years is the failure of hourly wages to keep pace with inflation, particularly for young workers and those with less than a college education. Another reason is the increase in the number of families headed by a single parent—usually the mother. Mother-only families are at high risk for poverty due to the absence of a second adult wage earner and the historically lower earning power of women.

The 1995 guidelines for poverty (see Table 12-1) are not planned to provide enough money to support a family but only to assist in survival. It means that families living below the poverty line must sacrifice, and often these sacrifices are in the area of necessities—medical care, adequate food and housing, and so forth.

REFLECTION...

Make a list of the costs for a middle-class family of four. Include the obvious (e.g., food, shelter, utilities, clothing, medical care, recreation, transportation) as well as those less obvious items (e.g., car, health, life insurance, funds for emergencies, the dentist/orthodontist, lessons, computer, vacations). Add up these costs and note the discrepancy between those living in poverty and those in the middle class.

Myths about Poverty

Myth: We have all heard the stereotypes concerning poor people: They are people of color who are too lazy to work. This stereotype is not only inaccurate and unfair, but it makes understanding the dynamics of poverty more difficult and, consequently, harder to consider appropriate interventions.

TABLE 12-1   1995 Poverty Guidelines for the Forty-Eight Contiguous States

One person	$7,470
Family of two	$10,030
Family of three	$12,590
Family of four	$15,150

From: Federal Register, 1995.

Reality: The reality is that the percentage of people of color in poverty may not be greater than that of white children. In fact, there are more poor white children than children of color.

Myth: Poor people live in the inner city.
Reality: More children in rural settings (27%) are poor than children in the inner city (11%) (Sherman, 1994).

Myth: Families are poor because they are lazy and don't work.
Reality: The reality is that most of the children of poor families have at least one parent who is working; these children receive twice as much support from the paid work their parents do than from welfare programs (Children's Defense Fund, 1996).

Myth: If they just worked harder, they wouldn't be poor.
Reality: The reality is that a person can work forty hours a week at minimum wage and the salary earned won't raise a family above the poverty line. And, finally, contrary to popular opinion, welfare is not a way of life for most poor people. The majority of families who receive welfare benefits receive them for less than two years (Sherman, 1994).

The Effects of Poverty

Poverty dims the future and creates stress and anxiety in the present. It limits opportunities and prospects. Although poor children can and often do succeed despite their poverty, researchers have documented a host of ways in which basic economic security helps children and poverty hurts them. Arloc Sherman (1994) has identified areas where money makes a big difference.

Money Buys Good Food

Money buys good food and good food results in healthy children. Lack of good food may result in iron deficiency, hunger, stunted growth, clinical malnutrition, and under-nutrition among low-income pregnant women.

Money Buys Safe and Decent Shelter

With poverty comes a lack of safe and decent shelter, homelessness, inadequate housing, moving from house to house and consequently from school to school. In addition, other problems include heating and electricity problems, utility shut-offs, cold and dampness, mold and allergies, cockroaches and rats, peeling paint and falling plaster, lead poisoning, crowded housing, and fire-prone mobile homes.

Money Buys Opportunities to Learn

Coming from a family in poverty means that the child(ren) probably will attend an inferior school, with inadequate supplies, which often is unable to retain the most skilled teachers and administrators. There will be fewer educational materials in the home, fewer stimulating activities (trips, lessons, museums, concerts, etc.), and less exposure to computers. While children from more affluent families often enter school with a strong educational background and degree of familiarity with computers, few children of poverty do. Also, children of poverty have greater home responsibilities that compete with school.

Money Reduces Family Stress and Conflict

As economic hardships increase so do the parents' level of stress and depression. Low incomes have an effect upon mental health both for the parent and for the child. Their lives are unpredictable—the loss of a job may result in homelessness. The inability to pay the heating bill may result in illness. Because of their poverty, they often feel shame, fear, and anger. There is apt to be conflict about how best to use the limited resources which are available. Furthermore, stress increases the chances of child abuse and neglect.

Money Buys a Decent Neighborhood

The lack of resources increases the chance that children will live in noisy, crime-ridden neighborhoods, and/or be more likely to live in neighborhoods that pose a threat from chemicals and pollution. The neighborhood is less likely to have libraries, organized recreational opportunities, and parks, and more likely to have gangs.

Money Buys Health Care, Health Supplies, and Safety Devices

Even with Medicaid, the families of poor children have trouble affording medical care—particularly preventive medicine, and their children receive lower quality medical care and less dental care. Due to the lack of funds, they are more apt to delay seeing health care providers and consequently are more apt to need the services of a hospital emergency room. The dollars available may not stretch far enough to cover basic health care supplies and safety devices such as vitamins, sterile bandages, antiseptics, safety locks for doors and windows, smoke detectors, child car-safety seats, and more.

Money Buys Healthy Recreation

Low-income families are less able to afford the expense of extracurricular school activities (sports equipment, fees, uniforms). There are fewer recreational facilities available and those that are available usually charge a fee (swimming pools, etc.).

Money Buys Transportation, Communication, and Economic Opportunity

People in poverty lack cars (only 42 percent have cars). If there is public transportation, it may be too expensive (the cost of a Sunday family outing to a city park may be prohibitive) or the public transportation may not provide needed routes. This lack of transportation may limit access to child care, health services, recreation, jobs, job-training programs, post-secondary education, and low-cost stores (grocery stores in an inner city are often more expensive than in other neighborhoods). A major communication problem is the lack of a telephone in many poor homes. This again limits access to opportunities, emergency services, contact with the school, and a means of reducing the feeling of isolation.

Having read the above list you can now begin to comprehend the effects of poverty on the lives of these families. Figure 12-1 is a valuable aid in furthering that understanding.

> *REFLECTION...*
>
> Select a name and grade level for a student. Now walk your student through the above table and then predict what that child's school experience is going to be. Most importantly, how can you best help this student?

The victims of poverty are our students and their families. Their lives are different from children with greater resources, but their needs are not. Without knowledge of, and concern for, the limitations imposed by poverty, educators will not be able to understand the functioning of these families. Consequently, we will be less effective as educators.

Schools and Families of Poverty

Poverty is a serious issue, both because the children it touches risk unsatisfied biological and safety needs (Reed & Sautter, 1990) and because the public schools are not designed to serve impoverished children (Fuller, 1992).

Since the students bring the effects of poverty with them to school, teachers must understand and deal with poverty and its consequences. This study provides insights into how teachers understand poverty and how they relate to children of poverty and their families. Hopefully, these insights will provide some direction in how to prepare pre-service teachers to better understand and teach children of poverty.

Children

Unlike their middle-class peers, children living in poverty often experience discontinuity between schooling and other areas of their lives (Banks, 1993). Studies focusing on the relationship between socioeconomic status and academic success equates standards that are based on middle-class experiences and opportunities. This includes middle-class social and language behaviors. Students from middle-class families generally acquire these behaviors prior to entering school, while students with limited resources may not have had these advantages and, consequently, enter schools that were designed for someone else.

The children frequently live with parents or a parent who may not have had positive school experiences. Substantial numbers of these parents dropped out of school before completing high school. Still other students live in homes with language-minority parents who did not attend school in the United States.

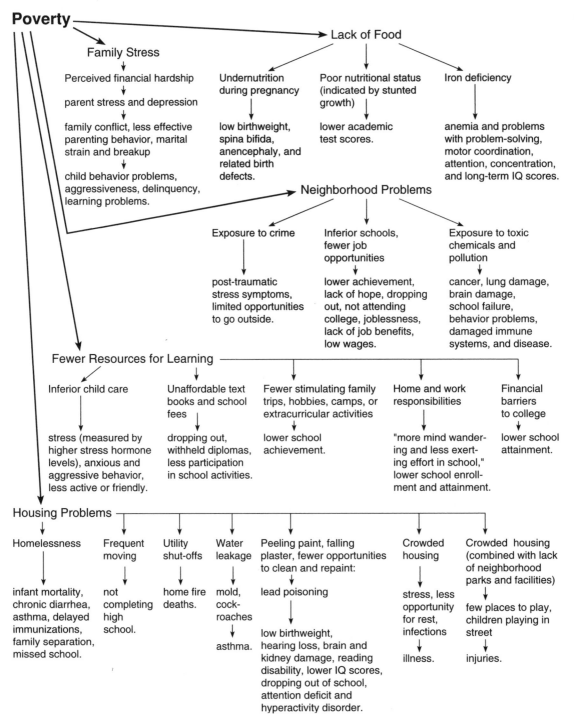

FIGURE 12-1 Examples of "pathways" from poverty to adverse child outcomes.

From: Wasting America's Future by Children's Defense Fund. © 1994 by Children's Defense Fund. Used by permission of Beacon Press, Boston.

The home environment is often cited as the reason for lack of academic achievement among low-income students. These parents are apt to be criticized for not being sufficiently involved. However, survival issues (e.g., money for food, clothing, affordable housing, adequate health care) command the time and energy of low-income parents, and they are often described as too distracted to attend to the educational needs of their children (Ascher, 1988). A list constructed by Ornstein and Levin (1989) outlines ten reasons for low achievement among low-income students, none of which refers to home environment. Ornstein and Levin (1989) suggest a need to transform the ways that teachers think about low-income students and their families.

With all their problems, these children must not be underestimated—they have impressive potential. A Kentucky science teacher describes how students in her highly impoverished school district won a statewide academic competition.

> *Some of them get up with the problem every morning: How do you wake up without an alarm clock or a parent there to wake you? How do you get up and go to school when you probably didn't have a bed to sleep in the night before? These kids could beat anybody.* **They solve problems all day.** *(Sherman, 1994, p. 78)*

Parents

Low-income parents are often thought to have little interest in the education of their children. The limited school involvement of low-income parents can be attributed, in part, to their lack of trust in the school personnel, as well as a lack of understanding of the way schools function. Often, differences in economic backgrounds between teachers and parents lead to discomfort on the part of parents when interacting with schools. This psychosocial distance between parents and teachers also leads to a lack of understanding of the dynamics operating within low-income families among teachers. Haberman (1995), in his book *Star Teachers of Children in Poverty,* discusses the difference between "star" teachers' perceptions of parents of poverty and those of other teachers.

Most teachers define "support from home" as parents helping children with assigned homework or supporting some action of school discipline. Star teachers, on the other hand, described parental support in terms of parents showing interest in what their children do in school and providing them with basics such as privacy, safety, sleep, nutrition, and health (Sherman, 1994, pp. 10–11).

Parents in poverty, like parents of all other socioeconomic groups, love their children, but may feel uncomfortable in their children's schools. They frequently feel helpless in their relationships with schools and teachers. In some cases, they may feel denigrated by the way in which schools and teachers communicate. Haberman says, "'Star' teachers do not blame parents. As much as they may find out about the child and/or the family, they see the information as a basis for helping children learn or want to learn more" (Haberman, 1995, pp. 11–12).

Poverty wears people down and defeats them, leaving little energy to deal with the problems within the family outside of fulfilling basic, daily needs (Webb & Sherman, 1989). They feel inadequate to participate in their children's learning, and their experience has been that the school assumes the responsibility to educate. Lack of information, skill, and transportation further isolates the parent from the school.

Working with Low-Income Families

In establishing a working partnership with low-income parents, you must remember that lack of resources doesn't indicate a lack of love or dreams for their children. Furthermore, although they may not be pedagogical experts, they are experts as far as their children are concerned and we need that expertise.

Teachers from middle- and lower-middle-class families have been enculturated into a middle-class world. Unless educators have had exposure to poverty and an understanding of the dynamics of poverty, they will subconsciously take middle-class expectations of parent–school relationships into their classrooms with them. Since most teachers are products of middle-class or lower-middle-class families, it is important that they not have inappropriate expectations for parents (Fuller, 1994).

The prolonged burdens and pressures of low-income families are considerable and not normally within the experience of most educators. Consequently, it is important to be well informed and sensitive when working with low-income families. The educator and the parent(s) have a strong common bond—all want the best for the child, and this can be the basis for a good working relationship.

Suggestions for Working with Low-Income Parents

Check Your Attitude

What is your attitude toward families who live in poverty? Do you blame the victim? Example: "If they just tried harder, they could significantly improve their financial situation." Do you deny the problems of poverty? Example: "If they can afford to have a television and VCR, they can't be doing too badly." Do you feel that people of poverty are intellectually inferior to those of the middle class? Example: "If they were more intelligent, they wouldn't be poor."

Educators are sensitive people who want the best for their students, but they still may have some unexamined attitudes toward poverty. How did you formulate your attitudes toward poverty? Have you checked the validity of your attitudes?

Know the Environment in Which
Your Low-Income Children Live

If your students come from an urban/suburban area or a small town, walk around the neighborhood. See where your students play and investigate the quality and quantity of the recreational facilities that are available to them. Where do families shop for groceries? Walk through the stores and observe the selections available and the cost. In many such stores in these settings, the items are more expensive and the choices more limited than those in some middle-class neighborhoods. Is there a library in the neighborhood? Churches? A disproportionate number of bars? What is the cultural make-up of the area? If you feel that this is not a safe environment to explore (although this is not usually the case), ask an appropriate person to join you in this adventure.

If your students live in a more rural environment, drive around the area until you know it well. Again, familiarize yourself with the stores in the area as well as identifying the churches, recreational facilities, bars, and so on. Who lives there? Ride the school bus on each of the routes of your students and see where they get off. How long a ride do they have to and from school? How long is their walk from the bus stop to their home? What is the nature of the housing in that area? It is important to remember not to criticize your low-income students' physical environment. The area is a part of the child, and, as a result, they will feel demeaned by negative comments. An objective discussion of a community problem (e.g., drugs, garbage collection, etc.) should not be negative. After exploring your low-income students' environment, identify the strengths and weaknesses of the area and determine how each will affect your teaching strategies.

Gathering Basic Information about Low-Income Families

The school office is a good place to start becoming acquainted with families. There you will find a record that can act as an introduction, and you will discover information that will help you understand some of the dynamics of the family. How many children are there in the household? What are their ages? Are any pre-school age? How many parents are in the home? Do one or both work? Is the place of work listed? What is the address of the family? Do they have a telephone? Is there a work number listed?

Communicate with the Low-Income Parents

The best communication model is two-way communication—parents and educators talking and listening to one another, and this should be every teacher's ultimate communication goal. Unfortunately, this is not always possible, for some parents are unable, unwilling, or uncomfortable in communicating with the schools. Nevertheless, it is important to actively endeavor to inform parents. Contacting parents about positive matters will make it easier and more productive if you need to work with them on a problem at a later date. Writing notes, assuming parents can read in your language, to a parent about their child's positive behaviors will demonstrate that you care about their child and that you recognize and appreciate their desirable behaviors. Phone calls can be particularly helpful in establishing positive parent–teacher communication. Also, brief calls to make a positive comment about a student encourages parents to become more actively involved in communicating with the school; after all, if a parent starts to believe, "That teacher likes my child," parental enthusiasm in school affairs will more likely result. Unfortunately, not all low-income families have phones, which means a letter or visit will be your options.

Getting Low-Income Families Actively Involved: Creating a Partnership

The view of parent involvement has changed over the last twenty-five years. In the past, high profile, low participation was the norm. This involvement often took the form of large meetings held in the evenings when parents listened to what educators had to say. The schedules of contemporary families no longer make this a viable activity. More importantly, these meetings no longer fit the contemporary goals of parental involvement—they were monologues rather than dialogues. The nature of parent involvement has changed, and true parent involvement is now seen as a partnership between the school and the home.

Low-income families have many demands on their time, as mentioned earlier in the chapter, and lack the economic resources necessary to reduce some of the stress caused by these demands. In addition, they may have had a negative school experience and not feel comfortable in the school environment. Flexibility, practicality, and creativity can help you mitigate some of these problems. For example, meetings with parents needn't always be held in the classroom. You can meet for a cup of coffee, make a home visit, and so forth. Moreover, while it is usually more productive to meet face to face with a parent, a phone call can also provide you with an opportunity for two-way communication. If there isn't a telephone available, you could provide your home phone number and the times you will be available.

Partnerships are based on respect, and it is imperative that parents are shown the same respect we show our colleagues. Also, in partnerships with low-income parents, it is important to remember that the stresses of life may be such that there will be times when parents do not have the emotional or physical energy to be full partners. A single father who has a minimum-wage job, a sick child, no day care, and is being evicted may have to expend his energies elsewhere.

Become Involved in the Community

To understand families, you must understand them as a part of a community as well as individual units. The following recommendations are suggestions of ways to become involved in a community. While understanding teachers are very busy people who work hard emotionally, intellectually, and even physically, at the end of the school day, or week, they need time to rejuvenate. However, the opportunities to learn about students and families continues beyond the classroom. You may not be able to participate in all of the suggested activities, but select those that interest you the most. In addition, your friends or family might want to join you in some of these activities.

If there is a community celebration, such as street fairs, ethnic holidays, and events such as pow-wows, attend. Accept as many invitations as you can: Bas- or Bar-Mitzvahs, confirmations, first communions, quinceneroes, and so forth. If you have a student singing a solo with a church choir, playing in the little league finals, or being honored for their talents in any way, attend.

Be Sensitive to the Financial Limitations of Low-Income Families

Low-income families may find it very difficult to send money for field trips, school projects, or special materials. Even requests for cookies for a party may be beyond some families. Also, some children are not able to participate in school sports due to the cost of the registration fee, equipment, and/or clothing. Imagine how demeaning and disappointing these situations are to the children and their parents.

Conclusion

In conclusion, as educators we have a wonderful opportunity, as well as a responsibility, to help the children and families of poverty. We must respect these families for a variety of reasons—their perseverance, hard work, and, of course, strong desire for success and a good life for their children. Not all educators are making positive contributions for a variety of reasons. Webb and Sherman (1989) take a rather dim view of educators' attitudes toward their students in poverty. They state, "The stigma of poverty is a powerful force in American classrooms. It manipulates teacher behavior in ways that educators themselves seldom realize. It can lower a teacher's expectations for a child, and can initiate a self-fulfilling prophecy of failure" (p. 487).

Lastly, well-informed teachers will not be influenced by the stereotypes of poor children. Educators that are knowledgeable and skillful can add to the quality of life for these children and their families and grow professionally themselves.

Recommended Activities

- Volunteer time at a homeless shelter and keep a journal of your experience.
- Interview a social worker about the lives of children and families living in poverty.
- Volunteer time working in a thrift shop. Write a description of three of the regular customers.
- Ask a social worker, Head Start teacher, and a nutritionist from WIC to speak to your class about the problems of children and families in poverty, either individually or as a panel.
- Volunteer in a Head Start classroom and keep a journal of your experience.
- Collect demographics about the resources of the poor as opposed to the middle class. Then use those figures to predict the kind of childhood experience each will have.
- Determine the income and expenses of a single parent making minimum wage and raising three children. Use your community to determine expenses: housing, food, transportation, health care, and so forth.

Additional Resources

Poverty and Students

Books:

Haberman, M. (1995). *Star teachers of children in poverty.*

Haberman is recognized as an expert in teacher education for urban schools—primarily schools that serve children of poverty. In this book he describes how those who have been recognized as "star" teachers work with children of poverty. It is practical and yet sensitive and makes specific suggestions. ISBN: 0-912099-08-9.

Director of Publications
Kappa Delta Pi
PO Box A
West Lafayette, IN 47906
Phone: 800-284-3167

Kozol, J. (1995). *Amazing grace: The lives of children and the conscience of a nation.* New York: Crown Publishers, Inc.

Amazing Grace is a book about the hearts of children who grow up in the South Bronx—the poorest congressional district in our nation. Kozol takes the reader into the lives of these children and their families and introduces them to a world they don't know. Kozol uses the words of his participants to help us understand the kindness of their hearts and the difficulty of their lives. This is a book that should be on every educator's bookshelf. ISBN: 0-517-79999-5.

> Crown Publishers
> 201 East 50th Street
> New York, NY 10022
> Phone: 212-751-2600

Sherman, Arloc. (1994). Introduction by Marian Wright Edelman. *Wasting America's future: The children's defense fund report on the costs of child poverty.*

For the first time in one place, there is sweeping evidence on the human, social, and economic costs of child poverty in the Unites States. This book gives surprising evidence that even a brief episode of poverty can do lasting damage to children and families. Also, we learn that low-income family background is a devastatingly powerful predictor of negative outcomes for children. For many readers, the essence of this book will lie in the stories of children and their families, many of whom endure unfair and damaging lives with grace, and who remind us that good things—whole and healthy lives—are worth paying for. ISBN: 0-8070-4107-6.

> Beacon Press
> 25 Beacon Street
> Boston, MA 02108
> Phone: 617-742-2110

Chapters:

Moles, O. C. (1993). Collaboration between schools and disadvantaged parents: Obstacles and opening. In N. F. Chavkin (Ed.), *Families and schools in a pluralistic society* (pp. 21–52). Albany, NY: State University Press.

Articles:

Children's Defense Fund. (1993). Child poverty hits record level. *CDF Reports, 14*(12), 11.

Children's Defense Fund. (1987). *Declining earnings of young men: Their relation to teenage pregnancy and family formation.* Washington, DC: Children's Defense Fund.

Children's Defense Fund. *Adolescent pregnancy and family formation.* Washington, DC: Children's Defense Fund, Adolescent Pregnancy Prevention Clearing House.

Videos:

Children of Poverty

This video examines some of the effects of poverty and the prognosis of children in poverty growing up to be healthy, both emotionally and physically. 1987. (26 minutes, color). Rental & purchase.

Films for the Humanities & Sciences
PO Box 2053
Princeton, NJ 08543
Phone: 800-257-5126

Organizations:

Children's Defense Fund
122 C Street, NW
Washington, DC 20001
Phone: 202-628-8787

Websites:

Child Welfare Home Page
http://www.childwelfare.com

Human Resource Policy Center
http://www.urban.org/ar95/resource.html

Institute for Children and Poverty
http://www.opendoor.com/hfh/icp.html

Institute for Research on Poverty
http://www.ssc.wisc.edu/irp/

National Center for Children in Poverty
http://www.cait.cpmc.columbia/edu/dept/nccp/

References

Ascher, C. (1988). Improving the school–home connection for poor and minority urban students. *The Urban Review, 20*(2), 109–123.

Baca Zinn, M. (1987). Structural transformation and minority families. In L. Beanery & C. Stimpson (Eds.), *Women, households, and the economy* (pp. 155–171). New Brunswick: Rutgers University Press.

Banks, C. R. (1993). Restructuring schools for equity: What have we learned in two decades. *Phi Delta Kappan, 75,* 42–44, 46–48.

Chavkin, N. F. (Ed.). (1993). *Families and schools in a pluralistic society.* Albany, NY: State University of New York Press.

Children's Defense Fund. (1996). Key facts about children. *Children's Defense Fund Reports, (17)*2, p. 5.

Coontz, S. (1995). The American family and the nostalgia trap. *Phi Delta Kappan, 76*(7), pp. K1–K20.

Federal Register. (1995). *60*(27), pp. 7772–7774.

Haberman, M. (1995). *Star teachers of children in poverty.* West Lafayette, IN: Kappa Delta Pi International Educational Honor Society.

Katz, M. (1986). *In the shadow of the poorhouse: A social history of welfare in America.* New York: Praeger Publishers, Inc.

Lasch, C. (1977). *Haven in a heartless world.* New York: Basic Books.

Latinos shift loyalties. (1994, April). *The Christian Century,* p. 344.

Lichter, D., & Eggebeen, D. (1993). Rich kids, poor kids: Changing income inequality among American children. *Social Forces, 71*(3), 761–780.

Ornstein, A., & Levine, D. (1989). Social class, race, and school achievement: Problems and prospects. *Journal of Teacher Education, 40*(5), 17–23.

Outtz, J. H. (1993). *The demographics of American families.* Santa Monica, CA: Milken Institute for Job and Capital Formation. (ERIC Document Reproduction Service No. ED 367 726)

Polakow, V. (1993). *Lives on the edge: Single mothers and their children in the other America.* Chicago: The University of Chicago Press.

Raintwater, L., & Smeeding, T. M. (1995). U.S. doing poorly—compared to others—policy points of view. *Child Poverty News.*

Sherman, A. (1994). *Wasting America's future: The children's defense fund report on the cost of child poverty.* Boston: MA: Beacon Press.

U.S. Census Bureau. (1993). Poverty in the United States. In *Current Population Research Series* (pp. 60–185). Washington, DC: U.S. Government Printing Office.

Webb, R. B., & Sherman, R. R. (1989). *Schooling and society* (2nd ed.). New York: MacMillan Publishing Company.

Fatherhood, Society, and School

CHARLES B. HENNON
Miami University

GLENN OLSEN
University of North Dakota

GLEN PALM
St. Cloud State University

This chapter will enable the reader to recognize the role of father in a child's life in the context of family, school, and society. The father's role in school will be discussed and change relating to that role will be presented. The purpose of this chapter is to help the reader to:

- Describe the culture of fatherhood
- Compare fathers of today to fathers of previous generations
- Identify fathering in the context of family systems
- Describe the relationships between fathers and school achievement
- Identify ways of involving fathers in schools and their child(ren)'s education
- Identify ways of making the community and school environment more father friendly

A new movement for reviving the faded image of the strong male parent ignited a debate in the mid 1990s. "Tonight, about 40 percent of American children will go to sleep in homes in which their fathers don't live." Are fathers really disappearing from the lives of children, as Blankenhorn (1995, p. 1) asserts? "Father hunger, or awareness of it, is especially acute in the United States. Some observers believe that the United States is in danger of becoming, in effect, a fatherless society, shorn of its male parents not by war or disease, but by choice." Is the United States becoming "fatherless" as lamented by Louv (1994, p. 2)?

The advantages of families being more in partnership with schools is recognized by educators (e.g., Epstein, 1995; Riley, 1994). Both schools and families benefit and techniques for building such partnerships are being disseminated. One aspect often overlooked, however, is the role fathers play in forming these partnerships as well as in the academic achievement of their children. The examination of fathers' roles is imperative to the understanding of family dynamics and how they influence children. It is widely believed that divorce and fatherless homes have dire consequences for school achievement (Amato, 1994). Perhaps less recognized is the influence of fathers in all types of family systems on school attendance, school work, and school and personal success. These influences are explored in this chapter.

In some people's view, the role of gender in parenting is swinging from clearly defined difference in roles and complement of functions of the 1950s (Parsons, 1955) to an ideal of androgynous parenting (Rotundo, 1985) in which gender differences grow smaller if socialization changes. The latest fatherhood movement, however, appears to emphasize gender differences. Gender as a concept is mired in a complex of social and political issues (Thompson & Walker, 1995) and often is discussed in emotionally charged atmospheres. Some writers express ambivalence about delineating parenting roles based on gender while understanding that changing roles of fathers represent both threats to the status quo and opportunities (Louv, 1993).

The authors of this chapter are advocating for more father involvement in all aspects of children's lives. Society, in general, and families and schools, in particular, benefit from supporting men in their roles as fathers. We believe that fathering is qualitatively different from mothering and that while some men and women desire more androgyny, others support more conventional approaches to parenting. Here we highlight some of the advantages of more androgynous approaches while articulating unique differences and strengths that fathers bring to parenting. We respect individual values and approaches to fathering and cultural differences in conceptions of what a father is and how fathering is done.

Our approach is not value free. We believe that more involvement by fathers with their children is valuable for the child, the father, the mother, the schools, and the society. We believe that fathers can be more involved regardless of their marital status and living arrangement relative to the child. Recognizing diversity in family forms and functioning, we believe that certain principles and practices can be more universally applied, while in other cases more selected interventions may be appropriate. For example, married fathers living with their children, divorced fathers living elsewhere, remarried fathers living with step-children while their own children are living with step-fathers, and fathers in intimate same-sex relationships who are living with their children, all face unique issues and may benefit from different resources, supports, and services.

Exploring fatherhood and father involvement, especially involvement with education and schooling, we first examine how the culture of fatherhood both pressures and reinforces fathers. Secondly, we discuss the conduct of fathering. Understanding fathers, social change, and how fathers can be part of negotiated social change allows a better appreciation of fathers' activities relative to their children's education and schooling. Next, we discuss how family systems influence fathering and thus how interventions must be sensitive to systemic rather than just individualistic characteristics. Finally, we turn to a discussion on involving fathers in schools and education.

Basic Premises

Four premises underlie the focus on the unique characteristics of men as parents. These underline the importance of fathers and fathering and are the guiding principles and rationale for making specific efforts to increase and support father involvement in families, schooling, and schools.

- *Fathers and mothers are different.* Not as clear cut as they used to be, gender boundaries for individuals have been stretched so that men can be nurturers and women providers. Individual differences aside, there are generic gender differences based on the interaction of biology and gender socialization (Biller, 1993; Roberts, 1996). Men and women tend to approach parenting with different goals, values, and styles. These differences are more subtle than the instrumental and expressive functions described by Parsons (1955).
- *Fathers are essential and not easily replaceable* by other male role models (Blankenhorn, 1995). Children benefit from the unique style and investment of male energy in their well-being (Roberts, 1996). The real importance of fathers may hinge more on their being different from mothers than being a clone of a good mother.

- *Standards for fatherhood must be revised to reflect a higher common ground* (Jackson, 1994). Fatherhood standards have eroded as family diversity and self-gratification are accepted as predominant values, changing the focus from clear expectations to fuzzy criteria for good fathering (Samuelson, 1996). It seems critical to create a set of high standards that respects diversity of family forms and cultural practices. At the same time, fathers must meet their own needs without diluting their commitment to their children. There is some consensus that caring, commitment, and leadership are areas where standards need to be emphasized (Palm, 1994).
- *Differences between mothers and fathers should be reframed from deficits to strengths* (Doherty, 1991). Men have unique characteristics based on their socialization that can be beneficial to the parent role. Some examples are problem-solving, sense of humor, playfulness, and risk-taking (Johnson & Palm, 1992). How men interact with their children forces youth to "stretch" both emotionally and physically. Fathers push children to deal with the world outside the mother–child bond. Children, consequently, develop a complex set of interactive and emotional communications skills. Fathers also encourage differentiation from the family and help adolescents, in particular, develop individual autonomy (Roberts, 1996). Men can benefit from learning more about empathy and expressing feelings and sensitivity, but are more likely to focus on these when feeling respected for some of the strengths they bring to parenting.

Differences must be acknowledged by schools in order to involve more men in the education process and to support their unique contribution to children as learners as well as to schools as institutions. The premises identified can be used by educators to develop a clearer understanding of how to facilitate fathers encouraging children to achieve their best, to take risks, and to solve problems.

> *REFLECTION...*
>
> What are the differences, from your experience and reading, between fathers and mothers? Are the differences based on biology and/or gender socialization? Because there are differences, how do we as a society deal with the differences? Do we change men, change women, and/or change society? Do we want androgynous males and females?

Fatherhood in Context

Culture of Fatherhood

Some authors suggest that a popular culture of fatherhood exists in the United States. This popular culture is fueled by the mass media and supported by many parenting experts (LaRossa, 1988; LaRossa & Reitzes, 1993) and can influence how fathers parent. Consumers of this culture are those attentive to the mass media's presentations about the fathering role and how fathers ought to parent. This popular culture includes ideals about the appropriate amount and type of father–child interactions, responsibilities of fathers, and such things as how fathers ought to be involved in their children's schooling. This culture exults androgynous, new, or modern fatherhood.

Some media, educators, and social scientists are portraying and advocating more nurturing fathering. Men should place less emphasis on being a distant and stern father who is a good provider, it is argued, and place more emphasis on playing, talking, caring, and nurturing. Some see this as new, better, and more responsive fathering. Others see it as feminizing the role of the father or, at least, having it be more androgynous. In any case, the roles of fathers may be becoming more complex and confused. Traditional measures for being a good father may no longer prevail. This focusing on new fatherhood is not confined to the United States. Similar questioning of fathers' roles is found in many societies including China, Ireland, Great Britain, Germany, and various countries in West Africa (Bruce, Lloyd, & Leonard, 1995; Lamb, 1987; Louv, 1994; Schmidt-Waldherr, 1992).

Reading about parenting is not likely to have a great influence on a father's behavior if there are other, more pressing desires and needs (LaRossa & Reitzes, 1993). These other desires and needs might include worries about unemployment, job security, career advancement, perpetual overworking, and so on. Attention to social and economic achievement and providing for one's family appears to be a major focus of men (Bruce, Lloyd, & Leonard, 1995). This is apparent even in the face of data suggesting that "family comes first" or that men are now more involved with and attuned to their families (Cohen, 1987).

LaRossa (1988) argues there has been more change in the culture of fatherhood than there has been in the conduct of fathering.

> *The idea that fathers have radically changed—that they now are intimately in-volved in raising their children—qualifies…as a folk belief, and it…is having an impact on our lives and that of our children. On the positive side, people are say-ing that at least we have made a start. Sure men are not as involved with their chil-dren as some of us would like them to be, but…the fact we are talking about change represents a step in the right direction. (p. 454)*

Discourse may be an important preliminary step and may lead to action. It can also be seen as more pressure on men to change and be something else, perhaps something they do not want to be. While some men relish involved fatherhood and appreciate information on and support for better nurturing and involvement, others do not. Some do not because fathering is a private affair, and some do not because they are already fulfilling the role in the way they think is best. It is their mode of fathering, perhaps the same as their fathers, and it works. "Best" may or may not include a lot of direct care giving and responsibility.

Modern Father

Given the popular parental culture and the sense of egalitarianism prevailing today in many segments of society, it is likely that fathering will continue to evolve. This is especially likely in the white middle class (LaRossa, 1988). The middle class is the driving force behind the changes, at least attitudinally, in the culture of fatherhood.[1] Thus men socialized to be fathers in a more conventional mode may feel pressure and tension to accept and change to a more modern mode.

Some modern fathers may be feeling pressured by more traditional wives to change their fathering activities. Research (LaRossa & LaRossa, 1981; Roberts, 1996) points to certain women protecting their "turf," and monitoring and evaluating men's household and child-care activities in ways men find uncomfortable. Or at least women do not expect men to be very involved (Marsiglio, 1991; Thompson & Walker, 1989).[2] Men and women tend to develop parenting/household management strategies along lines of believed competencies. Both parents assess their own abilities and preferences relative to those of the partner and their expectations of their partners (Kaplan & Hennon, 1992). Likely, each then assumes responsibility for tasks within the areas where they hold competencies and expertise (Anderson & Sabatelli, 1995).

Both parents can learn and master many tasks. However, earlier socialization and cultural and reference group expectations influence the perceptions of competencies as well as "what ought to be." Fathers tend to become involved when their wives expect them to be highly involved in household management and child care (Simons, Whitbeck, Conger, & Melby, 1990). Nevertheless, the distribution of household and child-care tasks may be more a function of power and its use than strict cultural norms about parenting. Women continue to do most of the work (Thompson & Walker, 1995).

REFLECTION ...

Who did most of the household and childcare tasks in your home? Will it be the same in your household? Does power have a role in their decisions?

Radoslav and Maria

For example, Radoslav and Maria Popescu immigrated twenty-five years ago from Eastern Europe and are living in an ethnic neighborhood in a large Midwestern city. They both grew up in a cultural context emphasizing more formal but loving relationships between fathers and children, especially sons. Fathers were stern and worked to care for and protect their families. In fact, Radoslav and Maria's fathers worked hard to get them to the United States where they could experience a better life. In the States, their families wanted to acculturate and be "like the rest." Radoslav and Maria grew up speaking English, listening to rock music, watching portrayals of family life on television and in movies, and made friends with American kids in their schools. In their neighborhood, some things remained more traditional and yet there was pressure to "be American."

After high school, Radoslav (or Rad as he is called) got work with a construction firm owned by his dad's brother. Maria pursued a nursing degree part-time at a community college, while working part-time. Being in love, they got married and soon had two children. Now, the older child is in fifth grade while the younger one is in third. Maria is back in school part-time, attending day classes so she can be home evenings with her family. A problem is arising with the older child. In school, she seems distracted and is falling behind the other students. The school psychologist wants to meet with the parents. A question thus arises, does Radoslav take time off work to go?

The macro-cultures (society) of the United States and that of the original homeland may be in conflict in this case. Perhaps not. Rad goes only if there is a behavioral problem and he needs to "straighten his daughter out," or perhaps if he perceives the school is at fault and he wants to straighten out the school. He remembers that his dad wanted him to do well in school, but Rad's father always respected and deferred to the school as the authority. His mother attended meetings; his dad never set foot inside a U.S. school. Rad's work buddies and the uncle who owns the company depend on him. Taking time off work would be a problem, and he would have to explain this to his uncle and work mates. Besides, even though Rad supports and loves his daughter, this is "women's stuff," not an issue for men (at least according to his friends).

But the meso-culture (community) may also offer some different and conflicting norms. Some neighbors seem to be involved in PTO, field trips, parent–teacher conferences, and the like. Some fathers help their children with homework. And the micro-culture (family) also influences thinking about what is right. Maria is working and going to school, and "modern." She expects and even demands that Rad get involved with his children, reminding him of how much he disliked the distant relationship he had with his dad. She would have to miss either work or class to go to the meeting. She thinks, "Why should I be the one to always make the sacrifices?" Besides, she remembers how Rad used to be so considerate in helping with housework and watching the children. What has happened? Why do their expectations about Rad's role as father seem to be at odds, and why is this creating conflict in their marriage?

Conduct of Fathering

On Time Activities

While some research indicates that today there is more male involvement in household and child-rearing activities, it is not clear exactly how widespread this change in family organization may be (Anderson & Sabatelli, 1995; LaRossa, 1988; Thompson & Walker, 1995). Empirical data are confusing and inconsistent concerning the amount of father involvement with their children and how much change, if any, there has been in this involvement. Sanik (1990) found that in 1986 fathers were spending an average of 1.7 hours per day in child care, compared to 0.5 hours in 1967. Other data (Bruce, Lloyd, & Leonard 1995) show that in 1986 men were spending an average of .8 hours per week in direct child care while women were spending 2.0 hours. Other research indicates the following:

> *Even as the concepts of shared parenting and shared breadwinning gain currency in Western media, the reality of emotional and physical fatherlessness grows.... a study of four year olds in 10 countries...discovered that the average daily time that fathers spent alone with their children was less than one hour, ranging from 6 minutes per day in Hong Kong and 12 minutes in Thailand to 54 minutes in China and 48 minutes in Finland. When the average time spent by both parents with their children was added to these amounts, the number of hours that fathers were present with their children ranged from 1 hour and 36 minutes per day in the United States to 3 hours and 42 minutes in Belgium. These findings suggest that even when fathers are present as an active member of a family, their direct involvement in child care can be very limited (Louv, 1994, p. 2).*

Robinson (1990) reports that U.S. men increased their average hours per week in housework from five hours in 1965 to twenty hours in 1985.[3] A *Parents* 1993 fatherhood poll finds that men are moving closer to child care parity with women, especially in households with mothers employed full-time outside the home (Louv, 1994). Lamb (1987) reports that fathers shoulder about one-tenth of the responsibility for children, regardless of the employment status of the mother in two-parent households. Thompson and Walker (1995) register that "women and girls do more than their share of housework in families" (p. 852) and note that feminist research does not forget that "over all, mothers, not fathers, are responsible for children" (p. 858). James Levine, director of the Fatherhood Project, is quoted in *American Health* (Schroepfer, 1991) as saying society is in the midst of an evolution, not a revolution, concerning fathers' involvement in child-related chores.

Research indicates that fathers are less likely than mothers to provide most of the continuous care for children and are less likely to sacrifice their own time to do so (LaRossa, 1988). Fathers are less involved in providing care, attending to, responding to, holding, soothing, and comforting their children (Darling-Fisher & Tiedje, 1990; LaRossa, 1988; Marsiglio, 1991; Thompson & Walker, 1989). Even fathers completing specially designed parent education programs are not especially involved in parent–child interaction. This is possibly due to work responsibilities, social obligations, and other factors (McBride, 1990).

While doing less "on time" activities with their children than mothers, men still report parenting to be an important role for them (Cohen, 1987). Other studies suggest that fathers consider their primary responsibility as being a good provider (Bruce, Lloyd, & Leonard, 1995; Lamb, 1987; Thompson & Walker, 1989). Given the available data, the involved father may be more apparent than real.

Popular culture aside, "real" culture would appear to be the place to intervene if more father involvement with children and with their children's schooling is desired. That is, popular media or the popular culture of parenting may not be the appropriate source for data and ideas concerning fathering nor the best intervention focus for enhancing father involvement.

In the real lives of men, fathers may not perceive the necessity or appropriateness of being involved with their children in other than playful or providing ways. Those wishing to negotiate a change in this social reality may find more profit from working directly with men and their families. These agents of change may want to pay special attention to what fathers say is important about what they do and what they see as shortcomings. Learning the meanings that real men attach to parenting and to how they may wish to change, may be more constructive in negotiating social change than writing one more prescriptive and preachy book on the topic of fathering, especially another father-bashing tome.

Conceptual Framework

Lamb (1987) provides a conceptualization for considering father involvement. He discriminates among *engagement* (time spent in one-on-one interaction with a child, in nurturing, playing, or disciplining), *accessibility* (less intense interaction where the father is engaged in another task but is available to respond to the child if needed), and *responsibility* (being accountable for the child's welfare and care, such as making and tracking appointments and being sure the child's needs are being met). Being responsible does not always require direct interaction with the child. A father can be anxious, worried, satisfied, or planning for contingencies while otherwise engaged (such as in driving a car, in employment, or in playing a round of golf).

The relative distribution of their saliency and the time and energy directed to these components of fathering may vary widely: (a) across cultural and socioeconomic groups; (b) by phase of the life cycle; (c) from family to family; (d) from child to child within a family; and (e) from day to day, not to mention from minute to minute. However, we argue here that each family establishes rules about the relative distribution of the various but interrelated components of parenting among the members of the parenting sub-system. These parenting strategies reflect each family's themes and thus exhibit some stability. However, these rules and strategies can be renegotiated and may change over time given different circumstances and needs (Anderson & Sabatelli, 1995).

One reflection of family system dynamics and themes is the *traditionalization of gender roles* (LaRossa, 1988). In general, regardless of how egalitarian their marriages are before the arrival of children, men do less household work after, relative to the increased total workload. On becoming parents, fathers and mothers experience a growing separation of roles (Belsky & Pensky, 1988; LaRossa, 1988). There is thus a regression to more familiar cultural expectations. Others suggest that often men maintain "role distance" from parenting while women embrace the parenting role (LaRossa & LaRossa, 1981).

One explanation for the traditionalization phenomenon suggests that spouses have biographic and socialization experiences giving them competencies in what are considered traditional domains (Jones, Brubaker, Ulrich, & Hennon, 1994). Gender socialization, cultural values, and expectations appear to play a part in how much and how fathers parent. Families can negotiate more or less egalitarian divisions of child care and other labor.

Understanding Fathering

Sometimes fathering might be perplexing, confusing, and/or frustrating for men. Sometimes it is forgotten or not in one's immediate stream of consciousness. But often fathering is joyful, involving, easy, unquestioned, and taken for granted. In the United States there is a *folk psychology* about fathering. It is distilled from living in and experiencing the culture. This folk psychology includes the readily understood, lived-out meaning of being a father, without attention to issues of race, ethnicity, and so on. It is what fathering "is." This folk psychology is one of the taken for granted, generally unquestioned, aspects of the natural world. It is the way things are. While being a father is complex and not easily understood, it is perhaps even harder for outsiders to grasp in a scientific way than it is for insiders who are experiencing it and understanding it in their natural, taken-for-granted, way. Outsiders, that is researchers and other professional experts, may also create and use "fictions"[4] to describe parenting that are not real to the lived experiences of fathers. That is, as fathers perceive how they are socially situated and act in their families, jobs, friendship groups, communities, and society in general.

To better understand fathering, one must include in the consideration the ethno-culture (or *stock of knowledge*) of fathers (in contrast to either the popular parental culture, or culture as known to the social scientist or educator). This ethno-culture consists of the values, norms, beliefs, attitudes, and material items as known to specific fathers. This stock of knowledge is the reality within which individual fathers operate. It is their reference world, with images of "who I am as a father" based at least partially upon expectations held by significant others and reference groups. It is the personal meaning of fatherhood. Fathers' transactions with this culture (or *life-world* as it is also known), as they understand and attend to it, influence their cognitive and behavioral actions. Other men, as well as children and women, help in shaping a father's life-world and stock of knowledge. Aspects of the popular parental culture may be a part of this lived culture. While it might be assumed that the predominate culture is hegemonic, in the contemporary United States, with all its diversity, one cannot assume that it is prevalent and directive everywhere and for everyone. That is, while there is some general, society-wide (macro) sharing of values and basic understandings concerning fatherhood, ethnic and other subcultural enclaves (meso) may provide a stronger context for behavior. And within these subtexts, idiosyncratic individual and family systems (micro) behavior will be found.

To reiterate, while there is a more hegemonic macro-cultural context for fathering in the United States, there are also important distinctions of a more meso- and micro-cultural level. For example, the environmental context differences that might be found within an Indian reservation in Wisconsin versus suburban Connecticut, or between a Jewish enclave in New York City and Afro-American Mennonites in North Carolina, or a divorced architect with one child both living in New Mexico and a married father of nine children all living in southern Idaho. To understand fathering in these various contexts, and to design better ways of increasing and enhancing involvement in schooling, it is important to (a) recognize difference, (b) be open to cultural definitions varying from one's own, (c) appreciate cultural context, (d) accept that a carefully constructed program may be culturally irreverent and/or culturally specific, (e) understand family system influences, and (f) consider fathering as part of the larger tapestry of men's lives.

Fathering and School Achievement

Some research indicates that fathers experience the same parental joys, worries, and frustrations as mothers (Entwisle, 1985; Thompson & Walker, 1989). There are, however, qualitative differences between mothers and fathers in how parenting is conducted. There are, as well, differences within groups of fathers. Fathers bring certain strengths to parenting. In some cases, fathers would like to change the way they father, perhaps becoming more involved, nurturing, skillful, close, and so forth. Some fathers want involvement in their children's schooling while others do not know how, feel alienated from school systems in general (especially if their own school experiences were not positive), or do not feel comfortable within a particular school setting. Some fathers may not realize that active school involvement is appropriate or useful.

Irrespective of other factors such as social class, family structure, or developmental characteristics and stage of the child, positive outcomes for children appear to be related to certain parenting styles. Various publications report positive developmental outcomes for children associated with parenting styles characterized by logical reasoning, clear communication, appropriate monitoring, support, involvement in the role and with the children, and love (Anderson & Sabatelli, 1995). Children raised with this style of parenting are observed to be successful in school, altruistic, cooperative, trusting, have good self-esteem, and are better able to enter into and maintain intimate relationships of high quality. Likewise, a style characterized by being sensitive to the children's developmental needs, nurturing without being overly restricting, acting responsive without being overly controlling, and stimulating without being overly directive is related with positive academic and other outcomes for children (Belsky & Vondra, 1985).

Research on school attendance, achievement and adjustment indicates that various aspects of family and household environments appear to influence educational outcomes of youth.[5] Some characteristics identified include socioeconomic status (SES), parents' employment status and educational backgrounds, and family structure (DuBois, Eitel, & Felner, 1994). For example, several studies, even when controlling for SES, demonstrate a relationship between father absence and poor academic performance and dropping out of school (Krantz, 1988; Samuelson, 1996). Some scholars (for example Bronfenbrenner, 1986; McLoyd, 1990) suggest that SES, household resources, and the like should be considered more distal influences, because "they do not directly describe the life circumstances and demands that result from them, nor the adaptive processes they require" (DuBois, Eitel, & Felner, 1994, p. 406).

Given the relationship between school adjustment and aspects of the family environment, including fathers' support (DuBois, Eitel, & Felner, 1994), it would appear that a better understanding of fathering and fathers' involvement with schools might provide better foundations for enhancing children's school adjustment and success. Bronfenbrenner (1986), for one, emphasizes transactions between families and schools. Transactions such as the quantity and quality of contact between parents and the child's school could be consequential for academic outcomes. While realizing that promoting this idea can create more pressure and higher expectations for father involvement, we believe that fathers' involvement in the schooling of their children is important and should be encouraged.

REFLECTION...

Given the fact that many children are living in female-headed households and have little or no contact with their fathers, what can teachers and schools do for these children? Are they "doomed" because their fathers are not involved in their lives? Or, given current norms of gender equality and inclusion, is it appropriate to design interventions specifically for fathers only?

Benefits of Involving Fathers in Schools

We believe there are several reasons for attempting to increase and support the involvement of fathers in schools and schooling. Included among these are:

- *Fathers* deserve, and some need, involvement support and services. Many men are interested in and open to this type of involvement, and others can be. The new father image has created a cultural expectation for more involvement in parenting, schooling, and schools (LaRossa, 1988). This expectation requires buttressing with new strategies by schools and other institutions to invite and engage fathers. An example would be the

Security Dads at Arlington High in Indianapolis. Fathers, instead of security guards, ride buses on field trips and to sporting events (Louv, 1994).

- There are many positive effects on *children* related to father involvement. Roberts (1996) reviews the many strengths that fathers confer on children's development and how this differs from the important contributions of mothers. Pruett's (1987) research points to father involvement as a significant influence on cognitive and emotional growth. Swick (1984) identifies fathers' contributions to academic achievement, self-esteem, moral development, and gender role identification. It appears logical that more involvement in a child's educational environment by fathers would extend the positive effects observed from increased involvement at home.

- *Families* benefit by increased participation of fathers in their children's schooling. Such attention and interest can strengthen and reinforce family interacting and ties in many important areas, including marriage and trans-generational relationships. A greater involvement by fathers also reinforces the importance placed upon education by the family.

- *Schools* benefit from more father involvement. This involvement enriches the resources to draw upon. That is, fathers' knowledge and skills can be tapped.

- Increased involvement in schools by fathers would also have positive influences on *society*. The style of male parenting in U.S. culture offers a number of important strengths that support school success. These include the encouragement to be independent, the fostering of competition that raises levels of achievement, and the high expectations that fathers often hold for their children that fosters competence. Social life can be more stable, with less violence, addictions, crime, and other pathologies. A more informed and involved citizen strengthens society. Father involvement can also strengthen society through strengthening the labor force and helping the economy remain productive and growing (Hennon et al., 1996).

Strategies for Involving Fathers in Schools

Efforts to enhance and support father involvement in schools and schooling should be sensitive to three levels of intervention: the macro-, meso-, and micro-cultures of fathers. In some cases, efforts to involve fathers more can be considered primary in nature. That is, efforts to *change* culture and social systems that provide the framework, guiding and shaping what men believe to be appropriate fathering. These primary interventions are attempts at negotiated social change that leads to new male socialization practices and values. They include expectations held by the military, religion, economic, education, or other institutions concerning appropriate male behavior toward children. These types of interventions are investments for the future of society by encouraging fathers supporting and investing in the human capital development of their children.

Other interventions are more secondary in nature in the sense that they are to *overcome* preexisting conditions and patterns. Such efforts are likely aimed at individual employers, churches, families, or men. These include attempts to convince fathers that, contrary to what they have learned and believe, other ways of acting are better. That is, fathers *are* to be nurturing, caring, involved, bringing the strengths and perspectives of men to parenting. Other interventions of this genre include those for fathers who are believers in more involvement, but are looking for more resources, support, and services to further this involvement.

Educators can design good interventions including appropriate resources, support, and services. Schools can assist in the provision of, or help in identifying, the *resources* available to fathers (such as family resource centers in schools that are father friendly, or parental leave policies and other employment benefits). Schools can also involve themselves in providing or assisting fathers in locating the *support* they deem necessary (such as a wife's words of encouragement or a network of other fathers in similar situations who can provide information and encouragement). Likewise, schools can offer empowering *services* (such as parenting classes for divorced fathers) that are useful tools for enhancing fathers' involvement with their children's schooling. However, this is not to discount the necessity of considering family- or relationship-level interventions.

Parenting is a relationship, and it is conducted under the influence of other relationships. "Fatherizing" a program or practice does not necessarily mean reducing interventions to individual characteristics or psychological terms. The support necessary may include information about how to talk with one's wife or ex-wife about the concerns the father has about parenting. Resources may include skills training on how fathers can achieve more involvement without trespassing on her turf. Other relationship-oriented practices could include school lessons to children about fathers in diverse families and working directly with fathers and children in ways that reinforce positive mutual interactions. Parenting or school involvement programs that authentically involve all parents may prove to be of more benefit than a program targeted only to fathers or mothers.

What efforts are needed to provide more resources, support, and services at the macro-, meso, and micro levels for families and fathers in order that men can be more involved with schools? Some ideas for such efforts to create and reinforce social change follow.

> ### REFLECTION...
>
> Why has there been this sudden change in how fathers want to be involved in schools? Why didn't this change take place in the 1960s or 1970s? Are the changes that are taking place an over-reaction to fathers' current and perhaps "less involved" roles? Do you think this discussion will be taking place twenty years from now?

Society-Level Interventions

People interested in negotiating social change that values father involvement in schooling should consider more primary interventions that are oriented to helping families and men develop values, themes, strategies, and rules that support and encourage father involvement with their children. These might include:

- Working for peace, social justice, equitable wealth distribution, safe neighborhoods, and sustainable development that considers the equitable distribution of the consequences of economic development (Hennon, Jones, & Schmenk, in press);
- Advocating policies of full employment in meaningful work at a living wage (Bruce, Lloyd, & Leonard, 1995);

- Supporting and encouraging the use of parental leaves, flex time, working at home, and other practices allowing fathers to be able to get time away from work to be engaged with their families (Bruce, Lloyd, & Leonard, 1995);
- Insuring equal opportunities for quality schooling that allows all people to achieve and maintain at least an adequate standard of living;
- Writing, preparing, or encouraging mass media portrayals of men in a diversity of positive family roles, including the unique strengths that fathers bring to parenting;
- Widely sharing the positive outcomes of efforts to have fathers be more involved, as well as sharing stories of how fathers are involved; and
- Advocating for fathers' rights, fair child support and visitation guidelines and strong enforcement of such, encouraging cooperative co-parenting (perhaps with joint custody), and other measures to keep fathers in contact, involved, and supportive of their children after divorce (or if unwed).

Community-Level Interventions

Fathers often are challenged in their efforts at achieving a reasonable balance of home and work life. This challenge can create additional stress, influencing their parenting. However, success at achieving an acceptable balance can be a source of support, and environmental factors such as regular work hours, vacations, job security, being able to attend school conferences in the early morning or late evening, communicating with school via electronic mail, and so on, might be resources helping fathers maintain a lower level of stress. Attitudes toward employment and specific work are also important. For example, research notes an elevated incidence of child abuse among unemployed fathers who would rather be working, compared to working fathers (Anderson & Sabatelli, 1995). Absorption in work, such as spending great amounts of time and energy, is related to fathers being more irritable and impatient with their children (Volling & Belsky, 1991).

School systems can work to encourage community development and economic growth. Holistic paradigms, rather than education-centered ones, can encourage viewing schools, employers, and families as all part of the same meso-culture. Working for what is good for the community as a whole appears to be an important strategy.

Proactive steps must be taken if fathers are to be involved in more appropriate and active ways in schools and schooling. Waiting for fathers to "show up at the door" may not prove strategic; other factors are required. We present here some ideas for resources, supports, and services that may prove essential in enhancing father involvement. These tips are offered for teachers, administrators, and school support staff (social workers, family educators, school psychologists, etc.) as well as parents and others concerned about schools and families. Staff and administration must:

- Help create family-friendly communities (Lawson et al., in press).
- Structure schools that are accessible and family (especially father) friendly, including flexibility in scheduling meetings with parents (Hooper-Briar & Lawson, 1994).
- Guarantee that schools are accountable and responsive to families.

- Commit to the importance of involving fathers. School personnel must understand the benefits and show courage and resiliency in facing difficult questions arising with this kind of change.
- Focus on uniqueness of fathers and the strengths they bring to parenting and in supporting children's education. Schools should capitalize on fathers' encouragement of students to solve problems and to excel. Many fathers like taking on the role of teacher/ mentor. This role reinforces feelings of competence and fathers feel they are doing something important. Inviting fathers to share skills or knowledge in schools is a way of taking advantage of these feelings. As a parent, one of the authors of this chapter was invited to share his expertise on future problem-solving with a sixth-grade class, and felt honored to be asked.
- Create environments that are father-friendly and portray fathers positively. The most obvious examples would be male teachers. Other ways to enhance the school environment are posters in the school and classroom of men at work, play, or with families. Videos, music, and other multimedia material about men in their varied roles can be used. Invite men to visit the classroom, not just on Father's Day or Career Day, to share something of themselves (work, hobbies, or special interests).
- Provide opportunities geared for fathers' interests. For example, building and setting up playground equipment, helping to coach a basketball team, or judging a science fair. These may be stereotypical opportunities but they can help fathers feel welcome and comfortable. They also encourage male openness to less stereotypical activities, perhaps directing a play or teaching a lesson.
- Sponsor more naturally occurring positive fathering activities involving fathers in clubs, scouts, outings, projects (including building and repairing), games, camping, fishing, and the like. More fun and active events can be opportunities for fathers to observe parenting and share information, as well as for "experts" to provide parenting information and model behavior.
- Include fathers in invitations. A generic invitation to "parents" can still be a code name for mothers. Fathers need explicit invitations to know that they are both expected and welcome.
- Offer father-only or father-child events and make special invitations to fathers. Be inclusive in invitations so that male father figures (e.g., uncles, grandfathers, mother's boyfriend) feel welcome.
- Sensitize to male communication styles. Fathers may want to get right to business and have relationship-building as a secondary priority.
- Establish family resources centers in the schools that are father-friendly, and that are as accessible as necessary in helping individuals and couples build capacity for better quality parenting. Such centers can help families in meeting the totality of their needs (such as health, financial management, stress management, leisure, etc.) (Hooper-Briar & Lawson, 1994; Strom, 1985).

Achieving more school involvement by fathers goes beyond the important step of making schools more father-friendly. Perhaps more primary interventions or comprehensive programs are necessary. These more comprehensive interventions can assist fathers in acquiring or enhancing their capacity for engaging with children and the other parent. Consequently, the importance of school involvement can be more readily understood, appreciated, and desired.

Parent Education

Palm (1995) identifies some specific gender differences that are pertinent to effective parent education. These differences include:

- Goals of mothers and fathers differ in parent education. Mothers appear more interested in getting support from other parents while fathers seem most interested in building a close relationship with their children and learning about discipline techniques.
- A second important area to acknowledge is the difference between mothers and fathers in relation to a knowledge and experience base (Palm & Palkovitz, 1988). Girls play more at being parents as part of their childhood experience while boys more often practice other roles. Girls and young women take classes on child development and family relations much more frequently than boys. These differences suggest that educational opportunities for boys and men are critical if fathers are to be more competent in skills and knowledge related to childrearing.
- Differences in interaction style is another area identified. Many earlier studies were based on research with infants. Fathers' interactions are described as being more physical, tactile, and arousing, while mothers are more verbal, soothing, and calming. Androgynous fathers appear to engage in the typical male styles of interactions (i.e., rough and tumble play) but are able to express affection (Palkovitz, 1984).
- Discipline is another area of perceived differences. Being strict and more harsh is characteristic of fathers (Bigner, 1994). Fathers seem able to be firmer, uphold limits, and be authoritative because of hierarchical views (Thevenin, 1993). Perhaps fathers focus more on the immediate outcomes (obedience and compliance) and less on longer term implications for relationships. This style difference may be changing as more men try to avoid the role epitomized by the phrase, "wait till your father gets home."
- Solving parenting problems also appears to differ by gender according to some recent research (Holden, 1988). Mothers appear more efficient and accurate at solving infant crying problems, for example. The differences are explained by mother's greater exposure to and experience with this type of problem.

Fathers' Involvement with Schools

Fathers are getting more involved in schools for a variety of reasons:

- Fathers are being specifically asked to be involved. This involvement includes PTO, riding buses in place of security guards, giving presentations to students, and inclusion in home–school communication and conferences.
- Fathers are creating work schedules or their companies have family-friendly policies allowing personal time off to engage in school activities. Some fathers are working at

or from their homes (including in their own or family businesses), which can allow more flexibility for involving themselves in their children's schools. Some men would like more flexibility in employment responsibilities, but face resistance from employers. Some men refuse promotions; some change jobs; some do not have this luxury or determination.

- Fathers are finding schools creating more father-friendly environments, including the curriculum. These "men-friendly" environments result in more fathers participating in schools as speakers, volunteer aides, or on the PTO/PTA board. Some school districts in Minnesota have young dad programs. These programs include young fathers talking to elementary children about the responsibilities and problems associated with being a teen father. Some school districts, in conjunction with other organizations, identify teen dads that want older fathers for a mentor. Pruett (1987) and Cunningham (1994) suggest ways of portraying fathers and other men in the curriculum.

There may be some negative reaction to these activities. Educators must listen to the needs of single mothers and others who may feel excluded when schools attempt to reach out to fathers. Providing opportunities for all parents, especially single parents or parents who may be left out when fathers are specifically invited, is encouraged.

REFLECTION...

Schools want to involve parents more, but if fathers don't get involved, how can schools just reach out to fathers? Is this a gender equity issue? Would you anticipate a backlash and what would it be?

Barriers to Fathers' Involvement in Schools

Fathers can offer various accounts and disclaimers for why they do, or do not, engage in certain behaviors (Kaplan & Hennon, 1992; LaRossa, 1988). These vocabularies of motive help in presenting to themselves and others the images of "father" they wish to offer. Self-image can be thought of as a retelling of a narrative (Schafer, 1983): "This is my story; this is who I am." Perhaps the telling of the fathering story is more often to self than to others. Fathers need to know who they are and give it justification so that they can be comfortable and secure. Father inclusion programs based primarily or exclusively on outsider expert knowledge and delivered in a prescription mode, are likely to be ineffective (Hennon & Arcus, 1993).

The real needs, desires, and wishes of men must be considered in order to overcome barriers to father involvement in schools. Likewise, those wishing to negotiate social change must understand the lived realities of the men they are targeting, as perceived by those men. This does not mean accepting at face value the excuses, justifications, and disclaimers offered by men. Fathers should be held accountable for their actions. But realizing that these actions and justifications are part of the "self" as constructed by each father is important. These narratives are aspects of the fathers' stock of knowledge and form part of the material that must be used for enhancing father involvement.

Palm (1985) examines types of father involvement in schools serving young children with disabilities. The results show that fathers tend to be most involved in events like holiday parties or concerts and conferences, but only 40 percent of fathers participate. In Palm's study, 20 percent of fathers observe a program, help with therapy at home, or attend parent meetings. Fathers are least likely to volunteer in the classroom, serve on a parent board, or help to make or repair classroom materials (less than 5 percent). These low proportions are surprising because early education, especially with children with disabilities, includes parent involvement as an integral part. What keeps fathers away from schools?

- The main barrier appears to be time and schedule conflicts (Johnson & Palm, 1992). Most fathers work full-time and many work during typical business and school hours. In comparison to fathers, mothers are involved more often in part-time employment.
- One barrier is the fathers' perceptions that the tasks are not part of their role. For example, one of the authors was meeting with a group of Even Start fathers and talking about the importance of reading to young children. The response from the men was that their wives did the reading; it was not their job.
- Another barrier is not feeling invited to a program. If a father walks into a program and looks around and only sees adult females and children, he gets the message that this place is for women and children. Mothers may also play a gatekeeper role and either decide to push for fathers going to an event or class, or discourage them from going. Often fathers do not know about opportunities for involvement because they are not in the direct line of communication. If the children come home to mother, they are likely to pass on information from the school directly to mother who then takes responsibility for requests from school.
- Programs may be hesitant to make specific efforts to reach out to fathers. With 40 percent of children not living with their dads on a regular basis (Blankenhorn, 1995), events and outreach targeted toward dads may seem offensive and disrespectful of family diversity. We know of a school that invited fathers to go to a school dance with their elementary-aged daughters. This was upsetting to a colleague who had a daughter whose father had died. She was upset for two reasons: first, her daughter was excluded, but perhaps more importantly, the event represented inappropriate gender role and age stereotypes. The fear of offending parents, especially single-female parents, makes it difficult to make specific overtures toward fathers.

The barriers listed suggest special efforts need to be made to capitalize on the benefits of father involvement. Understanding subtle barriers that can be addressed by schools is an important step in involving more fathers.

Family-Level Interventions

Marital stress influences the quality of parenting. In some cases, parents attempt to compensate for a poor marriage by using their children as a source of support and gratification. This might translate into more involvement with school activities. In other cases, parents blame children for the marital strife, or scapegoat the children to focus the problem elsewhere. Children will also keep the marital and family systems in balance by acting out or being compliant. Doing well or poorly in school, for example, can be a child's device to divert attention away from marital strife and toward the child and his or her needs. The outcome, as seen by school personnel, may be less or more father involvement in schools. In any situation, fathers will likely be less attentive to their children in appropriate ways when there are marital problems, or in the adjustment phase of divorce (Krantz, 1988).

Earlier in this chapter we documented some of the gender dynamics and turf issues involved with parenting. Mothers (especially divorced ones or others estranged from their children's fathers) can be non-supportive and resistant to father involvement. Even in good marriages there can be resistance to change. Ways for counteracting this tendency is for mothers to learn to expect such territorial feelings, and to talk about these with the fathers. Fathers should not rise to the competition (Schroepfer, 1991). However, fathers should not be "junior mothers" playing secondary roles, or be "competing mothers" for their children's attention and love. Children benefit from having parents who cooperate together as the parenting team, supporting each other while playing complementary roles (Anderson & Sabatelli, 1995; Louv, 1994).[6] One caution offered to fathers by Levine (Latham, 1992) is protecting against trying so hard to connect with their children in order to be superfathers, that their wives are neglected. Keeping marriages strong is one of the best ways to facilitate being a better father (Anderson & Sabatelli, 1995).

Here are some ways in which schools can facilitate family-level intervention:

- Schools can include in their curricula value-based family life education from the primary school years on through adulthood (Arcus & Daniels, 1993; Hennon & Arcus, 1993: Strom, 1985).
- School systems and individual school personnel, such as social workers or trained lay leaders, can encourage, support, advertise, and/or offer marital enrichment programs as well as interventions of a more therapeutic nature. Program possibilities include stress management, positive discipline techniques, parenting after divorce, couples' communication techniques, conflict management strategies, and exercises to help fathers and mothers become more self-aware and self-reflective about their behavior. Such resources can help parents realize how they respond to others' behavior and their influence on how others respond to them. Reflexivity is a critical process of increasing self-awareness and sensitivity to the experiences of both self and others. Reflexivity is a crucial component of any efforts directed toward change in the fathering role. Enrichment and education can be offered in conjunction with businesses, agencies, or religious institutions (Hennon & Arcus, 1993; Hooper-Briar & Lawson, 1994);
- Educators can help people in understanding that family interaction, interpersonal competency, and love for family, as well as spending engrossing time with family, are as important as occupational achievement.
- Importantly, school personnel can establish their own quality marriages or other interpersonal relationships.

Familial behavior is context sensitive, conditioned by where they occur (Gubrium & Holstein, 1993). Men experience what is termed as organizational embeddedness (Gubrium, 1987); that is, the social systems men are involved in are not discrete, but rather men carry the meanings of one into others. While analytically one can separate family from work, fathering from truck driving, in the wholeness of life as known to fathers, this may not be meaningful. To do so may be creating differences without distinction. But scholars and lay persons alike do discuss how one role impacts another. For example, how driving a long-haul truck interferes with or shapes fathering, due to time, energy, stress, and so on. (McCall, 1988). Interventionists need to take this embeddedness and wholeness into account. In this way, they can become more empathetic with fathers in how they concurrently perceive themselves as situated in family, employment, and community. Simple, one-factor or single-sector (such as education) interventions will miss the richness and interdependency of a father's total life. More family-centric (or if necessary father-centric) paradigms and practices might prove more effective (Hennon-Jones, Hooper-Briar, & Kopcanová, 1996).[7] In all, more holistic "fatherized" strategies for negotiated change in parenting and involvement in schools and schooling are called for.

Summary

In this chapter, we presented background information and conceptualizations helpful to educators in understanding men as a socially constructed gender and fathering as diverse social roles. We stressed that father involvement in families, schooling, and schools is valuable and should be further encouraged by educators. Men bring diverse strengths and capabilities to fathering, and no one model or mode is argued as being the best. Fathers are important; and while attempts to encourage more quality involvement with children is beneficial for families, schools, communities, and society, attempts to create androgynous fathers or to feminize the role may not be appropriate. Educators who appreciate the benefits of father involvement while respecting gender and individual differences are more likely to enjoy successful efforts at increasing father involvement. Negotiating social change is difficult; trying to do so without engaging with and being empathetic with those most affected (fathers especially, but also wives, lovers, ex-wives, and children) is extremely problematic. This chapter focused on fathers and their understanding of their roles, including their ethno-cultures and self-narratives about being fathers. Understanding flesh and blood fathers in one's own community, rather than generalities gained from the mass media and popular culture of disengaged or modern fathers, appears more profitable in creating the types of communities, schools, and families conducive to best educating and serving all children. The educator should thus focus on "real" culture as known to real men.

We offer a multitude of examples and general strategic ideas for making fathers more appreciated and respected for their strengths and abilities. These can be capitalized upon to make schools more father friendly and have fathers involved in quality ways with their families, schooling, and schools. While we believe that these ideas are solid, they only scratch the surface of the fertile soil of ideas. We are confident that the reader will generate and utilize other, equally good if not better, strategies. We hope that these ideas will also be shared.

What can we say in closing? Examine all ideas for parent involvement to check for gender bias. Provide for the needs of both mothers and fathers. Measure success of father involvement not by the numbers but the quality of the experience for men and children. Schools often must build programs slowly and expect some trial and error in learning what the men in their communities will respond to. For some communities it may mean bringing out a sports figure to draw men to an event, for others special invitations from the children to their fathers may work. There are many barriers in men themselves, their families, and in schools that make father involvement a real challenge.

Just inviting fathers into schools, or engaging in a discourse conducted in academic texts, magazines, and on PBS may not be enough. Reaching beyond the white, suburban, middle class would seem to be necessary if widespread change in fathering culture and conduct is desired. There are many ways of getting men involved. In addition to those discussed above, Arcus (1995) provides some parent education examples. Levine, Murphy, and Wilson (1993) suggest involvement strategies for early childhood education settings: (a) expect men to be involved—send notes; (b) put out the welcome mat and meet them at the door, recognizing the men's contributions; (c) find out what men want, ask questions, do surveys, establish focus groups; and (d) display images of men in brochures, posters, and other areas of education settings.

Engaging with fathers to learn their strengths, hearing their stories, taking advantage of their stocks of knowledge, participating in their lives, and appreciating their family themes and parenting strategies is important. This allows educators better recognition of: rationalizations versus role conflicts, desires to change but not knowing how versus not wanting to change, technically present fathers as well as functionally present fathers, and perhaps new ways to appreciate "old" fathering for what it offers to children and society, as well as the promise of "new" fathering.

One aspect of promoting good fathering and school involvement might be efforts to support, strengthen, and enrich marriages. This argument is advanced by those in the marriage and family enrichment fields (L'Abate & Weinstein, 1987; Lewis, 1979). School personnel demonstrate interest in promoting quality marriages because children are observed to have negative developmental outcomes when raised within family systems that include marital conflict and parental styles characterized by lack of supervision, hostility, rejection, or coercion. These outcomes include academic failure, substance abuse, aggressiveness, delinquency, and psychopathology (Anderson & Sabatelli, 1995). Divorced and other fatherless homes appear especially problematic.

Educators also concern themselves with community and society change. Making communities more family friendly and working to create a culture respectful and supportive of fathers' myriad roles in the nurturing of children can be useful devices. In some cases, educators can work to change culture in more primary ways; in other cases, the efforts are more secondary in that they are directed to change culture as a whole. Thinking holistically, acting assertively, listening to and respecting real fathers, and being committed to father involvement and resilient to criticism can allow educators to provide resources, services, and supports that men deserve and need. Ultimately, it is children and society that benefit.

Recommended Activities

1. Interview fathers from different generations, from the 1930s on. Discuss with the fathers their roles in the family regarding child care, work, nurturing children, activities

with children, quantity of time spent with children, responsibility for discipline, and gender issues relating to their children.

2. Interview fathers who had their first children when they were teenagers, in their 20s, in their 30s, and in their 40s. Ask them to address the following issues: their age in respect to raising children, responsibility of child rearing, types of interaction with their children, and their ability to father.

3. Observe a parent education class predominantly made up of males. What types of interaction do you observe between the father and his child(ren)? What types of interaction do you observe between the father and the parent educator?

4. Invite a panel of fathers into the class to describe parenting from their perspective. Is it different than mothering? Has the role of fathers changed over the years?

5. Locate a listserv group on WWW or email that was designed to be a fathers' discussion group. Monitor or speak through this medium to identify issues that fathers may be discussing.

6. Describe the role your father played or did not play in your life. If this is too difficult, describe the role any significant male played in your life prior to age 18.

Notes

1. LaRossa (1988) notes that most books and other texts about the "new" fatherhood have been authored by middle-class men.

2. Additionally, researchers like LaRossa (1988) show how couples socially construct gender relationships by offering accounts, justifications, and excuses for why fathers are not more involved in parenting.

3. In some studies, housework includes aspects of child care. Also, some families' strategies allocated the division of labor such that men do some housework tasks as a trade-off, in terms of egalitarianism, as women do some child care tasks. For example, see Barry (1993).

4. Deutscher (1973) and others (Hennon, 1992) note that social scientists create fictional concepts, or constructs known only to scientists, to explain everyday behavior. These concepts, such as personality and social structure, have no relevance for the average person, and do not explain their actions in the same way as "ethno-concepts," or terms and stories that people give to account for their actions.

5. Due to the research designs, the direction of causality and/or if there is mutual influencing (school achievement influences in family life, and vice versa) cannot be determined. From a systems viewpoint, the argument appears to be that they are mutually influencing and reinforcing of one another.

6. An article by Barry (1993) refers to complementary but not similar contributions to the division of parenting labor as the Jack Sprat approach.

7. That is, social policy and program from the inside out; practices that put families center stage (rather than schools or other systems) with their needs and strengths as the foundation for policy and practice agendas that are accountable to the end-users, that is, accountable to families.

Additional Resources

Involvement of Fathers in Schools

Agencies and Programs:

The Center on Fathers, Families & Public Policy
Family Resource Center
200 South Michigan Avenue
Chicago, IL 60601
Phone: 312-341-0902

DAD to DAD
3771 Admiral Drive
Atlanta, GA 30341
Phone: 404-457-1595

The Fatherhood Project
c/o Families & Work Institute
330 Seventh Ave., 14th Floor
New York, NY 10001
Phone: 212-465-2044

Father's Resource Center
Loring Park Office Bldg.
430 Oak Grove Street, Suite 105
Minneapolis, MN 55403
Phone: 612-874-1509

Father-to-Father
Children, Youth & Family Consortium
12 McNeal Hall
1985 Buford Avenue
University of Minnesota
St. Paul, MN 55108
Phone: 612-626-1312

MELD for Young Dads
123 North Third Street, Suite 507
Minneapolis, MN 55401
Phone: 612-332-7563

National Center for Fathering
10200 West 75th Street, Suite 267
Shawnee Mission, KS 66204-2223
Phone: 913-384-4661

National Center on Fathers & Families
Graduate School of Education
University of Pennsylvania
Philadelphia, PA 19104
Phone: 215-686-3910

National Fatherhood Initiative
600 Eden Road, Bldg. E
Lancaster, PA 17601
Phone: 717-581-8860

Teen Indian Parents Program
Division of Indian Work
3045 Park Avenue
Minneapolis, MN 55407
Phone: 612-827-1795

Videos:

Being a Single Parent
1987. (19 minutes). Films for the Humanities & Sciences.

For Dads Only: The #1 Childcare Survival Guide for Dads
1990. (39 minutes). Luxor Films/Aylmer Press.

On Being a Father with T. Berry Brazelton
1985. (70 minutes). Family Home Entertainment.

Fathering Issues and Concerns

Websites:

The American Family Network
http://www.customcpu.com:80/personal/mneligh/afn/links.htm

Dad and Son: Memoir
http://www.parentsplace.com/readroom/goodfathers/index.html

Dad Stuff
http://tam2000.tamu.edu/~phayes/dad-stuf.html

The Dad's Den
http://www.portage.net/~rborelli/dads.html

Discipline of Fatherhood
http://www.isl.net/wwyweb/wwy2595.html

Divorce Home Page
http://www.primenet.com/~dean

Fathering Issues and Resources
http://www.parentsplace.com/readroom/father.html

FatherNet Gopher
gopher://tinman.mes.umn.edu:80/11/FatherNet

FatherNet Web
http://www.fsci.umn.edu/cyfc/FatherNet.htp

Fathers' Resource Center
http://www.parentsplace.com/readroom/frc/index/html

Fathers Rights and Equality Exchange
http://www.vix.com/free/

Fathers Rights Foundation
http://www.intrnet.net/~risaacs/index.html

Life with Father
http://gertrude.art.uiuc.edu/ludgate/the/place/place2.html

M.E.N. Magazine
http://www.vix.com/menmag/

Men's Issue Page
http://www.vix.com/pub/men/index.html

San Diego Fathers' Group
ftp://ftp.cts.com/pub/jcb/fathers.html

Single Dad's Index
http://www.vix.com/pub/men/single-dad.html

Single Fathers
http://www.pitt.edu/~jsims/singlefa.html

Family Issues

Websites:

CYF Consortium
http://www.fsi.umn.edu/cyfc/cyfc.html

Family Planet
http://www.familyplanet.com

The Family Web
http://www.familyweb.com/

Family World
http://www.family.com/

For and About Children
http://www.ocsny.com/~mdm/children.html

Functional Family
http://pubweb.acns.nwu.edu/~rab/hnhome1.htm

Local Family Activities
http://111.family.com

The National Parenting Center
http://www.stpt.com/TNPC/

Parenting
http://iquest.com/~jsm/moms/parenting.html

Parents Helping Parents
http://www.portal.com:80/~cbntmkr/php.html

Parents Place
http://www.parentsplace.com/

Parents Soup
http://www.parentsoup.com

Positive Parenting Home Page
http://www.fishnet.net/~pparents/

Save the Children
http://www.winternet.com/~jannmart/nkcindex.html

Single Parent Project
http://www.alaska.net/~rwarner/spphtml.htm

References

Amato, P. R. (1994). Life-span adjustment of children to their parents' divorce. In E. N. Junn & C. J. Boyatzis (Eds.), *Child growth and development* (pp. 149–169). Guilford, CT: Dushkin/McGraw Hill.

Anderson, S. A., & Sabatelli, R. M. (1995). *Family interaction: A multigenerational developmental perspective.* Boston: Allyn and Bacon.

Arcus, M. E. (1995). Advances in family life education: Past, present and future. *Family Relations, 44,* 336–344.

Arcus, M. E., & Daniels, L. B. (1993). Values and family life education. In M. E. Arcus, J. D. Schvaneveldt, & J. J. Moss (Eds.), *Handbook of family of* *education (Vol. 1), Foundations of family life education* (pp. 76–105). Newbury Park, CA: Sage.

Barry, J. B. (1993, May/June). Daddytrack. *Utne Reader,* pp. 70–73.

Belsky, J. (1984). The determinants of parenting: A process model. *Child Development, 55,* 83–96.

Belsky, J., & Pensky, E. (1988). Marital change across the transition to parenthood. *Marriage and Family Review, 12,* 133–156.

Belsky, J., & Vondra, J. (1985). Characteristics, consequences, and determinants of parenting. In L. L'Abate (Ed.), *The handbook of family psychology and therapy* (pp. 523–556). Homewood, IL: Dorsey.

Bigner, J. (1994). *Parent–child relations: An introduction to parenting.* New York: Macmillan.

Biller, H. B. (1993). *Fathers and families: Paternal factors in child development.* Westport, CT: Auburn.

Blankenhorn, D. (1995). *Fatherless America: Confronting our most urgent social problem.* Dallas, TX: Harper Collins.

Bronfenbrenner, U. (1986). Ecology of the family as a context for human development: Research perspectives. *Developmental Psychology, 22,* 723–742.

Bruce, J., Lloyd, C. B., & Leonard, A. (1995). *Families in focus: New perspectives on mothers, fathers and children.* New York: The Population Council.

Cohen, T. (1987). Remaking men. *Journal of Family Issues, 8,* 57–77.

Cunningham, B. (1994, September). Portraying fathers and other men in the curriculum. *Young Children,* 4–13.

Darling-Fisher, C., & Tiedje, L. B. (1990). The impact of maternal employment characteristics on fathers' participation in child care. *Family Relations, 39,* 20–26.

Deutscher, I. (1973). *What we say/what we do: Sentiments & acts.* Glenview, IL: Scott, Foresman.

Doherty, W. J. (1991). Beyond reactivity and the deficit model of manhood: A commentary on articles by Napier, Pittman and Gottman. *Journal of Marriage and Family Therapy, 17,* 19–32.

DuBois, D. L., Eitel, S. K., & Felner, R. D. (1994). Effects of family environment and parent–child relationships on school adjustment during the transition to early adolescence. *Journal of Marriage and the Family, 56,* 45–414.

Entwisle, D. R. (1985). Becoming a parent. In L. L'Abate (Ed.), *The handbook of family psychology and therapy (Vol. 1)* (pp. 557–585). Homewood, IL: Dorsey.

Epstein, J. L. (1995, May). School/family/community partnerships: Caring for the children we share. *Phi Delta Kappan,* 701–712.

Gubrium, J. F. (1987). Organizational embeddedness and family life. In T. H. Brubaker (Ed.), *Aging, health, and family: Long term care* (pp. 23–41). Newbury Park, CA: Sage.

Gubrium, J. F., & Holstein, J. A. (1993). Phenomenology, ethnomethodology, and family discourse. In P. G. Boss, W. J. Doherty, R. LaRossa, W. R. Schumm, & S. K. Steinmetz (Eds.), *Sourcebook of family theories and methods: A contextual approach* (pp. 651–672). New York: Plenum.

Heck, R. K. Z., Owen, A. J., & Rowe, B. (Eds.). (1995). *Home-based employment and family life.* Westport, CT: Auburn House.

Hennon, C. B. (1992). Toward the turn of the century. *Journal of Family and Economic Issues, 13,* 355–372.

Hennon, C. B., & Arcus, M. (1993). Life-span family life education. In T. H. Brubaker (Ed.), *Family relations: Challenges for the future* (pp. 181–210). Newbury Park, CA: Sage.

Hennon, C. B., Jones, A., Hooper-Briar, K., & Kopcanová, D. (1996). A snapshot in time: Family policy and the United Nations International Year of the Family. *Journal of Family and Economic Issues, 17,* 9–46.

Hennon, C. B., Jones, A., & Schmenk, E. (in press). Family-linked policy and programs within the context of privatization. In D. Iatridis & J. Hoops (Eds.), *The social impact of privatization: Social justice and the welfare state in Central and Eastern Europe.* Westport, CT: Praeger.

Hennon, C. B., Jones, A., Schmenk, E., Roth, M., Popescu, L., & Kopcanová, D. (1996). *Family change and employment: Pressing issues and policy implications for Eastern and Central Europe.* Unpublished manuscript, Miami University, Family and Child Studies Center.

Holden, G. (1988). Adult's thinking about a child-rearing problem: Effects of experience, parental status, and gender. *Child Development, 59,* 1623–1632.

Hooper-Briar, K., & Lawson, H. A. (1994). *Serving children, youth and families through interprofessional collaboration and service integration: A framework for action.* Oxford, OH: The Danforth Foundation and the Institute for Educational Renewal at Miami University.

Jackson, J. (1994, June). The Role of Men in Children's Lives. Luncheon address to Family Re-Union III, Nashville, TN.

Johnson, L., & Palm, G. (1992). Planning programs: What do fathers want? In L. Johnson & G. Palm

(Eds.), *Working with fathers: Methods and perspectives* (pp. 59–77). Stillwater, MN: nu ink unlimited.

Jones, A., Brubaker, T. H., Ulrich, D. L., & Hennon, C. B. (1994, November). *Men's caring roles within the family: Changing images that challenge modern conceptions of gender.* Workshop presentation at the pre-conference, Anticipating the Future of Males in Families, to the annual conference of the National Council on Family Relations, Minneapolis, MN.

Kaplan, L., & Hennon, C. B. (1992). Remarriage education: The Personal Reflections Program. *Family Relations, 41,* 127–134.

Krantz, S. E. (1988). Divorce and children. In S. M. Dornbusch & M. H. Strober (Eds.), *Feminism, children, and the new families* (pp. 249–273). New York: Guilford.

L'Abate, L., & Weinstein, S. E. (1987). *Structured enrichment programs for couples and families.* New York: Brunner/Mazel.

Lamb, M. E. (1981). *The role of the father in child development.* New York: Wiley.

Lamb, M. E. (1987). Introduction: The emergent American father. In M. E. Lamb (Ed.), *The father's role: Cross-cultural perspectives* (pp. 3–25). Hillsdale, NJ: Lawrence Erlbaum.

LaRossa, R. (1988). Fatherhood and social change. *Family Relations, 37,* 451–457.

LaRossa, R., & LaRossa, M. M. (1981). *Transition to parenthood: How infants change families.* Beverly Hills, CA: Sage.

LaRossa, R., & Reitzes, D. C. (1993). Continuity and change in middle class fatherhood, 1925–1939: The culture-conduct connection. *Journal of Marriage and the Family, 55,* 455–468.

Latham, A. (1992, May). Fathering the nest. *M.,* pp. 66–75.

Lawson, H., Hooper-Briar, K., Hennon, C. B., & Jones, A. (in press). *Family policies and practices: International perspectives.* Thousand Oaks, CA: Sage.

Levine, J., Murphy, D., & Wilson, S. (1993). *Getting men involved: Strategies for early childhood programs.* New York: Scholastic.

Lewis, J. M. (1979). *How's your family?* New York: Brunner/Mazel.

Louv, R. (1993). *Fatherlove: What we need; what we seek; what we must create.* New York: Pocket Books.

Louv, R. (1994). *Reinventing fatherhood.* (Occasional Papers Series, No. 14.) Vienna: United Nations, International Year of the Family.

Marsiglio, W. (1991). Parental engagement activities with minor children. *Journal of Marriage and the Family, 53,* 973–986.

McBride, B. A. (1990). The effects of a parent education/play group program on father involvement in child rearing. *Family Relations, 39,* 250–256.

McCall, R. B. (1988, September). Real men do change diapers. *Parents,* p. 202.

McLoyd, V. C. (1990). The impact of economic hardship on black families and children: Psychological distress, parenting, and socioemotional development. *Child Development, 61,* 311–346.

Palkovitz, R. (1984). Parental attitudes and father's interaction with their five-month-old infants. *Developmental Psychology, 20,* 1054–1060.

Palm, G. (1985). Creating opportunities for father involvement. *Nurturing News, 7*(4), 12–13.

Palm, G. (1994). Future of fatherhood: A guiding image. *Family information services,* 62–64. Minneapolis, MN: M&M.

Palm, G. (1995). Understanding male involvement and promoting healthy male socialization. Workshop materials for Winter/Spring 1995 Early Childhood Education Regional Inservice Training. Minneapolis, MN: Department of Education.

Palm, G., & Palkovitz, R. (1988). The challenge of working with new fathers: Implications for support providers. In R. Palkovitz & M. Sussman (Eds.), *Transitions to parenthood* (pp. 357–376). New York: Haworth.

Parsons, T. (1955). Family structure and socialization of the child. In T. Parsons & R. F. Bales (Eds.), *Family socialization and interaction processes* (pp. 35–131). Glencoe, IL: Free Press.

Pruett, K. (1987). *The nurturing father: Journey toward the complete man.* New York: Warner Books.

Riley, R. (1994, November). Families come first. *Principal,* 30–32.

Roberts, P. (1996, May/June). Fathers' time. *Psychology Today,* pp. 48–56, 81.

Robinson, J. P. (1990, March/April). The hard facts about hard work. *Utne Reader,* p. 70.

Rotundo, E. A. (1985). America fatherhood: A historical perspective. *American Behavioral Scientist, 29,* 7–25.

Samuelson, R. J. (1996, April 8). Why men need family values. *Newsweek,* p. 43.

Sanik, M. M. (1990). Parents' time use: A 1967–1986 comparison. *Lifestyles: Family and economic issues, 11,* 299–316.

Schafer, R. (1983). *The analytic attitude.* New York: Basic Books.

Schmidt-Waldherr, H. (1992). From the "Fatherless Society" to the "New Fatherliness." In N. B. Leidenfrost (Ed.), *Families in transition* (pp. 85–90). Vienna: United Nations Office at Vienna, Centre for Social Development and Humanitarian Affairs, IYF Secretariat.

Schroepfer, L. (1991, June). Dad: New and improved. *American Health,* p. 64.

Simons, R., Whitbeck, L., Conger, R., & Melby, J. (1990). Husband and wife differences in determinants of parenting. *Journal of Marriage and the Family, 52,* 375–392.

Strom, R. D. (1985). Developing a curriculum for parent education. *Family Relation, 34,* 161–167.

Swick, K. (1984). *Inviting parents into the young child's world.* Champaign, IL: Stipes.

Thevenin, T. (1993). *Mothering and fathering: The gender differences in child rearing.* Garden City Park, NY: Avery.

Thompson, L., & Walker, A. (1989). Gender in families: Women and men in marriage, work and parenthood. *Journal of Marriage and the Family, 51,* 845–871.

Thompson, L., & Walker, A. J. (1995). The place of feminism in family studies. *Journal of Marriage and the Family, 57,* 847–865.

Volling, B. L., & Belsky, J. (1991). Multiple determinants of father involvement during infancy in dual-earner and single-earner families. *Journal of Marriage and the Family, 53,* 461–474.

Home Education

Personal Histories

J. GARY KNOWLES
The Ontario Institute for Studies in Education
of the University of Toronto

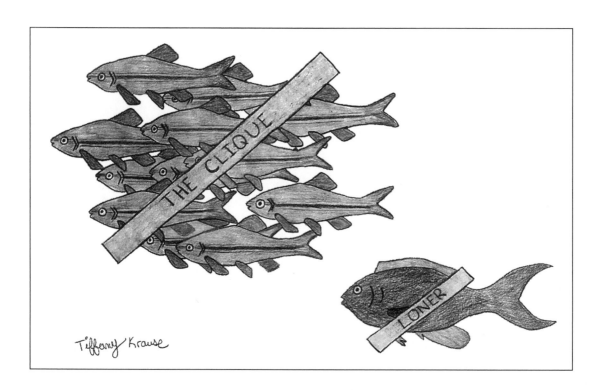

Tiffany Krause

> This chapter reviews home-education history and presents recent information about the home-education movement in the United States. Through use of observation and interviews, home-school educators are presented in a realistic manner. The future of home education and the relationship between the public and private schools is still evolving. The goals of this chapter are:
>
> - To help the reader understand why home education has developed
> - To describe the variety of reasons parents choose to home-educate their children
> - To compare home education to public or private education
> - To identify families that have home-educated their children and the strengths of home-educating their children

Often, when I meet with home-educating parents and they learn of my work as a university-based teacher educator they are outspoken about their dissatisfaction with public schools. Their complaints frequently focus on very specific practices of classroom teachers. As a one-time secondary school teacher and principal (although currently a university classroom teacher and researcher), I have had extensive experience observing public and private school classrooms and the teachers who work therein. Because I am also a parent and a teacher I understand, at least experientially, the basis for parents' concerns and complaints. On the other hand, I also understand some of the feelings that arise in teachers' minds when they are unjustly criticized.

As I prepared to write this chapter my 13-year-old, independent-minded son, John-Paul, declared to me that he does not want to go to school anymore. He has attended public schools up until this time. He refutes my suspicion that he is afraid of attending secondary school. Rather, he insists, for a multitude of well-articulated reasons that mainly have to do with issues of equity and social justice (but include his stated enthusiasm for exploring and learning about the world in concert with *his* special needs), and that a home education offers exciting possibilities. I cannot disagree with his reasoning, although I did raise many of my concerns with him, including ones related to the fact that he wanted (and was supported by his mother) to use commercially prepared curricular materials for some subject matter learning. The curriculum he desired to use was, I felt, a rather simplistic one, and I had great difficulty accepting that it had any substantial usefulness for his long-term intellectual development. Actually, the curriculum goes against the grain of my accumulated understandings about how children learn, and about good teaching, gleaned from many years working as a teacher and researcher, I am primarily against the underlying and expressed pedagogy! In other words, the particular prepared curriculum is contrary to my academic and experiential understandings about what constitutes good curriculum. Together, John-Paul and I will struggle with this issue. In the interim period John-Paul refined and assembled more arguments. A very interesting thing happened. Suddenly he became interested in the fact that I was researching home education issues, something that he had not been even vaguely interested in beforehand. In the few months prior to beginning his home education, then,

John-Paul voraciously read many of my published research reports on home education and engaged me in thoughtful discussions about many of my observations and the issues I raised. His arguments for learning at home rather than school are now also well grounded in some of my seasoned perspectives, although, as might be expected, he thinks my cautions regarding his situation are not valid. With regard to matters of curriculum, especially, he has not sensed anything like the full range of possibilities that are afforded home-educated children. He is thinking very narrowly about what it means to be a learner at home. But expanded possibilities may come to him! So, I anticipate that in the next few months we will, together, experientially explore the implications of some of my observations about home-educating parents and their practices as contained in this chapter.

REFLECTION...

It is important that you recognize your feelings about home education. Are they positive or negative? What was your source of information? Select four adjectives to describe your perception of home education. After completing this chapter, return to your adjectives and see if you wish to make any changes.

An Emerging Inquiry

Since 1983 I have spent extensive time researching "home schools"[1] and the parents who operate them. One of my consistent observations is that, despite claims to the contrary by both parent-teachers and formal school classroom teachers, there is considerable congruence between the teaching practices employed in both home education settings and public and private schools. As evident in my informal conversations with parents and casual observations of "school at home," some parents indeed seem to recreate the instructional contexts of schools and teach in ways, which they often highly criticize, of formal classroom teachers.

REFLECTION...

If your teaching was a reflection of how you were taught, how would you teach? What would the curriculum look like? What would your behaviors as a teacher be?

The apparent contradiction of this, given parents' expressions to me about public school teachers and their classrooms, prompted me to investigate the experiences and practices of parent-as-teacher. I originally wanted to know about the origins of parents' teaching methods, especially, the relationships between their biographies, their thinking about instruction, and their practices. To begin this work, I drew on my experiences as a secondary school teacher, the anecdotal unrecorded stories I heard from teachers (in staff rooms and informal discussions), and my experiences working and researching with pre-service and beginning (or first year) teachers (see, for example, Bullough, Knowles, & Crow, 1991;

Knowles, 1992, 1994; Knowles & Holt-Reynolds, 1991). My thinking went something like this: If—even after extensive formal preparation for classroom teaching—beginning public and private school teachers[2] fall back on their early experiences (of schools and teachers) as students to guide their thinking and practice in the classroom (Crow, 1987a; Knowles, 1988a, 1992, 1994), especially when they are having difficulties with their responsibilities, it is reasonable to imagine that parent-teachers working in the isolation of the home may do the same. As I thought about my own experiences as a classroom teacher and a home-educating parent (my two oldest children were taught at home for a very short time when we lived in a geographically isolated, rural location) this notion had considerable value.

Historical Overview

Home education in the United States as we know it in the 1990s has only a short history although, some would claim, a long heritage that rests in Judeo-Christian and colonial traditions. In this section, I draw heavily on an earlier, extensive, historical analysis of the home education movement from 1970 through 1990 (see, Knowles, Marlow, & Muchmore, 1992)[3] and extend it to the mid-1990s. A number of overlapping, interconnected phases distinguish the general development of the home education movement in the USA.[4]

Beginning of the Movement

In the late 1950s and the 1960s a number of parents across North America began questioning the hitherto largely unchallenged place and practices of formal and public schooling. Many of these parents, initially, simply wanted more influence over the pedagogies and curricular practices as found in public schools. These contentions (criticisms or challenges) came in an era of political and societal fermentation and, in a sense, symbolically represented the erosion of universal acceptance of the foundation of a whole social order, especially the assumptions behind aspects of public education and the development of socially conscious citizens. Parents' contentions and criticisms at that time—and as with parents through to the mid 1990s—rested in issues such as the perceived failure of public schools to meet their expectations and the perceived needs of their children, whether it be in matters of curriculum, pedagogy, personal safety, social justice, religious freedom, morality, and the like.

> **REFLECTION...**
>
> Why did the home education movement begin in the 1950s and 1960s and not in the 1990s or, even, 1950s? Was there a connection between the home education movement and other social issues taking place in the late 1950s and 1960s?

As parents removed their children from public schools, many school administrators and teachers felt the rebuff of such symbolic, intentional, and dramatic actions and a battle for control of the education of children ensued. (Essentially, from the time public schools were established in the nineteenth century, the responsibility of education was deemed to be solely in the domain of individual states within the Union; thus, parents were challenging a long-standing arrangement.) School boards, and some parents, ushered in a period of confrontation as they engaged in considerable litigious activity regarding the practice of teaching at home. School boards and superintendents took parents to court with arguments against the practice of home education typically resting in issues of parental expertise or preparedness to teach, matters of curriculum equivalency with public schools, claims of truancy based on compulsory attendance laws, issues regarding the appropriate socialization of children, and the state's right to educate children. Of no little consequence, also, was the fact that school districts depended on student attendance for funding from the states. Parents retaliated against these harsh responses with court cases of their own, many resting in matters of parental rights and challenges to the state's rights.

During the early periods of contention and confrontation, the mass media was largely on the side of schools. The stigma for parents that resulted, and their need to avoid litigious action, meant that a good number of families went underground, forced into a silence and isolation from neighbors and family as they endeavored to maintain what they claimed as their right and need. Thus it was, that researchers who first explored home education in the early 1980s (such as Delahooke, 1986; Gustavsen, 1981; Linden, 1983; Schemmer, 1985; Taylor, 1986; Van Galen, 1986, and myself) found it very difficult to locate willing families with whom to work. Many parents lived in a kind of fear, and did not want to be identified, prosecuted, or ostracized. They simply did not want others to know of their at-home practices and their children's absence from formal schools.

The 1980s and 1990s

One of the eventual results of these extensive court actions was that many of the cases resulted in decisions that were favorable to the parents, and many school superintendents were required by the courts to provide instructional or curricular alternatives for home-educated students. Essentially, beginning in the early 1980s, a period of cooperation between schools and parents began. Such artificially induced cooperation between schools and parents slowly increased, and changed in tone over the course of the decade, as schools became more responsive to parents (and as educators, in practice, acknowledged the importance of parental involvement, more generally, in the formal education of children). Cooperative relationships between schools and home-educating parents and their children have increased at an even more accelerated pace in the 1990s. School boards across the United States (and in other parts of North America, especially Canada) have worked to provide meaningful services for parents and their home-educated children. In particular, many school districts have developed inclusive policies that allow more flexible allocation of resources for students, accommodate flexible school attendance, and make provisions for home-educated students' participation in curricular and extra-curricular activities. Thus, as the notion of cooperation as mandated by the courts was implemented by schools it, along with changes in the thinking of professional educators, spawned various programmatic and structural responses helpful to home education students and their parents. Encouraged by considerable media activity, which viewed home education in more favorable ways, parents are now, in the mid 1990s, much more willing to acknowledge their educational activities than they were in the 1970s. Indeed, home-educating parents are now generally very vocal

and public in advocating and defending their practices; witness parents' extensive participation in legislative lobbying and their more open practices, for example—a stance far removed from the underground silence of the 1970s.

As the public responded more favorably to home education, not unexpectedly, the participation in its practice increased dramatically. Estimates of the home-education population vary greatly but extrapolations of its growth from a few thousand students in the 1960s
to upwards of a million in 1995 are not unrealistic. About 2 percent of school-age students,
according to my own estimates, are now educated at home. This growth signifies a number
of phenomena, not the least of which is the extensive consolidation of the movement
through the sheer growth of numbers coupled with the establishment of highly effective formal and informal networking groups. Such networking groups initially knitted the home
education population together by drawing on the most experienced or successful home-
educators for role modeling as well as advocacy, legal, and leadership roles. As parents
clustered together for moral, legal, instructional, and curricular assistance, a number of support services began to materialize, often led and developed by opportunistic religious educators and ministers, attorneys and those with legal expertise, publishers, and visionary
(many self-proclaimed) pedagogues. In addition, states have passed extensive legislation
supporting home education, and this fact alone bears witness to the effective way that the
networking capabilities of the home-education movement have been used.

Compartmentalization in the Home School Movement

Beginning in the early 1990s, as home education continued to grow—almost exponentially—
as an educational alternative, a fractionalization, or compartmentalization, appeared in the
ranks of the movement. Before the considerable growth in the numbers of home-educating
families, various ideological groups worked together for the "common good," for the general goals and needs of home education, broadly defined, and the needs of parents and their
children. This earlier cohesion was particularly evident in the late 1970s and early 1980s
when the legitimacy of such educational practices were questioned by many members of
the public. Not unexpectedly, then, this recent compartmentalization is evidenced by the
clustering of parents and groups of parents around more narrowly defined goals and purposes (which are for the most part ideologically defined). These are, in effect, special interest groups.

As in the greater society, the growth of special interest groups is fueled by both an increase in numbers and the potential for political influence. Whereas a decade earlier, parents of all perspectives largely worked together for the general acceptance and expansion
of home education as an alternative, in the 1990s, there are now visible divisions, and competition for political, religious, and educational influence is sometimes fierce.

As I look towards the end of the 1990s, I sense that the home education movement is
on the verge of another phase of its history, especially given relatively easy access to new
computer technologies and their communicative and educative possibilities.[5] But any enthusiasm I might have for the computer-based media is greatly tempered. I wonder and am
concerned about the long-term influence of the vast array of prepackaged materials (including computer media materials) on both the teaching of parents and the learning by students.
I wonder also whether the extensive use of such materials (many of which seem to be "cast-
offs" from educational publishers and schools, and are pedagogically less than forward-

looking) will eventually lead to home education developing the same kinds of pedagogical ills and complacency that many parents claim beset public schools. Replication of traditional school practices in the home (i.e., the creation of "home schools," miniature classrooms in spirit and practice, as opposed to "home education contexts"), and extensive reliance on externally produced curricula, diminishes many of the creative and educative possibilities of parents' teaching and the home education process. Whatever happens, I sense that the numbers of home educators will continue to grow until some plateau is reached, perhaps at about 3 percent of the total student population in the United States.[6] After all, to home-educate requires a great deal of commitment and allocation of family resources, resources that may not be so readily available to families in the coming decade given the uncertain economic, labor, and political horizons ushered in by the first six or so years of the 1990s.

Exploring Families

My understanding of home education originated in both my prior experiences and scholarly inquiries. Why do home-school parents adopt particular teaching practices? As I thought about this question, further questions came to mind and provided the initial framework for my inquiry. Such questions included: To what extent are prior experiences formative in the teaching practices of parent-teachers? What are the relationships between parent-teachers' practices and the teacher role models they hold? What are the elements of parents' teacher role identities? What are the formative experiences that drive parents into the realization of their conceptualizations of teaching at home? These were some of the questions that directed my work.

Some Terms

Keep in mind the meanings of several terms that I have used thus far. I use *teaching practices* to refer to the ways in which parent-teachers present educational materials, motivate their children as students, and generally achieve or facilitate the attainment of appropriate goals for their children's learning—this includes the many and varied activities that transpire in home education settings under the guidance of parents. In a sense I mean pedagogy; but *pedagogy* is a distancing word for many parents. *Teacher role model* refers to the experientially-based images and composite views of teachers and their practices which parent-teachers come to accept as being appropriate—or inappropriate—for facilitating their children's learning. *Teacher role identity* is the image of self-as-teacher that each parent-teacher comes to accept as appropriate for the educational guidance of their children.

Inquiring into Lives and Experiences

I selected twelve families from which to obtain extensive narrative information. These families lived along the Wasatch Front region of Utah—from Provo to Ogden, including Salt Lake City where, as of the early 1990s, there were over 1,000 families involved in home education.[7] The reason that I chose Utah families was simple. I was living in Utah at the time, and they were the families with which I was interacting and, in a general sense, reading about in the "bad press" of local newspapers. Because I wanted to gain a range of perspectives, I sought out diverse families along the lines of socioeconomic and occupational status, religious and political orientation, residential location, lifestyle, length of time involved in home education, parental education, and commitment to working with me. The last criterion was important because, after all, my work is by its very nature highly intrusive. I step into people's live and homes and often request very personal information, and I watch families at their work of teaching and learning—and of simply "being family." The twelve families were drawn from a pool of seventy-two families who had made their homes and educational endeavors available for my exploration.[8] Most families were in some way connected to the Utah Home Education Association, at that time a relatively young networking organization.

I did not restrict the length or breadth of parents' autobiographical accounts. Most parents chose to write or tape record their responses and most completed their accounts about the time I finished observing their at-home educating activities. The parents' accounts were up to 114 pages in length, although most were on the order of 15–35 pages (including those that were transcribed from audio tapes). Because I was dealing with people who were cautious about researchers such as myself, and very mindful about the public's view of their actions, I felt that the autobiographical approach was least intrusive because it removed me, somewhat, from the process of information gathering and gave the parents ample psychological and temporal space to tell their stories without my interference.

My findings suggest that there are a number of complex and intertwined sources of teacher role identity evident in the individual and collective biographies or personal histories of parent-teachers. Nevertheless, I observed, four major formative elements of teacher role identities stood out: childhood experiences of family, teacher role models, memories of school, and the impact of significant others or experiences. The first three components are outcomes of experiences they had early in their lives. The latter component, essentially an overlay experience, in most cases began and continued from a time just prior to when the parent-teachers began home-educating.[9] In the following sections I present a collective view of the families, the parents' perspectives, the practices I observed, and connections with their prior experiences.

The Families

Rather than sketch profiles of individual parents or families I provide, through a summary, a general sense of the families with which I had the privilege of working. They were diverse and not unlike (as a group) the profile of a much larger group of parents in a more recent study of home education in four western States—Utah, Nevada, Oregon, and Washington (see, Mayberry, Knowles, Ray, & Marlow, 1995).[10]

While a majority of the parents were from the mid- to lower socioeconomic groups of Utah society (based on available Census data), there was a considerable variety of family income. The lowest yearly income (less than $13,000, corrected for inflation as of 1995, and perhaps even as low as $8,000) was that of a single African American mother with three children who was working on a graduate degree in curriculum and early childhood education. At the other end of the income scale, was a family with an architect father, and another with a published writer mother and a media professional father. These two families, for example, resided in comfortable middle-class environments and had family incomes approaching $75,000 (also corrected for inflation). Other occupations represented in the families included that of an unskilled laborer, a number of skilled trades persons, clerical and semi-professional workers, paramedical professionals, salespersons, a computer programmer and communications technician, graduate students, and classroom teachers. Four of the parents had multiple professions and some of the parents (mainly fathers) were self-employed. About half of the mothers, and one father, had recently given up full-time employment to organize and guide the family home education enterprise.

About two thirds of the twenty-three parents (comprising twelve families) were either active or inactive members of the dominant religion in the state, the Church of Jesus Christ of Latter Day Saints (LDS or Mormon). Others were Roman Catholics, Evangelical Christians, adherents to the tenets of an Eastern religion, and agnostics. (The large number of LDS families somewhat reflected the proportion of LDS families in the state.) Almost half of the parents were born outside of Utah. Several had either traveled extensively or lived in a variety of settings in the United States, and at least three had traveled extensively outside of the country. Two were born overseas, one in Iran, the other in New Zealand, and had married Americans. Ages of the parents ranged from the mid-20s to nearly 50 years, with most in their late-20s to late-30s. The mean age was 33 years.

The size of the families varied, from two families with one child, to one family with six and another with seven children. Among the twelve families, there were thirty-three children being educated at home. Three families also had children attending public schools. Ages of the home-educated children ranged from four through fourteen years. Twenty-four of the children were in the equivalent of the early elementary grades (one through three), although there was a spread from Kindergarten through Grade Eight.

Most families lived in urban or suburban settings, although two lived in rural environments that were on the verge of being suburbanized. It was difficult to ascertain parents' political inclinations, although some parents voluntarily stated in our conversations or in their autobiographical accounts that they were Republican supporters. One parent, a father, was quite active in local political party organization and legislative lobbying. Of him (and others), I was cognizant of the apparent contradiction between working-class values, a heightened social conscience, and very conservative political values.

Several lifestyles were represented. One family, in particular, was highly "self-sufficient" in an ecological and environmental sense and somewhat socially isolated, although the children regularly interacted with other neighborhood children. Churchgoers regularly participated in social events centered in their respective religious communities. Some parents were highly active in the Utah Home Education Association. Three families also had loose connections with the Utah Christian Home School Association, then an embryonic organization. Involvement in both church and home education activities were high priorities in the affairs of most of the families, and often parents responsible for the daily home-educating activities had greatly reduced opportunities for social interactions with non-home-educating peers. Most of the families seemed to have some neighborhood responsibilities or connections with close-by families. The pastimes and lifestyles of these families appeared to be similar to other families in comparable occupational and socioeco-nomic situations as evidenced by casual observation of the neighborhoods in which they and other families lived.

For three families, the decision to home-educate was not a long deliberation—in con-trast to four of the families who had planned for it even before the birth of their children. Together, these parents had home-educated their children for time periods ranging from one to eight years. As a group they were well educated. Eleven of the parents had college de-grees with at least six having taken extensive post-baccalaureate studies or having earned graduate degrees. With the exception of those who were teachers, few among them had completed general or teacher education coursework. The remaining parents had high school diplomas. Those who were skilled workers or semi-professionals had attended trade schools or junior and community colleges.

For at least six parents, commitment to my inquiry into their family educating activities was important because they were interested in "dispelling mythologies in the public's mind" about the practice of home education.[11] In working with me they perceived an op-portunity to tell the "truth" as it were. (I was never sure whether they meant *truth* to have a capital *T*!) Perhaps because of my obvious connection with other home-educating families, and the fact that I, too, had home-educated my two oldest children when our family lived in a remote, rural place nearly a decade earlier, four parents assumed I would only report the good things about home schooling.

Other parents perceived benefits in regular communication with me since opportunities to interact with knowledgeable and sympathetic outsiders are considerably reduced when energies are focused almost exclusively on the activities associated with children's home learning. Most of the parents also bombarded me with questions on a range of educational issues, some of which I could answer and some I could not. Also, I shared printed and other resources with parents as they requested commentary or assistance with thinking about var-ious pedagogical/instructional, curricular, or school bureaucracy matters, and this was per-ceived as being helpful. But mostly, for those who wanted them, the transcripts of the conversational interviews were deemed to be "enlightening." One parent, for example, said that "[I] enabled [her] to make better sense of her feelings about schools and learning, and about a number of other educational matters."

Parents' Perspectives

Because of the extent and complexity of the information gathered, and the limitations in space, I present only some of my findings in this chapter.

Learning and Early Experiences

Parents' reflections upon childhood experiences revealed a range of feelings about learning, education, teachers, and schools—especially public schools. For some parents, for exam-ple, writing about their prior and early experiences produced fond memories but, for most, it presented a painful reminder of past ("preferred to be forgotten," as one parent put it) for-mal school experiences.

Most parents admitted that they had little experience in contemporary public schools—although one mother volunteered extensively in classrooms before committing to the work of home education. (She saw this activity as a way of understanding the problems with teachers and fellow students that her young son regularly experienced.) Previous teaching experiences in *any* setting—apart from Christian Sunday School—were minimal. There were, as mentioned, few parents with formal preparation to teach. Reading about other home-educating families and attending home education conventions were the predominant means of getting information about teaching at home and becoming prepared for the endeavor. Many expressed orientations that were, by their own admissions, distinctly Christian—"fundamental in the evangelical sense"—and conservative in character.

When asked to respond to a broad request, "Tell me about learning as a child," some parents quickly referred to schools and could not recognize, remember, or articulate any significant learning experience from childhood. "I can't remember learning anything as a kid in school." (After all, learning is often seamless!) As such, there could be some justification for regarding some of their responses as hyperbole. Nevertheless, responses such as this, coupled with other comments (some mild, such as "school was a bore, it was terrible...," and some more damning, such as, "school was sheer hell") emphasized the hostility and disengagement expressed by some parents toward aspects of their formal childhood learning activities and schools in general. In school "learning was infrequent and without joy," one parent noted. However, those same parents provided detailed accounts of other aspects of their personal history-based experiences, such as stories about negative teacher role models and their parents' educational philosophies. Their reticence, perhaps, evidences their needs for privacy, their selective memories, or merely their unwillingness to delve further into particularly unpleasant past experiences. "It has been very painful to remember this stuff," was not an infrequent response. Extremes of this position were taken by three parents and, despite my extensive and prolonged, sensitive questioning of them in our conversations, they continued to maintain their stance, seeking privacy, and rightly so. Clearly some parents had very unpleasant memories of schools (see, Knowles, 1988b, 1991a) but did not reveal the sources of their feelings.

Learning Defined

The substance of the parents' accounts and our conversations, together, drew attention to the ways in which they thought about questions such as "What is learning?" Many parents seemed unclear about the concept of "learning" and gave responses such as, "learning is doing schoolwork," or "learning takes place when kids are able to read well or do their math"—definitions close to that to which my son ascribes. Learning was generally defined narrowly: "Learning [occurs] when kids can do something properly, or can memorize the times table...or know the rules of grammar;" "learning has to do with focus on activities that give [children] definable skills." Defining the concept of learning, per se, was perhaps viewed as a useless task because parents were very much interested in the outcomes of learning. I was a little taken aback by the reaction of one parent. She made some comments about my questions of her (in which I inquired about the meanings of particular concepts) and then concluded by saying, "Obviously being an academic, a university professor, means you have high-flying ideas about meanings of words and ideas.... *My* understandings are much more *practical.*" More than a few said or implied that they "know learning when [they] see it."

Only a few parents articulated more complex perspectives. They said such things as: "Learning takes place when children are engaged on their own terms with the subject matter, making both simple and complicated meaning from the experience." Another took a similar position, but added (with slight overtones of educational philosopher John Dewey): "Learning takes place when there is evidence of changed behavior that can be recognized as relatively permanent…and as a result of a specific experience." These kinds of more elaborate perspectives, however, were in the minority. About half of the parents defined learning in terms of a product and a set of conditions rather than a process of engagement in educative experiences and personal change that takes place in the learner. Learning occurs most often, according to the former view, when there is quietness, organization, control of the activity and, perhaps more significantly, when children are learning by rote and are seated at their desks or work tables. A typical response was: "Learning takes place when the kids are able to produce great work—well written projects, neat drawings, and completion [of their] math [and other] assignments." As I reflected on these responses at the time of writing this chapter my son, John-Paul, came to mind. Somehow he has the notion in his mind that I, too, only believe he is learning when he is "producing." He has a fundamental understanding that learning is *only* evidenced by completed tasks. We have much to talk about and resolve regarding this matter. And, he thinks that learning is something to be, primarily, directed by someone else. Alas, this is the antithesis of my own views and I wonder about the experiential source of his perspectives. For example: What role have his experiences of (formal) school played in the formation of these views? Are they views of former peers? Are they the views of former teachers?

Childhood Learning Experiences

I asked the parents to describe some of their other learning experiences, ones not related to being in a formal school context. A consensus among several parents was that it is important "to learn by doing." These parents stated they had many happy memories of learning "fun things" in a variety of settings, from gardens, to workshops, to museums, to factories and warehouses, and other community settings. Another parent typified a slightly different position; she related the satisfaction of "using what we learned" and the "process of understanding that learning could be useful." Clubs such as the Girl Scouts and the Boy Scouts were mentioned as providing opportunities for different sorts of learning, something that was looked upon favorably by five of the parents. (In Utah, most LDS or Mormon children are exposed to the programs of these organizations because of their strong support within the Church of Jesus Christ of Latter Day Saints.) Modes of experiential learning—learning from experience, discovery learning, and learning by doing—were the predominant ways in which the parents favorably remembered learning. Learning, itself, was never couched in negative terms, though conditions peripheral to learning and teaching were: "I learned despite the mean, hateful teacher who stood over me with furrowed brows and knuckle-slapping ruler," said the parent who reflected on her experiences with a high school geography teacher.

As parents talked about their informal learning experiences I was struck by the stark contrasts to their school experiences. The informal experiences were couched in ways that reminded me of the rhetoric of "progressive pedagogy" which values educational processes; formal experiences were linked to repressive, authoritarian practices by adults and the focus on the more mechanical or structural aspects of learning. I was also taken with the apparent conflict between what they said about the concept of learning and their acknowledgments of the value of the experiential (learning by doing). But despite such acknowledgments, parents were not able to give more detailed explanations of the principles associated with such perspectives. For example, they did not acknowledge the importance of self-motivation, focus, guidance by others, or the place of prior learning experiences in crafting or facilitating new learning, and, in some sense, I was surprised by this. Yet, I often observed some of these very same principles in action within homes, a commentary, perhaps, about the gap between articulated, espoused perspectives of practice and the reality of practice itself.

School Experiences

The autobiographical accounts, when examined for themes, revealed two quite polar aspects of parents' experiences in schools. Some focused on the highly positive, while others dwelt on their very negative memories. Positive memories of schooling related to both student and teacher enthusiasm for particular subject matter and small group activities where they as students were made to "feel like human beings." Invariably, such situations denoted their enthusiasm for a particular context since they had "chosen to be there, where [they] could see improvement in themselves and others." Being able to do an activity or take a class voluntarily was also of paramount importance for some parents. While some of them "liked the opportunities to be alone at school" (perhaps isolated from peers), others were more enthusiastic about group activities. Experiential learning opportunities in art, music, science, and vocational training were especially applauded. By and large, however, the parents infrequently mentioned what I, as a teacher educator, call conditions highly conducive to healthy and enthusiastic individual and community learning. To say that such conditions did not exist for these parents is perhaps incorrect. What is important is that they were unable or unwilling to recollect many experiences which were highly memorable *and* educationally healthy. John-Paul, too, has argued that there were many barriers to his learning in school, barriers not unlike those recollected by the parents. As I honor his feelings, I also know that he was successful in a number of ways and enjoyed many aspects of his formal schooling. At thirteen years of age, his memory is short, yet, I do not want to be patronizing towards, or dismissive of, his views.

Many of the parents, especially the mothers, talked at length about their negative experiences in school. Of particular note were unhappy social events and "deplorable attitudes" of teachers and other students. One parent who grew up in the South remembered "being harassed by black children;" others wrote about being bullied by bigger kids or being frightened by gangs. Many wrote about being disliked either by peers or teachers. One young mother wrote: "The social experiences were usually bad. I was [constantly] 'left out' and felt I wasn't worth anything. I often had stomach pains as a result." This same person felt consolation in being alone and in quiet places where she could not be disturbed: "I yearned for quiet places to be alone—school was so traumatic." A few believed that teachers had showed extreme disrespect, or played favorites, and one claimed to be have been "treated like an animal." Indeed, there were three instances reported in the autobiographical accounts that in the 1990s would be labeled serious cases of harassment or abuse, with the worst case being quite obvious sexual abuse of a 13-year-old girl by a male teacher. School was indeed a terribly traumatic experience for this person. She had been so traumatized, she was unable to talk about the incident for many years; the teacher was never, to her knowledge, brought to justice.

Teacher Role Models

I wanted to get a sense of the kinds of teacher role models that helped shape the parents' practices. The categories of teacher role models which follow have been suggested by the parent-teachers themselves, while the distinction between positive and negative role models is mine. Not unexpectedly, the tendency in the accounts and conversations was for parents to emphasize the characteristics of negative role models. Negative role models are those associated with inappropriate teaching practices; practices that they deemed to be "not supportive of budding learners." Positive role models were those that were interpreted by the parents as representing appropriate teaching practice. As I reflected on my own experience of teachers as a student, I could readily identify most of the role models in my mind, even giving them names. Yet, my own experiences seemed glorious in comparison to the stories told me.

Positive Teacher Role Models

An underlying assumption in work with new classroom teachers (e.g., Crow 1987a, Knowles, 1992) is that notions of positive teacher role models are synonymous with particular teachers' views of good teaching. I also hold the same assumption in this work. There were at least three, identifiable, positive teacher role models evident in the parents' narratives.

The Disciplinarian
This teacher role model was strong on discipline, "took no disrespect, gave no sympathy," and required students to work hard. Descriptions of such teachers and their practices, included: "Strict," "well-disciplined students," "high expectations," and "personally detached from students," in that "there were no favorites." Several of the parents recognized that although such a role model "was not [their] favorite, [they] learned best" under this kind of teachers' tutelage; they were also "scared of being called on to respond to questions." (I was not able to satisfactorily clarify the meaning of "best" although I sense it embodies notions connected with satisfactory test or examination performance.)

The Enthusiast
An individual who was enthusiastic about the curriculum and subject matter, "[gave] the impression that the subject was delightful," and was "well-prepared and made the subject relevant." This type of teacher was a fondly remembered role model. Such a positive role example liked the students, encouraged a lot of student participation and, besides having high expectations of the students, was willing to involve students and help provide a sense of accomplishment. This same kind of teacher was also able to be thought provoking, challenging, and stimulating to students.

The Companion

There was a strong strand of support for the kind of teacher who could best be described as a "companion to the students," a character much more personable than the disciplinarian. Words and phrases that were used to describe this role model included: "The teacher had an understanding heart," "a sense of humor," and was a "gentle and comfortable companion" who was "non-threatening" and "lots of fun." Parents recollected that they learned well under the direction of this kind of teacher. More than anything, there was a sense of comfort in the parents' expressions about this kind of pedagogue who was "obviously able to put kids at ease."

Negative Teacher Role Models

The negative teacher role models were often remembered with intense passion. In both autobiographical accounts and in conversations they were given more attention than the positive role models. As one parent stated, "I had lots of bad teachers—the worst sort...." For her, there were no good teachers. Most of the teachers that fitted the negative role model "were against kids," "mechanical, and impersonal." I thought that, by eliciting responses about negative teacher role models, I would gain some notion of teaching practices which parents deemed inappropriate for their home education setting.[12] I was surprised, however, at the extent to which these parents recollected detailed accounts of these teachers' actions. And I wondered if this was a part of rationalizing their newfound roles as parent educators? Four negative teacher role models were evident in the autobiographical narratives.

The Bore

There was nothing much to excite students in this kind of teacher. Classroom teaching practices were recollected as boring, repetitive, lifeless, and not engaging the students in thoughtful and challenging pursuits. Classes were characterized by an emphasis on seat work and workbook activities. Although the teacher was usually a nice person and okay out of class, the students were "not swept away with the prowess—the teaching skills—of the teacher." One parent felt that teachers who fit this category were "more interested in [themselves] than students—and it showed because [they] could not see beyond [their] own viewpoints or interests."

The Critic

The critic embarrassed students. Students were subjected to the criticism of the teacher when they failed to understand, follow directions, or did not do things exactly as the teacher wanted. No individuality was allowed because it challenged the status of the teacher. Harsh criticism of students' work, abilities, and actions were characteristic of such a teacher. "I could never do anything—academic or anything else—right in [his] classroom," was a typical remark.

The Humiliator

A parent described this kind of teacher as being "rude, disrespectful, [and a person who did not] like teaching." The same parent expanded her position by citing a teacher "with a military mentality who yelled and humiliated." While this kind of role model may have been academically well-prepared, and presented interesting learning activities, such teachers were best remembered as providing often disconcerting and frightening outbursts of temper displays and fits of anger. They were offensive to students and did not seem to provide "any room for movement or accommodation of [young people]." Students of such teachers were "often terrified at the mere prospect of being in the room" with them.

The Deviant

Those teachers who represented a major departure from the "normal" teacher, as represented by all of previously mentioned categories, were typified by the "deviant." Normal was defined from the parent-as-student perspective as typical of the range of teacher types "usually experienced in schools." Seriously deviant behavior in teachers was mentioned or alluded to by a few parents. They felt that teachers' behaviors were not acceptable when they went beyond the traditional values of community and society. Descriptions of the actions of such teachers included the following statement: "The teacher made 'shocking' statements that outraged and brainwashed students." Disregard for individuals and for "the humanity of children" were central to the character of this type of teacher. Another parent described the deviant teacher as one who "declared truths to students which countered students' views on population control, homosexuality, and evolution." Not only did this comment suggest a conservative and fundamentalist religious perspective but it also reminded me of views of sexuality and "sexual deviance" commonly held in the 1960s through the early 1980s, the period when the parents were themselves in school.[13] One mother reported an alarming and frightening "pornographic experience with a male teacher" that bordered on molestation. Another mother, as noted, refused to talk about details concerning "a physical experience with a male teacher."

REFLECTION...

After reviewing the positive and negative teacher role models, can you add any other models? Which model would you prefer as a teacher and why? Which model engages you to learn? Can we look at teacher models in isolation or do other factors need to be taken into account? How do these models relate to home school parent/teachers?

Experiencing Schools as Adults

With the exception of the three parents who were teachers, most of the parents had not spent any time in schools as adults or parents. Several had originally enrolled their children in formal schools but had subsequently removed at least some of them. Their recent experiences of schools and classrooms were limited to meeting with teachers and principals, perhaps only fleeting visits or, at most, discussions in classrooms on "report card night" and in principals' offices.

Only one mother had volunteered in the school in which her child attended and, as I have mentioned, her serious attempts to understand and resolve her child's experiences were rebuffed by teachers and administrators. Another mother responsible for home-educating, a certified teacher, had previously taught in a senior high school and, from all accounts, was an exemplary and highly respected teacher who had a working knowledge of schools, recent educational changes, and typical school policies. A few other parents, as previously mentioned, had either teaching certificates or had taught in public schools, but did not have direct responsibility for the daily home learning activities.

Previous Teaching Experiences

Most parents with direct responsibility for educating their children had not taught in school-like settings before, perhaps a distinct advantage. Two of the three teachers represented by the families did not play major roles in the day-to-day home education activities—they were employed in schools. Besides the ex-secondary-school teacher, only one parent had taught in an educational institution—at the university level as a language instructor (while completing graduate studies). Of the parents involved daily in teaching at home, with the exception of the certified public school teacher, their previous teaching experiences were predominantly in religious settings. The kinds of prior experiences they mentioned in their narrative accounts included: "Scout den mother," "primary grades Sunday school teacher," teachers of preadolescent youth in recreational activities, music teacher, peer tutor, and teacherly roles in more traditional women's organizations (such as the Relief Society of the LDS Church). Work in "informal lesson [settings] with lots of discussion" were also mentioned and one parent tutored "exchange students in a junior high school." As mentioned, a number of parents who were fully employed did, however, have teaching experience, but their roles within the home-education contexts were predominantly supportive and their presence as teachers was not obvious in the day-to-day learning activities.

Learning to Teach

When I inquired about parents' preparation for becoming home-education teachers, I got responses that suggested the importance of contemporary role models. In Utah, at the time, there were a number of successful, well-publicized, and published home-educating parents, to whom nearly one third of the parent-teachers in the study either referred to, talked with or about, or emulated in their practice. In this regard, the networking organizations were highly successful, as were the self-publishing efforts of some "pioneer" Utah home educators such as Joyce Kinmont's, for example.

Access to the work or methods of other, "more appropriate," role models was gained through reading, and this was a preferred method for learning to think about teaching and teaching practices. Home education advocates such as Raymond and Dorothy Moore, and the late John Holt, were frequently mentioned as providing meaningful impetus for their home school practices. Other popular home school literature, such as the periodical *Growing without Schooling* and books by home educators (e.g., Colfax & Colfax, 1988), were mentioned, as was the published work of Marie Montessori and other well-known educators. Most of the literature cited by parents does not delve into detailed articulations of teaching methods appropriate for the home, although successful instructional and learning practices (usually in isolation from underlying philosophies or pedagogical intentions) are often discussed.

Networking opportunities were prominent in parents' explanations of their growth as teachers. Participation in the annual convention of the Utah Home Education Association, for example, was cited as providing several of the parents with "hands-on ideas about teaching." From my experience participating in this and other similar events, such conference instructional sessions are usually very prescriptive and structured either toward teaching particular content in very specific ways or resolving very context-specific instructional issues. At best, they provide workshop/cooperative learning kinds of environments which can be highly motivational. At worst, they encourage less than thoughtful teaching and selection of curricula. I have also noted at such conferences that there are experienced home educators who attempt to explore elements of their own experience, and the rationales behind their actions, in a public forum and in very authentic ways, and these kinds of sessions are often very thought provoking. A few parents reflected on the activities of the Association's district and neighborhood support groups, recognizing them as being useful for obtaining tips on teaching practices. All of the parents responsible for the daily home learning mentioned that they had attended at least one of the workshops conducted at the annual conventions. Two of the parents were even responsible for presenting workshops that were of the "this is what we did, and this is how we solved our problems…" kind.

Other chronologically recent sources of parents' views about teaching and education, and about appropriate role models, were the church congregations with which families were affiliated, particularly the LDS Church. The home-teacher, often a senior member who visits neighborhood families, has a valued role within the Church. Training by the Church for this activity provided, for at least one woman, "useful experiences for home schooling." Another family had taken classes in home and family management workshops offered through their church. Apart from the parents who were certified teachers, only one other had attended formal classes on teaching methods at the college level but this experience was incomplete. She never finished.

Teaching Practices Observed

Based on my observations of home education activities, I gained some insights into parents' teaching practices. Despite the fact I did not anticipate understanding, for instance, the underlying meanings ascribed to many of the parent–student interactions that I observed, it was at this relational boundary that many of the practices of the parents were made most visible.

Instructional Roles of Parents

Not unexpectedly, for example, few parents took on a traditional teacher-centered instructional role embodying a lecture format—informational talk followed by questions, answers, and activities—and I only observed this kind of pattern on two occasions (and for very short periods of time).[14] (Nevertheless, some parents said that they often used "something like lecturing" when they helped introduce new subject matter or deal with difficult topics.)

Rather, what predominated in many of the homes was a kind of close instructional talk between parents and learners, although here I mean closeness to denote the physical closeness or proximity of the interactions, a situation not unexpected given the close confines of most spaces allocated to home learning such as the kitchen table, a small study, or a special room set aside as "the school room" in the basement. I expected such quiet talk in the private confines of the home. Such talk was characterized best by the notion of question-and-answer sessions (usually controlled by the parent-teacher but sometimes dominated by inquisitive learners who sensed that their parents had particular understandings of the subject matter at hand) prefaced by informational or task-driven direct instructions (again usually given by the parent). In this context, most parents were either *very* prescriptive and directive in their facilitation of learning or, conversely, were nonspecific in the sense of providing only a loose framework for student activity and further inquiry.

In the first set of contexts, for example, parents gave specific, narrowly defined instructions that left little or no room for learners to make educative decisions. In the second group of cases, I noticed that parents wanted, it seemed, to encourage student-centered (or directed) learning experiences but were unable to articulate clear guidance or instructions for facilitating learning. (To be fair in my analysis, however, I acknowledge that my presence may have intimidated some parents and that, in other settings external to this study, I have witnessed some highly innovative guidance by parents who had very clear conceptions of both their pedagogy and their goals (see, e.g., Colfax & Colfax, 1988; Deakin, 1972; Hendy-Harris, 1983, for examples of highly innovative practices.) I also wondered whether at these times parents believed they were dealing with difficult subject matter or ideas which they were unfamiliar.

In my own work with John-Paul, I frequently fall into patterns of interaction not unlike "mini-versions" of formal lectures, something that greatly surprised me. Typically I have responded to a question posed by John-Paul by going into lengthy elaborations of some concept, even frequently sketching explanatory diagrams, which did not allow him opportunities to engage me in further dialog. This is contrary to how I know I operate in the university classroom. When I retreat from these sessions with John-Paul, I feel quite bothered by my less than engaging pedagogy. I have no explanation apart from the fact that I feel a great dissonance with the curriculum he is using and try to fill in some of the many gaps that are evident in it. It *does* have many gaps and presents incomplete accounts of many events and phenomena and I feel the need to "say my piece" as it were! So much for negotiating the curriculum. Interestingly, because his socialization to school-like practices seems so complete and ingrained, I find that I am, like so many classroom teachers, succumbing to the pressures exerted by the student.

In many interactions the children looked to the parents to provide solutions to problems but, to their credit, when parents were unsure they often deferred to other authorities, such as (authors of) books or family members (especially the other parent) who had particular expertise, situations not unlike that found in formal school classrooms. In this regard, the kinds of resources available to learners varied greatly, from the home with barely any print or non-print media resources to the family with over 10,000 books on the shelves (their very credible estimate). It was clear that most of the families spend a great deal of money buying teaching and learning aids. In four settings, parents' instructional directives frequently required children to seek information from a library, media center, through some other public/

community facility or agency (such as a national, regional, or state park), or a governing municipal body. One family extensively used community resources in addition to those mentioned: corporate manufacturers and wholesalers, small businesses, and professional people. These kinds of acknowledgments of authority I also made, libraries being the prominent site of such authority. (I also found myself taking a new look at textbooks, re-realizing their general paucity as vehicles for genuine, self-directed, relevant learning. There are simply too many pedagogically and substantively poor textbooks available to schools and to those who learn at home.)

Parents as "Traditional" Teachers

Despite the fact that parent-teachers were generally against using lecture-like practices in their teaching, a hallmark of traditional classrooms, some displayed other characteristics associated with more traditional school teacher roles, particularly those evidenced by teachers labeled "boring." Nearly half of the parents had their children laboriously involved in using detached (or not personally relevant), highly structured, commercially prepared workbooks and maintained the children in quiet seatwork for much of the time, much like the activities of the boring teacher reported by the parents in their narrative accounts. Such settings were more likely to look like miniature versions of traditional classrooms, where regularity, quietness, "back-to-basics" curricula, and individual repetitive work was highly valued. So, too, product was seen to be far superior to process. Educational products were *their* evidence of successful learning. This observation cuts to the quick; it has much more similarity with my situation that I would have envisaged six months earlier. My attempts to engage John-Paul in field work, for example, were only partially successful. He simply preferred seatwork. My guess is that he views seatwork as promoting completion of products with much less confusion, mess, and energy than schoolwork that occurs in the field.

Occasionally I observed some of the parents being quite critical with their children. (This was not criticism of the intellectual kind.) Such criticism, it seemed, came when parents were under pressure of some kind. The most obvious examples occurred when parents were preoccupied with work of their own (some had home businesses) or, perhaps, were tired and were interrupted by the children, or when children were obviously not engaged in what they were supposed to be doing—activities usually defined by being parent-mandated. At such times, the natural flow of the home education activities was interrupted. Parents, in these few cases, resorted to being critical of their children's work or action. The most apparent reasons for this were when children did not complete their work correctly (perhaps their work exhibited blatant and careless errors) or when they did not closely follow parent instructions.

Parents new to home education often prepared and presented lessons—not unlike that which a classroom teacher would do—that were highly structured at first; as their teaching proficiency increased over time, the structure was reduced. The same kind of loosening-up occurred with respect to selection and adherence to particular curriculum. This pattern was also noticeable in individual families over the duration of the time I spent with them. As parents acknowledged such, a progression was also evident with respect to the length of time that they had engaged in the process of home education. New home education contexts tended to be more structured than the old. Highly structured home schools tended to rely on commercially prepared curriculum materials, and parents were less involved with their children in many of the daily learning activities. In these cases, the parents acknowledged the limitations of their knowledge, instructional practices, and ways in which they believed they could constructively assist their children. By default they relied on a "correspondence school," distanced, hands-off approach. By their own definitions, the majority of the parent-teachers tended to teach in unimaginative ways that relied heavily on prepared materials (whether they be outdated or new text books, prepared curriculum materials, or outmoded views of the various subject matter) and imposed rigid structure. These were the practices that were congruent with their description of boring teachers.

With the exception of occasionally acting in ways that they—in their memories of being students—described as being "boring" and "critical," parents usually did not resort to the behaviors of the other highly negative teacher role models that they identified in their narrative accounts. More evident from my observations, however, were the actions characteristic of positive teacher role models. But, nevertheless, *their* practices were often, on an individual basis, much like those practices they had criticized. To be fair, however, I found myself in vaguely similar positions, a point of which I am not particularly proud.

Connecting Experience and Teaching Practices

When I asked the parents about the origin of some of their specific practices some were quite aware of the connections between their prior experiences and their actions as parent-teachers. Indeed, and as might be expected, there were strong parallels between parents' rationales for teaching at home and their actual practices—and the origins of those practices (see, Knowles, 1988b, 1991a). At the risk of some repetition I lay out some of the connections I observed below.

Childhood Experiences of Family

Family experiences as children laid the foundation of parents' views about teaching. Early positive family experiences suggested the acquisition of positive role model traits while, conversely it seemed, negative experiences and environments in their homes as children alerted parent-teachers to behaviors and strategies for dealing with children that they as adults wished to avoid. Patterns of family interaction and values were significant components of the early experiences and, as might be expected, these played out in the day-to-day educational guidance of their children. Some of the parents had "vowed to break [familial] patterns" of behavior.

Teacher Role Models

Most parents were greatly influenced by their experiences with both positive and negative teacher role models. They tended to have clear conceptions of the sort of teacher behaviors worthy of rejection (or replication, in a lesser number of cases). The mental pictures of teachers and teacher's actions acquired from their own experience as students were, not unexpectedly, important for making judgments about contemporary school teachers and their actions. Some parents did not express clear images of positive teacher role models, suggesting that the contribution to their own teacher role identity may be heavily weighted by negative experiences. They knew what they *did not* want to do, rather than what they wanted to do.[15]

Memories of School

Common judgments about what goes on in contemporary schools were often made from the framework of distant memories about school, and these memories were most influential for establishing home education (see, Knowles, 1991a). While specific teaching methods did not emerge from this remembrance, parents did have concepts of the atmospheres they wish to create as teachers in the home setting, often a counteractive and compensatory result of their own negative experiences (see, Mayberry & Knowles, 1989). More often, the images of school classrooms were replicated in the special places or rooms set aside for "home school."

Significant Others or Experiences

Because parents have a variety of backgrounds and experiences, they do not share, like classroom teachers, relatively similar professional development paths for becoming parent-teachers; thus, apart from their family and school learning experiences, a variety of other experiences helped formulate the basis for many of their practices. Some of these experiences include: prior teaching experiences, reading home education publications (sometimes they espoused the philosophies of one particular home education advocate), attending home education conventions and seminars, participating in home education networking organizations, experiencing particular religious contexts, and simply being immersed in the cultural milieu. In this regard, individuals such as John Holt and Raymond Moore (each with distinct ideological and pedagogical orientations) and local home educators of renown facilitated parents' thinking about teaching methods appropriate for the home. In the mid- to late-1980s in Utah, the Kinmont family and officers and workshop facilitators at the Utah Home Education Association annual conventions provided examples of influential local people.

The Strength of Teacher Role Identities

Parents with stronger positive images of self-as-teacher (images of teaching and learning couched in positive terms) seemed more able to implement a variety of teaching strategies and felt better about their teaching in the home. Similarly, many student and beginning teachers come to classroom teaching with positive images of self, a result of mainly positive experiences in schools. Such individuals tend to know their identities as teachers and engage in practices that are reasonably congruent with these identities. Moreover, they tend to have been successful students who enjoyed school. Many of the parent-teachers, however, tended to frame their teacher role identities in negative terms because that has been the tone of their experiences in schools. These parents were unsure about appropriate actions they should take in the home setting. They simply knew what they *did not* want to do (and their actions were part of their critique of formal schools). Unlike student or beginning teachers who have had an overlay of preparation for teaching and who usually have positive teacher role identities, the parent-teachers often did not have a great repertoire of positive experiences and appropriate teaching methods on which to fall back. And, they did not typically have many pleasant memories of schools. Not unexpectedly, some of these parents tended to teach as they were taught and in ways that they often criticized.

Isolation and Teaching Methods

Home education instruction, like teaching in public and formal school settings, is a rather lonely affair. Most parents were isolated, to varying degrees, in that they had little opportunities to observe other, perhaps more experienced, parent-teachers at work. As mentioned previously, it was at Utah Home Education Association business meetings and annual conventions, as well as opportune times with other home-educating parents, for example, that most exchanges of teaching ideas took place. However, most parents had at least one close home-educator friend and confidant with whom they occasionally consulted, usually by telephone.

The isolation of home education is one factor which places parents at a distinct disadvantage; when in difficult situations, they tend to use teaching methods that only allow them to cope with situations rather than employing methods that achieve certain sought-after and explicit goals. This was evident from my observations and discussions; often parents responded with pat answers to questions posed about quite difficult educational problems. Because a method worked for a friend, for example, it is likely to be tried and, if reasonably successful on the first try, implemented on a permanent basis without too much thought about the underlying rationales, ideological assumptions, and the long-term effects of such an approach. While many home educators are goal-oriented, goals are not necessarily translated into dynamic teaching methods; nor are various goals necessarily compatible or congruent. Despite my criticisms, I noted that two parents, in particular, seemed to possess an intuitive feel for their work as educators and their perception of their children's educational needs. These individuals stood out from their peers because of the appropriateness of their pedagogical decision-making. What was equally interesting to me was that these parents could not explain their good pedagogy (not unlike, as I have mentioned, many classroom teachers who sometimes cannot recognize their theories in practice).

The Home-Education Environment Reviewed

Structure

Parent-teachers typically cannot access a plethora of teaching methods that were acquired in teacher preparation programs as, perhaps, can certified teachers. Rather, they must rely on suggestions from friends, ideas from popular home education books, textbooks and workbooks, and their earlier experiences. Not infrequently, they teach in ways that reflect the manner in which they were taught. As already mentioned, this reliance on prior experiences is also evident in the methods used by certified teachers. With the exception of that which was learned through networking activities, for most parents exposure to different instructional methods only occurred during their years as students. As a result, their ability to draw on varieties of teaching methods is somewhat limited by their prior experiences.

Home educators tend to think about learning contexts as being either loosely or tightly structured (Knowles, 1987; c.f. Van Galen, 1986), a matter I raised earlier. Many parents in the beginning stages of their home-educating activities tightly structure the learning environments, and, as time progresses, they loosen up. Structure seems to be as much a factor of individual preference as it is of parent educational levels and personal accomplishment, for example. Yet, structure may also be a factor of prior experience. Those parents who feel more confident or accomplished in terms of their educational endeavors generally provided more flexible learning environments, with greater levels of responsibility for learning placed on the learners. Such people themselves were exposed to varieties of teaching methods or, as appeared to be the case in two instances, they have critically reflected on the negative aspects of their experience with a view to constructively determining more appropriate and innovative teaching methods. My envisioned, perfect context for my son would exhibit great flexibility and opportunities for self-direction. At this point, such a learning context is far from view, and even more distant from reality. We are grappling with very fundamental issues associated with learning informally. John-Paul has a great chasm to pass over before he can truly claim his power within the learning process. And John-Paul's mother and I have to resolve important pedagogical and curricular differences. It is these kinds of barriers to coherent, congruent educative experiences that, I suspect, get in the way of many more learners—both in the home and in schools—than I care to imagine.

Pedagogy

Experiential learning activities were primarily implemented by parents who had developed a flexible and less structured mode of daily and weekly operation of the home school. Further, experiential and discovery learning were implemented only by parents who felt secure in the particular subject area, had strong beliefs about the value of the particular approach, or were comfortable with a method because they, themselves, learned using similar approaches. Often teachers in schools had not met these parents' particular learning styles. Teaching methods often seemed to be directly related to parents' proficiency or experience in the particular subject area: the more proficient, the greater degree of flexibility in parents' teaching methods; the less proficient, the greater reliance on structure as evidenced by unimaginative assignments, workbooks, and other aids.

My findings generally support the notion that home-educating parents sometimes do teach much like they were taught, using approaches they often criticized in contemporary, formal schools. Each of the parent-teachers displayed some teaching that could be so classified. Central in the formulation of parents' teaching methods were their experiences in school, and, much like student and beginning teachers, the parents' teacher role identities were largely products of their biographies.

> *REFLECTION...*
>
> Discuss the similarities between the parent teacher, the pre-K teacher, and the K–12 teacher. Why are there similarities and what does it say about our teacher education programs?

Conclusion

My sense is that home education organizations and influential home education advocates ought to consider ways to facilitate the development of parents' responsive teaching methods. I see this as being crucial to the long-term health of the movement and the practice. While there are obviously parent-teachers who are able to provide exemplary educational opportunities for their children (see, e.g., Colfax & Colfax, 1988; Deakin, 1972; Hendy-Harris, 1983), many more home educators may be seriously limited as a result of their own limited experiences of learning and teaching (a mirror image of their criticism of public schools). On the other hand, there are parents who are able to break free of limiting or constraining school and learning experiences. Continued reliance on recollections of teachers' work and replications of schoolroom activities and methods to guide practice will do nothing to enhance the learning opportunities of home-education students who, after all, have the opportunities to capitalize on the advantages of one-on-one instruction and considerable learner freedoms. Recognizing the potential limitations of parents' instructional strategies may be an important motivation for networking groups to discuss and encourage appropriate parent-teacher professional development processes that honor the unique perceptions and orientations of families and do not obliterate the autonomy that they desire.

When analyzing the teaching practices of parents, one must take into consideration that many parent-teachers have had very little contact with formal theories of instruction. Lacking formal knowledge in this area, parents utilized the one apparent available option, their perceptions of instructional practices that they retained from their own learning and schooling. Yet being in charge of curriculum is very different from being on the receiving end as students, as any beginning classroom school teacher will tell. For beginning teachers, the reversal of roles (from student to teacher) is difficult to overcome. Home educators have similar experiences, and my observations suggest that they do not deviate far from the role models they experienced in schools or from images of learning and teaching established at some prior point in time. However, such connections are not linear. Attitudes about schooling, and the actual instructional patterns and practices implemented in the home are influenced by parents' learning and their intervening cultural knowledge—gained through their occupations, religious activities, community experiences and political expressions, and experiences of multiple cultures (through travel and life in multicultural contexts), for example.

My underlying intention in writing this chapter was to illustrate elements of the home-education experience—especially from the perspective of parents—as a way of raising awareness about some of the complex issues associated with this particular educational alternative. I focused on parents' personal history-based experiences as a way of exploring their day-to-day practices with their children. My very personal references to recent experiences with my son John-Paul were intended to round out my researcher perspective. Thus it is that I claim that parents' past experiences of schools and teachers are variously replicated in their teaching practices. Many parent-teachers may have negative recollections of their experiences in schools as students and relatively narrow conceptions of the role of teachers. Insights into parents' teacher role identities provides, at least, a partial explanation of why some parents teach in ways that they openly criticize of classroom teachers.

And finally, for me as a teacher educator, I am intent on conveying to pre-service teachers with whom I work the importance of understanding the perspectives of parents as an entry point for eventually working productively, collaboratively, and sensitively with them for the educational well-being of their children, the new teachers' pupils.

Recommended Activities

1. Invite in a panel of parents that are home-educating their children and have them address the reason for home education. Make sure to include parents that are home-educating elementary-aged children as well as high school students.
2. Interview children (ages 5–17) that have been or are being home-educated. Ask the students to describe the experience. Do they miss having more friends? What do they do when they are not being home-educated? If they have been in public/private school, ask how home education compares to this environment.
3. Try to locate college students or other young adults that were home-educated. As they look back, what were some of the strengths of home education and what were some of the challenges of being home-educated. Do these young adults think they are any different now because of their education? Would they home educate their own children?
4. Invite several superintendents to discuss the home education movement in the state and the impact home education has on the school district, extracurricular activities, and the school's resources.
5. Try to locate and compare a curriculum package being used in home education.
6. Find out how the local school district you are in works with parents that want to home-educate their children. Are there any limitations? How is testing/assessment done? What about extra-curricular activities?

Notes

1. I use *home school* here because it is a commonly used term meaning the setting in which home education takes place. I usually refrain from using the term because it connotes the replication of formal school structures and processes which I believe is contrary to the spirit of learning from and with parents at home. *Home education* implies the processes associated with learner growth rather than the processes associated with

the regimentation and constraints of formal schoolings. Home education suggests the possibilities for innovative practice.

2. Mostly these are teachers who have strong notions about their role as teachers (i.e., teacher role identities) based on their early (i.e., personal history-based experiences).

3. See, also, Mayberry, Knowles, Ray, & Marlow, 1995. Documentation of sources is included in both of these references.

4. In some ways the phases in the development of home education in the United States are similar, but expanded in scale and chronology, to those found in other national contexts such as Canada, Great Britain and Europe, Australia, and New Zealand. Home education as we know it today, simply has a much longer history in the United States.

5. I am not suggesting that computer technology is viewed as a panacea by home educators at large.

6. This estimate is well above figures often quoted for present populations (see Mayberry, Knowles, Ray, & Marlow, 1995).

7. Since the early 1990s, and as of 1995, the growth of home education in this area has grown, by some accounts, by as much as 300 percent.

8. The seventy-two families were part of a much larger study.

9. I also explored parent's rationales for teaching at home and, not unexpectedly, these same experiential elements fueled their thinking about becoming home educators (see, Knowles, 1992).

10. My sense is that this group of parents were very similar in practice and pedagocal orientation to families whose homes I have visited in many other settings beyond Utah. Apart from their religious affiliations they seem to be more like home-educators in other states than they are different. If anything, the Church of Jesus Christ of Latter Day Saints (LDS or Mormon—see discussion following this paragraph) families seem more liberal (than other conservative religious families I have visited in other states) in their thinking about and articulations of their pedagogies.

11. In the five years prior to beginning my work with these parent- teachers, I noted the predominance of negative press reports in both Utah and national newspapers (see, Knowles, Marlow, & Muchmore, 1992).

12. This was also an assumption made by Crow (1987a) and myself (Knowles, 1992) in our work with beginning teachers (see also Bullough, Knowles, & Crow, 1991).

13. Unlike my study of home-educated adults (see Knowles & Muchmore, 1995) these parent had, with two exceptions, attended public schools. Two of the parents had attended private schools.

14. On those occasions, however, I noticed a close relationship between the physical space and the instructional practice. For example, in one home, the arrangement of the physical space designated as "the home school" appeared to be a replication of a typical traditional school classroom—the space had a blackboard, bulletin boards, bookshelves with individual and sets of books, simple science equipment, wall maps and a globe, four students' desks in rows, a teacher's desk, and national and state flags in the corner. "School" types of behavior seemed more common in school-like settings!

15. This finding is not unlike that which I have learned about pre-service teachers entering into formal teacher preparation programs (Knowles, 1992).

Additional Resources

Home Schooling

Magazines and Newsletters:

Growing without Schooling
2269 Masschuesetts Avenue
Cambridge, MA 02140
Phone: 617-864-6100

Home Education Magazine
PO Box 1083
Tonasket, WA 98855
Phone: 509-486-1351

New Attitude
6920 SE Hogan
Grasham OR 97080
Phone: 503-253-9633

Parents' Choice Foundation
Box 185
Newton, MA 02168
Phone: 617-965-5913

Practical Homeschooling
Home Life
PO Box 1250
Fenton, MO 63026
Phone: 800-346-6322

The Teaching Home
PO Box 20219
Portland, OR 97220
Phone: 503-253-9633

Electronic Forums:

America Online's Home Schooling Forum
keyword: homeschool

The Home Education Resource Center

Jon's Homeschool Resource Page
http://www.armory.com/~jon/hs/home-school.html

Prodigy's Home Schooling Information Center
http://antares.prodigy.com/hmsccoi.html

Web Chapel Home-School Link
http://www.iadfw.net/webchap/links-hs.html

References

Bullough, Jr., R. V., Knowles, J. G., & Crow, N. A. (1991). *Emerging as a teacher*. London, UK, & New York: Routledge.

Colfax, D., & Colfax, M. (1988). *Homeschooling for excellence*. New York, NY: Warner Books, Inc.

Crow, N. A. (1987a). *Socialization within a teacher education program: A case study*. Unpublished doctoral dissertation, The University of Utah, Salt Lake City, UT.

Crow, N. A. (1987b, April). *Preservice teachers' biography: A case study*. A paper presented at the Annual Meeting of the American Educational Research Association, Washington, DC.

Deakin, M. (1972). *The children on the hill*. London: Quartet Books.

Delahooke, M. M. (1986). *Home educated children's social/emotional adjustment and academic achievement: A comparative study*. Unpublished doctoral dissertation, California School of Professional Psychology, Los Angeles, CA.

Feiman-Nemser, S., & Buchmann, M. (1987). *When is student teaching teacher education?* (Reserved Series No. 178). East Lansing, MI: Michigan State University, Institute for Research on Teaching.

Gustavsen, G. A. (1981). *Selected characteristics of home schools and parents who operate them*. Unpublished doctoral dissertation, Andrews University, Berrien Springs, MI.

Hendy-Harris, J. (1983). *Putting the joy back into Egypt: An experiment in education*. Auckland, NZ: Hodder and Stroughton.

Knowles, J. G. (1987). *Instructional patterns and practices in the home school: An exploratory case study of three Utah families*. A paper presented at the Northern Rocky Mountain Educational Research Association Annual Meeting, Park City, UT.

Knowles, J. G. (1988a). A beginning teacher's experience: Reflections on becoming a teacher. *Language Arts, 65*(7), 702–712.

Knowles, J. G. (1988b). Parents' rationales and teaching methods for home schooling: The role of biography. *Education and Urban Society, 21*(1), 69–84.

Knowles, J. G. (1989). Cooperating with home school parents: A new agenda for public schools? *Urban Education, 23*(4): 392–411.

Knowles, J. G. (1991a). Parents' rationales for operating home schools. *Journal of Contemporary Ethnography, 20*(2), 203–230.

Knowles, J. G. (1991b, January/February). Fox in the chicken coop or goose in the nest laying a golden egg? Reflections on researching home schools. *Home Education Magazine, 8*(1), 15–17, 39–41, 49.

Knowles, J. G. (1992). Models for understanding preservice and beginning teachers' biographies: Illustrations from case studies. In I. F. Goodson (Ed.), *Studying teachers' lives* (pp. 99–152). London, UK, & New York: Routledge.

Knowles, J. G. (1993). Life history accounts as mirrors: A practical avenue for the conceptualization of reflection in teacher education. In J. Calderhead & P. Gates (Eds.), *Conceptualizing reflection in teacher development* (pp. 70–92). London, UK: Falmer Press.

Knowles, J. G. (1994). Metaphors as windows on a personal history: A beginning teacher's experience. *Teacher Education Quarterly, 21*(1), 37–66.

Knowles, J. G. (forthcoming). *Reflections of home education*. New York, NY: St. Martins Press.

Knowles, J. G., & Cole, A. L., with Presswood, C. S. (1994). *Through preservice teachers' eyes: Exploring field experiences through narrative and inquiry*. New York: Merrill.

Knowles, J. G., & Hoefler, V. B. (1988, April). *An exploratory case study of how parents think about enhancing parent–child relationships in home school settings: Bonding or tying the apron strings*. A paper presented at the Annual Meeting of the American Educational Research Association, New Orleans, LA, April 5–9.

Knowles, J. G., & Hoefler, V. B. (1989). *The student teacher who wouldn't go away: Learning from failure*. Journal of Experiential Education, 12(2), 14–21.

Knowles, J. G., & Holt-Reynolds, D. (1991). Shaping pedagogies against personal histories in preservice teacher education. *Teachers College Record, 93*(1), 87–113.

Knowles, J. G., Marlow, S. E., & Muchmore, J. A. (1992). From pedagogy to ideology: Origins and phases of home education in the United States,

1970–1990. *American Journal of Education, 100* (1), 195–235.

Knowles, J. G., & Muchmore, J. A. (1995). "We're grown up home schooled kids—and we're doing just fine, thank you very much." *Journal of Research of Christian Education, 4*(1), 35–56

Kohli, M. (1980). Biography: Account, text, method. In D. Bertaux (Ed.), *Biography and society: The life history approach in the social sciences* (pp. 61–76). Beverly Hills, CA: Sage Publications Inc.

Leslie, L. L., Swiren, J. M., & Flexner, N. (1977). Faculty socialization and instructional productivity. *Research in Higher Education, 71,*127–143.

Linden, N. J. F. (1983). *An investigation of alternative education: Home schooling.* University Microfilms International, No. 8403319.

Lortie, D. C. (1975). *Schoolteacher.* Chicago, IL: University of Chicago Press.

Mayberry, M. (1988). *Doing it their way: A study of Oregon's home schoolers.* Unpublished doctoral dissertation, University of Oregon, Eugene, OR.

Mayberry, M., & Knowles, J. G. (1989). Family unity objectives of parents who teach their children: Ideological and pedagogical orientations to home schooling. *The Urban Review, 21*(4), 209–226.

Mayberry, M., Knowles, J. G., Ray, B. D., & Marlow, S. E. (1995). *Home schooling: Parents as educators.* Beverly Hills, CA: Crown Press/Sage Publications.

Schemmer, B. A. S. (1985). *Case studies of four families engaged in home education.* University Microfilms International No. 8525190.

Sprinthall, N. A., & Theis-Sprinthall, L. (1983a). The need for theoretical frame-works in educating teachers: A cognitive-developmental perspective. In K. R. Howey & W. F. Gardner (Eds.), *The education of teachers.* New York, NY: Longman.

Sprinthall, N. A., & Theis-Sprinthall, L. (1983b). The teacher as an adult learner: A cognitive-developmental view. In G. A. Griffin (Ed.), *Staff development: The eighty-second yearbook of the National Society for the Study of Education* (Pt. 2). Chicago, IL: The University of Chicago Press.

Stephens, J. (1969). *The processes of schooling.* New York, NY: Holt, Reinhart, & Winston.

Taylor, J. W. (1986). *Self-concept in home-schooling children.* Unpublished doctoral dissertation, Andrews University, Berrien Springs, MI.

Van Galen, J. (1986). *Schooling in private: A study of home education.* Unpublished doctoral dissertation, The University of North Carolina at Chapel Hill, Chapel Hill, NC.

Watson, L. C. & Watson-Franke, M. B. (1985). *Interpreting life histories: An anthropological inquiry.* New Brunswick, NJ: Rutgers University Press.

Weinstein, C. S. (1989). Teacher education students' preconceptions of teaching. *Journal of Teacher Education, 40*(2), 53–60.

Wells, K. (1984). *Teacher socialization in the educational organization: A review of the literature.* Paper presented at the Convention of the Western Speech Communication Association, Seattle, WA.

Zeichner, K., & Grant, C. (1981). Biography and social structure in the socialization of student teachers: A re-examination of the pupil control ideologies of student teachers. *Journal of Education for Teaching, 3,* 299–314.

Zeichner, K. M., & Tabachnick, B. R. (1981). Are the effects of university teacher education washed out by school experience? *Journal of Teacher Education, 2,* 7–11.

Zeichner, K. M., & Tabachnick, B. R. (1985). The development of teacher perspectives: Social strategies and institutional control in the socialization of beginning teachers. *Journal of Education for Teaching, 11,* 1–25.

Chapter 15

Educational Policy and the Role of Advocacy

SHIRLEY L. ZIMMERMAN
University of Minnesota

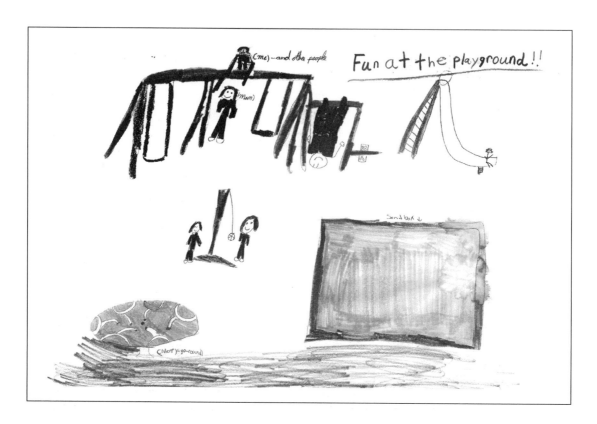

Public policy and advocacy are two topics that are interwoven. Both merit discussion because of the importance of local, sate, or national educational policy initiatives. Teachers, parents, and students need to be aware of the role of advocacy in their lives.

The purpose of this chapter is to help the reader to:

- Describe the history of educational policy in the United States with an emphasis on home–school relations
- Describe a model of social change
- Distinguish between the different educational policy initiatives in the 1900s
- Show the effect of one policy, Goals 2000: Educate America Act, on families and schools in this country
- Describe how people, including educators, become advocates for children and schools
- Identify any legislative policy initiated by parents rather than educators or politicians

This chapter is intended to acquaint readers with the range of policy issues confronting education in the United States today. To help in this endeavor, it employs a social change model or framework (Smelser & Halpern, 1978; Zimmerman, 1982, 1995). A *model* is a set of concepts or ideas that fit together in a particular way that help in understanding what is being observed or experienced. Readers can use this model to better understand some of the confusions and contradictions that underlie many of these issues and that affect the education of children. The chapter identifies some of the values underlying these issues as major sources of such contradictions, and reveals the historical background and the philosophical foundations of these values. It also identifies some of the changes that have occurred in American society that have added to the confusions surrounding educational policy developments in this country.

Using the ideas and concepts from the social change model presented in the discussion, the author continues to provide a brief historical review of educational policy in the United States. The review focuses in particular on those developments that relate to home–school relations and give readers a broad perspective of the issues involved in preschool and K–12 educational policy. The chapter concludes with a discussion of Goals 2000: The Educate America Act as a culminating social action resulting from the mobilization of activity to address perceived problems in the education of our nation's children.

The chapter has been written not only to give readers a broad perspective of the issues involved in educational policy but also a broad perspective from which to view their role as teachers and teachers-in-training, and some understanding of the context in which they are performing that role. Educational policy is part of that context, shaping educational practice in ways of which they may be only dimly aware—whether with regard to child abuse reporting laws, equal educational opportunities for children, child safety, child learning objectives, or resources sufficient for teachers to do their job. It is important that readers understand that just as policy helps shape practice, they can help shape policy and thereby effect the conditions under which children can best grow and learn.

What Is Educational Policy? What Is Advocacy?

Public policy in the area of education is really a story about the decisions of thousands of individual schools, school boards, and state legislatures pertaining to the education of children. More recently, public policy has come to include decisions of the Federal government also. The latter's decisions pertain to school desegregation, federal aid to education, educational access for disabled children, early childhood education, and national voluntary educational standards that schools throughout the country are encouraged to meet. Educational policy in the United States—which may be defined as an agreed upon course of action with respect to the education of children—mirrors the changes that have occurred in American society in which education as an institution is embedded. As readers shall see, educational policy is *a temporarily agreed upon course of action* that reflects the role that advocates play and have played in shaping it.

Advocacy refers to the espousal of a cause that often leads to social action or policy change (Kahn, Kamerman, & McGowan, 1972; Zimmerman, 1971), whether such action pertains to school choice, home schooling, school funding, school financing, or parent involvement. Advocacy involves speaking before and working with community groups, doing media presentations, participating in TV and radio talk shows, writing letters to the editor and to policy makers at all levels of government on matters pertaining to children's education, and lobbying and testifying before official bodies to effect desired action(s) and changes. Advocacy is a role that many teachers have played in the development of programs in this country, and thereby in helping to effect social change. Let us now turn to the model of social change that frames the discussion that follows.

The Social Change Model: Its Component Parts

The model of social change that provides the framework for the discussion in this chapter consists of: (a) a novel situation or a situation perceived as novel; (b) different perceptions and definitions of the situation; (c) the mobilization of activity in support of different perceptions of the situation, and; (d) the social action or policy that addresses the situation (Zimmerman, 1982, 1995). Although the component parts of the model are easy to identify, because the processes involved in the model are highly interactive, dynamic, and complex, they are not easily followed in detail. For this reason, only the broad outlines of the model are illustrated in this discussion, beginning with the assumptions that underlie it.

One of the assumptions underlying the social change model presented here is that the values that have emerged as dominant in the history of the United States have provided the bases for the ways in which the country has chosen to meet the educational needs of the nation's children and youth. These values, as they pertain to educational policy, include: freedom, individual rights, self-realization through individual achievement, and equality of opportunity (Williams, 1960). Such values, which are based on certain beliefs about human nature and the nature of society, have grown out of a variety of cultural traditions and ideological positions that took root when our country was founded (Smelser & Halpern, 1978). The philosophical foundations of such values are *utilitarianism* and *individualism* supported by a Protestant republican ideology.

Utilitarianism is a philosophy which holds that individuals seek to avoid pain and achieve pleasure; that they derive pleasure from the acquisition and consumption of material goods and pain from economic loss; that they have biological needs that instinctively cause them to act in their own self-interest; and that the interests of all are served by individuals who act in their own self-interest (Ball & Dagger, 1990; Zimmerman, 1992). Utilitarianism asserts that whatever helps people avoid pain and achieve pleasure or happiness has utility, but because that which gives pleasure and happiness or utility is seen to be scarce, it assumes that the pleasures of some will be gained at the expense or pain of others. Since education, if measured in terms of income, family stability, and self-reports, has been found to be key to happiness (Zimmerman, 1992), and because the government is heavily involved and invested in education, government's role in promoting such happiness might be evaluated accordingly.

Individualism, like utilitarianism, also justifies individuals acting in their own self-interest with minimal government interference (Kahn, 1969; Zimmerman, 1992; 1995). Individualism holds that individuals are obligated to try to achieve and get ahead and have equal opportunities for doing so. If they fail, the doctrine goes, they fail because of defects, deficiencies, and imperfections in their personalities and characters. For this reason, the pain and shame they and their families may experience as a result of failure are seen as justifiable. In keeping with this view, nineteenth century educators taught that hard work, loyalty, and good character led to success, and that laziness and character deficiencies led to failure, putting the individual and not society on trial (Tyack & Hansot, 1981).

The *Protestant republican ideology* which was the basis for nineteenth century public education, supported both utilitarianism and individualism as social philosophies. It was based on the conviction that America was selected by God as a redeemer nation. This conviction gave coherence and vibrancy to the rhetoric of common school crusaders who combined economic with religious and political arguments in making the case for public education. School crusaders were the school and child advocates or moral entrepreneurs of their time. Believing that a modest amount of schooling would prepare everyone to compete on an equal footing, they embraced the view that life is a contest in which those who worked hard would win and those who did not would lose, in keeping with the doctrine of individualism. Typically British-American in origin, evangelical Protestant in religion, and middle-class in economic outlook, nineteenth century education crusaders and reformers were the elites of their communities who earned their livings as ministers, lawyers, politicians, college presidents, and professors. Praising the United States as a land of economic opportunity and justice, and promulgating the view that the poor and marginalized individuals were responsible for their own plight, they were unaware of how the views they espoused were shaped by their status in the society. The implication of their views was that if children worked hard, learned to read and write, and achieved in school, they would grow up to be successful winners in the contest of life.

With the growing secularization of American society in the late nineteenth century, public education came to be seen as necessary, not only for personal success and advancement,

---

> ### *REFLECTION ...*
>
> Are we, in the United States, in a period of utilitarianism, individualism, and/or Protestant republican ideology? Explain the basis of your decision.

---

but also for responsible participation in a democratic political order (Tyack & Hansot, 1981). Education reformers, including Horace Mann, held that if the United States was to be an open society, all children had to have the same educational opportunities (Lipset, 1993). This view, in theory, justified expanding educational opportunities as a means of ensuring the later success of children in what was later to become a highly specialized and credentialed society. Equality of educational opportunity, in turn, justified the view that if everyone had equal access to public schooling, the inequalities resulting from the nation's economic and social order—namely capitalism—could hardly be regarded as unjust.

Contradiction and Conflicts in Educational Policy

Although educators in the nineteenth century recognized that educational opportunities in the United States were not equal and sought to correct them, they had a stake in promoting the "contest mentality," that is, the view that individuals who rise to the top are best. This view promoted competition, which at the time was confined to competition between individuals, not groups based on differences with regard to gender, race, religion, and/or disability, as was later to be the case. The contest mentality reflected the values underlying public education in the United States at the time: individual achievement, hard work, and success—setting the stage for many of the contradictions in and conflicts over public policy in the domain of education and home–school relations in the years to come. The reasons for such contradictions and conflicts in educational policy in the United States are three-fold (Smelser & Halpern, 1978):

1. Different value premises cannot be fully realized to the same degree at the same time by those who hold them. For example, many who may regard the equalization of educational opportunities of prime importance also may regard low property taxes to be equally important. Because tax revenues are the means of financing public education, equalizing educational opportunities and keeping taxes low cannot be achieved to the same degree at the same time.

2. Because the United States is such a pluralistic and heterogeneous society, individuals and groups differ in their ranking of values on matters pertaining to the education of children. Thus, for example, some individuals and groups rank equality of educational opportunity higher than other individuals and groups who rank freedom of choice in educational policy higher.

3. The multiplicity of value premises available within the society encourages different groups to mobilize and counter-mobilize around those issues involving the values they hold to be most important. Thus, in the United States, different groups can be found to mobilize and counter-mobilize around such issues as: school choice, school prayer, property tax relief, school finance reform, school dress codes, school safety, school curricula, funding for education, and so forth. Underlying these issues are such values as: freedom, individual rights, equality of opportunity, equity and fairness, and others.

Different Values at Different Times

Over time, according to the social change model, competing value themes in educational policy can be observed to oscillate just as they do in other policy domains. Thus, egalitarian values came to predominate in the Progressive era of the late 1900s, the New Deal era of the 1930s, and the years of the Great Society in the 1960s. Such values in educational policy in the 1930s were reflected in concerns about the equal treatment of children, and in the 1960s, with desegregation and equal opportunity for *all* children. Egalitarian values receded in importance during the Eisenhower era of the 1950s, the Nixon years of the 1970s (Smelser & Halpern, 1978), the Reagan–Bush period of the 1980s, and the Clinton/Gore era of the 1990s. The 1950s, for example, were marked by a preoccupation with individual achievement in the context of Sputnik (Smelser & Halpern, 1978), and in the Nixon years and Reagan–Bush years in the context of a heightened emphasis on individualism.

> *REFLECTION...*
>
> What do you anticipate the value theme being after the year 2000?

In the context of an increasingly competitive global economy and technological developments effecting major changes in the structure of America's economy and families, individual achievement values continue to predominate in the 1990s. With regard to families, such changes pertain to the growth in single-parent families, stepparent families, families with mothers who work outside the home, and so forth. With regard to the economy, such changes, domestically, refer to the shift from a manufacturing to a service economy, and internationally, to the rise of other countries as competitors of the United States in world markets. Such changes in this discussion represent the *novel situation* in the social change model that provides the conceptual framework for the chapter.

Defining the Novel Situation and the Role of Moral Entrepreneurs

According to the social change model depicted here, with the advent of structural change of the nature described above in relation to families and the economy, certain social processes appear to unfold. To the extent such changes diverge or are different from the ways in which people have learned to perceive and make sense of the world around them, that is, their *normative, cognitive frameworks,* different individuals and groups begin to emerge to express alarm about the changes they observe—whether these pertain to families, the economy, schools, or all three. In the model, such individuals are called *moral entrepreneurs.* Moral entrepreneurs, or advocates, are individuals and groups who attempt to define, evaluate, and make understandable to others the novel situation—as *they* perceive and understand it to be. Their perceptions are shaped by the values and attitudes they hold and the values of the larger society. Every state and local community has its moral entrepreneurs who speak out on educational and other policy issues. William Bennett, Secretary of the United States Department of Education during the Reagan years, is an example of a moral entrepreneur in the area of education at the national level. Richard Riley serves in that capacity in the Clinton Administration.

REFLECTION...

Identify individuals and groups/organizations in your local community that could be called "moral entrepreneurs." What do they have in common? What are their differences? How did they get started? What individuals or groups in your local community were there before these recent moral entrepreneurs?

Competing Definitions of the Situation

According to the social change model, the initial period of defining the problem or novel situation with regard to the education of children is likely to be confused and confusing, in part because of the multiplicity of value premises and perspectives the culture provides for assigning meaning to the novel situation. Thus, different people are likely to perceive and define the novel situation differently. Differences in perceptions help to explain why some may perceive low test scores and high rates of school drop out as reflecting the failure of families to be sufficiently involved in the education of their children and others as reflecting the failure of schools to adequately address the diverse learning needs of children. The issue of bilingual education is pertinent here, as are special schools for immigrant children and the inclusion of children with special disabilities in all classrooms—in that different individuals and groups perceive and define these issues differently. The initial struggle over competing definitions of the situation is likely to be a cultural one with different individuals and groups that specialize in commenting on the society playing a prominent role: public and religious leaders, academics, journalists, artists, and writers are examples of such commentators.

The Social Action Component of the Model

According to the model, the cultural struggle over competing perceptions and definitions of the situation assumes a political dimension as different moral entrepreneurs attempt to spread their definitions of the situation to politically significant groups and mobilize them to press for some kind of social action that fits with the moral entrepreneurs' definition of the situation. Moral entrepreneurs may even create a politically significant group or movement for this purpose. An example of a politically significant group is the Children's Defense Fund, a group that does research and lobbies on behalf of children, often on matters pertaining to educational policy. The group was founded by Marion Wright Edelman, who is a moral entrepreneur who speaks out on behalf of children and attempts to persuade others to adopt her definition of their needs and problems.

> **REFLECTION...**
>
> Why is the Children's Defense Fund a politically significant group? What does it do that other groups (NEA, AFT, NAEYC, ACLU) do not do? How and why does it advocate for children?

The social action that results from the mobilization of such activity may be a moral crusade, as for example, the civil rights movement that led to the desegregation of public schools in the United States; a legal regulation such as the ban on guns in the schools; a new institution like the Office of Educational Technology in the Department of Education that is part of the Goals 2000: Educate American Act, 1994; or an organizational reform like the extension of the school day and year. Such action(s) constitute(s) the condition(s), or novel situation, for initiating another cycle of conflict and change, similar to that which gave impetus to the initial action. In short, change in public policy in the area of education is ongoing and interactive. The ongoing and oscillating nature of policy developments in education is illustrated in the brief discussion of the history of educational policy and home–school relations in the United States that follows, based on the social change model presented here.

Educational Policy Developments in the United States: Illustrating the Social Change Model

The Novel Situation

Infant Schools
The history of the oscillating nature of educational policy in the United States reflects the dynamics that have been outlined in the presentation of the social change model above. During the colonial period, young children were taught the basics of reading at an early age at home. Later, in the late eighteenth and early nineteenth centuries, infant schools were established, largely as a result of the infant school movement that promulgated the importance of such schools as a means of helping poor families and their children, or in the language of the times, as a means of uplifting the poor. As education came to be viewed in terms of the future development of children, and good for all children, infant schools in turn gave impetus to the idea of early education outside the home for other children (Kaestle & Vinovskis, 1978).

The Victorian Family
In addition to the infant school movement, the early nineteenth century marked the beginning of a movement to establish a new type of family. Known as the *Victorian family,* this new type of family was characterized by sharply defined work and domestic roles and

responsibilities for husbands and wives. The movement to establish a new type of family was fostered primarily by changes in the economy and labor force, and given meaning by an ideology concerning the nature of men, women, and children and the proper role of each. The ideology was sufficiently powerful to temporarily reverse the shift of responsibility for children's education from their homes to schools, but not for long. By and large, children were required to spend a certain number of hours and days of each year outside the home, in school, and steadily progress in their development from skill to skill and grade to grade.

Standardized Curriculum and Individual Achievement
With the establishment of more uniform expectations regarding the school behaviors of children, teachers were confronted with the task of having to impose uniform curriculum on children. Accordingly, children who did not conform to emerging childhood norms became a source of anxiety for parents. This included precocious children who came to be seen as deviant and off schedule, even though individual achievement was prized and regarded an asset in the pursuit of competitive excellence and in keeping with the contest mentality. Those placing greater importance on equality or the common good, however, were apt to downgrade the importance of individual achievement and democratize it (Kett, 1978). With the movement toward the standardization of curriculum and child behavioral norms and the growing numbers of young children attending school, large numbers of children were increasingly subject to the systematic normative regulation of their behaviors in their early years.

Recognition of Home–School Differences
Nineteenth century educators were keenly aware of trends toward the greater standardization of school curriculum and children's behaviors, and recognized differences in the normative features of home and school. Schools separated siblings according to age and grade, but families did not (Dreeben, 1968). School size contributed to child anonymity, family size to intimacy among members. While school curriculum and text books were standardized, families attended to children's idiosyncrasies and individual preferences. Schools encouraged independence and self-reliance, while families, normatively at least, encouraged cooperation and support. Schools accorded merit on the basis of individual achievement while parents loved their children regardless of their achievements. Schools were governed by norms of impersonality and impartiality; family norms were particularistic and affective. Finally, specialization and organizational size fostered secondary relationships in schools, that is, relationships that were temporary and purposeful; family relationships, on the other hand, were primary, ongoing, and diffuse. Thus, the norms governing the two institutions—families and schools—were vastly different in their institutional and historical roots.

Different Definitions of the Situation, and the Mobilization of Activity in Opposition to Infant Schools

Gradually, differences in the institutional norms that governed school and family life and the perception that early intellectual activity led to insanity caused reformers to question infant schools and then oppose them. Indeed, during the period from 1830 to 1880, advocates of progressive education, and also medical authorities, counseled against the early education of children because of the association that had been made between early intellectual activity and insanity (Kaestle & Vinovskis, 1978). Reformers waged a slow but successful effort with parents to keep three- and four-year-old children at home. Concerns about early education were heightened by the increasingly bureaucratic structure of public schools and the belief that home child rearing would prevent the moral and spiritual deterioration of American society—and insanity.

Thus, the attitudes that supported the growth of infant schools and the education of children outside the home in the early nineteenth century shifted. While children in the late eighteenth and early nineteenth centuries were expected to learn to read at an early age, by the mid-nineteenth century, they were discouraged from doing so by educators who cautioned against it. The percentage of young children attending infant schools declined accordingly (Kaestle & Vinovskis, 1978). The strongest predictors of child school attendance during this period were children's ages and the communities in which they lived, not their ethnicity, sex, or parents' literacy and socio-economic status. Between 1860 and 1880, school attendance declined significantly for every subgroup in the population, attributable largely to changes in perceptions of infant schools.

Redefinition of the Pre-School Years, Subsequent Actions and Counteractions, and Different Definitions of the Situation

Attitudes toward preschools began to change again when the preschool years came to be perceived and defined as a distinctive childhood stage. Such redefinition of the childhood stage represented the novel situation that resulted in part from the ascendance of Lockean views that spoke to the uniqueness of the emotional, physical, and intellectual needs of children. Such views drew attention to the importance of early child care and the long-term implications of existing child-rearing practices. As early childhood came to be seen as a developmental stage that required special attention and care, child-rearing theorists and school advocates began to initiate a new relationship between school and family. As theory once again promoted early institutional learning, many parents followed. Nonetheless, for most children, the child's transition at age five from a protective, personal family to an age-graded, task-oriented school persists as a major life course event.

The last several years have seen a dramatic change in the care of very young children. Children today are entering school at earlier and earlier ages. Nursery schools and day-care centers for three- and four-year-olds, and even infants, have developed, in part, in response to the increased numbers of mothers who work outside the home, and, in part, in response to welfare policies mandating that mothers receiving welfare benefits work or prepare themselves for work. While 40 percent of all three- and four-year-old children were enrolled in preprimary school in 1970, by 1992, this figure had doubled to 80 percent (U.S. Bureau of Census, 1994). The percentage of children attending pre-school was almost as high for black as it was for white children, 55.1 and 55.8 percent respectively; for Hispanics, it was lower, 48.4 percent.

Despite episodic enthusiasm for infant schools, kindergartens, and later for programs like Head Start, the shift toward the institutionalization of very young children has not gone unchallenged. Some scholars fault early education because they say it has failed to produce significant improvements in children's development over the long term. Others counter by emphasizing, for example, Head Start's immediate positive effects on children's academic skills, and say that despite the diminution of its effects over time, the program provides health and social benefits that are important to children and their parents. They emphasize the program's role in parents' lives—in encouraging parents' involvement in their children's education and in providing jobs for parents—as Head Start teachers, for example. Many, in fact, argue that parents are more properly the educators of very young children than pre-school teachers and child-care providers. Indeed, in the 1970s President Richard Nixon vetoed legislation providing for a comprehensive early childhood education program on grounds that it usurped parental authority. Part of the confusion over Head Start stems from the different and shifting arguments that have been used to justify and evaluate the program (DeParle, 1993), such as parental employment, parental involvement, early childhood development, and child care for working parents, especially for parents receiving Aid to Families with Dependent Children (AFDC). Reports of unqualified staff and insufficient space have contributed to the confusions surrounding the program. Underlying many of the debates about early childhood education today are issues of race and social class and the allocation of scarce resources.

Education of First through Twelfth Graders

Just as home–school relations are affected by policy related to early childhood education, they also are affected by policy pertaining to elementary and secondary education (Kaestle & Vinovskis, 1978). Public schools developed at a time when older patterns of family and community control over youth had become ineffectual. By assuming tasks the family could no longer perform, or chose not to perform, educational institutions helped to effect the transition from family control to parent influence over child behaviors. The expansion of schools and the establishment of school norms prescribing age-appropriate behaviors were useful in helping to effect this transition. Contemporary examples of such norms are school dress and behavioral codes—and also bans on guns in schools.

By the 1950s, older sources of authority and consensus with respect to education came under attack. While educational reformers of the nineteenth and twentieth centuries shared an evangelical confidence in their mission, by the 1950s and 1960s, such confidence had begun to diminish. The early 1950s marked the end of an era of continuity in the values and institutional complexities that education administrators promoted earlier in the twentieth century (Smelser & Halpern, 1978). White male leaders and education experts no longer commanded the authority and respect they once did. New actors in school politics challenged the old order and began to dismantle the system of school governance that had evolved over the previous half century. The initial impetus for change came largely from a series of social movements that began with the Civil Rights Movement and gathered momentum after the *Brown* v. *Topeka School Board* decision in 1954 ordering school desegregation.

Attempts to End Discrimination and Racism

Angry protest movements, emulating the methods of the Civil Rights Movement, emerged as groups began to define themselves on the basis of their race, sex, and social class. Newly conscious of their separate interests, these groups were unwilling to let the experts define their interests. Many groups—students, minorities, women, teachers, the students with disabilities, school finance reformers—learned the law and how to use it as an instrument for effecting social change. As a consequence, older processes involving the political accommodation of differences eroded as offended parties turned increasingly to the courts. Techniques of protest, court action, and new legislation pioneered by blacks and their white allies spread rapidly to other groups—feminists, Hispanics or Latinos, families of special needs children, Native Americans, and others. By joining together, these groups hoped to achieve greater power and equity through their collective efforts and actions.

The aim of these protest movements was to end discrimination and neglect in education. Advocates based their appeal for social justice on traditional egalitarian and democratic ideals. Blacks, for example, cast their arguments in moral and political terms. While the groups differed in their demands, they all shared the conviction that education offered the means of increasing and advancing their economic and social opportunities. The mission of these groups was to force those in positions of power to attend to their neglected educational needs.

Black protest movements called attention to the contradictions between professed American values of freedom and equality of opportunity and the realities of black lives. Similar protest movements demanding redress and recognition for other dispossessed groups followed the black rebellion in rapid succession. Unlike education crusaders and moral entrepreneurs of the past, the leaders of these protest movements viewed themselves as outsiders. They made protest an everyday occurrence for leaders in the most universal of all American institutions—the public schools. As attacks against the caste system in the South proceeded, protest leaders discovered institutional racism and black powerlessness in abundance in the North.

The challenges these protest leaders presented were a new or novel situation for educational leaders. Such challenges diverged markedly from the ways in which educational leaders were accustomed to looking at or understanding the world around them. They were not prepared, either by experience, ideology, or training to address fundamental differences over school goals, governance, and programs (Tyack & Hansot, 1981). Seeking to maintain their initiative, educational leaders tried to redefine the issues that protest groups raised with regard to education. Thus they defined the educational needs of minority groups in terms of educational deficiencies that required such remedies as compensatory education, better vocational offerings, and early childhood education.

Minority groups refused to accept white experts' definitions of and solutions for their problems, however. Like the ethnic groups of the nineteenth century, minority groups in the 1960s wanted the public schools to legitimize their cultures and interests by offering courses in African American studies, Hispanic studies, and Native American heritage. Women wanted the schools to legitimize their concerns through more offerings of classes focusing on women's issues. Advocates of ethnic self-determination went a step further in campaigning for community control of schools and for hiring minority staff, using persuasion and confrontation in advocating for the education reforms they were seeking.

Several social actions or changes in school policies and programs followed as result of the mobilization of their activity. Liberal reformers in education, foundations, and governments responded with programs designed to use education to wage war against poverty and increase equity and educational opportunities for minority groups. Head Start and Follow Through, both federal programs, were designed to equalize educational opportunities by providing special training for underserved children. State and federal governments created dozens of other programs to serve neglected groups. Unfortunately, the rapid growth and expansion of such programs often led to services that duplicated one another or worked at cross purposes. Such fragmentation and duplication of services was the result of the way services were funded—namely by funding category, such as day care or Head Start, rather than by function, such as early childhood education or child development, allowing administrators little flexibility in defining effective education. In the meantime, school districts experimented with plans for decentralization, community control, and community advisory councils to make the governance of education programs more responsive to the needs of community groups.

During the 1960s and 1970s, funding for public education increased at a rate unparalleled in U.S. history. It increased, in part, because of the growth of the school age population which forced schools to expand accordingly, and in part because of the infusion of federal funds to states and local communities for the education of children. Some of the increase also may be attributed to the efforts of public interest lawyers who assisted plaintiffs in demanding fundamental changes in educational policies, such as the equalization of state financing for public education and the elimination of institutional racism and sexism. Public interest lawyers also may be credited with establishing students' right to free speech and due process in cases of suspensions, and the elimination of racial bias in pupil classification.

Increasingly, federal legislation guaranteeing everyone's civil rights, regardless of sex or race, and the decisions of state and federal courts in class action suits, came to dominate state and local decisions in education, education traditionally being the domain of local school districts and states, not of the federal government. Such legislation served to increase the possibility of law suits by individuals seeking redress to education policies and practices they viewed as exclusionary. The adversarial mode of legal debate polarized views and opinions and sharpened group differences. Litigation arising from injustices and unmet education needs signaled a breakdown in other forms of persuasion for dealing with disputes. It also signaled a loss of trust in administrative compromise and school board and legislative action in dealing with group conflict.

REFLECTION...

Is there a difference between elementary/secondary and early childhood education and the role of public policy and advocacy for children? Should there be a difference? Why?

Different Perceptions/Definitions of the Situation in Education in the 1990s

The problems in education today are seen as the outgrowth of the educational successes of the past and the disillusionment that followed the *Brown* v. *Topeka Board of Education* decision in 1954 (Tyack & Hansot, 1981) ending segregation in education. Much of the disillusionment stems from the unrealistic expectations that followed from that momentous decision and exaggerated promises of reforms that would work where others in the past had failed. Social scientists, whose perceptions and definitions of the situation differed, contributed to this disillusionment. Some, discouraged by what they perceived to be the disappointing results of compensatory education, decried such efforts for failing to effect long term positive change. Others blamed the schools for failing to equalize outcomes, whether with respect to academics or lifetime incomes. Over time, public confidence in education has declined, from 49 percent of those who said they had a great deal of confidence in education as an institution in 1974 to 22 percent in 1993 (Confidence in institutions, 1993). Indeed, in 1993, public satisfaction with education was lower than it was for almost all other social institutions: the press, the executive branch of government, congress, organized labor, television, and organized religion.

The list of problems associated with education is long, according to Goals 2000 which Congress enacted in 1994. The preamble to Goals 2000 states that seventy-five million American adults are functionally illiterate and cannot read or write; that almost half of all infants in the United States are born with one or more problems that place them at risk for educational failure in the future; that roughly 75 percent of all students fail to achieve a basic level of proficiency in math and science; that almost 13 percent of all 16–24-year-olds are high school dropouts, nearly 35 percent of whom are Hispanic and almost 20 percent black; and that over half of all high school graduates lack the skills for an entry-level job or college (*Goals 2000,* 1994). And even though the United States spends more for education than other countries, 9- and 13-year-old U.S. children score lower in math than children in other countries: Korea, Taiwan, Italy, Israel, Spain, Canada, and England (Educational outputs: Comparative student performance, 1993).

Seymour Lipset (1993) argues against drawing comparisons between children in the United States and other countries, contending that if comparisons are to be made, they should be made between children in the top 10 to 20 percent of their class in the United States and the 10 percent of the children in other countries who go to quality schools (Lipset, 1993). He holds that unlike other countries, the United States attempts to educate *all* children—in the same institutional setting—regardless of their social class and parents' status and whether they are rich or poor, immigrant or native born. Universal public education, he says, is a conscious policy which holds that if the United States is to be a free and open society, all children must have the same educational opportunities. The assumption was and is that while the best students might not learn as much or as fast as they otherwise might, they will not suffer long-term damage as a consequence. Beyond the importance of the decision itself, Lipset (1993) holds that the *Brown* v. *Topeka Board of Education* decision was important in sensitizing the country to the anti-democratic implications of separate systems of education, one for black and another for white children. However, because public schools attempt to educate children from all groups and social classes, Lipset acknowledged that the quality of public education cannot be the same as in private schools or in schools attended by only 10 percent of the children in other countries, nor should this be expected, he added.

Despite declining confidence in public education as an institution, public support for education in the United States remains strong (Education: Seen important everywhere, 1993). Almost everyone thinks education is very important or essential (85%). Most in the United States in 1993 thought too little was being spent on it and that as a consequence, the education of children suffered (Education...high levels of support for spending everywhere, 1993). Yet, compared to other countries—Italy, France, Japan, and Germany—the United States spends more for education at all levels: preprimary, primary, and secondary (Educational inputs: Comparative spending levels in the G-7, 1993).

Today, unlike the 1950s and 1960s when the political tension in American education was between disadvantaged groups and the producers of education, the political tension is between the producers of education and the power elites—business leaders and elected officials. In contrast to countries like Japan, where employers and schools work together to achieve common goals and strategies, employers and educators in the United States in the 1990s do not. Their estrangement persists despite national education and labor policy calling for their collaboration (Applebome, 1995). Many employers in the United States in fact have retreated from the schools in the face of opposition from educational leaders (Institute for Educational Leadership, 1995).

In the late 1980s, governors, educators, business executives, and parents joined in the debate about the future of public education in the United States and whether the United States should set national standards for the education of children as European countries and Japan do (Chira, 1989). According to opinion polls, the adoption of national educational standards has broad public support although national standards run counter to American traditions of state and local responsibility for the education of children. Advocates, in making the case for national standards, argue that national standards could be used as a basis for testing children's knowledge and for determining the state of education for the nation as a whole. The latter in turn could be used for issuing a national report card on education. Scores also could be used as incentives for schools whose students score below acceptable standards to do better in educating children. Indeed, Charles Finn, chair of the board of governors of the National Assessment of Educational Progress, argued that national standards were necessary to improve poor schools.

Not everyone agrees with the move to establish national standards for assessing the knowledge of American children, however. While advocates of different persuasions agree that education consists of learning how to think, write, calculate, and analyze, and not just how to memorize facts, and that U.S. students were not learning enough to get and hold good jobs or be good citizens, advocates did not agree on how to address these problems. Governors welcome the idea of national standards. Some hold that national standards would allow teachers to teach in ways that work best for them. Opponents argue that lack of consensus about what children should know would make the identification of good schools problematic.

Arguments over curriculum are based on personal experiences and self-interest. While business leaders emphasize skills in math and science, educators argue that such skills should not be acquired to the exclusion of knowledge acquisition for its own sake. Ethnic groups charged that the cognitive frameworks of educators often excluded women, minority groups, and non-Western cultures. Other voices say that while a revamped curriculum would have to include the contributions of excluded groups, it would have to emphasize a common American heritage also. These are only some of the arguments emanating from different perceptions of national educational standards that led up to the enactment of Goals 2000: Educate America Act in 1994, the culminating social action of the social change model in this discussion.

REFLECTION...

Investigate whether there are national and/or state standards the students in your state must meet. How were the standards determined and how is the assessment done? What is the role of alternative assessment in the standards?

Goals 2000 and National Standards: The Social Action of 1994

On March 31st, 1994, Congress enacted and President Clinton signed into law the Goals 2000: Educate America Act. The Act represents both continuity and change in public policy in the domain of education in the United States. It represents change in terms of the recognition it gives to the importance of parents in children's school achievement. It represents continuity in terms of defining educational achievement as a measure of child success. It also represents continuity in terms of the institutional arrangements that were established when Congress enacted the Elementary and Secondary Education Act (ESEA) in 1965. Such arrangements pertain to the role of the Federal government in supporting the efforts of state governments and local school districts in the education of the nation's children. ESEA, in putting the educational needs of poor and disadvantaged children on the national agenda, committed the federal government to investing large sums of money to meet their needs (Maeroff, 1985). Similarly, Goals 2000, by defining children's school achievement in terms of the national interest, legitimizes the role of the federal government in collaborating with states and local school districts in establishing and implementing national educational standards that schools are expected to meet.

However, while ESEA defined the schools as the problem with respect to the education of disadvantaged children, Goals 2000 defines poor student achievement as the problem in 1994. Goals 2000 places into law six national education goals promulgated by President Bush and all fifty governors, adding two more and additional language describing the intent of each. The eight goals pertain to: 1) school readiness, 2) school completion, 3) student achievement and citizenship, 4) teacher education and professional development, 5) student achievement in math and science, 6) adult literacy and lifelong learning, 7) alcohol and drug free schools, and 8) parent participation and involvement. According to the Act, by the year 2000:

1. All children in America will start school ready to learn.
2. The high school graduate rate will increase to at least 90 percent.

3. All students will complete 4th, 5th, and 12th grades with demonstrated competency over such subject matter as English, math, science, foreign languages, civics and government, economics, arts, history, and geography; and every school in America will ensure that all students are prepared for responsible citizenship, further learning, and productive employment.

4. The nation's teachers will have access to programs for the continued improvement of their professional skills and the opportunity to acquire the knowledge and skills needed to instruct and prepare all students for the 21st century.

5. The nation's students will be first in the world in math and science achievement.

6. Every adult will be literate and possess the knowledge and skills necessary to compete in a global economy and exercise the rights and responsibilities of citizenship.

7. Every school in the United States will be free of drugs, violence, and the unauthorized presence of firearms and alcohol, and will offer a disciplined environment conducive to learning.

8. Every school will promote partnerships to increase the involvement of parents of preschool and school-age children and the participation of parents in promoting the social, emotional, and academic growth of their children. It is this eighth goal that relates most explicitly and directly to home–school relations.

The act, in keeping with the American value of freedom, emphasizes the *voluntary* nature of the content and performance standards that define what students should know and be able to do. It also delineates the roles of state and federal governments in standard setting and enforcement. It establishes the structures (Office of Educational Technology in the Department of Education) and procedures by which such standards are to be *voluntarily* set and certified. It underscores the importance of providing a *fair* opportunity for all students to acquire the knowledge and skills described in the *voluntary* national content and student performance standards. Its goal is to make all students technologically competent to compete in the new global economy in the new technological age.

Home–School Relations under Goals 2000: The Role of Families

Goals 2000 not only is based on the assumption that schools and families must do better in preparing children for the technological society of the twenty-first century but also, as in the eighteenth and nineteenth centuries, the assumption that personal deficiencies—lack of skills and motivation—are synonymous with personal failure. As national education policy, Goals 2000 represents, in part, a return to the philosophy espoused by John Watson (Kagan, 1981), that the home is responsible for what the child becomes. Modern writers are persuaded that interactive social experience, especially experience in the home, is the central basis for the development of children and their extraordinary variation. This belief is supported by research documenting the influence of home and family on children's school achievement (Achenbach & Howell, 1993; Christenson, Rounds, & Gorney, 1992).

The importance of home and family for children's school achievement is underscored in a study undertaken by the Rand Corporation. Rand researchers found that while improvements in minority students' test scores seemed to be related to changes that occurred in *both* the home and school, improvements in white students' scores seemed to be related primarily to family (Grissmer, Kirby, Berends, & Williamson, 1994). Better educated parents seemed to be the most important factor in children's school achievement as measured by their test scores. Given declining school drop-out rates, this finding portends well for child school achievement in the future. Between 1970 and 1990, the percentage of mothers with high school degrees increased 21 percent, from 62 to 83 percent. Smaller families also made a difference in that students from smaller families seemed to fare better in school. From this, the researchers reasoned that although family incomes had not grown, family resources per child were greater because average family size was smaller. The increased number of working mothers and single mothers—two trends that have worried policy makers—seemed to have no significant effect on children's scores when examined alone. Based on their findings, Rand researchers concluded that desegregation and increased spending on education, especially early education and nutrition programs for poor and minority children, were paying off. In the face of anticipated cuts in federal spending, Rand researchers cautioned against dismantling programs until it was known which programs deserved to continue and which did not.

Threatened Actions Related to Goals 2000

In 1995, threatened cuts to education included $173.5 million from Goals 2000: The Educate America Act, eliminating not only the increased funding in President Clinton's budget proposal for 1996, but reducing the appropriation for 1995 as well (Celis, 1995). As of late summer 1995, in addition to anticipated spending cuts in Goals 2000, cuts were anticipated in spending for bilingual education; the Safe Schools and Drug Free Act; vocational education; the school to work transition program; and Title I, the program designed to help disadvantaged students reach grade level in reading and math. Some of these threats stemmed from perceptions that programs, such as those funded by Title I, did not work, and others, such as bilingual education, ran counter to organized interests favoring English-only education. Several teachers of bilingual education said immigrant children needed the extra help that bilingual education provides to help in their transition from being new immigrants to being productive citizens. The underlying and overriding issue with regard to the budget cuts, however, was not the failure of schools and families to help children learn, but the federal budget deficit and the priority given to its reduction and other matters (Grissmer et al., 1994). Although threatened program cuts represented just 10 percent of all Federal spending on education, according to many school officials, the cuts would fall disproportionately on urban schools, which educate the poorest and neediest of the country's children.

In the meantime, one father in Northern Virginia launched an initiative to add parents' rights to state constitutions (Clark, 1995). He viewed the movement for parental involvement in the schools as a "well-intentioned elitist effort that is doomed to failure." He argued that the reason parents have not been involved in schools is because society has contracted out to schools responsibilities that belonged to parents in the first place, cautioning parents to be more skeptical and militant about "the latest educational directive coming down from on high." According to a survey conducted by the National PTA in 1992, the major reason for parents' lack of involvement in the schools is lack of time, followed by a feeling that they have nothing to contribute, and the lack of child care. Although the response to the call for parent involvement in general has been positive, parents were rated as highly involved in only 46 percent of the schools attended by students in the future high school class of 2000, according to data from the 1993 National Household Education Survey (Clark, 1995).

Conclusion

As can be seen from the foregoing discussion, the story of public policy in education is a continuing saga—in keeping with the social change model that frames the discussion. It is a story of social actions that come to be perceived as novel situations and the mobilization of activity around different perceptions and definitions of the situation. The application of the model to policy developments in education hopefully helped to identify some of the sources of confusion and contradiction surrounding these developments. By extending observations beyond Goals 2000 to include anticipated budget cuts that threaten Goals 2000 and other educational efforts, especially those related to home–school relations and parent involvement, the discussion hopefully also illuminated the repetitive and dynamic nature of the policy process as it relates to education, and also the iterative and dynamic nature of social change itself.

Although American public education traditionally has been an expanding and optimistic undertaking, today there is far greater ambivalence and uncertainty about education as the route to personal success (Tyack & Hansot, 1981). The 1990s are different from earlier periods of U.S. history when individuals could, simply by working hard and exercising self-control, acquire positions of status. Today people are more dependent on the actions of others and how others perceive them. Also, despite current challenges to affirmative action, race, sex, and class continue to be important determinants of opportunity. Educators, who by and large tend to believe in the U.S. social order and the beliefs that support it, have tried to prevent opposition to the educational enterprise from organizing by giving everyone who matters a say in it.

Now the times demand hard choices for a variety of reasons. Citizen revolts against higher taxes, increased demands for educational services, changing demographics, and a growing preference for the private over the public sector compound the difficulties in making such choices. Indeed, the rebirth of faith in the free market and a growing hostility toward the public sector have caused some people to ask why public schools should be supported at all. While different groups want something different from education—employers better-trained and more productive workers, parents better opportunities and jobs for their children, and teachers more diligent learners—educational policy requires diverse groups pursuing their separate interests to join together and arrive at a common definition of the purpose of education. Because schools are close at hand everywhere, they can provide a forum for different groups to join together in forging such a definition, one that will help us arrive at an agreed upon course of action with regard to the education of our nation's children in the twenty-first century.

Teachers can play an important role in this process. Their's is a foundational role that begins the long term, ongoing process of the formal education of children. Based on evidence they carefully accumulate and document, preschool teachers can become advocates for children and the learning supports that children need to grow and develop: they can write letters to the editor, speak before groups, and lobby and testify before official bodies when they perceive situations that might be defined as harmful to children's educational progress or that threaten to undermine the achievement of the nation's educational goals.

Teachers seldom have the opportunity to step back and view their role from a broader perspective. Hopefully, this chapter has provided the opportunity for them to do that and in addition, some conceptual tools that they themselves can use to better understand some of the contradictions, confusions, and conflicts that surround educational policy and affect their practice. Hopefully, it also has given them some insights into the role that advocates play in shaping educational policy and that they too can play in helping to shape educational policy so that it better supports learning—and the education of children.

Recommended Activities

1. Pretend you are a U.S. Senator. You want to improve the quality of home–school relations. Write a bill, if you think this is a role for the federal government, that would improve home–school relations.
2. Visit a school superintendent or other administrator and ask about the impact Goals 2000 had on their district/building relative to families.
3. Develop a timeline from the early 1900s to the present and identify certain educational policy initiatives on the timeline.
4. Interview preschool teachers and/or directors and ask them if the educational policy decisions in the 1960s and 1970s for preschool has had an influence on the K–12 system.
5. Follow the history of Goals 2000. How did Goal 2000 develop from an idea into educational policy in the United States?
6. Go through a school board's minutes to determine the number of family issues relating to schools. Determine which issues are mandated by the state, federal government, or by local authorities.
7. Write or email your representative or senator and ask for a listing of all bills that have dealt with parent involvement or families and education in the last five years. In addition, find out if there are any bills pending in those areas.

Additional Resources

Education Policy and Advocacy

Organizations:

American Federation of Teachers
555 New Jersey Avenue, NW
Washington, DC 20001
Phone: 202-879-4400

Center for the Future of Children
The David & Lucile Packard Foundation
300 Second Street, Suite 102
Los Altos, CA 94022
Phone: 415-948-3696
http://www.futureofchildren.org

Center on Families, Communities, Schools and Children's Learning
John Hopkins University
3505 North Charles Street
Baltimore, MD 21218
Phone: 401-516-0370

Child Welfare League of America
440 First Street, NW
Washington, DC 20001
Phone: 202-638-2952

Children Now
1212 Broadway, Suite 530
Oakland, CA 94612
Phone: 800-CHILD-44
http://www.dnai.com:80/~children/
(mostly CA, but deals with some national issues)

Children's Defense Fund
25 E Street, NW
Washington, DC 20001
Phone: 202-628-8787
http://www.tmn.com/cdf/index.html

Children's Institute International
711 South New Hampshire Avenue
Los Angeles, CA 90005
Phone: 213-385-5100
http://childrensinstitute.org
(mostly CA, but deals with some national issues)

Council for Exceptional Children
1920 Association Drive
Reston, VA 22091-1589
Phone: 800-845-6232

Institute for Responsive Education
605 Commonwealth Avenue
Boston, MA 02215
Phone: 617-353-3309

National Association for Bilingual Education
Union Center Plaza
810 First Street, NE, 3rd Floor
Washington, DC 20002
Phone: 202-898-1829

National Association for the Education of Young Children
1834 Connecticut Avenue, NW
Washington, DC 20009-5786
Phone: 800-424-2460

National Association of Child Advocates
1522 K Street, NW, Suite 600
Washington, DC 20005
Phone: 202-289-0777
FAX: 202-289-0776
Email: hn1315@handset.org

National Black Child Development Institute
1023 15th Street, NW, Suite 600
Washington, DC 20005
Phone: 202-387-1281

National Education Association
1201 16th Street, NW
Washington, DC 20036
Phone: 202-833-4000

Stand For Children
1834 Connecticut Avenue, NW
Washington, DC 20009
Phone: 800-663-4032
FAX: 202-234-0217
http://www.stand.org

Websites:

Administration for Children and Families
  (U.S. Dept. of Health and Human Services)
http://www.act.dhhs.gov/

Brookings Institute
http://www./brook.edu/

Electronic Policy Network
http://www.epn.org/

Legal Needs of Children
http://www/newcollege.edu/personal/homes/rshepard/nchildre.html

Native American Policy Group
http://www.swcp.com/~napg/

Rand Corporation
http://www.rand.org/

The Urban Institute
http://www.urban.org/

References

Achenbach, T. M., & Howell, C. (1993). Are American children's problems getting worse? A 13-year comparison. *Journal of American Academy of Child Adolescent Psychiatry, 32*(6), 1145–1154.

Applebome, P. (1995, February 20). Employers wary of school system. *New York Times,* p. A1.

Ball, T., & Dagger, R. (1990). The "L-Word": A short history of liberalism. *The Political Science Teacher, 3*(1), 1–9.

Celis, W. III. (1995, March 18). Deepest U.S. cuts since '81 are proposed for education. *New York Times,* p. 6.

Chira, S. (1989, December 26). National standards for schools gain. *New York Times,* p. 38.

Christenson, S. L., Rounds, T., & Gorney, D. (1992). Family factors and student achievement: An avenue to increase students' success. *School Psychology Quarterly, 7*(1), 178–206.

Clark, C. (1995, January 20). Parents and schools: Will more parental involvement help students? *CQ Researcher.*

Confidence in institutions: The public perspective. (1993). *Roper Center Review of Public Opinion and Polling, 5*(1), 94–99.

DeParle, J. (1993, March 19). Sharp criticism for Head Start, even by friends. *New York Times,* p. A1.

Dreeben, R. (1968). *On what is learned in school.* Reading, MA: Addison-Wesley.

Education...high levels of support for spending everywhere. (1993). *The Public Perspective 5*(1), 12.

Education: Seen important everywhere. (1993). *The Public Perspective, 5*(1), 14.

Educational inputs: Comparative spending levels in the G-7. (1993). *The Public Perspective 5*(1), 7.

Educational outputs: Comparative student performance. (1993). *The Public Perspective, 5*(1), 9.

Finn, C. (1993). U.S. educational performance: A failing grade. *The Public Perspective, 5*(1), 3–5.

Grissmer, D., Kirby, S. N., Berends, M., & Williamson, S. (1994). *Student achievement and the changing American family.* Santa Monica, CA: Rand Corporation.

Institute for Educational Leadership. (1995). *National Employers Survey.* Washington, DC: U.S. Bureau of Census.

Kaestle, C. F., & Vinovskis, M. A. (1978). From apron strings to ABCs: Parents, children and schooling in nineteenth century Massachusetts. In J. Demos & S. S. Boocock (Eds.), *Turning points: Historical and sociological essays on the family* (pp. S39–80). Chicago: Chicago University Press.

Kagan, J. (1981). The moral function of the school. *Daedalus, 110*(3), 151–165.

Kahn, A. (1969). *Theory and practice of social planning.* New York: Russell Sage Foundation.

Kahn, A., Kamerman, S., & McGowan, B. (1972). *Child advocacy: Report of a national baseline study.* New York: Columbia University School of Social Work.

Kett, J. F. (1978). Curing the disease of precocity. In N. Smelser & S. Halpern (Eds.), *Turning points: Historical and sociological essays on the family* (pp. S183–212). Chicago: University of Chicago Press.

Lipset, S. (1993). A contrarian perspective. *The Public Perspective, 5*(1), 6–7.

Maeroff, G. I. (1985, September 30). After 20 years, education programs are a solid legacy of Great Society. *New York Times,* p. 11.

Smelser, N., & Halpern, S. (1978). The historical triangulation of family, economy, and education. In J. Demos & S. S. Boocock (Eds.), *Turning points:*

Historical and sociological essays on the family (pp. S288–315). Chicago: University of Chicago Press.

The Goals 2000: Educate America Act. (1994, April 11). *Washington social legislation bulletin, 33,* 31.

Tyack, D., & Hansot, E. (1981). Conflict and consensus in American public education. *Daedalus, 110*(3), 1–25.

U.S. Bureau of Census. (1994). *Statistical abstract of the United States, 1994.* Washington DC: U.S. Government Printing Office.

Williams, R. M. (1960). *American society: A sociological interpretation.* New York: Knopf.

Zimmerman, S. L. (1971). *Information and referral services: The role of advocacy.* Washington, DC: U.S. Department of Health, Education, and Welfare Social and Rehabilitation Service (Working Draft).

Zimmerman, S. L. (1982). Confusions and contradictions in family policy developments: Application of a model. *Family Relations, 31*(3), 455–456.

Zimmerman, S. L. (1992). *Family policies and family well-being: The role of political culture.* Newbury Park, CA: Sage Publications.

Zimmerman, S. L. (1995). *Understanding family policy: Theories and applications.* (2nd ed.). Newbury Park, CA: Sage Publications.

About the Authors

Mary Lou Fuller

Mary Lou Fuller is a Chester Fritz Distinguished Professor in the Department of Teaching and Learning in the College of Education and Human Development at the University of North Dakota. She has been a school psychologist and a classroom teacher in the primary grades and Head Start. She has co-authored one book, *The Adult Learner,* written chapters for other books, and written over thirty articles. Her areas of research include the family, multicultural education, the adult learner, and home–school relations.

Sara Fritzell Hanhan

Sara Fritzell Hanhan is Associate Professor in the Department of Teaching and Learning at the University of North Dakota. She teaches undergraduate and graduate courses in Early Childhood Education, including a course in home–school relations. In addition to advocating for a strong presence of parent voices in schools, she is interested in ways of documenting the work that teachers, children, and families do in schools. Her most stable interest, however, is her family, which consists of husband, Ugur, and sons, Tolga and Kenan.

Charles B. Hennon

Charles B. Hennon is Professor in the Department of Family Studies and Social Work and is the Associate Director of the Family and Child Studies Center at Miami University, Oxford, Ohio. Previously, Dr. Hennon was Professor of Child and Family Studies at the University of Wisconsin–Madison. His areas of specialization include rural families, the allocation of resources to various family roles, and family stress and its effective management. He is past editor of the *Journal of Family* and *Economics Issues,* has co-edited two books, and has published over forty-five journal articles and book chapters.

J. Howard Johnston

J. Howard Johnston is a Professor of Secondary Education at the University of South Florida. Until 1990, he served as Professor of Curriculum and Instruction at the University of

Cincinnati, where he has also served as Dean of the Graduate School of Education and Acting Dean of the College of Education. Dr. Johnston is a well-established author, lecturer, and researcher. He has written over 100 works on middle level education and has presented over 500 invited papers and lectures in the United States, Canada, the Caribbean, Europe, and Asia. Two of his most recent books, *The New American Family and the School* (1990) and *Teaching Disadvantaged, At-Risk Youth* (1992), reflect his interest in the changing nature of the American population and the need to structure schools for success.

J. Gary Knowles

J. Gary Knowles has explored issues of teacher development and home education since the early 1980s. He is a co-author (with M. Mayberry, B. D. Ray, and S. E. Marlowe) of *Home-Schooling: Parents as Educators* (Sage, 1995) and has authored many articles on home education. He is presently working on a book about his research experiences with home educators.

Douglas D. Knowlton

Douglas D. Knowlton is a clinical psychologist and an associate professor in the special education program at the College of Education and Human Development at the University of North Dakota. In addition, he maintains a private practice in adolescent and child psychology at the Family Institute in Grand Forks, North Dakota.

Judith E. MacDonald

Judith E. MacDonald began her teaching career as an elementary school teacher in the New York City Public School System. At present she is an Associate Professor in the Department of Curriculum and Instruction at Montclair State University. Her research interests have focused on the reciprocal effects of being a teacher and parent. She is currently investigating how prospective teachers who are parents use their parenting knowledge in their development as teachers.

Carol Marxen

Carol Marxen is an Assistant Professor of Education at the University of Minnesota–Morris. She teaches kindergarten, science, and mathematics methods courses. Her research focuses on kindergarten education and science/mathematics curriculum for primary grades.

Mary McLean

Mary McLean is currently Professor and Chair of the Graduate Special Education Department at Cardinal Stritch College in Milwaukee, Wisconsin. She also teaches in the undergraduate Early Childhood Education program. Before moving to Milwaukee, Dr. McLean directed programs in Early Childhood Special Education at Auburn University and the University of North Dakota. She currently serves as President of the Division for Early Childhood of the Council for Exceptional Children.

Tara Lea Muhlhauser

Tara Lea Muhlhauser is the director of the Children and Family Services Training Center at the University of North Dakota and is a faculty member in the Department of Social Work. She is a licensed social worker and attorney, specializing in child welfare, family law, and domestic relations issues.

Glenn Olsen

Glenn Olsen is Associate Professor in the Department of Teaching and Learning at the University of North Dakota. He has taught at community and technical colleges in Minnesota and Wisconsin. He has taught preschool, middle, and secondary students in twenty-seven years of teaching. His research interests include conflict resolution, fathering, home–school relations, and parent education.

Glen Palm

Glen Palm is Professor of Child and Family Studies at St. Cloud State University, where he teaches courses in child development and parent education. He also coordinates the Parent Education licensure program at SCSU. He is a Parent Educator in the St. Cloud Early Childhood Family Education program where he has taught parent education classes for fathers for twelve years. Dr. Palm was Co-Editor of the book, *Working with Fathers: Methods and Perspectives* and writes a regular column for Family Information Services on working with fathers. He is also the father of three children ages 9–18.

AmySue Reilly

AmySue Reilly is Assistant Professor at Auburn University. She received her Ph.D. from the University of New Mexico. Dr. Reilly is Co-Director of Project AIM (Auburn Intervention Model), an early intervention program for very young children and their families. Currently, she is the Project Director of a U.S. Department of Education project that helps prepare professionals to work in the field of Early Childhood Special Education.

Elizabeth J. Sandell

Elizabeth J. Sandell is currently the Executive Director of Minneapolis-based MELD, a national, private, not-for-profit family support organization. MELD also provides training, curriculum, and other resources to family education services around the world. Prior to MELD, Dr. Sandell was Division Manager for Early Childhood Family Education with the Saint Paul Public Schools. She has been a Lecturer in Early Childhood Education and in Family Education for the University of Minnesota, Mankato State University, Macalester College, and Saint Paul Bible College.

Gloria Jean Thomas

Gloria Jean Thomas is an Associate Professor in Educational Leadership at the University of North Dakota in Grand Forks. She teaches all of the law classes for the College of Education and Human Development, including Law for Teachers, School Law for School Administrators, Special Education Law, and Higher Education Law. She also teaches in higher education administration. Her Ph.D. is from Brigham Young University, where she specialized in school law. She has written many articles on school law, the principalship, and rural schools and is the lead author of *The Law and Teacher Employment.*

Sandra Winn Tutwiler

Sandra Winn Tutwiler is Associate Professor and Chair of the Education Department at Hamline University in St. Paul, Minnesota. She teaches courses in educational psychology, urban education, and foundations of education. Dr. Tutwiler has also been a teacher and/or a counselor in elementary school, middle school, high school, and community college settings. Her research interests include school and family relations and the impact of educational experiences on the quality of life for African American girls and women. She is currently working on an anthology of mothering experiences among women of color.

Karen W. Zimmerman

Karen W. Zimmerman is a Professor in the Human Development, Family Living and Community Educational Services Department at the University of Wisconsin–Stout. She received her Ph.D. with co-majors in family environment and home economics education from Iowa State University. She teaches courses in child development, parent education, family life issues, and family and consumer education. She is the undergraduate program director for Family and Consumer Educational Services and the graduate program director in Home Economics.

Shirley L. Zimmerman

Shirley L. Zimmerman is Professor of Family Social Science at the University of Minnesota, where she teaches courses on family policy, family policy research, and family policy from an international perspective. She is the author of *Understanding Family Policy: Theoretical Approaches* (1988), *Family Policies and Family Well-Being: The Role of Political Culture* (1992), and *Understanding Family Policy: Theories and Applications* (2nd edition) (1995). She is the author of numerous articles dealing with family policy and related issues. Her research focuses on policy choices that mediate the connections between families and government, factors that influence such choices, and the outcomes of such choices for families.

Index

Post-traumatic stress disorder (PTSD), 242
Poverty, 257–272
 activities to learn more about, 269
 child abuse/neglect and, 240
 children in, 6, 258, 260, 263–265
 educators' understanding of, 6–7
 effects of, 261–263
 family implications of, 24
 myths about, 260–261
 nature of, 258–260
 parents in, 265–268
  working with, 266–268
 resources on, 269–271
 War on Poverty, 19
Power of their ideas: Lessons for America from a small school in Harlem, The (Meier), 103
Practical Homeschooling, 329
Prayer in public school, 221
Prehistorical families, 13
Preschools
 attitudes toward, 339–342
 policy on, 339–342
Pride, family, 30
Problems in school, avoidance of, 193
Process of parenting, The (Brooks), 83
Progressive pedagogy, 314
Progress reports, 201
Project DAKOTA, 174
Protecting Children, 247
Protection of children, family's role in, 3
Protestant denominations, 53–54
Protestant republican ideology, 335
Protest movements, 343
PTSD, 242
Public Law 94–142, 155, 156, 223
Public Law 99–457, 155, 156–157, 172
Public Law 102–119 (IDEA), 156, 163, 171, 172, 223–224, 226
Public schools. *See* School(s)
Puerto Ricans, 51
Punctuality, 46

Racial harassment, 231
Racism
 African American view of, 48
 attempts to end, 343–344
Rand Corporation, 348–349
Recognition, to facilitate parent involvement, 135
Recreation, 262
Recruitment of parent volunteers, 134–135
Referrals, 196–197
Reformation families, 14–15
Rehabilitation Act of 1973, 223
"Related services," legal definition of, 225
Religion, legal disputes involving, 214–215
Renaissance families, 14–15
Report cards, 201
Reporting family violence, 250–251
Reports
 narrative, 115

progress, 201
Republican ideology, Protestant, 335
Reserved Powers Clause of the Tenth Amendment, 211
Resource Center on Child Protection and Custody, 251
Resources
 of family, school requirements vs., 195–196
 family involvement in middle school and, 197–198
 information. *See* Articles; Books; Chapters; Organizations; Videos; Websites
Responsibility of father, 280
Rights
 of parents
  fundamental, 210, 213, 217
  under IDEA, 224
  in state constitutions, 349
 of schools, 213
 of student, 226–228
Riley, Richard, 338
Role ambiguity, 78
Role identity, teacher, 308, 323–324
Role models
 in blended families, 28
 teacher, 308, 315–317, 322–323
Role of educators in the protection and treatment of child abuse and neglect, The (Tower), 255
Roles
 gender, 281
 prioritizing, 73–74
Role strain (overload and conflict), 72–73, 75–76
Roman period families, 13–14
Roosevelt, Franklin D., 154
Rousseau, J. J., 15
Rural schools, 5

Safety devices, 262
Schechter, Susan, 246
Schedules, attention to, 46
School(s)
 emergence of mandatory, 17–18
 father involvement and, 284, 288–290
 infant, 339, 340–341
 memories of, 323
 parents' perspectives on, 96–101
 in the past, 5
 prayer in, 221
 rights of, 213
 rural, 5
 segregation of, 216–217
 urban, 5
School and family partnership: Case studies for special educators (Buzzell), 164
School and the Military Family (booklet), 62
School councils, 138–139
School Development Program (SDP), 185–186

School Development Team, 185
School fees, 219–220
School-home journal, 115
Search Institute, The, 205
Second chance: Men, women, and children a decade after divorce (Wallerstein), 24–25
Secular humanism, 221
Segregation of schools, 216–217
Self-concept, of abused/neglected children, 242
Self-esteem, low, 31
Sensitivity of parents, 92–93
"Separate but equal" doctrine, 216
Sequin, Edouard, 153–154
Services
 for children with disabilities, 155, 160
 related, legal definition of, 225
Sex education, 218
Sexual abuse, intra-familial child, 239
Sexual harassment, 230, 231
Sexually transmitted diseases, 218
Shame, dysfunctional families and, 32
Shared Decision Making (video), 147
Shelter, 261
Siblings, of child with disabilities, 161–162
Sibshops: Workshops for siblings of children with special needs (Meyer & Vadasy), 165
"Significant others: Teachers' perceptions on relationships with parents" (Hulsebosch), 103
Single-parent families, 8, 21, 23–26
 child abuse/neglect and, 240
 children from, 25
 financial concerns of, 75
 perspectives of, 98–99
 resources on, 35–37
Single Parenting (video), 37, 84
"Single teenage parent families: Hispanic-American families" (Hildebrand et al.), 36
Six stages of parenthood, The (Galinsky), 83
Skip generation parenting, 22
Socialization, ethnic (enculturation), 3, 45. *See also* Assimilation/enculturation
Social support, from functional families, 30–31
Society
 father involvement and, 284
 preparing children for, 3
Sociological definition of families, 2–3
Somewhere a child is crying: Maltreatment causes and prevention (Fontana), 252
Special education. *See also* Children with disabilities
 court decisions on, 223–226
 family involvement model in, 171–177